Dakota Grammar
With Texts and Ethnography

Dakota Grammar

With Texts and Ethnography

STEPHEN R. RIGGS

Edited with a preface by James Owen Dorsey
Introduction by John D. Nichols

MINNESOTA HISTORICAL SOCIETY PRESS

First published in 1893 by the Department of the Interior, U.S. Geographical and Geological Survey of the Rocky Mountain Region, as Contributions to North American Ethnology, volume 9

www.mnhs.org/mhspress

The Minnesota Historical Society Press is a member of the
Association of American University Presses.

Manufactured in the United States of America

10 9 8 7 6 5 4 3 2 1

∞ The paper used in this publication meets the minimum requirements of the American National Standard for Information Sciences—Permanence for Printed Library materials, ANSI Z39.48-1984.

Front cover: Dakota camp, 1890; back cover: Stephen R. Riggs's Hazelwood Mission on the Minnesota River (in present-day Yellow Medicine County), ca. 1860 (Minnesota Historical Society collections)

International Standard Book Number 0-87351-472-6

Library of Congress Cataloging-in-Publication Data

Riggs, Stephen Return, 1812–1883.
   [Dakota grammar, texts, and ethnography]
   Dakota grammar : with texts and ethnography / Stephen R. Riggs ;
edited with a preface by James Owen Dorsey ; introduction by John D. Nichols.
      p.   cm.
   "First published in 1893 by the Department of the Interior, U.S. Geographical and
Geological Survey of the Rocky Mountain Region, as Contributions to North American
ethnology, volume 9."
   Includes bibliographical references and index.
   ISBN 0-87351-472-6 (pbk. : alk. paper)
   1. Dakota language.
   2. Dakota Indians.
   I. Dorsey, James Owen, 1848–1895.
   II. Title.
PM1021.R48 2004
497′.5243—dc22   2004004186

Introduction

Dakota Grammar with Texts and Ethnography contains information about the Dakota language and people collected in the mid-nineteenth century by members of the Protestant-sponsored Dakota Mission in present-day Minnesota and published by the United States government in 1893. The first part is a description of the Santee dialect of the Dakota language; the second, a collection of traditional stories in Dakota with word-by-word and running English translations; the third, an ethnography with notes on the history and customs of the Dakota. This book remains an important document for the study of Dakota culture and history, and a source of continuing interest to students of the language.

Dakota Language and People

The Dakota and Lakota people, known in English as the Sioux, live today on reservations and reserves in Minnesota, Montana, Nebraska, North Dakota, South Dakota, Manitoba, and Saskatchewan, and in cities throughout the United States and Canada. Recorded in this book is their division into bands known as the "seven council fires." In the early and mid-nineteenth century, the eastern Santee (Isanti) group of bands—the Mdewakanton (Mdewakantonwan), Wahpekute, Wahpeton (Wahpetonwan), and Sisseton (Sisitonwan)—lived west of the Mississippi River in present-day Minnesota and northern Iowa. In eastern South and North Dakota was a central group of bands, the Yankton (Ihanktonwan) and the Yanktonai (Ihank-tonwanna). The western group, the Teton (Titonwan), lived west of the Missouri River in the Dakotas, and in northwestern Nebraska and eastern Wyoming. Each group speaks a major regional variety (dialect) of a single Sioux language.

The name *Sioux*, like many other tribal names in English, derives not from the people's name for themselves but from a neighboring tribal group's name for them. The people's self-designation is *Dakota* (a more accurate spelling of which is *Dakhota*), generally interpreted as meaning "allies, friends," although this is the form of the word only among the eastern group (Santee) and the central group (Yankton and Yanktonai). The Yankton and Yanktonai have been referred to as *Nakota*, even though they call themselves Dakota (Dakhota) in their own form of the language. The parallel term in the western group (Teton) is *Lakota* (*Lakhota*). There is no single shared name in the language for the people and the language. Although many still find the name *Sioux* acceptable, a recent suggestion to be considered is to call the language *Dakotan* in English to prevent confusion between the use of *Dakota* as a name for the eastern and central groups and their language varieties, and its use as a cover term for Dakota and Lakota. Two other nations, the Assiniboine of Montana and Saskatchewan and the Stoney of Alberta, also speak dialects of Dakotan and call themselves *Nakoda* or *Nakota.*

Strikingly similar to the Dakotan language in the sounds they use, their vocabularies, and their word and sentence structures are a number of other indigenous languages. To the west is Crow, between Teton and Yankton are Hidatsa and Mandan on the Missouri River, and to the south are Chiwere (Iowa, Otoe, and Missouria, all no longer spoken) and Dhegiha (Omaha-Ponca, Osage-Kansa, and Quapaw, with Kansa and Quapaw no longer spoken). Hocak or Hochunk (Winnebago) is spoken mainly in Wisconsin and Nebraska. Ofo, Biloxi, and Tutelo, as well as others less well documented, were once spoken in the southeastern United States. The deepest similarities among all of these languages are due to their common genetic origin. They form a family of languages, the Siouan family, descended from a single ancient spoken language that scholars call *Proto-*

Siouan. The Siouan languages in turn are related to the now-extinct Catawba and Woccon languages of North and South Carolina within a larger language family called Siouan-Catawban.

Dakota and Lakota are today, like other North American indigenous languages, endangered, although they rank among the strongest in terms of numbers, with at least six thousand speakers. Only in a few communities, however, is a significant percentage of the population fluent in the ancestral language. Few children now acquire the language naturally at home. A wave of concern on the part of the Dakota people has brought about language-maintenance efforts, including language classes at all school levels, university courses, new writing systems and dictionaries, recorded lessons, language societies, and a variety of language-oriented websites.

The Dakota Mission

The first sustained efforts by European Americans to learn and write the Dakota language began in 1834 at Prairie du Chien in present-day Wisconsin when the volunteer missionary brothers Gideon H. and Samuel W. Pond picked up a single phrase of trader Dakota and used it to elicit the names of things from Dakotas they encountered on their trip up the Mississippi River to Fort Snelling. Not only did they need the Dakota language for communication in their daily life with the Dakota at the missions they established in Minnesota, but their Protestant Christianity, a religion centered on a written sacred text, demanded the creation of a written mode of Dakota, the translation of the Bible into that new mode of language, and the spread of native-language literacy among the Dakota themselves.

The Ponds claimed that they had learned most of the words in common use during their first five or six years among the Dakota. They also consulted a vocabulary of words supplied by Scott Campbell, a Dakota interpreter for St. Peter's Indian Agency at Fort Snelling (located between present-day Minneapolis and St. Paul). As the Ponds refined their writing system, they made their own vocabularies. These lists of words grew into manuscript dictionaries and grammars, shared with and added to by newly arrived missionaries, most notably the Presbyterians Stephen Return Riggs and Thomas S. Williamson, who worked primarily at Lac qui Parle up the St. Peter's (now the Minnesota) River.

Riggs and Williamson were part of the Dakota Mission, a body of Christian missionaries sent into the field by the American Board of Commissioners for Foreign Missions. Organized in 1810 by the General Association of Congregational Churches of Massachusetts, the board sponsored members of several Protestant denominations. Eventually the Ponds, too, became allied with the Dakota Mission.

It took more than forty years to finish the Dakota Bible. Along the way there were numerous other books published, beginning with a spelling book in 1836, followed soon by Bible passages, a catechism, a reader, and a hymnal. The most prolific translator was Joseph Renville Sr. of Lac qui Parle, a trader of Dakota and French descent. He had little English and no literacy but was a master of spoken Dakota and Canadian French. Williamson read aloud passages from a French edition of the Bible, and, after some negotiation of French dialects, Renville dictated the Dakota translation, with Riggs and others attempting to write it down. Thus began a tradition of Dakota literacy that flourished in the late-nineteenth century and continues to live today.

By 1850 the Dakota Mission's documentation of the Dakota language was attracting attention locally and in Eastern missionary and scholarly circles. Riggs wrote an address on Dakota that was read in 1851 at the second annual meeting of the Minnesota Historical Society. Also in 1851, he was selected to carry the linguistic collections of the mission to New York City and to work there with a distinguished linguist, Professor William Wadden Turner of Union Theological Seminary, and reshape them into professional publications. Riggs and Turner made significant revisions in the orthography, forming new complex letters with diacritics to represent more systematically the Dakota sounds that differed most widely from the sounds of English, what Riggs called the "clicks and gutturals." [1] To incorporate the changes for publication, new characters had to be designed and cast as metal type.

The resulting volume, published in 1852 under the auspices of the Smithsonian Institution and the patronage of the Minnesota Historical Society, included a grammar, a few extracts from the Bible translations and the Lord's Prayer in an interlinear format, a Dakota-English dictionary, and an English-Dakota dictionary. The whole work was credited to the members of the Dakota Mission with Riggs listed as its editor. Samuel Pond was not pleased about this, and his memoirs reveal resentment at Riggs for taking top billing for the collaborative work. Pond later disowned his connection with the grammar and the dictionary. A comparison, however, of the published grammar with a manuscript in the Pond Family Papers at the Minnesota Historical Society suggests that little of the Ponds' work appeared in the heavily revised grammar.

The development of the Dakota Mission's language materials continued with additions from the Santee, Teton, and Yankton dialects. Riggs corresponded with James Owen Dorsey, a missionary turned linguist and ethnologist at the Bureau of American Ethnology, about a new publication and submitted manuscripts, but died in 1883 before the editing was completed. Dorsey reworked the Riggs submissions, adding material from his own research into Siouan languages and cultures other than Santee, and drawing on the notes of other missionaries to pro-

---

1. Stephen R. Riggs, *Tah-koo wah-kan; or, The Gospel among the Dakotas* (Boston: Congregational Publishing Society [1869?]), 12.

duce the new Dakota-English dictionary in 1890 and *Dakota Grammar, Texts, and Ethnography* (the original title of the present volume) in 1893. A proposed companion English-Dakota dictionary was not completed in time; it was published independently by John P. Williamson, a son of Thomas Williamson, in 1902. These three books, along with the religious translations and the original writings in Dakota published in various mission newspapers, constitute the main documentation of the Santee dialect made down to the present.

Dorsey began *Dakota Grammar with Texts and Ethnography*, now attributed solely to Riggs as author, with a long preface showcasing Dorsey's disagreements with Riggs as well as Dorsey's passion for understanding Dakota within a comparative framework in relation to the other Siouan-speaking tribal groups. It adds little to the work and shifts the focus away from the book's core subjects, the Dakota people and their language. Footnotes bearing Dorsey's initials as well as those of members of the mission correct, add to, or dispute with the text. The first part is essentially the same as the 1852 grammar, although notes on the Teton dialect were inserted here and there, some technical terms revised, and a few new sections inserted, especially speculative ones on the origin and analysis of words. Although much outdated, the Riggs version of the Dakota Mission grammar remains the only grammar of the Santee dialect. Despite the changes made earlier in the writing system, one whole set of Dakota consonants was not distinguished by the missionaries, and other inconsistencies in recording significant sound distinctions in Dakota were common in their writings. Like all of the linguistic works of the mission, the grammar falls short of complete accuracy in the writing of Dakota sounds.

The Dakota language texts in Santee and Yankton included in the second part, with the samples of religious translations carried over from the 1852 work, were submitted for publication by Riggs as early as 1877. They are among the earliest examples of

North American indigenous oral literature written by native speakers. They remain among the few available texts in these dialects not having their origin in translations from other languages. The authors were Michael (Michel) Renville, a son of the translator Joseph Renville; David Grey Cloud and James Garvie, both Dakota Presbyterian ministers; and Walking Elk, a Yankton tribal leader.

While the authentic traditions reported by Riggs from Dakota sources in the third, or ethnography, part are invaluable, a number of sections of it derive from published works by other authors of the time. Some sections contain little more than Christian testimony. The reader must carefully evaluate the influence of Riggs's commitment to the nineteenth-century ideals of "Christian civilization" on his reporting. Read critically, the account is still a valuable source of historical and ethnographic information. Riggs's etymological explanations of the meaning of names, however, should be reexamined in light of continuing Dakota oral tradition and more recent linguistic analysis. The list of tribal and other group names, long the standard source, has now been supplemented with lists from other contemporary and earlier sources.[2]

Dakota Language Studies since Riggs

Later grammars built on the Dakota Mission tradition. The anthropologists Franz Boas and John R. Swanton revised Riggs's Santee grammar and added information on the Teton dialect Lakota in a 1911 publication. Most subsequent work has been on this dialect. Ella Deloria, a Lakota speaker and scholar of Yanktonai ancestry, joined Boas in an indispensable grammar of her own dialect, published in 1941, which replaced the 1911 work.

2. "Sioux until 1850" by Raymond J. DeMallie in *Plains*, ed. DeMallie, vol. 13 of *Handbook of North American Indians* (Washington, DC: Smithsonian Institution, 2001), 2: 736–48. See the following Suggestions for Further Reading for more information about this publication and others mentioned below.

Deloria's Lakota and Yanktonai text collection of 1932 is central to any study of the language and traditional literature. A Roman Catholic missionary, Eugene Buechel, wrote a grammar of Lakota (published in 1939) in the Riggs manner and a dictionary (published in a revised edition by Paul Manhart in 2002). Buechel's work is unusual among those documenting the language as it was directed at Lakota speakers, rather than at language scholars.

The best contemporary grammatical materials are a 1996 sketch of Lakota by David S. Rood and Allan R. Taylor, and the lesson and dictionary materials prepared by them for the University of Colorado's Lakhota Project. Newer materials by native-speaking language teachers are now appearing, the most interesting published by Albert White Hat Sr. in 1999. Many of the older documents of Dakota and Lakota linguistics are available on-line, as are dictionaries, lessons, and texts. A computer search using the headings "Sioux language," "Dakota language," or "Lakota language" will uncover much of value.

Every major published work on Dakota and Lakota since Riggs's efforts has revised the writing system. Local language-revitalization projects and curricula follow in the same tradition. There is still no single standard way to write the language. To aid in matching Riggs's work (including the dictionaries of both Riggs and Williamson) with some of the newer writing systems, a brief comparative table has been added to this edition of *Dakota Grammar with Texts and Ethnography*. Written Dakota without the diacritics is quite usable by fluent speakers; the less experienced who want to use written materials as a learning aid, however, will need to supplement unmarked systems with one of the marked ones, such as those of Albert White Hat and the University of Colorado project. An emerging trend in writing is the use of letters and letter combinations without diacritics to represent fully Dakota sounds, returning to something like the missionaries' earliest writing systems but with improved accuracy.

Spelling systems, transcriptions, grammars, and dictionaries cannot be the language itself, of course, and are only imperfect representations on paper of the authentic spoken words. Yet they can still be tools for use both by the Dakota in maintaining their living language and by others studying it. The members of the Dakota Mission were humble about their achievements as linguists, but their endeavors continue today to contribute to the revitalization and appreciation of a vibrant Dakota linguistic heritage.

JOHN D. NICHOLS
Department of American Indian Studies
University of Minnesota—Twin Cities

Suggestions for Further Reading

For the main starting point for further reading in Dakota language, history, and culture, as well as the best general guide to both primary and secondary sources, see:

DeMallie, Raymond J., ed. *Plains.* Vol. 13 (in 2 parts) of *Handbook of North American Indians.* William C. Sturtevant, general editor. Washington, DC: Smithsonian Institution, 2001. The main essays of interest are "Siouan Languages" by Douglas R. Parks and Robert L. Rankin (1: 94–114); "Sioux until 1850" by DeMallie (2: 718–60); "Santee" by Patricia C. Albers (2: 761–76); "Yankton and Yanktonai" by DeMallie (2: 777–93); "Teton" by DeMallie (2: 794–820); "Sioux, 1930–2000" by Dennis M. Christafferson (2: 821–39); and "Tribal Traditions and Records" by DeMallie and Parks (2: 1062–73).

The nature of the dialect situation, the dialect affiliation of the contemporary reservations and reserves, and the relation of Assiniboine and Stoney to Dakota are treated in:

Parks, Douglas R., and Raymond J. DeMallie. "Sioux, Assiniboine, and Stoney Dialects: A Classification." *Anthropological Linguistics* 34 (1992): 233–55.

The classic documents on the Santee dialect are:

Riggs, Stephen R. *A Dakota-English Dictionary.* Ed. James Owen Dorsey. Department of the Interior, U.S. Geographical and Geological Survey of the Rocky Mountain Region; Contributions to North American Ethnology, vol. 7. Washington, DC: Government Printing Office, 1890. Reprint with foreword by Carolynn I. Schommer. Borealis Books. St. Paul: Minnesota Historical Society Press, 1992.

———. *Dakota Grammar, Texts, and Ethnography.* Ed. James Owen Dorsey. Department of the Interior, U.S. Geographical and Geological Survey of the Rocky Mountain Region; Contributions to North American Ethnology, vol. 9. Washington, DC: Government Printing Office, 1893. Reprinted as *Dakota Grammar with Texts and Ethnography* with introduction by John D. Nichols. St. Paul: Minnesota Historical Society Press, 2004.

———, ed. *Grammar and Dictionary of the Dakota Language.* Smithsonian Contributions to Knowledge, vol. 4. Washington, DC: Smithsonian Institution, 1852.

Williamson, John P. *An English-Dakota Dictionary.* New York: American Tract Society, 1902. Reprint with foreword by Carolynn I. Schommer. Borealis Books. St. Paul: Minnesota Historical Society Press, 1992.

The early writings in and on the Dakota language are described in:
Pilling, James Constantine. *Bibliography of the Siouan Languages.* Smithsonian Institution; Bureau of American Ethnology, bulletin no. 5. Washington, DC: Government Printing Office, 1887.

The main sources for the study of grammar, replacing Riggs's work, but concentrating on Lakota, are:
Boas, Franz, and Ella Deloria. *Dakota Grammar.* National Academy of Sciences (U.S.) Memoirs, vol. 23, 2nd memoir. Washington, DC: Government Printing Office, 1941.
Buechel, Eugene. *A Grammar of Lakota, the Language of the Teton Sioux Indians.* St. Louis, Chicago, etc.: Planographed by John S. Swift Co., 1939.
Rood, David S., and Allan R. Taylor. "Sketch of Lakhota, a Siouan Language." In *Languages,* ed. Ives Goddard (440–82). Vol. 17 of *Handbook of North American Indians.* William C. Sturtevant, general editor. Washington, DC: Smithsonian Institution, 1996

The classic collection of bilingual texts in Lakota and Yanktonai is:
Deloria, Ella. *Dakota Texts.* American Ethnological Society; Publications, vol.14. New York: G. E. Stechert, agents, 1932.

Dakota oral traditions in English from a variety of historical sources have been conveniently gathered, along with the bilingual texts from *Dakota Grammar with Texts and Ethnography,* in:
Woolworth, Alan R., comp. and ed. *Santee Dakota Indian Legends.* Tales of the Santee (Eastern) Dakota Nation, vol. 2. St. Paul: Prairie Smoke Press for Sisseton-Wahpeton Tribe, 2003.

Language lessons for Dakota include:
Beardy, Sheila, et al. *A Sioux Phrase Book Based on the Dialects of Manitoba.* Brandon, MB: Departments of Native Studies and Languages, Brandon University, n.d.
Flute, Rebecca, Carolynn I. Schommer, Timothy Dunnigan, and Ann Rynde. *Dakota Iapi.* 3rd ed. Revised by Neil McKay and Lisa

Elbert. Minneapolis: Department of American Indian Studies, University of Minnesota, 2002.

Language lessons for Lakota include:

Rood, David S., and Allan R. Taylor. *Beginning Lakhota.* 2 vols. Boulder: Lakhota Project, University of Colorado, 1976. Distributed by the Department of Linguistics, University of Colorado, Boulder.

White Hat, Albert, Sr. *Reading and Writing the Lakota Language.* Ed. Jael Kampfe. Foreword by Vine Deloria Jr. Salt Lake City: University of Utah Press, 1999.

Some recent dictionaries, all of Lakota, are:

Buechel, Eugene, and Paul Manhart, comps. and eds. *Lakota Dictionary: Lakota-English / English-Lakota.* Lincoln: University of Nebraska Press, 2002.

Ingham, Bruce. *English-Lakota Dictionary.* Richmond, Surrey, UK: Curzon Press, 2001.

Rood, David S., and Allan R. Taylor. *Elementary Bilingual Dictionary: English-Lakhota / Lakhota-English.* Boulder: Lakhota Project, University of Colorado, 1976. Distributed by the Department of Linguistics, University of Colorado, Boulder.

COMPARATIVE TABLE OF SELECTED DAKOTA AND LAKOTA ORTHOGRAPHIES

Dakota Writing   Lakota Writing

Consonants

DM	RW	BU	UM	IPA	BM	DB	RT	WH
b	b	b	b	[b]	b	b	b	b
c	ć,c[1]	c	c	[tʃ]	c=c,c[2]	c	č	c̄
c	ć,c[1]	ć	c	[tʃʰ]	c=c,ċ[2]	c'	čh	c
c	ć,ç[1]	ç	c'	[tʃ']	c'	c'	č?	c'
d	d	d	d	[d]		d[3]	d[3]	
g	g	g	g	[g]	g	g	g	g
g	ġ	ġ	g	[ɣ],[ʁ]	g=ġ[2]	ġ	ğ	ġ
h	h	h	h	[h]	h	h	h	h
r	ħ	ħ	ħ	[x]	ḣ	ḣ	ñ	ḣ
r	ħ	ḥ	ħ'	[xʔ]	h'=ħ'[2]	ḣ'	ñ?	ħ'
k	k	k	k	[k]	k=k̇,k[2]	k	k	k̄
k	k	k̇	ḳ	[kʰ]/[kˣ][4]	k=k,k̇[2]	k'	kh	k/k[4]
q	ḳ	ḳ	k'	[k']	k'	k'	k?	k'
	l[5]			[l]	l	l	l	l
m	m	m	m	[m]	m	m	m	m
n	n	n	n	[n]	n	n	n[6]	n
p	p	p	p	[p]	p=ṗ,p[2]	p	p	p̄
p	p	ṗ	ḅ	[pʰ]/[pˣ][4]	p=p,ṗ[2]	p'	ph	p/p[4]
p	ḅ	ḅ	p'	[p']	p'	p'	p?	p'
s	s	s	s	[s]	s	s	s	s
s	s'	ṣ	s'	[sʔ]	s'	s'	s?	s'
x,ś	ś,ś[1]	š	ṡ	[ʃ]	š	s	š	s
x,ś	ś',s'[1]	ṣ̌	ṡ'	[ʃʔ]	š'	ṡ'	š?	s'
t	t	t	t	[t]	t=ṫ,t[2]	t	t	t̄
t	t	ṫ	ṭ	[tʰ]/[tˣ][4]	t=t,ṫ[2]	t'	th	t/t[4]
t	ṭ	ṭ	t'	[t']	t'	t'	t?	t'
w	w	w	w	[w]	w	w	w	w
y	y	y	y	[y]	y	y	y	y
z	z	z	z	[z]	z	z	z	z
j	ź,ż[1]	ž	ż	[ʒ]	j	z	ž	j
	'	ɔ	'	[ʔ]	'	'	?	

Vowels

DM	RW	BU	UM	IPA	BM	DB	RT	WH
a	a	a	a	[a]	a	a	a	a
an	aŋ	añ	aŋ	[ã]	an=aŋ[2]	ą	ą	aŋ
e	e	e	e	[e]	e	e	e	e
i	i	i	i	[i]	i	i	i	ɪ
ɪn	iŋ	iñ	iŋ	[ĩ]	in=iŋ[2]	į	į	ɪŋ
o	o	o	o	[o]	o	o	o	o
on	oŋ	uñ	uŋ	[õ][7]	on=oŋ[2]	ų	ų	uŋ
u	u	u	u	[u]	u	u	u	u
un	uŋ	uñ	uŋ	[ũ]	un=uŋ[2]	ų	ų	uŋ

Sources for Table

DM Dakota Mission. This system is a generalized one formed from systems used in publications of the Dakota Mission, especially those published before 1852.

RW Riggs-Williamson. This system is used in the Riggs Dakota-English dictionary (1890, 1992) and grammar (1893, 2004), and in the Williamson English-Dakota dictionary (1902, 1992).

BU Brandon University. This system is used in *A Sioux Phrase Book* by Beardy et al. (n.d.) and in Dakota language classes at Brandon University.

UM University of Minnesota. This system is used in *Dakota Iapi* by Flute et al. (2002) and in Dakota language classes at the University of Minnesota—Twin Cities.

IPA International Phonetic Alphabet. This standard phonetic alphabet indicates the main pronunciations of Dakota and Lakota sounds.

BM Buechel and Manhart. This system is used in *Lakota Dictionary* by Buechel and Manhart (2002).

DB Deloria and Boas. This system is used in *Dakota Texts* by Deloria (1932) and in *Dakota Grammar* by Boas and Deloria (1941).

RT Rood and Taylor. This system is used in the grammar of Lakhota in "Sketch of Lakhota" by Rood and Taylor (1996) and in their materials written for the University of Colorado's Lakhota Project (1976).

WH White Hat. This system is used in *Reading and Writing the Lakota Language* by White Hat (1999).

Notes for Table

1. The Riggs grammar and dictionary use the first symbol; the Williamson dictionary uses the second.

2. A form shown before an equal-sign (=) appears in the headword for an entry; a form shown after an equal-sign appears in the pronunciation indication following the headword. A plain stop is indicated variably by a letter with a dot over it or by an unmarked letter. An aspirated stop is indicated variably by an unmarked letter or by a letter followed closely by an aspirate mark.

3. Required only for Dakota.

4. Variation in the pronunciation of aspirates is reported for Lakota. Some speakers have a glottal release after the stop (indicated here with a small raised h [ʰ] in IPA phonetics), and some have a velarized release (indicated here with a small raised x [ˣ] in IPA phonetics). White Hat provides characters for both, using an unmarked letter for a stop with a glottal release and a letter with a dot over it for a stop with a velarized release.

5. Required only for Lakota.

6. This source also uses an n with a hacek over it (ň) for a velar nasal consonant.

7. Nasalized o is a variant pronunciation of nasalized u; the distinction is not written in some modern orthographies.

DEPARTMENT OF THE INTERIOR

U. S. GEOGRAPHICAL AND GEOLOGICAL SURVEY OF THE ROCKY MOUNTAIN REGION

J. W. POWELL in Charge

CONTRIBUTIONS

TO

NORTH AMERICAN ETHNOLOGY

VOLUME IX

WASHINGTON

GOVERNMENT PRINTING OFFICE

1893

DEPARTMENT OF THE INTERIOR

U. S. GEOGRAPHICAL AND GEOLOGICAL SURVEY OF THE ROCKY MOUNTAIN REGION

J. W. POWELL in Charge

DAKOTA GRAMMAR, TEXTS, AND ETHNOGRAPHY

BY

STEPHEN RETURN RIGGS

EDITED BY JAMES OWEN DORSEY

WASHINGTON
GOVERNMENT PRINTING OFFICE
1893

CONTENTS.

CONTENTS.

LETTER OF TRANSMITTAL.

SMITHSONIAN INSTITUTION, BUREAU OF ETHNOLOGY,

Washington, D. C., April 25, 1893.

SIR: I have the honor to transmit to you the copy for " Contributions to North American Ethnology, Vol. IX, Dakota Grammar, Texts, and Ethnography," by the late Stephen Return Riggs, having edited it according to your instructions.

I am, with respect, your obedient servant,

JAMES OWEN DORSEY,

Ethnologist.

To HON. J. W. POWELL,

Director, Bureau of Ethnology

PREFACE.

By the Editor, JAMES OWEN DORSEY.

In consequence of the death of the author in 1883, the copy furnished by him for the present volume was left in such a shape that some editing was necessary before it could be sent to the printer.

By order of the Director of the Bureau of Ethnology, the editorship of the manuscript was committed to me. I was requested also to prepare the table of contents and index, and to see that the arrangement of the chapters, headings, etc., conformed to the general plan of the publications issued by this Bureau.

That such disposition of the manuscript was in harmony with the wishes of the author will appear after a perusal of the following extract from a letter, dated April 20, 1881, sent by Dr. S. R. Riggs to Mr. J. C. Pilling, then chief clerk of the Bureau. After speaking of an article that he was preparing, to be entitled "Unwritten Laws," Dr. Riggs continues thus: "This letter, I think, will partly cover Ethnology. But I do not profess to be skilled in Ethnology as a science, and shall be glad of any suggestions from Maj. Powell and yourself."

In the manuscript as received from the author were sundry quotations from my letters to him. But as several years had elapsed since these were written and as I had been enabled to revise the quoted statements, bringing the information down to date, it was but proper that such revisions should appear as footnotes, each followed by my initials.

During the process of editing the manuscript it was ascertained that, as there had been additional investigations among the Dakota and other tribes of the Siouan stock since the death of the author, several questions treated by him deserved further elucidation. When one considers the many years in which the venerable author was associated with the work among the Dakota Indians (1837–1883) it would seem to many persons very pre-

sumptuous for one whose life among the Indians began as late as 1871 to
question his conclusions, unless abundant facts could be shown to confirm
the assertions of the critic.

The author's life among the Indians was spent chiefly with a single
division of the Dakota, known as the Santee or Mdewakantonwan. A few
of the Teton words in his dictionary were furnished by one of his sons,
Rev. T. L. Riggs, but most of them were obtained from Rev. W. J. Cleveland. The author, moreover, knew very little about the languages of those
cognate tribes that are not Dakota, such as the Ponka, Omaha, Kansa,
Winnebago, etc., while I have lived among many of these tribes and have
devoted considerable time to the comparison of most of the Siouan languages,
having engaged in original investigation from time to time, as late as
February, 1893, when I visited the Biloxi Indians in Louisiana.

In order, therefore, to furnish the readers of this volume with the latest
information, and to give more fully than was possible in those footnotes for
which I am responsible my reasons for hesitating to accept some of the
author's conclusions, as well as evidence confirmatory of some of the author's
statements this preface has been written.

In my notation of Dakota words, both in this preface and in the footnotes, the author's alphabet has been used, except where additional characters were needed; and such characters are described in the following section
of this preface. But in recording the corresponding words in the cognate
languages the alphabet used is that of the Bureau of Ethnology.

All footnotes followed by " S. R. R." were contributed by the author.
Those furnished by his son, Rev. Alfred L. Riggs, are signed " A. L. R."
" T. L. R." stands for Rev. T. L. Riggs, and " J. P. W." for Rev. J. P.
Williamson. " J. O. D." marks those footnotes for which I am responsible.

LIST OF SOUNDS PECULIAR TO INDIAN WORDS IN THE PREFACE.

The alphabet given by the author on pages 3 and 4 has no characters
representing certain sounds heard in the Teton dialect of the Dakota and
in some of the cognate languages. Besides these, there are other sounds,
unknown in Teton and the other dialects of the Dakota, but common to
the other languages of the Siouan family. These peculiar sounds and some
additional ones which are described are given in the characters adopted by
the Bureau of Ethnology. The authority for the Hidatsa words is Dr.
Washington Matthews, U. S. Army.[1] The Tutelo words were recorded

---

[1] U. S. Geol. and Geogr. Surv., Hayden, Miscell. Publ. No. 7, 1877: Ethnog. and Philol. of the
Hidatsa Indians.

chiefly by Dr. Horatio Hale, though a few were acquired since 1882 by Mr. J. N. B. Hewitt and myself. The Mandan words are taken from the vocabularies of Dr. F. V. Hayden, Dr. W. J. Hoffman, and Prince Maximilian, of Wied.

ă   as a in *what* or as o in *not.*

c   sh, given as ś by the author and Matthews.

ɔ   a medial sound, between sh (ś) and zh (ź).

ç   as th in *thin*, the surd of ꜩ.

d̨ȼ   a d sound followed by a dh sound which is scarcely audible. This combination is peculiar to the Biloxi, Hidatsa, and Kwapa languages. Given as d by Matthews.

ȼ   dh, or as th in *the*, the sonant of ç.

e   a short e as in *get.*

ꜧ   a sound heard at the end of certain syllables, but slightly audible, nearer h than kh. Given by Matthews as an apostrophe after the modified vowel.

ɪ   as in *it.*

j   zh, or as z in *azure*. Given as ź by the author and as z by Matthews.

ꞣ   a medial k, between g and k, heard in Teton, Ꝑegiha, etc.

k'   an exploded k. Given as ꝁ by the author.

ⁿ   a vanishing n, scarcely audible, as the French n in *bon, vin*, etc., occurring after certain vowels. Given as ŋ by the author.

ñ   as ng in *sing, singer*, but not as ng in *finger;* heard sometimes before a k-mute, at others just before a vowel, as in Ʇᵒiwere (i-çŭñ-e, i-yŭñ-e, wañ-e, etc.). Given as ŋ by the author.

q   kh or as ch in German *ach*. Given as ḣ by the author and Matthews.

ꞩ   a medial sound, between d and t.

ŭ   as oo in *foot.*

û   as u in *but*, given by Matthews as "a" with a dot subscript.

tc   as ch in *church*. Given as ć by the author.

tç   a t sound followed by a ç (th) sound, as th in *thin*, but scarcely audible. It is the surd of d̨ȼ, and is peculiar to the Biloxi, Hidatsa, and Kwapa languages. Given as t by Matthews.

ꞩɔ   a medial sound, between dj (j as in judge) and tc.

ꞩs   a medial sound, between dz and ts.

SEPARATE PRONOUNS.

On page 11 it is said that the separate personal pronouns "appear to be capable of analysis, thus: To the incorporated forms mi, ni, and i, is added the substantive verb, e, the y coming in for euphony. So that miye is equivalent to *I am*, niye to *thou art*, and iye to *he is*." On page 12 the author informs us that "miś, niś, and iś would seem to have been formed from miye, niye, iye; as, miye eś contracted into miś; niye eś contracted into niś, etc." On the same page we find the emphatic forms of the pronouns, miś miye, I myself; niś niye, thou thyself; iś iye, he himself, etc.

Now, if the author has made correct analyses, miye = mi+y+e; niye = ni+y+e; iye = i+y+e; miś = mi+y+e+eś; niś = ni+y+e+eś; iś = i+y+e+eś; miś miye = mi+y+e+eś mi+y+e. He tells us, too, that the forms miś, niś, and iś were originally subjective, while miye, niye, and iye were originally objective.

On examining a myth in the Bushotter (Teton) collection, the following sentences were extracted, as they show how the Teton Indians use the separable pronouns. When the Giant Anuŋg-ite or Two Faces discovers the presence of his adversary, Haχela, he exclaims, Niś eya kakiśćiya yaćiŋ na ćl
<small>You too I make you suffer you wish and to</small>
mayau he: Are you coming to me because you wish me to make you
<small>me you are coming ?</small>
suffer, too? (Here niś is subjective or nominative.) Haχela replies, Hiya, niyeś pha χiŋ hmŭŋyela kaksa iyećiyiŋ kta ća ćl ćihi: No, I
<small>No, you indeed head the with a whizzing cutting it I make yours will when to I come (and no one else) sound off go suddenly to you</small>
come to you in order to cut off your head (making) a whizzing sound (with my sword) as I send it (your head) suddenly (or forcibly) to the ground. Here niyeś, which is objective in this sentence, marks a contrast: it is you only, not I, who must suffer. After killing the giant, Haχela takes the rescued infant to the lodge of his parents, who are afraid to let him enter, as they think that he is the giant. So Haχela says, Ina, he
<small>O mother, that</small>
miye ća wahi ye lo: O mother, this is I who have come, not he (the
<small>I as I have indeed . come</small>
giant). Here miye is subjective. When Haχela is taken to the lodge of the chief who has two daughters, the elder daughter says to the younger, Ito, miyeś le bluha kte: Well, I (not you) will have this one (for my
<small>Well, I (not you) this I have will</small>
husband). But the younger sister laughs as she retorts, He yaćin śni ća
<small>That you wanted not as</small>
miyeś hiŋgna wayiŋ kte ćiŋś: As you did not want him (when you
<small>I (not you) a husband I have him will .(female for speaking)</small>

could have had him.) Subsequently, when the elder sister had turned
Haxela into a dog, iŋś eya ih́a na heya, Niś ehaŋ nićakiźiŋ kte, eya: She,
_{she too laughed and said as You yourself you suffer shall said what}
_{follows   precedes}
too, laughed and said, "You yourself shall suffer (now)."

INSEPARABLE PRONOUNS.

On page 13 the author remarks, "These forms md and d may have
been shortened from miye and niye, the n of niye being exchanged for d."
In addition to the objections given in the foot note on p. 13, the editor
offers the following table:

Siouan languages.	Verbs having their 3d sing. in—	make their 2d sing. in—	and their 1st sing. in—	Personal pronouns.
Dakota	ya- yu-	da-(la-) du-(lu-)	mda-(bda-, bla-) mdu-(bdu-, blu-)	1st, miye 2d, niye
Ȼegiha	ȼa- ȼi-	na-(ona-) ni-(oni-)	ḅa- ḅi-	1st, wie, etc. 2d, ȼi, ȼie, etc.
Kansa	ya- yü-	hna- hnü-	bla- blü-	1st, mi 2d, yi
Osage	ȼa- ȼü-	cta-, ctsa- ctü-, ctsü-	dȼa- dȼü-	1st, wie 2d, ɥie
Kwapa	dȼa- dei-	ta- ti-	ptȼa- ptȼi-	1st, wie 2d, dȼi, dȼie
Ɉoiwere	ra- ru-	ora- oru-	hata- hatu-	1st, mire 2d, dire
Winnebago	ɥa- ru-	cara- curu-	ɥa- ɥu-	1st, ne 2d, ne
Hidatsa	da-(da-) du-(dȼu-)	da-(dȼa-) da-(dȼu-)	ma- mu-	1st, ma, mi 2d, da (dȼa), di (dȼi)
Biloxi	da- du-	ida- idu-	nda- ndu-	1st, ñxindi (nom.) ñxint-kaⁿ (obj.) 2d, ayindi (nom.) ayint-kaⁿ (obj.)

N. B.—The Hidatsa and Biloxi modal prefixes da- and du- are not
exact equivalents of the Dakota ya- and yu-, the Ȼegiha ȼa- and ȼi-; etc.
The following appears on page 15: "Perhaps the origin of the 't' in
'tku' may be found in the 'ta' of the 3d person used to denote property.'
How can this apply to dekśi-tku, his or her mother's brother, even if it
could be said of taŋkśi-tku, his younger sister, and ćiŋhiŋ-tku, his or her
son? While a son or a sister might be transferred to another person's
keeping, a mother's brother could not be so transferred. Such an uncle had
greater power over his sister's children than the father had, among the
Omaha and cognate tribes, and presumably among the Dakota. Among
the Omaha even an adoptive uncle was conceded this power, as when
Susette La Flèche (now Mrs. T. H. Tibbles) was invited by her father's
brother (a Ponka chief) to remove from the Omaha Reservation in Nebraska

to the Ponka Reservation in the Indian Territory, for the purpose of accepting a position as teacher in the agency school. The real father, Joseph La Flèche, consented, but Two Crows, an adoptive mother's brother, and no real kinsman, objected, and for that reason Susette did not go. It appears, then, that the 't' in 'dekśi-tku' does not imply "transferable possession."

CONTINUATIVES.

On page 45 the author translates two proper names thus: Iŋyaŋg-mani, One-who-walks-running, and Anawaŋg-mani, One-who-walks-as-he-gallops-on. As mani is used here as a continuative, it would be better to render the two names, One-who-continues-running, and One-who-continues-galloping-on. In all of the Siouan languages which have been studied by the editor we find these continuatives. They are generally the classifiers, words denoting attitude, the primary ones being those denoting standing, sitting, or reclining. In the course of time the reclining is differentiated from the moving; but at first there is no such differentiation.

The author agreed with the editor in thinking that some of these Dakota continuative signs, haŋ, waŋka, and yaŋka, were originally used as classifiers; and a comparison of the Teton texts with those contained in the present volume shows that these words are still used to convey the idea of action that is (1) continuous or incomplete and (2) performed while the subject is in a certain attitude. Thus haŋ means to stand, stand upright or on end, but when used after another verb it means the standing object. The other verbs used as classifiers and continuatives are waŋka (Teton, yuŋka), to recline, yaŋka (Teton, yaŋḳa), to sit, hence to be. Yaŋka occurs as a classifier on pp. 83, 85, 86, 87, 88, 89, etc. That it conveys the idea of *sitting* is shown by the context on p. 89, where the Star born *sat* (iyotaŋke) on the ridge of the lodge and was fanning himself (ihdadu yaŋka). Waŋka, to recline: on p. 83, the twin flowers abounded (*lay* all along) in the star country. On the next page, the infant Star born was kicking out repeatedly (naġaŋgata waŋka, he *lay* there kicking). On page 110 we read, Uŋktomi waŋ kaken ya waŋka, An Unktomi was going (literally, going he reclined).

CARDINAL BIRTH-NAMES.

The Dakota names which belong to children, in the order of their birth, up to fifth child, are given on page 45. Thus the first child, if a boy, is called Ćaske; if a girl, Winona. The second, if a boy, is called Hepaŋ.

and if a girl, Hapaŋ, and so on.   While this class of birth-names is found among the Ponka, Omaha, Osage, Kansa, Kwapa, the Ḻɔiwere tribes, and the Winnebago, all these tribes observe a different rule, i. e., the first son is always called Ingȼaⁿ, or some equivalent thereto, even though he may not be the first child, one or more daughters preceding him in the order of birth; and in like manner the first daughter is always called Winaⁿ or by some one of its equivalents, although she may have several brothers older than herself.   On the other hand, if there should be in a Dakota household first a daughter, next a son, the elder or first born would be Winona and the next Hapaŋ (there being no Ćaske), while if the first born was a boy and the next a girl the boy would be Ćaske and his sister Hapaŋ (there being no Winona).

KINSHIP TERMS.[1]

The following are the principal kinship terms in most of the Siouan languages, all of which, except those in the Dakota, Hidatsa, Mandan, and Tutelo, having been recorded by me.   Most of the terms may be used by females as well as males; but when the use of a term is restricted to persons of one sex a note to that effect will be found in the proper place. In the Biloxi column, the algebraic sign ($\pm$) denotes that the ending following it may be used or omitted at the will of the speaker.

[1] See pp. 45, 203, 204, 207.

English.	Dakota.	Ҫegiha.	Kwapa.	Kansa.	Osage.
Father	atkuku (<ate)	iȼadi	edȼatĕ	iyadje	iȼaʇse
Mother	huŋku (<huŋ)	iha^{n}	eha^{n}, chŭ^{n}	ihŭ^{n}	ihŭ^{n}
Mother's brother	dekśitku (<dekśi)	inegi	eteʞe	idjegi	iqʇseʞi, i^{n}ʇseʞi }
Father's sister	tuŋwiću (<tuŋwiŋ)	iʞimi	etimi	itcimi	iqtsimi
Grandfather	tuŋkaŋśitku, tuŋkaŋśidaŋ, etc. (<tuŋkaŋ)	iʞiga^{n}	etiʞa^{n}	itcigu	iqtsiʞu
Grandmother	kuŋku (<kuŋ)	iʞa^{n}	eʞa^{n}	iʞu	iʞu, iqʞu
Elder brother (his)	ćiŋću <ćiŋye)	iji^{n}ȼĕ	eji^{n}dȼĕ	ijiye, iji^{n}ye	ioi^{n}ȼe, ioi^{n}e
Elder brother (her)	timdoku (<timdo)	iʞinu	etitu	itcidu	itsi^{n}ʇu, iqtsiʞu
Elder sister (his)	taŋkeku (<taŋke)	iʞañge	etûⁿʞe	itañge	itañʞe, iqtañʞe
Elder sister (her)	ćuŋku, ćuŋweku	ija^{n}ȼĕ	ejû^{n}dȼĕ	ijuwe	ioñ^{n}we
Younger brother	suŋkaku (<suŋka)	isañga [fem. voc., wisa^{n}ȼa^{n}']	esû^{n}ʞa	isûñga, *his* isŭ^{n}ya^{n}, *her*	isañʞa, isûñʞa
Younger sister (his)	taŋkśitku (<taŋkśi)	iʞañge		itañge	iteeoiûʞa
Younger sister (her)	taŋkaku (<taŋka)	iʞañge			
Son	ćiŋhiŋtku(<ćiŋkśi)	ijiñge	ejiñʞe	ijiñge	ioiñʞe
Daughter	ćuŋkśitku, ćuŋwiŋtku (<ćuŋkśi)	ijañge	ejañʞe	ijûñge	ioññʞe
Grandchild	takoźakpaku (<takoźa)	iʞucpa	etucpa	itucpa, itcucpa	itcucpa, iqtsucpa

Ɉoiwere.	Winnebago.	Mandan.	Hidatsa.	Tutelo.	Biloxi.
aⁿtce	hiaⁿɉoi-rȟ		atçc, tçaɨçic	{ daɨ (Hewitt); eati; tat,yat(Hale)	adi-yaⁿ (<adi)
ihŭⁿ	hiŭⁿni-na			{ ehĕⁿ, *his;* ehiⁿ, *her* (Hewitt) ina; hena; henŭⁿ (Hale)	ŭⁿni, ŭⁿni-yaⁿ
itceka	hitek, hiteꭓara		(itçadɇn)	{ enek (Hewitt); eiuek (Hale)	tukaⁿni noqti, his mother's elder brother; tukaⁿni aka, younger do.
itumi	hitcŭⁿwiⁿ-rȟ	ko-tomi-nikoc, *the* aunt (Wied)	icami, icawi tomin		toⁿni, toⁿniyaⁿ, elder sister; toⁿni aka, etc., younger do.
ituka iku	hitcoke-rȟ hikoroke, hikorokĕ-rȟ Voc., kŭⁿnikȟ		adɇutçaka iku	eɟoꭓĕⁿ (Hewitt) higuⁿ (Hale) egoⁿq (Hewitt)	kaⁿqo ꭓŭⁿꭓŭⁿ, ꭓŭⁿꭓŭⁿyaⁿ
iyina	hini-rȟ hitcito-rȟ		iaka Itçametsa	ewahyek (Hewitt)	iui, ini-yaⁿ tando noqti
iyuna	hinŭⁿktcapa-rȟ, *his sister.*	ptañkoc	itçamia	tahañk, *sister* (Hale); etahĕñk (Hewitt)	tañk-qohi-yaⁿ
iyuna	hinu-rȟ,hinŭⁿ-rȟ		idɇu	enoⁿq (Hewitt)	inoⁿni
içŭñe	hisŭñk-rȟ		itsuka	sŭⁿtka (Hale) esoⁿɟk (Hewitt)	soⁿtkaka, sontka-kayaⁿ, *his* tando akayaⁿ, *her*
itañe	waitcke-rȟ hitcañka-rȟ	ptañka	itçakica itçaku		tañkaka (+yaⁿ) taⁿskɔ (+yaⁿ)
iyiñe (Iowa); iɔiñe (Oto)	hinɪk	ko-nike	idɇici	eteka	yiñꭓiyaⁿ
iyŭñe	hinŭk, hinŭꭓa-rȟ, hinŭñꭓa-rȟ	iko-nuhañke	ika	eteka (prob. his or her *child*)	yŭñꭓɪyaⁿ
itaꭓwa, grandson; itaꭓwami, granddaughter.	hitcuⁿcke-niñꭓe-ra his grandson		itçamapica		yiñꭓadodi, son's son; yŭñꭓadodi, son's daughter; yŭñꭓayiñ i, daughter's son; yŭñꭓayŭñꭓɨ, daughter's daughter.

English.	Dakota.	Ȼegiha.	Kwapa.	Kansa.	Osage.
Brother-in-law (his)	tahaŋku (<tahaŋ)	iⱥaha^n	etaha^n	itaha^n	itaha^n
Brother-in-law (her)	śiȼeȼu, śiȼeku (<śiȼe)	ici'e	ecik'e	icik'e	icik'e
Sister-in-law (his)	haⱥkaku (haⱥka)	ıbañga	ehañɥa	ihŭñga	ibañɥa
Sister-in-law (her)	iȼepaŋku (<iȼepaŋ)	iciɥa^n	ecika^n	iciɥa^n	icika^n
Sister's son (his)	toŋśkaku(<tonśka)	iⱥa^{n}cka	etû^{n}cka	itcucka	iⱥtsucka
Brother's son (her)	tośkaku (tośka)	iⱥucka		itcuckaya^n	iⱥtsucka^n
Sister's daughter (his)	tuŋźaŋku (<tuŋźaŋ)	iⱥija^n	eⱥijû^n	itciju	itsioŭ^n, iⱥtsioŭ^n
Brother's daughter (her)	tozaŋku (<tozaŋ)	iⱥujañge	etujañɥe	itcujañge	iⱥtsuɔañɥe
Son-in-law	takośku (takoś)	iⱥande	etû^{n}tĕ	itŭndje	iⱥtŭnⱥse
Daughter-in-law	takośku (<takoś)	iⱥini	etini	itcini	iⱥtsini
Husband (her)	hihna-ku (<hihna)	egȼañge	ektçañɥe, eⱥnŭñɥĕ		
Husband (my)	mihihna	wiegȼañge	wiktçañɥe		
Wife (his)	tawiȼu (<tawiŋ)	igaqȼa^n	eⱥaqna^n eⱥaqnû^n	igaqla^n	
Wife (my)	mitawiŋ	wigaqȼa^n			

Ꞩoiwere.	Winnebago.	Mandan.	Hidatsa.	Tutelo.	Biloxi.
itaha^n icike	hitcă^n-ră hicik'ĕ-ră		id¢aų̆tçi icikici	etahĕ^{n}ĕ^n (Hewitt)	taha^{n}niya^n yiñꭓa yiꭓi
ihaña icika^n	hiwañke-ră		uaka, his brother's wife itç a-da¢amia, i-tçarawia, his wife's sister, his wife.		tcka^{n}niya^n
	hitcŭ^{n}cke-ră hitca^{n}cke-ră			etoskaii (Hewitt)	tûksiki (±ya^n), elder sister's son; tûksikiaka(±ya^n), younger sister's son.
				etosiñk (Hewitt)	tusûñꭓi (±ya^n), elder sister's daughter; tusûñ-kiaka (±ya^n), younger sister's daughter.
	hitcujañk-ră				Name forgotten by Indians.
	waꭓohotci-ră hinŭk-tcek-hani-ră, "the one whom I have for a new daughter."			eohĕñk (Hewitt)	tondi-ya^n toho^{n}ni-ya^n
	hikana-na		ikid¢a	eta-mañki	yiñꭓaꭓi-ya^n
itami	hikana-hară hitcawi^n-na		ua	eta-mihĕ^n, "his woman" (Hale) ("his spouse," Hewitt)	nyiñꭓaꭓi-ya^n yiñꭓo^{n}ni-ya^n
	hitcawi^n-hară			witamihĕ^{n}e^n, "my spouse" (Hewitt)	nyiñꭓo^{n}ni-ya^n

The "hna" in the Dakota term should not be compared with the
Dakota verb, ohnaka, to place in, but with the Ƈegiha verb, gȼaⁿ, to take a
wife (see "gȼañ" in egȼañge, a husband, her husband), which answers to the
Kansa lañge, the Osage ᶄȼañᶄe, and the ᒐoiwere ᶄrañe, all of which are
related to the verb, to take hold of, seize, apparently pointing to a time when
marriage by capture was the rule. (See the Dakota verb yuza.) The
original meaning of "my husband" therefore may have been my capturer or
seizer. Ohnaka, when applicable to a person, refers to a sitting one, otherwise it is applicable to what is curvilinear, a part of a whole, a garment,
book, etc. This is not brought out by the author, though attitude is
expressed or implied in nearly all the verbs of placing or putting in the
various Siouan languages. The Tutelo word for her husband, etamañki,
does not mean, "her man." Mañki, a husband, differs materially from the
several words which are said to mean "man" in Tutelo. "To take a
husband," in Tutelo, is tamañkŭⁿse (<mañki), and "to take a wife" is
tamihŭⁿse (from etamihĕⁿĕⁿ, a wif⊕, his wife). "To take a husband" in
Biloxi, is yiñᶄadoⁿni, very probably from yiñᶄaᶅi and oⁿni, probably
meaning "to make or have for a husband or child's father." "To take a
wife" in Biloxi, is yiñᶄoⁿni (yiñᶄi and oⁿni, to do, make), literally, "to
make a young one." The Biloxi term for "my wife," nyiñᶄoⁿniyaⁿ, may
have been derived from yiñᶄi, little one, child, and oⁿni an occasional form
of ŭⁿni or ŭⁿniyaⁿ, a mother, the whole meaning, "my little one his or her
mother." In like manner, "my husband," nyiñᶄaᶅiyaⁿ, may have been
derived from yiñᶄi, child, and aᶅiyaⁿ or adiyaⁿ, his or her father, the compound meaning, "my little one his or her father."

Among the Dakota names for kinship groups (see page 45), there are
several which admit of being arranged in pairs, and such an arrangement
furnishes hints as to the derivation of at least one name in each pair, in
connection with present and probably obsolete forms of marriage laws. In
each pair of names, the second invariably ends in kśi or śi, the exact
meaning of which has not been ascertained, though it may be found to
imply a prohibition. Thus, ćinću, his elder brother, ćiŋye, an elder brother
(of a male); but ćiŋ-kśi, a son (who can not marry the widow of the
speaker, though one whom that speaker calls ćiŋye can marry her.) A
woman's elder sister is ćuŋ, ćuŋwe, or ćuŋwi, her elder sister being ćuŋku
or ćuŋweku; but a daughter is ćuŋ-kśi (she can not marry her mother's
husband, though the mother's elder sister can do so). A man's elder sister
is taŋke, a woman's younger sister, taŋka; but a man's younger sister is
taŋ-kśi; it is not certain whether there is any restriction as to marriage

contained in this last kinship name. A father is ate, and a mother's brother is de-kśi (in Teton, le-kśi); we find in the cognate languages (excepting Ȼegiha and Winnebago) some connection between the two names, thus in Kwapa, the syllable te is common to edȼate and etexe; in Kansa, dje is common to iyadje and idjegi; in Osage, ɪse is common to iȼaɪse and iqɪsexi; in Ɉoiwere, tce is common to aⁿtce and itceka. At present, my mother's brother can not marry my father's widow (who is apt to be his own sister). A man's brother-in-law (including his sister's husband) is tahaŋ, and a man's male cousin is tahaŋ-śi (who can not marry that sister). A woman's brother-in-law or potential husband is śiȼe, but her male cousin, who can never become her husband, is iȼe-śi or śiȼe-śi. A man's sister-in-law (including his potential wife), is haŋka; but a man's female cousin (whom he can not marry) is haŋka-śi. A woman's sister-in-law (including her husband's sister and her brother's wife) is iȼepaŋ, but a woman's female cousin (who can become neither the husband's sister nor the brother's wife) is iȼepaŋ-śi. The editor proposes to group together in like manner the corresponding terms in the cognate languages, such as ijiⁿȼĕ, his elder brother, and ijiñge, his or her son; ijaⁿȼĕ, her elder sister, and ijañge, his or her daughter; but that must be deferred to some future time.

CARDINAL NUMERALS.

On pages 48 and 49 the author undertakes to analyze the Dakota names for the cardinal numerals. He does this without comparing the Dakota names with those in the cognate languages. A knowledge of the latter will enable the student to correct some of the statements of the author, and for that reason these names are now given.

ONE.

Dakota, waŋȼa, waŋźi or waŋźidaŋ (waŋźina, waŋźila). Said by the author to be derived from waŋ, an interjection calling attention perhaps, at the same time *holding up a finger*. N. B. This is only a supposition.

Ȼegiha, wiⁿ, wiⁿaqtci (just one).
Kansa, miⁿ, miⁿqtci.
Osage, wiⁿ, wiⁿqtsi.
Kwapa, miⁿqti.
Ɉoiwere, iyaⁿ, iyañke.
Winnebago, hijaⁿ, hijañkida.
Mandan, maqana.

Hidatsa, duetsa (d¢uetsa) luetsa.

Tutelo, noⁿsa, also nos, nosai, noⁿsai, etc.

Biloxi, soⁿsa.   I have not yet found in these cognate languages any interjection resembling the Dakota waɳ *in use*, from which the respective forms of the numeral could be derived.

TWO.

Dakota, noɳpa, "from eɳ aoɳpa, to bend down on, or place on, as the second finger is laid over the small one; or perhaps of nape oɳpa, nape being used for finger as well as hand.   N. B.   The second finger laid down (that next to the little finger of the left hand) is not laid *over*, but *beside* the small one.

Ȼegiha, naⁿba, in composition ¢aⁿba, as in the proper name xaxe ¢aⁿba, Two Crows.   See seven, a derivative.   To place a horizontal object on something would be, a'aⁿhe, which could not have been the source of naⁿba.

Kansa, nŭⁿba.

Osage, ¢ŭⁿda.

Kwapa, naⁿpa, to place a horizontal object on something, ak'ŭⁿhe.

Ⱡᵓiwere, nowe.

Winnebago, noⁿp, noⁿpa, noⁿpi, nŭⁿp.   The root in the Winnebago verb *to place a horizontal object* is, t'ŭⁿp.

Mandan, nuⁿpa.

Hidatsa, dopa (d¢opa, nopa).

Tutelo, noⁿp, noⁿbai, etc.

Biloxi, noⁿpa, naⁿpa; to place a horizontal object on something, iⁿpi.

THREE.

Dakota, yamni: "from mni (root), *turning over* or *laying up*."

Ȼegiha, ¢ab¢iⁿ: compare roots, b¢iⁿ and b¢iⁿ¢a, beb¢iⁿ, *twisted;* etc.

Kansa, yabli, yabliⁿ: root bliⁿ, *turned.*

Osage, ¢ad¢iⁿ or na¢idⁿ.

Kwapa, d¢abni.

Ⱡᵓiwere, tanyi.

Winnebago, tani.

Mandan, namni.

Hidatsa, dami (d¢ami) or nawi.

Tutelo, nan, nani, lat, etc.

Biloxi, dani: many roots in which na, ne and ne are syllables convey the ideas of *bending, turning,* or shaking.

FOUR.

Dakota, topa, "from opa, to follow; (perhaps ti, *a house,* and opa, *follow with*) as we say, 'in the same box' with the rest. The three have banded together and made a 'ti' or 'tidaŋ,' as we should say *a family,* and the fourth joins them." N. B.—Is not this rather fanciful?

Ƈegiha, duba; to follow is u¢uhe; to join a party, ĕd uihe (in full, ĕdi uihe).

Kansa, duba or ¡uba; to follow, uyupye.

Osage, ¡u**d**a; to follow, u¢upce.

Kwapa, ¡uwă.

Ꞁᵓiwere, towe; to follow a road or stream, owe; to join or follow a party, oyuᶍe.

Winnebago, tcop tcopa-ra, tcopi; to follow, howe.

Mandan, tope.

Hidatsa, topa (tçopa).

Tutelo, tob, top.

Biloxi, topa.

FIVE.

Dakota, zaptaŋ, "from za (root), holding (or perhaps whole, as in zani) and ptaŋyaŋ or ptaya, together. In this case the thumb is bent down over the fingers of the hand, and *holds them together.*"

Ƈegiha, Kansa, and Osage, sată^n.

Kwapa, sata^n.

Ꞁᵓiwere, çata^n.

Winnebago, satc, satca^n.

Mandan, kequ^n.

Hidatsa, kihu (=kiqu).

Tutelo, gisa^n, kise, kisa^n.

Biloxi, ksa^n, ksani.

To hold is u¢a^n in Ƈegiha, uyiñge in Kansa, u¢iñᶍe in Osage, unañe in Ꞁᵓiwere, ad¢aqeqe and ûkcie in Hidatsa, and dusi in Biloxi.

SIX.

Dakota, śakpe "from śake, nail, and kpa or kpe (root), lasting as some kinds of food which go a good ways, or filled, as a plump grain. This is the second thumb, and the reference may be to the other hand being completed. Perhaps from the idea of bending down as in nakpa, the ear." No satisfactory analysis of this numeral can be given in the cognate languages, and that given by the author needs further examination.

Ȼegiha, cade̯.
Kansa, cápe.
Osage, cápe̯.
Kwapa, cape̯'.
Ꞁoiwere, caꞃwe.
Winnebago, akewe.
Mandan, kima.
Hidatsa, akama or akawa.
Tutelo, agasp, agas, akes, akaspe.
Biloxi, akûqpe.

SEVEN.

Dakota, śakowiꞃ, " from śake, nail, and owiꞃ, perhaps from owiꞃġa, to bend down; but possibly from oiꞃ, to wear as jewelry, this being the forefinger of the second hand; that is the ring finger." Do the Dakota Indians wear rings on their index fingers?

Ȼegiha, deȼaⁿba, -de appearing in cade̯, *six*, and ȼaⁿba being *two;* as if seven were or, the *second of the new series, beginning with six.* Kansa, peyuⁿba.   Osage, peȼŭⁿda or pe(ȼ)aⁿda.   Kwapa, penaⁿda.   Ꞁoiwere, cahma.   Winnebago, caꞃowe.   Mandan, kupa.   Hidatsa, śapua (capua). Tutelo, săgum, sagom.   Biloxi, naⁿpahudi, from variants of noⁿpa, *two,* and udi, *stock,* or ahudi, *bone,* the "second stock" or "second bone."

EIGHT.

Dakota, śahdoġaꞃ, "from śake, nail, probably, and hdoġaꞃ, possessive of yuġaꞃ, to open (hduġaꞃ is the true form, J. O. D.); but perhaps it is oġaꞃ or oġe, cover, wear; the nail covers itself. Two fingers now cover the thumb." How can the nail "cover itself?" Ȼegiha, deȼabȼiⁿ, as if from -de and ȼabȼiⁿ, *three or the third of the new series, beginning with six.* Kansa, kiya-ꞁuba, "again four," and peyabli (cape and yabli). Osage, kiꞃȼe-ꞁuda, "again four."   Kwapa, pedȼabniⁿ (cape and dȼabniⁿ).   Ꞁoiwere,

krerapriⁿ (incapable of analysis, tanyi being *three*). Winnebago, haru-
wañke or ha¢uwañke (can not yet be analyzed). Mandan, titûki. Hidatsa,
dopapi (d¢opapi), from dopa (d¢opa), two and pi-, which appears to be the
root of pitika (pitçika), *ten*, the whole probably signifying *ten less two*.
Tutelo, palan, palan (pa and *three*). Biloxi, dan-hudi, the "third stock" or
"third bone."

<h3 style="text-align:center">NINE.</h3>

Dakota, napćiŋwaŋka, "from nape, hand, ćistiŋna, small, and waŋka,
lies—hand small lies; that is, the remainder of the hand is very small, or
perhaps, the hand now lies in a small compass. Or, from napćupe (marrow
bones of the hand), or "the finger lies in the napćoka, inside of the hand."
Query by the editor: May not the name refer to the little finger of the
right hand which alone remains straight?

Ɖegiha, Kansa and Kwapa, cañka.

Osage, ꭓ¢ed¢aⁿ tse ¢iñꭓe or ꭓ¢ed¢aⁿ tsĕ wiⁿ ¢iñꭓe, "ten less one."

Ꝇoiwere, cañke.

Winnebago, hijañkitcaⁿckuni or hijañkitcŭⁿqckuni, "one wanting," i. e.
to make ten.

Mandan, maqpi (from maqạna, *one*, and piraq, *ten*), "ten less one." (?)

Hidatsa, duetsapi (d¢uetsa and pi-), "ten less one."

Tutelo, sa, saⁿ, ksañk, ksäⁿꝗk.

Biloxi, tckane.

<h3 style="text-align:center">TEN.</h3>

Dakota, wikćemna, "from wikće or ikće, common, and mnayaŋ, gathering, or from mna, to rip, that is, let loose. It would mean either that the
common or first gathering of the hands was completed, or, that being completed, the whole were loosed, and the ten thrown up, as is their custom;
the hands in the *common position*."

Ɖegiha, g¢eba or g¢eb¢aⁿ (in which g¢e=kće of the Dakota, and
b¢aⁿ=mna of the Dakota).

Kansa, lebla or leblaⁿ.

Osage, ꭓ¢ed¢aⁿ.

Kwapa, ktçebna or ktçeptçaⁿ.

Ꝇoiwere, kepraⁿ.

Winnebago, kerepana.

Mandan, piraq.

Hidatsa, pitika (pitçika).

Tutelo, butck, putck.

Biloxi, ohi, "completed, filled, out, to have gone through the series."

ELEVEN.

Dakota, ake waŋźi, "again one," or wikćemna saŋpa waŋźidaŋ. "ten more one."

Ȼegiha, agȼiⁿ-wiⁿ, "one sitting-on (ten)."

Kansa, aliⁿ-miⁿqtci, same meaning.

Osage, aᴚȼiⁿ-wiⁿqtsi, same meaning.

Kwapa, miⁿqti-aᴚniⁿ, "one sitting-on," or ktçeptçaⁿ-taⁿ miⁿqti aᴚniⁿ, "ten-when one sitting-on."

Ɫoiwere, aᴚriⁿ-iyañke, "one sitting-on."

Winnebago, hijañkida-cina, meaning not certain (hijañkida, *one*).

Mandan, aga-maqana (maqana, *one*).

Hidatsa, ahpi-duetsa (aqpi-dȼuetsa), "portioned one."

Tutelo, agi-noⁿsaii.

Biloxi ohi soⁿsaqehe, "ten one-sitting-on."

TWELVE.

Dakota, ake noŋpa, "again two," or wikćemna saŋpa noŋpa, "ten more two."

Ȼegiha, caᑐĕ-naⁿba, "six times two."

Kansa, aliⁿ-nŭⁿba, "two sitting-on."

Osage, aᴚȼiⁿ-ȼŭⁿᑐa, same meaning.

Kwapa, naⁿpa-aᴚniⁿ, same meaning.

Ɫoiwere, aᴚriⁿ-nowe, same meaning.

Winnebago, noⁿpa-cina (noⁿpa, *two*).

Mandan, aga-nuⁿpa (nuⁿpa, *two*).

Hidatsa, ahpi-dopa (aqpi-dȼopa), "portioned two."

Tutelo, agi-noⁿpaii; see noⁿbai, *two*.

Biloxi, ohi noⁿpaqĕhe, "ten two-sitting-on."

NINETEEN.

Dakota, uŋma napćiŋwaŋka, "the other nine."

Ȼegiha, agȼiⁿ-cañka, "nine sitting-on."

Kansa, ama cañka, "the other nine," or aliⁿ-cañka, "nine sitting-on."

Osage, aᴚȼiⁿ ᴚȼeᑐȼaⁿ tse ȼiñᴚe, "sitting-on ten less (one)."

Kwapa, cañka-aχniⁿ, "nine sitting-on."

Ɫoiwere, aχriⁿ-cañke, same meaning.

Winnebago, hijañkitcŭⁿqckuni-cina (see *nine*).

Mandan, aga-maqpi (see *nine*).

Hidatsa, ahpi-duetsapi (aqpi-d¢uetsapi), "portioned ten less one."

Tutelo, agi-ksañkaii (see *nine*).

Biloxi, ohi tckanaqĕhe, "ten nine-sitting-on."

ONE HUNDRED.

Dakota, opawiŋġe, "from pawiŋġa, to bend down with the hand, the prefixed o indicating perfectness or roundness; that is, the process has been gone over as many times as there are fingers and thumbs."

Ɔegiha, g¢eba-hi-wiⁿ, "one stock of tens."

Kansa, leblaⁿ hü tcüsa (leblaⁿ, *ten*, hü, *stock*, tcüsa, meaning unknown).

Osage, χ¢ed¢aⁿ hü ɔiⁿa, "ten stock small," or "small stock of tens."

Kwapa, ktçeptçaⁿ hi, "stock of tens."

Winnebago, okihijaⁿ.

Mandan, isuk maqana (maqana, *one*).

Hidatsa, pitikictia (pitçikiqtçia), "great ten."

Tutelo, ukeni nosa, or okeni.

Biloxi, tsipa.

ONE THOUSAND.

Dakota, kektopawiŋġe, or koktopawiŋġe "from opawiŋġe and ake or kokta, *again* or *also*."

Ɔegiha, g¢eba-hi-wiⁿ χañga, "one great stock of tens," or χuge wiⁿ, "one box," so called because annuity money before the late civil war was paid to the Indians in boxes, each holding a thousand dollars in specie.

Kansa, leblaⁿ hü jiñga tcüsa (leblaⁿ, *ten*, hü, *stock*, jiñga, *small*, tcüsa, meaning uncertain) or leblaⁿ hü tañga, "large stock of tens."

Kwapa, ktçeptçaⁿ hi tañχa, "a large stock of tens."

Winnebago, kokijaⁿ (koke, *box*, hijaⁿ, *one*), "one box."

Mandan, isuki kakuhi.

Hidatsa, pitikictia akakodi (pitçikiqtçia akakod¢i), exact meaning not known.

Tutelo, ukeni putskai, "ten hundred."

Biloxi, tsipiⁿtciya, "old man hundred," from tsipa, *hundred*, and iⁿtciya, *old man*.

THE TERMS FOR "WHITE MAN" IN SIOUAN LANGUAGES.

On p. 174 Dr. Riggs, in speaking of Hennepin's narrative, says: "The principal chief at that time of this part of the tribe, is called by Hennepin 'Washechoonde.' If he is correct, their name for *Frenchmen* was in use, among the Dakota, before they had intercourse with them, and was probably a name learned from some Indians farther east." The author's supposition as to the eastern origin of waśićuŋ as an appellation for white men might stand if there were no explanation to be found in the Dakota and cognate languages. Hennepin himself is a witness to the fact that the Dakota Indians of his day called spirits waśićuŋ (as Dr. Riggs states on p. 175). And this agrees with what I have found in the Teton myths and stories of the Bushotter collection, where waśićuŋ is given as meaning guardian spirit. Dr. Riggs himself, in his Dakota-English dictionary, gives waśićuŋ as "nearly synonymous with wakaŋ" in the opinion of some persons. He appends the following Teton meanings: "A familiar spirit; some mysterious forces or beings which are supposed to communicate with men; mitawaśićuŋ he omakiyaka, my familiar spirit told me that." This phrase he gives as referring to the Takuśkaŋśkaŋ, the Something-that-moves or the Wind powers. The Mandan use waci and the Hidatsa maci for white man. Though the Hidatsa word was originally applied only to the French and Canadians, who are now sometimes designated as maśikat'i (maci-kûtçi, in the Bureau alphabet), the true whites. The Ɉoiwere tribes (Iowa, Oto, and Missouri) call a Frenchman maç okenyi, in which compound maç is equivalent to maci of the Hidatsa, waci of the Mandan, and waśićuŋ of the Dakota. The Ponka and Omaha call a white man waqĕ, one who excels or goes beyond (the rest), and a Frenchman waqĕ ukeɟiⁿ, a common white man. The Winnebago name for Frenchman is waqopinina, which may be compared with the word for mysterious.

NOTES ON THE DAKOTA MYTHS.

On p. 84, lines 8 to 13, there is an account of the wonderful result produced by tossing the Star-born up through the smoke hole. In the Biloxi myth of the Hummingbird there is an account of a girl, a boy, and a dog that were cared for by the Ancient of Crows. One day, in the absence of the fostermother, the girl tossed four grains of corn up through the smoke hole, and when they came down they became many stalks filled with ears of excellent corn. The girl next threw the tent itself up into the air, causing it to come down a beautiful lodge. When she threw her little brother into the air he came down a very handsome warrior. The girl then asked her brother to toss her up, and when he had done this, she came down a very beautiful woman, the fame of her loveliness soon spreading throughout the country. The dog and such clothing as the sister and brother possessed were tossed up in succession, each act producing a change for the better.

On p. 85, from line 33 to p. 86, line 5, there is an account of the deliverance of the imprisoned people by the Star-born when he cut off the heart of the monster that had devoured them. In like manner the Rabbit delivered the people from the Devouring Mountain, as related in the Ꝙegiha myths, "How the Rabbit went to the Sun," and "How the Rabbit killed the Devouring Hill," in "Contributions to North American Ethnology," Vol. VI, pp. 31, 34.

Note 2, p. 89. Eya after a proper name should be rendered by the initial and final quotation marks in the proper places, when eċiya follows, thus: Mato eya eċiyapi, They called him, " Grizzly bear."

When heya precedes and eya follows a phrase or sentence the former may be rendered, *he said as follows*, and the latter, *he said what precedes*. Heya answers to ge, gai or ga-biama of the Ꝙegiha, and eya to e, ai or a-biama. In like manner the Dakota verbs of thinking may be rendered as follows: heċiŋ (which precedes, answering to geꝗegaⁿ of the Ꝙegiha), by *he thought as follows*, and eċiŋ (which follows, answering to eꝗegaⁿ in Ꝙegiha), by *he thought what precedes*.

The myth of the Younger Brother (p. 139–143) contains several incidents which find their counterparts in the Biloxi myth of the Thunder-being. In the Dakota myth the wife of the elder brother plots against the younger brother; she scratches her thighs with the claws of the prairie chicken which the brother-in-law had shot at her request, and tells her husband on his return that his brother had assaulted her. In the Biloxi myth it is the aunt, the wife of the Thunder-being's mother's brother, who scratched herself in many places. In the Dakota myth the Two Women are bad at first, while the mother was good. But in the Biloxi myth the Old Woman was always bad, while her two daughters, who became the wives of the Thunder-being, were ever beneficient. In the Dakota myth the old woman called her husband the Uŋktehi to her assistance, prevailing on him to transport her household, including the Younger Brother, across the stream. In the Biloxi myth the two wives of the Thunder-being, after the death of their mother, call to a huge alligator, of the "salt water species called box alligator" by the Biloxi, and he comes

XXXII   DAKOTA GRAMMAR, TEXTS, AND ETHNOGRAPHY.

to shore in order to serve as the canoe of the party.   Doubtless there were more points of resemblance in the two myths, but parts of the Biloxi one have been forgotten by the aged narrator.

NOTES ON THE DAKOTA DANCES.[1]

The Begging dance is known among the Ponka as the Waṇa watcigaxe (See "Omaha Sociology," in 3d Ann. Rept. Bur. Ethn., p. 355.)   The No flight dance is the Make-no-flight dance or Maȼa watcigaxe of the Ponka and Omaha.   It is described in "Omaha Sociology" (in 3d Ann. Rept. Bur. Ethn., p. 352).   The Scalp dance is a dance for the women among the Ponka and Omaha, who call it Wewatci.   (See "Omaha Sociology," in 3d Ann. Rept. Bur. Ethn., p. 330).

The Mystery dance is identical with the Wacicka of the Omaha.   A brief account of that dance was published by the editor in "Omaha Sociology," in 3d Ann. Rept. Bur. Ethn., pp. 342–346.

The Grass dance, sometimes called Omaha dance, is the dance of the Heȼucka society of the Omaha tribe, answering to the Ilucka of the Kansa, and the Iñ꜀ȼüⁿcka of the Osage.   For accounts of the Heȼucka see "Omaha Sociology," in 3d Ann. Rept. Bur. Ethn., pp. 330–332, and "Hae-thu-ska society of the Omaha tribe," by Miss Alice C. Fletcher, in the Jour. of Amer. Folk-Lore, April–June, 1892, pp. 135–144.   For accounts of the sun-dance, with native illustrations, see "A Study of Siouan Cults," Chapter V, in the 11th Ann. Rept. of the Bureau of Ethnology.

BUREAU OF ETHNOLOGY,
    Washington, D. C., September 15, 1893.

---

[1] See pp. 224–232.

DAKOTA GRAMMAR, TEXTS, AND ETHNOGRAPHY.

PART FIRST.

GRAMMAR.

DAKOTA GRAMMAR.

CHAPTER I.

PHONOLOGY.

THE ALPHABET.

VOWELS.

The vowels are five in number, and have each one uniform sound, except when followed by the nasal " ŋ," which somewhat modifies them.

a   has the sound of English *a* in *father*.

e   has the sound of English *e* in *they*, or of *a* in *face*.

i   has the sound of *i* in *marine*, or of *e* in *me*.

o   has the sound of English *o* in *go*, *note*.

u   has the sound of *u* in *rule*, or of *oo* in *food*.

CONSONANTS.

The consonants are twenty-four in number, exclusive of the sound represented by the apostrophe (').

b   has its common English sound.

ć   is an aspirate with the sound of English *ch*, as in *chin*. In the Dakota Bible and other printing done in the language, it has not been found necessary to use the diacritical mark.*

ċ   is an emphatic *ć*. It is formed by pronouncing " ć " with a strong pressure of the organs, followed by a sudden expulsion of the breath.†

d   has the common English sound.

g   has the sound of *g* hard, as in *go*.

ġ   represents a deep sonant guttural resembling the Arabic *ghain* (غ). Formerly represented by *g* simply.‡

h   has the sound of *h* in English.

ḣ   represents a strong surd guttural resembling the Arabic *kha* (خ). Formerly represented by *r*.‡

---

* For this sound Lepsius recommends the Greek χ.

† This and ķ, p, ţ, are called *cerebrals* by Lepsius.

‡ This and ż correspond with Lepsius, except in the form of the diacritical mark.

3

k   has the same sound as in English.

ķ   is an emphatic letter, bearing the same relation to *k* that "ç" does to "ć." In all the printing done in the language, it is still found most convenient to use the English *q* to represent this sound.*

l   has the common sound of this letter in English. It is peculiar to the Titoŋwaŋ dialect.

m   has the same sound as in English.

n   has the common sound of *n* in English.

ŋ   denotes a nasal sound similar to the French *n* in *bon*, or the English *n* in *drink*. As there are only comparatively very few cases where a full *n* is used at the end of a syllable, no distinctive mark has been found necessary. Hence in all our other printing the nasal continues to be represented by the common *n*.

p   has the sound of the English *p*, with a little more volume and stress of voice.

p   is an emphatic, bearing the same relation to *p* that "ç" does to "ć."*

s   has the surd sound of English *s*, as in *say*.

ś   is an aspirated *s*, having the sound of English *sh*, in in *shine*. Formerly represented by *x*.

t   is the same in English, with a little more volume of voice.

ţ   is an emphatic, bearing the same relation to "t" that "ç" does to "ć."*

w   has the power of the English *w*, as in *walk*.

y   has the sound of English *y*, as in *yet*.

z   has the sound of the common English *z*, as in *zebra*.

ź   is an aspirated *z*, having the sound of the French *j*, or the English *s* in *pleasure*. Formerly represented by *j*.

The apostrophe is used to mark an hiatus, as in s'a. It seems to be analogous to the Arabic *hamzeh* (ᴄ).

NOTE.—Some Dakotas, in some instances, introduce a slight *b* sound before the *m*, and also a *d* sound before *n*. For example, the preposition "om," *with*, is by some persons pronounced *obm*, and the preposition "en," *in*, is sometimes spoken as if it should be written *edn*. In these cases, the members of the Episcopal mission among the Dakotas write the *b* and the *d*, as "ob," "ed."

---

* These are called *cerebrals* by Lepsius. In the alphabet of the Bureau of Ethnology these sounds are designated by tc' (=ć, of Riggs), k' (=ķ), p' (=p), and t' (=ţ), respectively, and are called *explosives*.

SYLLABICATION.

§ 3. Syllables in the Dakota language terminate in a pure or nasalized vowel, as ti-pi, *house*, taŋ-yaŋ, *well*. To this rule there are some exceptions, viz. :

a. The preposition ' en,' *in*, and such words as take it for a suffix, as, petan, *on the fire*, tukten, *where*, etc.; together with some adverbs of time, as, dehan, *now*, hehan, *then*, tohan, *when*, etc.

b. When a syllable is contracted into a single consonant (see § 11), that consonant is attached to the preceding vowel; as, om, *with*, from o-pa, *to follow;* waŋ-yag, from waŋ-ya-ka, *to see;* ka-kiś, from ka-ki-źa, *to suffer;* bo-śim-śi-pa, *to shoot off*, instead of bo-śi-pa-śi-pa. But, in cases of contraction in reduplication, when the contracted syllable coalesces readily with the consonant that follows, it is so attached; as, śi-kśi-ća; sa-psa-pa.

c. There are some other syllables which end in ś; as, iś, *he*, niś, *thou*, miś, *I*, ṛakaeś, *indeed*, etc. These are probably forms of contraction.

ACCENTS.

PLACE OF ACCENT.

§ 4. 1. In the Dakota language all the syllables are enunciated plainly and fully; but every word that is not a monosyllable has in it one or more accented syllables, which, as a general thing, are easily distinguished from such as are not accented. The importance of observing the accent is seen in the fact that the meaning of a word often depends upon it; as, mága, *a field*, maġá, *a goose;* ókiya, *to aid*, okíya, *to speak to.*

2. More than two-thirds, perhaps three-fourths, of all Dakota words of two or more syllables have their principal accent on the *second* syllable from the beginning, as will be seen by a reference to the Dictionary; the greater part of the remaining words have it on the *first.*

3. (*a*) In polysyllabic words there is usually a secondary accent, which falls on the second syllable after the primary one; as, hewóskantúya, *in a desert place;* íćiyópeya, *to barter.*

(*b*) But if the word be compounded of two nouns, or a noun and a verb, each will retain its own accent, whether they fall two degrees apart or not; as, aġúyapi-ićápaŋ, (*wheat-beater*) *a flail;* inmú-śúŋka, (*cat-dog*) *a domestic cat;* akíćita-náźiŋ, *to stand guard.*

REMOVAL OF ACCENT.

§ 5. 1. Suffixes do not appear to have any effect upon the accent; but a syllable prefixed or inserted before the accented syllable draws the accent back, so that it still retains the same position with respect to the beginning of the word; as, napé, *hand*, minápe, *my hand;* baksá, *to cut off with a knife*, bawáksa, *I cut off;* mdaská, *flat*, ćaŋmdáska, *boards;* máġa, *a field*, mitámaġa, *my field.*

When the accent is on the first syllable of the word the prefixing syllable does not always remove it; as, nóġe, *the ear*, manóġe, *my ear.*

2. The same is true of any number of syllables prefixed; as, kaśká, *to bind;* wakáśka, *I bind;* wićáwakaśka, *I bind them.*

3. (*a*) If the verb be accented on the second syllable, and pronouns be inserted after it, they do not affect the primary accent; as, waśtédaka, *to love;* waśtéwadaka, *I love something.*

(*b*) But if the verb be accented on the first syllable, the introduction of a pronoun removes the accent to the second syllable; as; máni, *to walk;* mawáni, *I walk.*

In some cases, however, the accent is not removed; as, óhi, *to reach to;* ówahi, *I reach.*

4. When 'wa' is prefixed to a word commencing with a vowel, and an elision takes place, the accent is thrown on the first syllable; as, iyúśkiŋ, *to rejoice in;* wíyuśkiŋ, *to rejoice;* amdéza, *clear*, wámdeza; amdóśa, *the redwinged black-bird*, wámdośa.

5. When 'wo' is prefixed to adjectives and verbs forming of them abstract nouns, the accent is placed on the first syllable; as, pidá, *glad;* wópida, *gladness;* waóŋśida, *merciful;* wówaoŋśida, *mercy;* iháŋgya, *to destroy;* wóihaŋgye, *a destroying.*

6. So also when the first syllable of a word is dropped or merged into a pronominal prefix, the accent is removed to the first syllable; as, kiksúya, *to remember;* míksuya, *remember me.*

CHANGES OF LETTERS.

SUBSTITUTION AND ELISION.

§ 6. 1. 'A' or 'aŋ' final in verbs, adjectives, and some adverbs, is changed to 'e,' when followed by auxiliary verbs, or by certain conjunctions or adverbs. Thus—

(*a*) When an uncontracted verb in the singular number ending with 'a' or 'aŋ' precedes another verb, as the infinitive mood or participle, the 'a' or 'aŋ' becomes 'e;' as, ya, *to go;* ye kiya, *to cause to go;* niwaŋ, *to swim;* niwe kiya, *to cause to swim;* niwe uŋ, *he is swimming;* but they also say niwaŋ wauŋ, *I am swimming.*

(b) 'A' or 'aŋ' final in verbs, when they take the sign of the future tense or the negative adverb immediately after, and when followed by some conjunctions, is changed into 'e;' as, yuke kta, *there will be some;* mde kte śni, *I will not go.*

To this there are a number of exceptions. Ba, *to blame,* and da, *to ask* or *bèg,* are not changed. Some of the Mdewakaŋtoŋwaŋ say ṭa kta, *he will die.* Other dialects use ṭiŋ kta. Ohnaka, *to place* any thing *in,* is not changed; as, "minape kiŋ takudaŋ ohnaka śni wauŋ," *I have nothing in my hand.* Ipuza, *to be thirsty,* remains the same; as, ipuza kta; "tuwe ipuza kiŋhaŋ," etc., "*let him that is athirst come.*" Some say ipuze kta, but it is not common. Yuha, *to lift, carry,* in distinction from yuha, *to have, possess,* is not changed; as, mduha śni, *I cannot lift it.*

(c) Verbs and adjectives singular ending in 'a' or 'aŋ,' when the connexion of the members of the sentence is close, always change it into 'e;' as, ksape ċa waśte, *wise and good;* waŋmdake ċa wakute, *I saw and I shot it.*

(d) 'A' and 'aŋ' final become 'e' before the adverb 'hiŋċa,' the particle 'do,' and 'śni,' *not;* as, śiċe hiŋċa, *very bad;* waśte kte do, *it will be good;* takuna yute śni, *he eats nothing at all.* Some adverbs follow this rule; as, taŋye hiŋ, *very well;* which is sometimes contracted into taŋyeh.

But 'a' or 'aŋ' final is always retained before tuka, uŋkaŋ, uŋkaŋś, eśta, śta, keś, and perhaps some others.

(e) In the Titoŋwaŋ or Teton dialect, when 'a' or 'aŋ' final would be changed into 'e' in Isaŋyati or Santee, it becomes 'iŋ;' that is when followed by the sign of the future; as, 'yukiŋ kta' instead of ' yuke kta,' 'yiŋ kta' instead of 'ye kta,' 'ṭiŋ kta' instead of 'ṭe kta,' 'ċaŋtekiyiŋ kta,' etc. Also this change takes place before some conjunctions, as, epiŋ na wagli, *I said and I returned.*

2. (a) Substantives ending in 'a' sometimes change it to 'e' when a possessive pronoun is prefixed; as, śuŋka, *dog;* mitaśuŋke, *my dog;* nitaśuŋke, *thy dog;* taśuŋke, *his dog.*

(b) So, on the other hand, 'e' final is changed to 'a,' in forming some proper names; as, Ptaŋsiŋta, the name given to the south end of Lake Traverse, from ptaŋ and siŋte.

§ 7. 1. (a) When 'k' and 'ḳ,' as in kiŋ and kiŋhaŋ, ḳa and ḳehaŋ, etc., are preceded by a verb or adjective whose final 'a' or 'aŋ' is changed for the sake of euphony into 'e,' the 'k' or 'ḳ' following becomes 'ċ' or 'ċ;' as yuhe ċiŋhaŋ, *if he has,* instead of yuha kiŋhaŋ; yuke ċehaŋ, *when there was,* instead of yukaŋ ḳehaŋ.

(b) But if the proper ending of the preceding word is 'e,' no such change takes place; as, waśte kiŋhaŋ, *if he is good;* Wakaŋtaŋka ape ḳa waśtedaka wo, *hope in God and love him.*

2. When 'ya,' the pronoun of the second person singular and nominative case, precedes the inseparable prepositions 'ki,' *to*, and 'kíći,' *for*, the 'ki' and 'ya' are changed, or rather combined, into 'ye;' as, yećaġa, *thou makest to*, instead of yakićaġa; yećićaġa, *thou makest for one*, instead of yakićićaġa. In like manner the pronoun 'wa,' *I*, when coming in conjunction with 'ki,' forms 'we;' as, wećaġa, not wakićaġa, from kićaġa. Wowapi wećaġe kta, *I will make him a book*, i. e. *I will write him a letter.*

3. (*a*) When a pronoun or preposition ending in 'e' or 'i' is prefixed to a verb whose initial letter is 'k,' this letter is changed to 'ć;' as, kaġa, *to make*, kićaġa, *to make to* or *for one;* kaksa, *to cut off*, kićićaksa, *to cut off for one.*

(*b*) But if a consonant immediately follows the 'k,' it is not changed; as, kte, *to kill*, nikte, *he kills thee*. In accordance with the above rule, they say ćićute, *I shoot thee;* they do not however say kićute, but kikute, *he shoots for one.*

(*c*) This change does not take place in adjectives. They say kata, *hot*, nikata, *thou art hot;* kuźa, *lazy*, nikuźa, *thou art lazy.*

§ 8. 1. 'T' and 'k' when followed by 'p' are interchangeable; as iŋkpa, iŋtpa, *the end* of any thing; wakpa, watpa, *a river;* siŋkpe, siŋtpe, *a muskrat.*

2. In the Ihaŋktoŋwaŋ dialect, 'k' is often used for 'h' of the Waħpetoŋwaŋ; as, kdi, *to arrive at home*, for ħdi; ćaŋpakmikma, *a cart or wagon*, for ćaŋpaħmihma. In the same circumstances the Titoŋwaŋ use 'g,' and the Mdewakaŋtoŋwaŋ 'n;' as, ćaŋpagmigma, ćaŋpanminma.

3. Vowel changes required by the Titoŋwaŋ:

(*a*) 'a' to 'u,' sometimes, as 'iwaŋġa' to 'iyuŋġa;'

(*b*) 'e' to 'i,' sometimes, as 'aetopteya' to 'aitopteya;'

(*c*) 'e' to 'o,' as 'mdetaŋhuŋka' to 'blotaŋhuŋka;' 'ķehaŋ' to 'ķohaŋ' or 'ķoŋhaŋ;'

(*d*) 'i' to 'e,' as 'ećoŋpi ye do' to 'ećoŋpe lo;'

(*e*) 'i' to 'o,' sometimes, as 'ituya' to 'otuya;'

(*f*) 'i' to 'u,' as 'odidita' to 'oluluta;' 'itaħaŋ' to 'utuħaŋ,' etc.;

(*g*) 'o' to 'e,' sometimes, as 'tiyopa' to 'tiyepa;'

(*h*) 'a' or 'aŋ' final, changed to 'e,' before the sign of the future, etc., becomes 'iŋ,' as 'yeke kta' to 'yukiŋ kta,' 'ţe kta' to 'ţiŋ kta.'

4. Consonant changes required by the Titoŋwaŋ:

(*a*) 'b' to 'w,' (1) in the prefixes 'ba' and 'bo,' always; (2) in some words, as 'waħbadaŋ' to 'waħwala;'

(*b*) 'b' to 'm,' as 'śbeya' to 'śmeya;'

(*c*) 'd' to 'l,' always; as the 'd' sound is not in Titoŋwaŋ;

(*d*) 'h' to 'g,' always in the combinations 'hb,' 'hd,' 'hm,' 'hn,' which become 'gb,' 'gl,' 'gb' and 'gn;'

(*e*) 'ḳ' to 'n,' as 'ḳa' to 'na;'

(*f*) 'm' to 'b,' as (1) in 'md' which becomes 'bl;' and (2) in 'm' final, contracted, as 'om' to 'ob,' 'tom' to 'tob;'

(*g*) 'm' to 'p,' as in the precative form 'miye' to 'piye;'

(*h*) 'n' to 'b,' as (1) in contract forms of 'ć,' 't,' and 'y,' always; e. g., 'ćaŋteśin' to 'ćaŋteśil,' 'yun' to 'yul,' and 'kun' to 'kul,' etc.; (2) in certain words, as 'nina' to 'lila,' 'mina' (*Ih.*) to 'mila;' (3) 'n' final in some words, as 'en' to 'el,' 'hećen' to 'hećel,' 'waŋkan' to 'waŋkal,' 'taŋkan' to 'taŋkal,' etc.;

(*i*) 't' to 'ć,' as 'ćistiŋna' to 'ćisćila;'

(*j*) 't' to 'g,' as 'itokto' to 'itogto;'

(*k*) 't' to 'k,' as 'itokam' to 'ikokab.'

(*l*) 'w' to 'y,' in some words, as 'owasiŋ' to 'oyasiŋ,' 'iwaŋġa' to 'iyuŋġa,' 'waŋka' to 'yuŋka,' etc.;

(*m*) 'y' to 'w,' as 'ećoŋ ye do' to 'ećoŋ we lo;'

(*n*) 'daŋ' final generally becomes 'la,' as 'hokśidaŋ' changed to 'hokśila;' but sometimes it changes to 'ni,' as 'waŋźidaŋ' to 'waŋźini,' 'tuwedaŋ' to 'tuweni,' etc.;

(*o*) 'waŋ,' as indicated above, in 'a' to 'u,' in some words, becomes 'yuŋ,' as 'ḣewaŋke' to 'ḣeyuŋke,' 'napćiŋwaŋka' to 'napćiŋyuŋka,' 'iwaŋġa' to 'iyuŋġa,' etc.

§ 9. 1. When two words come together so as to form one, the latter of which commences and the former ends with a vowel, that of the first word is sometimes dropped; as, ćaŋtokpani, *to desire* or *long for*, of ćaŋte, *the heart*, and okpani, *to fail of;* wakpićahda, *by the side of a river*, from wakpa and ićahda; wićota, *many persons*, from wića and ota. Tak eya, *what did he say?* is sometimes used for taku eya.

2. In some cases also this elision takes place when the second word commences with a consonant; as, napkawiŋ and namkawiŋ, *to beckon with the hand*, of nape and kawiŋ.

3. Sometimes when two vowels come together, 'w' or 'y' is introduced between them for the sake of euphony; as, owihaŋke, *the end*, from o and ihaŋke; niyate, *thy father*, from the pronoun ni, *thy*, and ate, *father*.

§ 10. The 'yu' of verbs commencing with that syllable is not unfrequently dropped when the pronoun of the first person plural is used; as, yuhá, *to have*, úŋhapi, *we have;* yúza, *to hold*, úŋzapi, *we hold.* Yúza also becomes oze, which may be oyúze contracted; as, Makatooze, *the Blue Earth River,* lit. *where the blue earth is taken;* oze śiċa, *bad to catch.*

CONTRACTION.

§ 11. 1. Contractions take place in some nouns when combined with a following noun, and in some verbs when they occupy the position of the infinitive or participle. The contraction consists in dropping the vowel of the final syllable and changing the preceding consonant usually into its corresponding sonant, or *vice versâ,* which then belongs to the syllable that precedes it; as yus from yuza, *to hold;* tom from topa, *four.* The following changes occur:

·z into s; as, yuza, *to hold* any thing; yus naźiŋ, *to stand holding.*

ź into ś; as kakiźa, *to suffer;* kakiś wauŋ, *I am suffering.*

ġ into h; as, máġa, *a field,* and maġá, *a goose,* are contracted into mah.

k into g; as, waŋyaka, *to see* any thing, is contracted into waŋyag.

p into m; as, topa, *four,* is contracted into tom; watopa, *to paddle* or *row* a boat, is contracted into watom.

t into d; as, odota, the reduplicated form of ota, *many, much.*

t into g; as, boźagźata, the reduplicated form of boźata, *to make forked by punching.*

ċ, t, and y, into ŋ; as, waniċa, *none,* becomes wanin; yuta, *to eat* any thing, becomes yuŋ; kuya, *below,* becomes kun.

2. The article 'kiŋ' is sometimes contracted into 'g;' as, oyate kiŋ, *the people,* contracted into oyateg.

3. Ċaŋte, *the heart,* is contracted into ċan; as, ċanwaśte, *glad* (ċaŋte *and* waśte, *heart-good*).

4. When a syllable ending in a nasal (ŋ) has added to it 'm' or 'n,' the contracted form of the syllable that succeeded, the nasal sound is lost in the 'm' or 'n,' and is consequently dropped; as, ċaŋnuŋpa, *to smoke a pipe,* ċaŋnum mani, *he smokes as he walks;* kakiŋċa, *to scrape,* kakin iyeya.

Contracted words may generally be known by their termination. When contraction has not taken place, the rule is that every syllable ends with either a pure or nasalized vowel. See § 3.

CHAPTER II.

MORPHOLOGY.

PRONOUNS.

§ 12. Dakota pronouns may be classed as *personal* (*simple* and *compound*), *interrogative, relative,* and *demonstrative pronouns,* together with the *definite* and *indefinite pronouns* or *articles.*

PERSONAL PRONOUNS.

§ 13. To personal pronouns belong *person, number,* and *case.*

1. There are three persons, the *first, second,* and *third.*

2. There are three numbers, the *singular, dual,* and *plural.* The dual is only of the first person; it includes the person speaking and the person spoken to, and has the form of the first person plural, but without the termination 'pi.'

3. Pronouns have three cases, *subjective, objective,* and *possessive.*

§ 14. The simple pronouns may be divided into *separate* and *incorporated;* i. e. those which form separate words, and those which are prefixed to or inserted into verbs, adjectives, and nouns. The incorporated pronouns may properly be called *article pronouns* or *pronominal particles.*

Separate.

§ 15. 1. (*a*) The separate pronouns in most common use, and probably the original ones, are, Sing., miye, *I,* niye, *thou,* iye, *he.* The plural of these forms is denoted by 'uŋkiye' for the first person, 'niye' for the second, and 'iye' for the third, and adding 'pi' at the end either of the pronoun itself or of the last principal word in the phrase. Dual, uŋkiye, (*I and thou*) *we two.*

These pronouns appear to be capable of analysis, thus: To the incorporated forms 'mi,' 'ni' and 'i,' is added the substantive verb 'e,' the 'y' coming in for euphony. So that 'miye' is equivalent to *I am,* 'niye' to *thou art,* and 'iye' to *he is.*[1]

---

[1] A knowledge of the cognate languages of the Siouan or Dakotan stock would have led the author to modify, if not reject, this statement, as well as several others in this volume, to which attention is called by similar foot-notes. 'Mi' and 'ni' can be possessive (§ 21) and dative (§ 19, 3), or, as the author terms it, objective (though the act is *to* another); but he did not show their use in the subjective or nominative, nor did he give 'i' as a pronoun in the 3d singular. Besides, how could he reconcile his analysis of miś, niś, and iś (§ 15, 1, *b*) with that of miye, niye, and iye?—J. O. D.

(*b*) Another set of separate pronouns, which are evidently contracted forms, are, Sing., miś, *I*, niś, *thou*, iś, *he*. The Plural of these forms is designated by employing 'uŋkiś' for the first person, 'niś' for the second, and 'iś' for the third, and adding 'pi' at the end of the last principal word in the phrase. Dual, uŋkiś, (*I and thou*) *we two*. These contracted forms of miś, niś, and iś would seem to have been formed from miye, niye, iye; as, miye eś contracted into miś; niye eś contracted into niś, etc.

2. These pronouns are used for the sake of emphasis, that is to say, they are employed as emphatic repetitions of the subjective or objective pronoun contained in the verb; as, miś wakaġa, (*I I-made*) *I made;* miye mayakaġa, (*me me-thou-madest*) *thou madest me.* Both sets of pronouns are used as emphatic repetitions of the subject, but the repetition of the object is generally confined to the first set. It would seem in fact that the first set may originally have been objective, and the second subjective forms.

3. Miś miye, *I myself;* niś niye, *thou thyself;* iś iye, *he himself;* uŋkiś uŋkiyepi, *we ourselves*, etc., are emphatic expressions which frequently occur, meaning that it concerns the person or persons alone, and not any one else.

§ 16. 1. The possessive separate pronouns are: Sing., mitawa, *my* or *mine*, nitawa, *thy* or *thine*, tawa, *his;* Dual, uŋkitawa, (*mine and thine*) *ours;* Plur., uŋkitawapi, *our* or *ours*, nitawapi, *your* or *yours*, tawapi, *their* or *theirs:* as, wowapi mitawa, *my book*, he nitawa, *that is mine.*

2. The separate pronouns of the first set are also used as emphatic repetitions with these; as, miye mitawa, (*me mine*) *my own;* niye nitawa, *thy own;* iye tawa, *his own;* uŋkiye uŋkitawapi, *our own.*

INCORPORATED OR ARTICLE PRONOUNS.[1]

§ 17. The incorporated pronouns are used to denote the subject or object of an action, or the possessor of a thing.

Subjective.

§ 18. 1. The subjective article pronouns, or those which denote the subject of the action, are: Sing., wa, *I*, ya, *thou;* Dual, uŋ, (*I and thou*) *we two;* Plur., uŋ-pi, *we*, ya-pi, *ye*. The Plur. term, 'pi' is attached to the end of the verb.

---

[1] "Article pronoun" is adopted by the author from Powell's Introduction to the Study of Indian Languages, 2d ed., p. 47. But the article pronoun of Powell differs materially from that of Riggs. The *classifier* which marks the gender or *attitude* (standing, sitting, etc.) should not be confounded with the *incorporated pronoun*, which performs a different function (§ 17).—J. O. D.

2. (*a*) These pronouns are most frequently used with active verbs; as, wakaġa, *I make;* yakaġa, *thou makest;* uŋkaġapi, *we make.*

(*b*) They are also used with a few neuter and adjective verbs. The neuter verbs are such as, ti, *to dwell*, wati, *I dwell;* itoŋśni, *to tell a lie*, iwatoŋśni, *I tell a lie.* The adjective verbs with which 'wa' and 'ya' are used are very few; as, waoŋśida, *merciful*, waoŋsiwada, *I am merciful;* duzahaŋ, *swift*, waduzahaŋ, *I am swift of foot;* ksapa, *wise*, yaksapa, *thou art wise.*

(*c*) The neuter and adjective verbs which use the article pronouns 'wa' and 'ya' rather than 'ma' and 'ni,' have in some sense an active meaning, as distinguished from suffering or passivity.

3. When the verb commences with a vowel, the 'uŋ' of the dual and plural, if prefixed, becomes 'uŋk;' as, itoŋśni, *to tell a lie*, uŋkitoŋśni, *we two tell a lie;* au, *to bring*, uŋkaupi, *we bring.*

4. When the prepositions 'ki,' *to*, and 'kíći,' *for*, occur in verbs, instead of 'waki' and 'yaki,' we have 'we' and 'ye' (§ 7. 2.); as, kićaġa, *to make to one*, wećaġa, *I make to;* kićićaġa, *to make for*, yećićaġa, *thou makest for*, yećićaġapi, *you make for* one. Kiksuya, *to remember*, also follows this rule; as, weksuya, *I remember.*

5. In verbs commencing with 'yu' and 'ya,' the first and second persons are formed by changing the 'y' into 'md' and 'd;' as, yuwaśte, *to make good*, mduwaśte, *I make good*, duwaśte, *thou makest good*, duwaśtepi, *you make good;* yawa, *to read*, mdawa, *I read*, dawa, *thou readest.* In like manner we have iyotaŋka, *to sit down*, imdotaŋka, *I sit down*, idotaŋka, *thou sittest down.*

6. In the Titoŋwaŋ dialect these article pronouns are 'bl' and 'l;' as, bluwaśte, luwaśte, etc.

7. These forms, 'md' and 'd,' may have been shortened from miye and niye, the 'n' of niye being exchanged for 'd.' Hence in Titoŋwaŋ we have, for the first and second persons of 'ya,' *to go*, mni kta, ni kta.[1]

8. The third person of verbs and verbal adjectives has no incorporated pronoun.

Objective.

§ 19. 1. The objective pronouns, or those which properly denote the object of the action, are, Sing., ma, *me*, ni, *thee;* Plur., uŋ-pi, *us*, and ni-pi, *you.*

---

[1] I am inclined to doubt this statement for two reasons: 1. Why should one conjugation be singled out to the exclusion of others? If md (bd, bl) and d (l) have been shortened from miye and niye, how about wa and ya (§ 18, 1), we and ye (§ 18, 4), ma and ni (§ 19, 1–2, *b*)? 2. See footnote on §15, 1, *a*. This could be shown by a table if there were space. See § 54. J. O. D.

2. (*a*) These pronouns are used witn active verbs to denote the object of the action; as, kaġa, *he made*, makaġa, *he made me*, niċaġapi, *he made you* or *they made you.*

(*b*) They are also used with neuter verbs and adjectives; as, yazaŋ, *to be sick*, mayazaŋ, *I am sick;* waśte, *good*, mawaśte, *I am good.* The English idiom requires that we should here render these pronouns by the subjective case, although it would seem that in the mind of the Dakotas the verb or adjective is used impersonally and governs the pronoun in the objective. Or perhaps it would better accord with the genius of the language to say that, as these adjective and neuter-verb forms must be translated as passives, the pronouns 'ma' and 'ni' should not be regarded in all cases as objective, but, as in these examples and others like them, subjective as well.

(*c*) They are also incorporated into nouns where in English the substantive verb would be used as a copula; as, wiċaśta, *man*, wimaċaśta, *I am a man.*

3. In the same cases where 'we' and 'ye' subjective are used (see § 18, 4), the objective pronouns have the forms 'mi' and 'ni,' instead of 'maki' and 'niċi;' as, kiċaġa, *he makes to one*, miċaġa, *he makes to me*, niċaġa, *he makes to thee*, niċaġapi, *he makes to you.*

4. There is no objective pronoun of the third person singular, but 'wiċa' (perhaps originally *man*) is used as an objective pronoun of the third person plural; as, waśtedaka, *to love any one*, waśtewiċadaka, *he loves them*; wiċayazaŋ, *they are sick.* When followed by a vowel, the 'a' final is dropped; as, eċawiċuŋkiċoŋpi, *we do to them.*

§ 20. Instead of 'wa,' *I*, and 'ni,' *thee*, coming together in a word, the syllable 'ċi' is used to express them both; as, waśtedaka, *to love*, waśteċidaka, *I love thee.* The plural of the object is denoted by adding the term 'pi;' as, waśteċidakapi, *I love you.* The essential difference between 'ċi' and the 'uŋ' of the dual and plural is that in the former the first person is in the nominative and the second in the objective case, while in the latter both persons are in the same case. (See § 24, 1.)

The place of the nominative and objective pronouns in the verb, adjective, or noun, into which they are incorporated, will be explained when treating of those parts of speech.

Possessive.

§ 21. Two forms of possession appear to be recognized in Dakota, *natural* and *artificial.*

(*a*) The possessive article pronouns of the first class are, Sing., mi or ma, *my*, ni, *thy;* Dual, uŋ, (*my* and *thy*) *our;* Plur., uŋ-pi, *our*, ni-pı, *your.* These express natural possession; that is, possession that can not be alienated.

(*b*) These pronouns are prefixed to nouns which signify the different parts of oneself, as also one's words and actions, but they are not used alone to express the idea of property in general; as, mitaŋćaŋ, *my body;* minaġi, *my soul;* mitawaćiŋ, *my mind ;* mitezi, *my stomach;* misiha, *my foot;* mićaŋte, *my heart;* miiśta, *my eye;* miisto, *my arm;* mioie, *my words;* miohaŋ, *my actions;* uŋtaŋćaŋ, *our two bodies;* uŋtaŋćaŋpi, *our bodies;* nitaŋćaŋpi, *your bodies;* uŋnaġipi, *our souls;* uŋćaŋtepi, *our hearts.*

(*c*) In those parts of the body which exhibit no independent action, the pronoun of the first person takes the form 'ma;' as, mapa, *my head;* manoġe, *my ears;* mapoġe, *my nose;* mawe, *my blood*, etc.

§ 22. 1. The pronouns of the first and second persons prefixed to nouns signifying relationship are, Sing., mi, *my*, ni, *thy;* Dual, uŋki, (*my* and *thy*) *our;* Plur., uŋki-pi, *our*, ni-pi, *your:* as, mićiŋća, *my child;* nidekśi, *thy uncle;* nisuŋka, *thy younger brother;* uŋkićiŋćapi, *our children.*

2. (*a*) Nouns signifying relationship take, as the pronouns of the third person, the suffix 'ku,' with its plural 'kupi;' as, suŋká, *the younger brother* of a man, suŋkaku, *his younger brother;* taŋká, *the younger sister* of a woman, taŋkaku, *her younger sister;* hihna, *husband*, hihnaku, *her husband;* ate, *father*, atkuku, *his* or *her father.*

(*b*) But after the vowel 'i,' either pure or nasalized, the suffix is either 'tku' or 'ćiu;' as, dekśi, *uncle*, dekśitku, *his* or *her uncle;* taŋkśi, *the younger sister* of a man, taŋkśitku, *his younger sister;* ćiŋkśi, *son*, ćiŋhiŋtku, *his* or *her son;* tawiŋ, *a wife*, tawićiu, *his wife;* ćiŋye, *the elder brother* of a man, ćiŋćiu, *his elder brother.*

Perhaps the origin of the 't' in 'tku' may be found in the 'ta' of the third person used to denote property. See the next section.

§ 23. 1. The prefixed possessive pronouns or pronominal particles of the second class, which are used to express property in things mainly, possession that may be transferred, are, 'mita,' 'nita,' and 'ta,' singular; 'uŋkita,' dual; and 'unkita-pi,' 'nita-pi,' and 'ta-pi,' plural: as, mitaoŋspe, *my axe;* nitaśuŋke, *thy horse;* they say also mitahokśidaŋ, *my boy.* These pronouns are also used with koda, *a particular friend*, as, mitakoda, *my friend*, nitakoda, *thy friend*, takodaku, *his friend;* and with kićuwa, *comrade*, as nitakićuwa, *thy comrade;* also they say, mitawiŋ, *my wife*, tawićiu, *his wife.*

2. (*a*) 'Mita,' 'nita,' and 'ta,' when prefixed to nouns commencing with 'o' or 'i,' drop the 'a;' as, owiŋźa, *a bed*, mitowiŋźe, *my bed;* ipahiŋ, *a pillow*, nitipahiŋ, *thy pillow;* itazipa, *a bow*, tinazipe, *his bow.*

(*b*) When these possessive pronouns are prefixed to abstract nouns which commence with 'wo,' both the 'a' of the pronoun and 'w' of the noun are dropped; as, wowaśte, *goodness,* mitowaśte, *my goodness;* woksape, *wisdom,* nitoksape, *thy wisdom;* wowaoŋśida, *mercy,* towaoŋśida, *his mercy.*

(*c*) But when the noun commences with 'a,' the 'a' of the pronoun is usually retained; as, akićita, *a soldier,* mitaakićita, *my soldier.*

3. 'Wića' and 'wići' are sometimes prefixed to nouns, making what may be regarded as a possessive of the third person plural; as, wićahuŋku, *their mother;* wićiatkuku, *their father.*

4. 'Ki' is a possessive pronominal particle infixed in a large number of verbs; as, bakiksa, bokiksa, nakiksa, in the Paradigm; and, okide, *to seek one's own,* from ode; waśtekidaka, *to love one's own,* from waśtedaka; iyekiya, *to find one's own—to recognize*—from iyeya, etc. In certain cases the 'ki' is simply 'k' agglutinated; as, kpaksa, *to break off one's own,* from paksa; kpaġaŋ, *to part with one's own,* from paġaŋ, etc.

5. Other possessive particles, which may be regarded as either pronominal or adverbial, and which are closely agglutinated, are, 'hd,' in Isaŋyati; 'kd,' in Yankton, and 'gl,' in Titoŋwaŋ. These are prefixed to verbs in 'ya,' 'yo,' and 'yu.' See this more fully explained under Verbs.

Tables of Personal Pronouns.

	SEPARATE PRONOUNS.		
	Subjective.	Objective.	Possessive.
Sing. 3.	iye; iś	iye	tawa
2.	niye; niś	niye	nitawa
1.	miye; miś	miye	mitawa
Dual 1.	uŋkiye; uŋkiś		uŋkitawa
Plur. 3.	iyepi;	iyepi	tawapi
2.	niyepi;	niyepi	nitawapi
1.	uŋkiyepi; uŋkiś	uŋkiyepi	uŋkitawapi

	INCORPORATED PRONOUNS.		
	Nominative.	Objective.	Possessive.
Sing. 3			-ku, -tku; ta-
2	ya; ye	ni; ni	ni-; ni-; nita-
1	wa; we	ma; mi	mi-; ma-; mita-
Dual 1	uŋ; uŋki		uŋ-; uŋki-; uŋkita-
Plur. 3		wića	-kupi, -tkupi; ta-pi
2	ya-pi; ye-pi	ni-pi; ni-pi	ni-pi; ni-pi; nita-pi
1	uŋ-pi; uŋki-pi	uŋ-pi; uŋki-pi	uŋ-pi; uŋki-pi; uŋkita-pi

§ 24. These are ' ći,' 'kići,' and ' ići.'

1. The double pronoun ' ći,' combines the subjective *I* and the objective *you;* as, waśtećidaka, *I love you,* from waśtedaka. (See § 20.)

2. The form 'kići,' when a double pronoun, is *reciprocal,* and requires the verb to have the plural ending; as, waśtekićidapi, *they love each other.* But sometimes it is a preposition *with* and *to:* mići hi, *he came with me.* The Titoŋwaŋ say kići waki, *I came with him.*

3. The reflexive pronouns are used when the agent and patient are the same person; as, waśteićidaka, *he loves himself,* waśtenićidaka, *thou lovest thyself,* waśtemićidaka, *I love myself.*

The forms of these pronouns are as follows:—

Sing.	Dual.	Plur.
3. ići		ići-pi
2. nići		nići-pi
1. mići	uŋkići	uŋkići-pi.

RELATIVE PRONOUNS.

§ 25. 1. The relative pronouns are tuwe, *who,* and taku, *what;* tuwe kaśta and tuwe kakeś, *whosoever* or *anyone;* taku kaśta and taku kakeś, *whatsoever* or *any thing.* In the Titoŋwaŋ and Ihaŋktoŋwaŋ dialects 'tuwa' is used for tuwe, both as relative and interrogative.

2. Tuwe and taku are sometimes used independently in the manner of nouns: as, tuwe u, *some one comes;* taku yamni waŋmdaka, *I see three things.*

3. They are also used with 'daŋ' suffixed and 'śni' following: as, tuwedaŋ śni, *no one;* takudaŋ mduhe śni, *I have not anything;* tuktedaŋ uŋ śni, *it is nowhere;* uŋmana ećoŋpi śni, *neither did it.*

INTERROGATIVE PRONOUNS.

§ 26. These are tuwe, *who?* with its plural tuwepi; taku, *what?* which is used with the plural signification, both with and without the termination 'pi;' tukte, *which?* tuwe tawa, *whose?* tona, tonaka, and tonakeća, *how many?*

DEMONSTRATIVE PRONOUNS.

§ 27. 1. These are de, *this,* and he, *that,* with their plurals dena, *these,* and hena, *those;* also, ka, *that,* and kana, *those* or *so many.* From these are formed denaka and denakeća, *these many;* henaka and henakeća, *those many;* and kanaka and kanakeća, *so many as those.*

2. 'Daŋ' or 'na' is sometimes suffixed with a restrictive signification; as, dena, *these*, denana, *only these;* hena, *those*, henana, *only so many.*

3. 'E' is used sometimes as a demonstrative and sometimes as an impersonal pronoun. Sometimes it stands alone, but more frequently it is in combination, as, 'ee,' 'dee,' 'hee,' *this is it.* Thus it indicates the place of the copula, and may be treated as the substantive verb. (See § 155.)

ARTICLES.

§ 28. There are properly speaking only two articles, *the definite* and *indefinite.*

Definite Article.

§ 29. 1. The definite article is kiŋ, *the;* as, wićaśta kiŋ, *the man,* maka kiŋ, *the earth.*

2. The definite article, when it occurs after the vowel 'e' which has taken the place of 'a' or 'aŋ,' takes the form 'ćiŋ' (§ 7. 1.); as, wićaśta śiće ćiŋ, *the bad man.*

3. Uses of the definite article: (*a*) It is generally used where we would use *the* in English. (*b*) It is often followed by the demonstrative 'he'—kiŋ he—in which case both together are equivalent to *that which.* In the place of 'kiŋ,' the Titoŋwaŋ generally use 'kiŋhaŋ.'[1] (*c*) It is used with verbs, converting them into verbal nouns; as, ećoŋpi kiŋ, *the doers.* (*d*) It is often used with class nouns and abstract nouns; when in English, *the* would be omitted; as, woksape kiŋ, *the wisdom,* i. e., *wisdom.* See this more at large under Syntax.

4. The form of kiŋ, indicating past time, is koŋ, which partakes of the nature of a demonstrative pronoun, and has been sometimes so considered; as, wićaśta koŋ, *that man,* meaning some man spoken of before.

5. When 'a' or 'aŋ' of the preceding word is changed into 'e,' 'koŋ' becomes 'ćikoŋ' (§ 7. 1.); as, tuwe waŋmdake ćikoŋ, *that person whom I saw,* or *the person I saw.*

In Titonwaŋ, koŋ becomes çoŋ, instead of ćikoŋ. W. J. CLEVELAND.

Indefinite Article.

§ 30. The indefinite article is 'waŋ,' *a* or *an,* a contraction of the numeral waŋźi, *one;* as, wićaśta waŋ, *a man.* The Dakota article 'waŋ' would seem to be as closely related to the numeral 'waŋźi' or 'waŋća,' as the

---

[1] While *some* of the Titoŋwaŋ may use "kiŋhaŋ" instead of "ɧiŋ," this can not be said of those on the Cheyenne River and Lower Brule reservations. They use ɧiŋ in about two hundred and fifty-five texts of the Bushotter and Bruyier collection of the Bureau of Ethnology.—J. O. D.

English article 'an' to the numeral *one*. This article is used a little less frequently than the indefinite article in English.

VERBS.

§ 31. The Verb is much the most important part of speech in Dakota; as it appropriates, by agglutination and synthesis, many of the pronominal, prepositional, and adverbial or modal particles of the language.

Verbal Roots.

§ 32. The Dakota language contains many verbal roots, which are used as verbs only with certain causative prefixes, and which form participles by means of certain additions. The following is a list of the more common verbal roots:—

baza, *smooth*
ġa, *open out*
ġaŋ, *open out*
ġapa, *open out*
ġata, *spread*
ġuka, *spread out*
hiŋta, *brush off*
hmuŋ, *twist*
hna, *fall off*
hnayaŋ, *deceive*
huhuza, *shake*
ħća, *open out, expand*
ħći, *crumble, gap*
ħdata, *scratch*
ħdeća, *tear, smash*
ħdoka, *make a hole*
ħepa, *exhaust*
ħića, *arouse*
ħpa, *fall down*
ħpu, *crumble off*
ħtaka, *catch, grip*
ħu, *peel*
ħuġa, *jam, smash*
kawa, *open*
kća, *untangle*
kiŋća, *scrape off*
kiŋza, *creak*

koŋta, *notch*
ksa, *separate*
kśa, *bend*
kśiźa, *double up*
ktaŋ, *bend*
mdaza, *spread open*
mdaźa, *burst out*
mdu, *fine, pulverize*
mna, *rip*
mni, *spread out*
pota, *wear out*
psaka, *break in two*
psuŋ, *spill*
pśuŋ, *dislocate*
pta, *cut out, pare off*
ptaŋyaŋ, *turn over*
ptuźa, *crack, split*
sba, *ravel*
sbu, *dangle*
sdeća, *split*
skića, *press*
skita, *draw tight*
smiŋ, *scrape off*
sna, *ring*
sni, *cold, gone out*
sota, *clear off, whitish*

śaka, *press down*
śka, *tie*
śkića, *press*
śna, *miss*
śpa, *break off*
śpi, *pick off*
śpu, *fall off*
śuźa, *mash*
taka, *touch, make fast*
taŋ, *well, touch*
tepa, *wear off*
tića, *scrape*
tipa, *contract*
titaŋ, *pull*
tkuġa, *break off*
tpi, *crack*
tpu, *crumble, fall off*
weġa, *fracture*
wiŋźa, *bend down*
zamni, *open out*
źa, *stir*
źaźa, *rub out, efface*
źiŋ, *stiff*
źipa, *pinch*
źuŋ, *root out*
źuźu, *come to pieces.*

Verbs formed by Modal Prefixes.

§ 33. The modal particles 'ba,' 'bo,' 'ka,' 'na,' 'pa,' 'ya,' and 'yu' are prefixed to verbal roots, adjectives, and some neuter verbs, making of them active transitive verbs, and usually indicating the mode and instrument of the action.

(*a*) The syllable 'ba' prefixed shows that the action is done by *cutting* or *sawing*, and that *a knife* or *saw* is the instrument. For this the Titoŋwaŋ use 'wá' for the prefix.

(*b*) The prefix 'bo' signifies that the action is done by *shooting* with a gun or arrow, by *punching* with a stick, or by any instrument thrown endwise. It also expresses the action of *rain* and *hail;* and is used in reference to *blowing* with the mouth, as, bosni, *to blow out.*[1]

(*c*) The prefix 'ka' denotes that the action is done by *striking*, as with an axe or club, or by *shaving*. It is also used to denote the effects of *wind* and of *running water*.

(*d*) The prefix 'na' generally signifies that the action is done with the *foot* or *by pressure*. It is also used to express the involuntary action of things, as the bursting of a gun, the warping of a board and cracking of timber, and the effects of freezing, boiling, etc.

(*e*) The prefix 'pa' shows that the action is done by *pushing* or *rubbing* with the hand.

(*f*) The prefix 'ya' signifies that the action is performed with *the mouth*.

(*g*) The prefix 'yu' may be regarded as simply *causative* or *effective*. It has an indefinite signification and is commonly used without any reference to the manner in which the action is performed.

Usually the signification of the verbal roots is the same with all the prefixes, as they only have respect to the *manner* and *instrument* of the action; as, baksa, *to cut in two with a knife*, as a stick; boksa, *to shoot off;* kaksa, *to cut off with an axe;* naksa, *to break off with the foot;* paksa, *to break off with the hand;* yaksa, *to bite off;* yuksa, *to break off*. But the verbal root śka appears to undergo a change of meaning; as, kaśka, *to tie*, yuśka, *to untie*.

§ 34. These prefixes are also used with neuter verbs, giving them an active signification; as, nażiŋ, *to stand*, yunażiŋ, *to raise up, cause to stand;* ćeya, *to cry*, naćeya, *to make cry by kicking*.

§ 35. 1. We also have verbs formed from adjectives by the use of such of these prefixes as the meaning of the adjectives will admit of; as, waśte, *good*, yuwaśte, *to make good;* teća, *new*, yuteća, *to make new;* śića, *bad*, yaśića, *to speak evil of*.

2. Verbs are also made by using nouns and adjectives in the predicate, in which case they are declined as verbs; as, Damakota, *I am a Dakota;* mawaśte, *I am good*.

---

[1] For the Titoŋwaŋ use, see 'wo' and 'yu' in the Dictionary.

3. Sometimes other parts of speech may be used in the same way, i. e., prepositions; as, emataŋhaŋ, *I am from.*

§ 36. There are several classes of verbs which are compounded of two verbs.

1. 'Kiya' and 'ya' or 'yaŋ,' when used with other verbs, impart to them a causative signification and are usually joined with them in the same word; as naźiŋ, *he stands,* naźiŋkiya, *he causes to stand.* The first verb is sometimes contracted (see § 11); as, waŋyaka, *he sees,* waŋyagkiya, *he causes to see.*

2. In the above instances the first verb has the force of an infinitive or present participle. But sometimes the first as well as the second has the force of an independent finite verb; as, hdiwaŋka, *he comes home sleeps* (of hdi and waŋka); hinaźiŋ, *he comes stands* (of hi and naźiŋ). These may be termed *double verbs.*

§ 37. To verbs in Dakota belong *conjugation, form, person, number, mode,* and *tense.*

§ 38. Dakota verbs are comprehended *in three conjugations,* distinguished by the form of the pronouns in the first and second persons singular which denote the agent. Conjugations I and II include all common and active verbs and III includes all neuter verbs.

(*a*) In the *first conjugation* the subjective singular pronouns are 'wa' or 'we' and 'ya' or 'ye.'

(*b*) The *second conjugation* embraces verbs in 'yu,' 'ya,' and 'yo,' which form the first and second persons singular by changing the 'y' into 'md' and 'd,' except in the Titoŋwaŋ dialect where these are 'bl' and 'l.'

(*c*) Neuter and adjective verbs form the *third conjugation,* known by taking what are more properly the objective pronouns 'ma' and 'ni.'

1. Of neuter verbs proper we have (*a*) the complete predicate, as, ṭa, *to die;* asni, *to get well;* (*b*) with adjectives; as waśte with aya or iċaġa; waśte amayaŋ, *I am growing better.*

2. Of predicate nouns; as, Wamaśiċuŋ, *I am a Frenchman.*

3. Of predicate adjectives; as, mawaśte, *I am good.* All adjectives may be so used.—A. L. Riggs.

§ 39. Dakota verbs exhibit certain varieties of form which indicate corresponding variations of meaning.

1. Most Dakota verbs may assume *a frequentative form*, that is, a form which conveys the idea of frequency of action. It consists in doubling a syllable, generally the last; as, baksa, *to cut off with a knife*, baksaksa, *to cut off in several places*. This form is conjugated in all respects just as the verb is before reduplication.

2. The so-called *absolute* form of active verbs is made by prefixing 'wa' and is conjugated in the same manner as the primitive verb, except that it can not take an objective noun or pronoun. The 'wa' appears to be equivalent to the English *something;* as manoŋ, *to steal*, wamanoŋ, *to steal something;* taspaŋtaŋka mawanoŋ (*apple I-stole*), *I stole an apple*, wamawanoŋ, *I stole something*, i. e., *I committed a theft*.

3. When the agent acts on *his own*, i. e. something belonging to himself, the verb assumes the *possessive* form. This is made in two ways: First, by prefixing or inserting the possessive pronoun 'ki' (and in some cases 'k' alone); as, waśtedaka, *to love* anything; ćiŋća waśtekidaka, *he loves his child*. Secondly, in verbs in 'yu,' 'ya,' and 'yo,' the possessive form is made by changing 'y' into 'hd;' as, yuha, *to have* or *possess* any thing; hduha, *to have one's own;* śuktaŋka wahduha, *I have my own horse*.

It has already been noted that in the Yankton dialect the 'y' becomes 'kd' and in the Teton dialect 'gl;' thus in the three dialects they stand, hduha, kduha, gluha. The verb 'hi,' *to come to*, forms the possessive in the same way: hdi, kdi, gli, *to come to one's own home*. Examples of 'k' alone agglutinated forming the possessive are found in kpataŋ, kpaǵaŋ, kpaksa, etc. It should be also remarked that the 'k' is interchangable with 't,' so that among some of the Dakotas we hear tpataŋ, etc.

4. When the agent acts on *himself*, the verb is put in the *reflexive* form. The reflexive is formed in two ways: First, by incorporating the reflexive pronouns, ići, nići, mići, and uŋkići; as, waśteićidaka, *he loves himself*. Secondly, verbs in 'yu,' 'ya,' and 'yo,' that make the possessive by changing 'y' into 'hd,' prefix to this form 'i;' as, yuźaźa, *to wash* any thing; hduźaźa, *to wash one's own*, as one's clothes; ihduźaźa, *to wash oneself*.

5. Another form of verbs is made by prefixing or inserting prepositions meaning *to* and *for*. This may be called the *dative* form.

(*a*) When the action is done *to* another, the preposition 'ki' is prefixed or inserted; as, kaǵa, *to make* any thing; kićaǵa, *to make to* one; wowapi kićaǵa (*writing to-him-he-made*), *he wrote him a letter*. This form is also used when the action is done on something that *belongs to* another; as, śuŋka kikte, (*dog to-him-he-killed*) *he killed his dog*.

(b) When the thing is done *for* another, 'kíći' is used; as, wowapi kićićaga, (*writing for-him-he-made*) *he wrote a letter for him.* In the plural, this sometimes has a reciprocal force; as, wowapi kićićagapi, *they wrote letters to each other.*

6. In some verbs 'ki' prefixed conveys the idea that the action takes effect *on the middle* of the object; as, baksa, *to cut in two with a knife*, as a stick; kibaksa, *to cut in two in the middle.*

7. There is a causative form made by 'kiya' and 'ya.' (See § 36. 1.)

8. (a) The locative form should also be noted, made by inseparable prepositions 'a,' 'e,' 'i,' and 'o': as, amani, ewaŋka, inaźiŋ and ohnaka.

(b) Verbs in the "locative form," made by the inseparable 'a' have several uses, among which are: 1. They sometimes express location *on*, as in amani, *to walk on.* 2. Sometimes they convey the idea of what is *in addition to*, as in akaġa, *to add to.*

PERSON.

§ 40. Dakota verbs have three *persons*, the *first*, *second*, and *third.* The third person is represented by the verb in its simple form, and the second and first persons by the addition of the personal pronouns.

NUMBER.

§ 41. Dakota verbs have three *numbers*, the *singular, dual,* and *plural.*

1. The *dual* number is only of the first person. It includes the person speaking and the one spoken to, and is in form the same as the first person plural, but without the termination 'pi;' as, waśteuŋdaka, *we two love him;* mauŋni, *we two walk.*

2. The *plural* is formed by suffixing 'pi;' as, waśteuŋdakapi, *we love him;* manipi, *they walk.*

3. There are some verbs of motion which form what may be called a *collective plural*, denoting that the action is performed by two or more acting *together* or *in a body.* This is made by prefixing 'a' or 'e;' as, u, *to come*, au, *they come;* ya, *to go*, aya, *they go;* naźiŋ, *to stand*, enaźiŋ, *they stand.* These have also the ordinary plural; as, upi, yapi, naźiŋpi.

MODE.

§ 42. There are three *modes* belonging to Dakota verbs: the *indicative, imperative,* and *infinitive.*

1. The *indicative* is the common form of the verb; as, ćeya, *he cries;* ćeyapi, *they cry.*

2. (a) The *imperative* singular is formed from the third person singular indicative and the syllables ' wo ' and ' ye ;' as, ćeya wo, ćeya ye, *cry thou.* Instead of 'ye,' the Mdewakaŋtoŋwaŋ has ' we,' and the Titoŋwaŋ ' le.' The Yankton and Titoŋwaŋ men use ' yo.'

(b) The imperative plural is formed by the syllables ' po,' ' pe,' ' m,' and ' miye ;' as, ćeya po, ćeya pe, ćeyam, and ćeya miye. It has been suggested that ' po' is formed by an amalgamation of ' pi,' the common plural ending, and ' wo,' the sign of the imperative singular. In like manner, ' pi ' and ' ye,' may be combined to make ' pe.' The combination of ' miye ' is not so apparent.[1]

By some it is thought that the Titoŋwaŋ women and children use ' na ' for the imperative.[2]

The forms 'wo,' 'yo,' and 'po' are used only by men; and 'we,' 'ye,' 'pe,' and 'miye' by women, though not exclusively. From observing this general rule, we formerly supposed that sex was indicated by them; but lately we have been led to regard 'wo' and 'po' as used in *commanding,* and 'we,' 'ye,' 'pe,' and 'miye,' in *entreating.* Although it would be out of character for women to use the former, men may and often do use the latter.

When 'po,' 'pe,' and 'miye' is used it takes the place of the plural ending 'pi;' as, ćeya po, ćeya miye, *cry ye.* But with the negative adverb 'śni,' the 'pi' is retained; as, ćeyapi śni po, *do not cry.*

Sometimes in giving a command the 'wo' and 'ye,' signs of the imperative, are not expressed, The plural endings are less frequently omitted.

3. The *infinitive* is commonly the same as the ground form of the verb, or third person singular indicative. When two verbs come together, the first one is usually to be regarded as the infinitive mood or present parti-

---

[1] Instead of 'po,' 'pe' and 'miye,' the Titoŋwaŋ make the imperative plural by the plural ending 'pi' and 'ye,' or 'yo;' as, ećoŋpi yo. In the Lord's prayer, for example, we say, "Wauŋhtanipi kiŋ uŋkićićaźuźupi ye;" but we do not say in the next clause, "Ḳa taku wawiyutaŋ kiŋ ekta uŋkayapi śni piye," but "uŋkayapi śni ye." Possibly the plural termination 'pi' and the precative form 'ye' may have been corrupted by the Santee into ' miye,' and by the Yankton and others into ' biye.'—W. J. C. Then it would seem plain that ' po' is formed from ' pi' and ' yo;' and we reduce all the imperative forms, in the last analysis, to 'e' and 'o.'—S. R. R.

[2] 'Na' can hardly be called a sign of the imparative, as used by women and children. (1) It appears to be an abbreviation of wanna. *now*: as, maḳu-na, *i. e.,* maḳu wanna, *Give me, now!* A corresponding use of *now* is found in English. (2) It is, at best, an interjectional adverb. (3) It is not used uniformly with an imperative form of the verb, being often omitted. (4) It is used in other connections; (a) as a conjunction—when used by women it may be only such, as, maḳu na, *Give it to me, and*—an incomplete sentence; it is often used between two imperative verbs, as, iḳu na yuta, *take and eat,* whereas, if it was an imperative sign, it would follow the last verb; (b) it is used to sooth crying children, as, Na! or, Nana! (c) Na! and Nana! are also used for reproving or scolding. (5) 'Na' is used possibly as the terminal 'la,' and will drop off in the same way. (6) If 'na' were a proper sign of the imperative, men would use it (or some corresponding form) as well as women. But they do not. We find 'wo' and 'we,' 'yo' and 'ye,' 'po' and 'pe;' but nothing like 'na' used by men.—T. L. R.

ciple; and is contracted if capable of contraction (§ 11); as, waŋyaka, *to see* any thing, waŋyag mde kta, (*to see* it *I-go will*) *I will go to see it;* nahoŋ wauŋ, (*hearing I-am*) *I am hearing,* or *I hear.*

What in other languages are called *conditional* and *subjunctive* modes may be formed by using the indicative with the conjunctions uŋkaŋś, kiŋhaŋ or ćiŋhaŋ, tuka, eśta or śta, and keś, which come after the verb; as, ćeya uŋkaŋś, *if he had cried;* ćeye ćiŋhaŋ, *if he cry;* ćeye kta tuka, *he would cry, but* he does not: wahi uŋkaŋś wakaśke kta tuka, *if I had come, I would have bound him.*

TENSE.

§ 43. Dakota verbs have but two *tense forms,* the *aorist,* or *indefinite,* and the *future.*

1. The *aorist* includes the present and imperfect past. It has commonly no particular sign. Whether the action is past or now being done must be determined by circumstances or by the adverbs used.

2. The sign of the *future* tense is 'kta' placed after the verb. It is often changed into 'kte;' for the reason of which, see § 6. 1. *b.*

What answers to a *perfect past* is sometimes formed by using 'koŋ' or 'ćikoŋ,' and sometimes by the article 'kiŋ' or 'ćiŋ;' as taku nawahoŋ koŋ, *what I heard.*

PARTICIPLES.

§ 44. 1. The addition of 'haŋ' to the third person singular of some verbs makes an *active participle;* as, ia, *to speak,* iahaŋ, *speaking;* naźiŋ, *to stand,* naźiŋhaŋ, *standing;* mani, *to walk,* manihaŋ, *walking.* The verbs that admit of this formation do not appear to be numerous.[1]

2. The third person singular of the verb when preceding another verb has often the force of an active participle; as, nahoŋ wauŋ, *I am hearing.* When capable of contraction it is in this case contracted; as, waŋyaka, *to see,* waŋyag nawaźiŋ, *I stand seeing.*

§ 45. 1. The verb in the plural impersonal form has in many instances the force of a *passive participle;* as, makaśkapi wauŋ, (*me-they-bound I-am*) *I am bound.*

2. Passive participles are also formed from the verbal roots (§ 33) by adding 'haŋ' and 'wahaŋ;' as, ksa, *separate,* ksahaŋ and ksawahaŋ, *broken*

---

[1] Judging from analogy, haŋ (see haŋ, *to stand, to stand upright on end,* in the Dictionary) must have been used long ago as a classifier of attitude, *the standing object.* Even now we find such a use of taŋ in Ƈegiha (Omaha and Ponka), kaŋ in Kansa, tqaŋ and kqaŋ in Osage, taha in Ꞁoiwere, and teeka in Winnebago. The classifier in each of these languages is also used after many primary verbs, as haŋ is here, to express incomplete or continuous action. See "The comparative phonology of four Siouan languages," in the Smithsonian Report for 1883.—J. O. D.

in two, as a stick. In some cases only one of these forms is in use; but generally both occur, without, however, so far as we have perceived, any difference in the meaning.

A few of the verbal roots are used as adjectives; as, mdu, *fine;* but they also take the participle endings; as, mduwahaŋ *crumbled fine.*

CONJUGATION I.

§ 46. Those which are embraced in the *first conjugation* are mostly active verbs and take the subjective article pronouns 'ya' or 'ye' and 'wa' or 'we' in the second and first persons singular.

FIRST VARIETY.

§ 47. The *first variety* of the first conjugation is distinguished by *prefixing* or *inserting* 'ya' and 'wa,' article pronouns of the second and first persons singular.

A. PRONOUNS PREFIXED.

Kaśka, *to tie* or *bind* anything.

INDICATIVE MODE.

Aorist tense.

Sing.	Dual.	Plur.
3. kaśka, *he binds* or *he bound.*		kaśkápi, *they bind.*
2. yakáśka, *thou bindest.*		yakáśkapi, *ye bind.*
1. wakáśka, *I bind.*	uŋkáśka, *we two bind.*	uŋkáśkapi, *we bind.*

Future tense.

3. kaśke kta, *he will bind.*		kaśkápi kta, *they will bind.*
2. yakáśke kta, *thou wilt bind.*		yakáśkapi kta, *ye will bind.*
1. wakáśke kta, *I will bind.*		uŋkáśkapi kta, *we will bind.*
	uŋkáśke kta, *we two will bind.*	

IMPERATIVE MODE.

Sing.	Plur.
2. kaśká wo, ye, or we, *bind thou.*	kaśká po, pe, or miye, *bind ye.*

PARTICIPLE.

kaśkáhaŋ, *bound.*

B. Pronouns Inserted.

Manoŋ, *to steal* anything.

INDICATIVE MODE.

Aorist tense.

Sing.	Dual.	Plur.
3. manóŋ, *he steals* or *stole.*		manóŋpi, *they steal.*
2. mayánoŋ, *thou stealest.*		mayánoŋpi, *ye steal.*
1. mawánoŋ, *I steal.*	maúŋnoŋ, *we two steal.*	maúŋnoŋpi, *we steal.*

Future tense.

3. manóŋ kta, *he will steal.*		manóŋpi kta, *they will steal.*
2. mayánoŋ kta, *thou wilt steal.*		mayánoŋpi kta, *ye will steal.*
1. mawánoŋ kta, *I will steal.*		maúŋnoŋpi kta, *we will steal.*
	maúŋnoŋ kta, *we two will steal.*	

IMPERATIVE MODE.

Sing.	Plur.
2. manóŋ wo, ye, or we, *steal thou.*	manóŋ po, pe, or miye, *steal ye.*

§ 48. The verb yúta, *to eat* anything, may be regarded as coming under the *first variety* of this conjugation. The 'yu' is dropped when the pronouns are assumed; as, yúta, *he eats*, yáta, *thou eatest*, wáta, *I eat*.

SECOND VARIETY.

§ 49. The *second variety* of the first conjugation is distinguished by the use of 'ye' and 'we' instead of 'yaki' and 'waki' (§ 18. 4), in the second and first persons singular.

A. Pronouns Prefixed.

Kiksuya, *to remember* any thing.

INDICATIVE MODE.

Aorist tense.

Sing.	Dual.	Plur.
3. kiksúya, *he remembers.*		kiksúyapi, *they remember.*
2. yéksuya, *thou rememberest.*		yéksuyapi, *ye remember.*
1. wéksuya, *I remember.*	uŋkíksuya, *we two remember.*	uŋkíksuyapi, *we remember.*

IMPERATIVE MODE.

Sing.	Plur.
2. kiksúya wo, ye, or we, *remember thou.*	kiksúya po, pe, or miye, *remember ye.*

Future tense.—It is deemed unnecessary to give any further examples of the future tense, as those which have gone before fully illustrate the manner of its formation.

B. Pronouns Inserted.

Ećakićoŋ, *to do* anything *to* another.

INDICATIVE MODE.

Aorist tense.

Sing.	Dual.	Plur.
3. ećákićoŋ, *he does to* one.		ećákićoŋpi, *they do to.*
2. ećáyećoŋ, *thou doest to.*		ećáyećoŋpi, *ye do to.*
1. ećáwećoŋ, *I do to.*	ećáuŋkićoŋ, *we two do to.*	ećáuŋkićoŋpi, *we do to.*

IMPERATIVE MODE.

Sing.	Plur.
2. ećákićoŋ wo, ye, or we, *do thou* it *to* one.	ećákićoŋ po, pe, or miye, *do ye* it *to* one.

CONJUGATION II.

§ 50. Verbs in 'yu,' 'ya,' and 'yo,' which change 'y' into 'd' for the second person, and into 'md' for the first person singular, belong to this conjugation. They are generally active in their signification.

FIRST VARIETY.

A.—VERBS IN 'YU.'

Yuśtaŋ, *to finish* or *complete* any thing.[1]

INDICATIVE MODE.

Aorist tense.

Sing.	Dual.	Plur.
3. yuśtáŋ, *he finishes* or *finished.*		yuśtáŋpi, *they finish.*
2. duśtáŋ, *thou dost finish.*		duśtáŋpi, *ye finish.*
1. mduśtáŋ, *I finish.*	úŋśtaŋ, *we two finish.*	úŋśtaŋpi, *we finish.*

IMPERATIVE MODE.

Sing.	Plur.
yuśtáŋ wo, etc., *finish thou.*	yuśtáŋ po, etc., *finish ye.*

First person plural —Verbs in 'yu' generally form the first person plural and dual by dropping the 'yu,' as in the example; but occasionally a speaker retains it and prefixes the pronoun, as, uŋyúśtaŋpi for úŋśtaŋpi.

---

[1] In the Titoŋwaŋ dialect, yuśtaŋ has luśtaŋ in the second person singular, and bluśtaŋ in the first.

B. Verbs in 'ya.'

Yaksa, *to bite* any thing *in two.*

INDICATIVE MODE.

Aorist tense.

Sing.	Dual.	Plur.
3. yaksá, *he bites in two.*		yaksápi, *they bite in two.*
2. daksá, *thou bitest in two.*		daksápi, *you bite in two.*
1. mdaksá, *I bite in two.*	uŋyáksa, *we two bite in two.*	uŋyáksapi, *we bite in two.*

IMPERATIVE MODE.

Sing.	Plur.
yaksá wo, etc., *bite thou in two.*	yaksá po, etc., *bite ye in two.*

Ya, *to go,* is conjugated in the same way in Isaŋyati, but in the Ihaŋk-toŋwaŋ and Titoŋwaŋ dialects it gives us a form of variation, in the singular future, which should be noted, viz: yiŋ kta, ni kta, mni kta; dual, uŋyiŋ kta.

C. Verbs in 'yo.'

Iyotaŋka, *to sit down.*

INDICATIVE MODE.

Aorist tense.

Sing.	Dual.	Plur.
3. iyótaŋka, *he sits down.*		iyótaŋkapi, *they sit down.*
2. idótaŋka, *thou sittest down.*		idótaŋkapi, *you sit down.*
1. imdótaŋka, *I sit down.*	uŋkíyotaŋka, *we two sit down.*	uŋkíyotaŋkapi, *we sit down.*

IMPERATIVE MODE.

Sing.	Plur.
iyótaŋka wo, etc., *sit thou down.*	iyótaŋka po, etc., *sit ye down.*

SECOND VARIETY.

§ 51. The *second variety* of the second conjugation embraces such verbs as belong to the same class, but are irregular or defective.

Irregular Formations.

(*a*) **Hiyu,** *to come* or *start to come.*

INDICATIVE MODE.

Aorist tense.

Sing.	Dual.	Plur.
3. hiyú, *he comes.*		hiyúpi, *they come.*
2. hidú, *thou comest.*		hidúpi, *you come.*
1. hibú, *I come.*	uŋhíyu, *we two come.*	uŋhíyupi, *we come.*

IMPERATIVE MODE.

Sing.   Plur.

hiyú wo, etc., *come thou.*   hiyú po, etc., *come ye.*

(b) Yukaŋ, *to be* or *there is.*

Sing.	Dual.	Plur.
3. yukáŋ, *there is* some.		yukáŋpi, *they are.*
2.		~~dukáŋpi, *you are.*~~
1.	uŋkáŋ, *we two are.*	úŋkaŋpi, *we are.*

The verb 'yukaŋ' in the singular is applied to things and not to persons except as considered collectively.

(c) *Plur.* Yakoŋpi, *they are.*

Sing.	Dual.	Plur.
3.		yakóŋpi, *they are.*
2. dakánoŋ, *thou art.*		dakánoŋpi, *you are.*
1.	uŋyákoŋ, *we two are.*	uŋyákoŋpi, *we are.*

These last two verbs, it will be observed, are defective. Kiyukaŋ, formed from yukaŋ, is used in the sense of *to make room for* one and is of the first conjugation.

VERBS WITH OBJECTIVE PRONOUNS.

§ 52. 1. The objective pronoun occupies the same place in the verb as the subjective; as, kaśka, *he binds,* makaśka, *he binds me;* manoŋ, *he steals,* maninoŋ, *he steals thee.*

2. When the same verb contains both a subjective and an objective pronoun, the objective is placed first; as, mayakaśka, *thou bindest me,* mawićayanoŋ, *thou stealest them.* An exception is formed by the pronoun of the first person plural, which is always placed before the pronoun of the second person, whether subjective or objective; as, uŋnićaśkapi, *we bind you.*

KAŚKA, *to tie* or *bind.*							
		him, her, it.	*thee.*	*me.*	*them.*	*you.*	*us.*
Indicative.	*Sing.* 3. kaśká	nićáśka	makáśka	wićákaśka	nićáśkapi	uŋkéśkapi
	2. yakáśka		mayákaśka	wićáyakaśka		uŋyákaśkapi
	1. wakáśka	ćićáśka		wićáwakaśka	ćićáśkapi	
	Dual. uŋkáśka			wićúŋkaśka		
	Plur. 3. kaśkápi	nićáśkapi	makáśkapi	wićákaśkapi	nićáśkapi	uŋkáśkapi
	2. yakáśkapi		mayákaśkapi	wićáyakaśkapi		uŋyákaśkapi
	1. uŋkáśkapi	uŋnićaśkapi		wićúŋkaśkapi	uŋnićaśkapi	
Imperat.	*Sing.* kaśká wo, etc.		makáśka wo	wićákaśka wo		uŋkáśka po
	Plur. kaśká po, etc.		makáśka po	wićákaśka po		uŋkáśka po

Impersonal Forms.

§ 53. Active verbs are frequently used impersonally in the plural number and take the objective pronouns to indicate the person or persons acted upon, in which case they may be commonly translated by the English passive; as, kaśkapi, (*they-bound-him*) *he is bound;* nićaśkapi, (*they-bound-thee*) *thou art bound;* makaśkapi, (*they bound me*) *I am bound;* wićakaśkapi, (*they bound them*) *they are bound.*

Neuter and Adjective Verbs.

§ 54. Neuter and adjective verbs seem likewise to be used impersonally and are varied by means of the same pronouns; as, ṭa, *dies* or *he dies* or *he is dead,* niṭa, *thee-dead* or *thou art dead,* maṭa, *me-dead* or *I die* or *am dead,* ṭapi, *they die* or *are dead;* possessive form, kiṭa, *dead to,* as, ate makiṭa, *father to me dead;* waśte, *good,* niwaśte, *thee-good, thou art good,* mawaśte, *me-good, I am good,* uŋwaśtepi, *we are good.*

It is suggested by Prof. A. W. Williamson that the so-called objective pronouns in these cases are used as datives and that they find analogy in our English forms *methinks, meseems.*[1] A further careful consideration of these Dakota article pronouns and the manner in which they are used leads to the conclusion that these were the original forms, as fragments of 'miye' and 'niye.' In the progress of the language it was found convenient, and even necessary, for the active transitive verbs to have other forms, as, 'wa' and 'ya,' to be used solely as subjective pronominal particles.[2] Whence they were obtained is not manifest. But as children, in their first efforts to speak English, are found disposed invariably to use the objective for the subjective, as, *me want, me cold, me sick, me good,* etc., it would be natural that where the necessity of changing does not exist the original forms should be retained as subjectives. The form for the first person plural has been retained both as subjective and objective. Many of this class of verbs are best translated as passives.

It appears practically convenient to include these verbs and a few others which are varied in a similar manner in one group, to which we will give the name of *third conjugation.*

---

[1] See foot-note on the Paradigm after § 59, 4. Prof. A. W. Williamson is correct with reference to possessive or dative verbs in 'ki,' as kiṭa, makiṭa. Compare the use of the Latin *sum: Est mihi liber.* But niwaśte, mawaśte, uŋwaśtepi, niṭa, maṭa, uŋṭapi cannot be said to convey a dative idea. The cognate languages show that these are pure objectives.—J. O. D.

[2] How about md (bd, bl) and d (l), mentioned in § 18, 7?—J. O. D.

CONJUGATION III.

§ 55. This conjugation is distinguished by the pronouns 'ni' in the second and 'ma' in the first person singular. Those verbs included under the *first variety* take these pronouns in *their full form*. The *second variety* embraces those in which the pronouns appear in *a fragmentary state* and are irregular in their conjugation.

FIRST VARIETY.

§ 56. To this variety belong *neuter* and *adjective* verbs. The proper adjective verbs always prefix the pronouns; but, while some neuter verbs prefix, others insert them.

A. Pronouns Prefixed.

Ṭa, *to die* or *be dead.*

INDICATIVE MODE.

Aorist Tense.

Sing.	Dual.	Plur.
3. ṭa, *he is dead* or *he dies.*		ṭápi, *they are dead.*
2. niṭá, *thou art dead* or *thou diest.*		niṭápi, *you are dead.*
1. maṭá, *I am dead* or *I die.*	uṇṭá, *we two are dead.*	uṇṭápi, *we are dead.*

IMPERATIVE MODE.

Sing.		Plur.
2. ṭa wo, etc., *die thou.*		ṭa po, etc., *die ye.*

Waśté, *good* or *to be good.*

Sing.	Dual.	Plur.
3. waśté, *he is good.*		waśtépi, *they are good.*
2. niwáśte, *thou art good.*		niwáśtepi, *you are good.*
1. mawáśte, *I am good.*	uṇwáśte, *we two are good.*	uṇwáśtepi, *we are good.*

B. Pronouns Inserted.

Asni, *to get well* or *be well, recover from sickness.*

INDICATIVE MODE.

Aorist Tense.

Sing.	Dual.	Plur.
3. asní, *he is well.*		asnípi, *they are well.*
2. anísni, *thou art well.*		anísnipi, *you are well.*
1. amásni, *I am well.*	uṇkásni, *we two are well.*	uṇkásnipi, *we are well.*

IMPERATIVE MODE.

Sing.	Plur.
asní wo, etc., *be thou well.*	asní po, etc., *be ye well.*

§ 57. Verbs in this variety have only 'n' and 'm,' fragments of the article pronouns 'ni' and 'ma,' in the second and first persons singular. These appear to be mostly active transitive verbs.

A. PRONOUNS PREFIXED.

1. The fragmentary pronouns 'n' and 'm' are prefixed to the verb in its entirety.

Uŋ, *to use* any thing, as a tool, etc.

INDICATIVE MODE.

Aorist Tense.

Sing.	Dual.	Plur.
3. uŋ, *he uses.*		úŋpi, *they use.*
2. nuŋ, *thou usest.*		núŋpi, *ye use.*
1. muŋ, *I use.*	uŋkúŋ, *we two use.*	uŋkúŋpi, *we use.*

In this and the following examples only the indicative aorist is given, the formation of the remaining parts having been already sufficiently exhibited.

Uŋpa and caŋnúŋpa, *to smoke a pipe*, are conjugated like uŋ, *to use.*

The *reflexive form* of verbs, which in the third person singular commences with ·ihd' (see § 39. 4.), is also conjugated like 'uŋ ;' as, ihdáśka, *to bind oneself;* nihdáśka, *thou bindest thyself;* mihdáśka, *I bind myself.*

2. The agglutinated 'n' and 'm' take the place of the initial 'y.'

(*a*) **Yaŋka**, *to be.*

Sing.	Dual.	Plur.
3. yaŋká, *he is.*		yaŋkápi, *they are.*
2. naŋká, *thou art.*		naŋkápi, *ye are.*
1. maŋká, *I am.*	uŋyáŋka, *we two are.*	uŋyáŋkapi, *we are.*

(*b*) **Yaŋka**, *to weave*, as snowshoes.

Sing.	Dual.	Plur.
3. yáŋka, *he weaves.*		yáŋkapi, *they weave.*
2. náŋka, *thou weavest.*		náŋkapi, *you weave.*
1. mnáŋka, *I weave.*	uŋyáŋka, *we two weave.*	uŋyáŋkapi, *we weave.*

Yáŋka, *to weave*, differs in conjugation from yaŋká, *to be*, only in the first person singular.

B. PRONOUNS INSERTED.

3. 'N' and 'm' take the place of 'w.'

(*a*) **Owiŋźa**, *to make a bed of* or *use for a bed.*

Sing.	Dual.	Plur.
3. owíŋźa, *he uses for a bed.*		owíŋźapi, *they use for a bed.*
2. oníŋźa, *thou usest for a bed.*		oníŋźapi, *you use for a bed.*
1. omíŋźa, *I use for a bed.*		uŋkówiŋźapi, *we use for a bed.*
	uŋkówiŋźa, *we two use for a bed.*	

(*b*) **Iwaŋġa**, *to inquire of* one.

Sing.	Dual.	Plur.
3. iwáŋġa, *he inquires of.*		iwáŋġapi, *they inquire of.*
2. inúŋġa, *thou inquirest of.*		inúŋġapi, *you inquire of.*
1. imúŋġa, *I inquire of.*	uŋkíwaŋġa, *we two inquire of.*	uŋkíwaŋġapi, *we inquire of.*

This second example differs from the first in the change of vowels, 'u' taking the place of 'a.'

Wáŋka and iwáŋka, *to lie down, go to bed*, are conjugated like iwáŋġa.

In the Titoŋwaŋ dialect iyuŋġa is used instead of iwaŋġa, thus:

Sing.	Dual.	Plur.
3. iyuŋġa.		iyuŋġapi.
2. inuŋġa.		inuŋġapi.
1. imuŋġa.	uŋkiyuŋġa.	uŋkiyuŋġapi.

Ićiyuŋġa, *I inquire of thee;* uŋkiniyuŋġapi, *we inquire of you;* etc.

They also say yuŋka and iyuŋka, instead of waŋka and iwaŋka. The like change of 'wa' to 'yu' is found in other words.

4. 'N' and 'm' inserted with an 'a' preceding.

Ećoŋ, *to do* anything.

Sing.	Dual.	Plur.
3. ećóŋ, *he does.*		ećóŋpi, *they do.*
2. ećánoŋ, *thou doest.*		ećánoŋpi, *you do.*
1. ećámoŋ, *I do.*	ećóŋku, *we two do.*	ećóŋkupi and ećóŋkoŋpi, *we do.*

Héćoŋ, kéćoŋ, and tókoŋ are conjugated like ećóŋ.

C. PRONOUNS SUFFIXED.

5. The pronouns when suffixed take the forms 'ni' and 'mi.

a. **Ećiŋ**, *to think.*

Sing.	Dual.	Plur.
3. ećíŋ, *he thinks.*		ećíŋpi, *they think.*
2. ećáŋni, *thou thinkest.*		ećáŋnipi, *you think.*
1. ećáŋmi, *I think.*	uŋkéćiŋ, *we two think.*	uŋkéćiŋpi, *we think.*

Héćiŋ, kéćiŋ, wáćiŋ, and awáćiŋ are conjugated like ećíŋ.

Iŋ, *to wear*, as a shawl or blanket.

Sing.	Dual.	Plur.
3. iŋ, *he wears.*		iŋpi, *they wear.*
2. hiŋní, *thou wearest.*		hiŋnípi, *you wear.*
1. hiŋmí, *I wear.*	uŋkíŋ, *we two wear.*	uŋkíŋpi, *we wear.*

This example differs from the preceding in receiving a prefixed 'h.'

DOUBLE VERBS.

§ 58. These are formed of two verbs compounded (§ 37. 2.). They usually have the pronouns proper to both verbs, though sometimes the pronouns of the last verb are omitted; as, hdiyotaŋka (hdi and iyotaŋka), *to come home and sit down;* wahdimdotaŋka, *I come home and sit down;* they also say wahdiyotaŋka.

CONJUGATIONS I AND II.

Hiyotaŋka, *to come and sit down.*

Sing.	Dual.	Plur.
3. híyotaŋka, *he comes,* etc.		híyotaŋkapi, *they come,* etc.
2. yahídotaŋka, *thou comest,* etc.		yahídotaŋkapi, *you come,* etc.
1. wahímdotaŋka, *I come,* etc.	uŋhíyotaŋka, *we two come,* etc.	uŋhíyotaŋkapi, *we come,* etc.

Hdiyotaŋka is conjugated like híyotaŋka. Hinaźiŋ, hdinaźiŋ, and kinaźiŋ, in both parts, are of the first conjugation; as, wahinawaźiŋ, yahinayaźiŋ, etc.

CONJUGATIONS I AND III.

Iŋyaŋka, *to run* (prob. i *and* yaŋka).

Sing.	Dual.	Plur.
3. íŋyaŋka, *he runs.*		íŋyaŋkapi, *they run.*
2. yaínaŋka, *thou runnest.*		yaínaŋkapi, *you run.*
1. waímnaŋka, *I run.*	uŋkíŋyaŋka, *we two run.*	uŋkíŋyaŋkapi, *we run.*

Hiwaŋka, kiwaŋka, and hdiwaŋka are conjugated like kaśka of the first conjugation and iwaŋga of the third.

IRREGULAR AND DEFECTIVE VERBS.

§ 59. 1. Eya, *to say,* with its compounds héya and kéya, are conjugated *irregularly,* 'h' and 'p' taking the place of 'y' in the second and first persons singular.

Eya, *to say* anything.

Sing.	Dual.	Plur.
3. éya, *he says.*		éyapi, *they say.*
2. ehá, *thou sayest.*		ehápi, *you say.*
1. epá, *I say* or *said.*	uŋkéya, *we two say.*	uŋkéyapi, *we say.*

2. The Ihaŋktoŋwaŋ and Titoŋwaŋ forms of 'eya,' in the singular and dual, when followed by the sign of the future, are worthy of note; as, eyiŋ kta, ehiŋ kta, epiŋ kta, uŋkeyiŋ kta.

3. Epća, *I think,* with its compounds hepća and kepća, are *defective,* being used only in the first person singular.

4. On the use of 'eya' and its compounds it is proper to remark that 'eya' is placed *after* the matter expressed, while 'heya' immediately precedes, it being compounded of 'he' and 'eya,' *this he said.* On the other hand, 'keya' comes in at the close of the phrase or sentence. It differs from 'eya' and 'heya' in this, that, while *their* subject is in the *same person* with that of the verb or verbs in the same sentence, the subject of 'keya' is in a different person or the expression preceding is not in the same form, *as regards person,* as when originally used; as, mde kta, eya, *I will go, he said;* mde kta, keya, *he said that I would go;* hećamoŋ kta, epa, *that I will do, I said;* hećamoŋ kta, kepa, *I said that I would do that.* Kećiŋ and kećaŋkiŋ follow the same rule that governs keya and kepća.

The annexed paradigm will present, in a single view, many of the facts and principles which have been already presented in regard to the synthetic formations of active verbs.

KSA, to break off, separate.

		him, etc.	*thee.*	*me.*	*them.*	*you.*	*us.*
baksa, to cut off with a knife or saw.	Sing. 3. baksá	baníksa		bamáksa	bawićáksa	baníksapi	baúŋksapi
	2. bayáksa			bamáyaksa	bawićáyaksa		baúŋyaksapi
	1. bawáksa	baćíksa			bawićáwaksa	baćíksapi	
	Dual baúŋksa				bawićúŋksa		
	Plur. 3. baksápi	baníksapi		bamáksapi	bawićáksapi	baníksapi	baúŋksapi
	2. bayáksapi			bamáyaksapi	bawićáyaksapi		baúŋyuksapi
	1. baúŋksapi	baúŋniksapi			bawićúŋksapi	baúŋniksapi	
boksa, to shoot off or punch off.	Sing. 3. boksá	boníksa		bomáksa	bowićáksa	boníksapi	boúŋksapi
	2. boyáksa			bomáyaksa	bowićáyaksa		boúŋyaksapi
	1. bowáksa	boćíksa			bowićáwaksa	boćíksapi	
	Dual boúŋksa				bowićúŋksa		
	Plur. 3. boksápi	boníksapi		bomáksapi	bowićáksapi	boníksapi	boúŋksapi
	2. boyáksapi			bomáyaksapi	bowićáyaksapi		boúŋyaksapi
	1. boúŋksapi	boúŋniksapi			bowićúŋksapi	boúŋniksapi	
kaksa, to cut off with an ax.	Sing. 3. kaksá	nićáksa		makáksa	wićákaksa	nićáksapi	uŋkáksapi
	2. yakáksa			mayákaksa	wićáyakaksa		uŋyákaksapi
	1. wakáksa	ćićáksa			wićáwakaksa	ćićáksapi	
	Dual uŋkáksa				wićúŋkaksa		
	Plur. 3. kaksápi	nićáksapi		makáksapi	wićákaksapi	nićáksapi	uŋkáksapi
	2. yakáksapi			mayákaksapi	wićáyakaksapi		uŋyákaksapi
	1. uŋkáksapi	uŋnićaksapi			wićúŋkaksapi	uŋnićaksapi	
naksa, to break off with the foot.	Sing. 3. naksá	naníksa		namáksa	nawićáksa	naníksapi	naúŋksapi
	2. nayáksa			namáyaksa	nawićáyaksa		naúŋyaksapi
	1. nawáksa	naćíksa			nawićáwaksa	naćíksapi	
	Dual naúŋksa				nawićúŋksa		
	Plur. 3. naksápi	naníksapi		namáksapi	nawićáksapi	naníksapi	naúŋksapi
	2. nayáksapi			namáyaksapi	nawićáyaksapi		naúŋyaksapi
	1. naúŋksapi	naúŋniksapi			nawićúŋksapi	naúŋniksapi	
paksa, to break off by pushing.	Sing. 3. paksá	nipáksa		mapáksa	wićápaksa	nipáksapi	uŋpáksapi
	2. yapáksa			mayápaksa	wićáyapaksa		uŋyápaksapi
	1. wapáksa	ćipáksa			wićáwapaksa	ćipáksapi	
	Dual uŋpáksa				wićúŋpaksa		
	Plur. 3. paksápi	nipáksapi		mapáksapi	wićápaksapi	nipáksapi	uŋpáksapi
	2. yapáksapi			mayápaksapi	wićáyapaksapi		uŋyápaksapi
	1. uŋpáksapi	uŋnípaksapi			wićúŋpaksapi	uŋnípaksapi	
yaksa, to bite off.	Sing. 3. yaksá	niyáksa		mayáksa	wićáyaksa	niyáksapi	uŋyáksapi
	2. daksá			mayádaksa	wićádaksa		uŋyádaksapi
	1. mdaksá	ćiyáksa			wićámdaksa	ćiyáksapi	
	Dual uŋyáksa				wićúŋyaksa		
	Plur. 3. yaksápi	niyáksapi		mayáksapi	wićáyaksapi	niyáksapi	uŋyáksapi
	2. daksápi			mayádaksapi	wićádaksapi		uŋyádaksapi
	1. uŋyáksapi	uŋníyaksapi			wićúŋyaksapi	uŋníyaksapi	
yuksa, to break off in any way.	Sing. 3. yuksá	niyúksa		mayúksa	wićáyuksa	niyúksapi	uŋyúksapi
	2. duksá			mayáduksa	wićáduksa		uŋyáduksapi
	1. mduksá	ćiyúksa			wićámduksa	ćiyúksapi	
	Dual uŋyúksa				wićúŋyuksa		
	Plur. 3. yuksápi	niyúksapi		mayúksapi	wićáyuksapi	niyúksapi	uŋyúksapi
	2. duksápi			mayáduksapi	wićáduksapi		uŋyáduksapi
	1. uŋyúksapi	uŋníyuksapi			wićúŋyuksapi	uŋníyuksapi	

Frequentative.	Absolute.	Reflexive.	Possessive.¹	Dative.¹
Sing. 3. baksáksa	wabáksa	baíćiksa	bakíksa	bakíćiksa
2. bayáksaksa	wabáyaksa	baníćiksa	bayákiksa	bayéćiksa
1. bawáksaksa	wabáwaksa	bamíćiksa	bawákiksa	bawéćiksa
Dual baúŋksaksa	wabáuŋksa	baúŋkićiksa	baúŋkiksa	baúŋkićiksa
Plur. 3. baksáksapi	wabáksapi	baíćiksapi	bakíksapi	bakíćiksapi
2. bayáksaksapi	wabáyaksapi	baníćiksapi	bayákiksapi	bayéćiksapi
1. baúŋksaksapi	wabáuŋksapi	baúŋkićiksapi	baúŋkiksapi	baúŋkićiksapi
Sing. 3. boksáksa	wabóksa	boíćiksa	bokíksa	bokíćiksa
2. boyáksaksa	wabóyaksa	boníćiksa	boyákiksa	boyéćiksa
1. bowáksaksa	wabówaksa	bomíćiksa	bowákiksa	bowéćiksa
Dual boúŋksaksa	wabóuŋksa	boúŋkićiksa	boúŋkiksa	boúŋkićiksa
Plur. 3. boksáksapi	wabóksapi	boíćiksapi	bokíksapi	bokíćiksapi
2. boyáksaksapi	wabóyaksapi	boníćiksapi	boyákiksapi	boyéćiksayi
1. boúŋksaksapi	wabóuŋksapi	boúŋkićiksapi	boúŋkiksapi	boúŋkićiksapi
Sing. 3. kaksáksa	wakáksa	ihdáksa	hdaksá	kíćićaksa
2. yakáksaksa	wayákaksa	nihdáksa	yahdáksa	yéćićaksa
1. wakáksaksa	wawákaksa	mihdáksa	wahdáksa	wéćićaksa
Dual uŋkáksaksa	waíŋkaksa	uŋkíhdaksa	uŋhdáksa	uŋkíćićaksa
Plur. 3. kaksáksapi	wakáksapi	ihdáksapi	hdaksápi	kíćićaksapi
2. yakáksaksapi	wayákaksapi	nihdáksapi	yahdáksapi	yéćićaksapi
1. uŋkáksaksapi	waúŋkaksapi	uŋkíhdaksapi	uŋhdáksapi	uŋkíćićaksapi
Sing. 3. naksáksa	wanáksa	naíćiksa	nakíksa	nakíćiksa
2. nayáksaksa	wanáyaksa	naníćiksa	nayákiksa	nayéćiksa
1. nawáksaksa	wanáwaksa	namíćiksa	nawákiksa	nawéćiksa
Dual naúŋksaksa	wanáuŋksa	naúŋkićiksa	naúŋkiksa	naúŋkićiksa
Plur. 3. naksáksapi	wanáksapi	naíćiksapi	nakíksapi	nakíćiksapi
2. nayáksaksapi	wanáyaksapi	naníćiksapi	nayákiksapi	nayéćiksapi
1. naúŋksaksapi	wanáuŋksapi	naúŋkićiksapi	naúŋkiksapi	naúŋkićiksapi
Sing. 3. paksáksa	wapáksa	ićípaksa	kpaksá	kíćipaksa
2. yapáksaksa	wayápaksa	nićípaksa	yakpáksa	yéćipaksa
1. wapáksaksa	wawápaksa	mićípaksa	wakpáksa	wéćipaksa
Dual uŋpáksaksa	waúŋpaksa	uŋkíćipaksa	uŋkpáksa	uŋkíćipaksa
Plur. 3. paksáksapi	wapáksapi	ićípaksapi	kpaksápi	kíćipaksapi
2. yapáksaksapi	wayápaksapi	nićípaksapi	yakpáksapi	yéćipaksapi
1. uŋpáksaksapi	waúŋpaksapi	uŋkíćipaksapi	uŋkpáksapi	uŋkíćipaksapi
Sing. 3. yaksáksa	wayáksa	ihdáksa	hdaksá	kíćiyaksa
2. daksáksa	wadáksa	nihdáksa	yahdáksa	yéćiyaksa
1. mdaksáksa	wamdáksa	mihdáksa	wahdáksa	wéćiyaksa
Dual uŋyáksaksa	waúŋyaksa	uŋkíhdaksa	uŋhdáksa	uŋkíćiyaksa
Plur. 3. yaksáksapi	wayáksapi	ihdáksapi	hdaksápi	kíćiyaksapi
2. daksáksapi	wadáksapi	nihdáksapi	yahdáksapi	yéćiyaksapi
1. uŋyáksaksapi	waúŋyaksapi	uŋkíhdaksapi	uŋhdáksapi	uŋkíćiyaksapi
Sing. 3. yuksáksa	wóksa	ihdúksa	hduksá	kíćiyuksa
2. duksáksa	wadáksa	nihdúksa	yahdúksa	yéćiyuksa
1. mduksáksa	wamdúksa	mihdúksa	wahdúksa	wéćiyuksa
Dual úŋksaksa	waúŋyuksa	uŋkíhduksa	uŋhdúksa	uŋkíćiyuksa
Plur. 3. yuksáksapi	wóksapi	ihdúksapi	hduksápi	kíćiyuksapi
2. duksáksapi	wadúksapi	nihdúksapi	yahdúksapi	yéćiyuksapi
1. úŋksaksapi	waúŋyuksapi	uŋkíhduksapi	uŋhdúksapi	uŋkíćiyuksapi

¹In some of the cognate Siouan languages there are two datives in common use, with an occasional third dative. Some Dakota verbs have two of these; e. g., from kaǧa, to make, come kićaǧa (first dative) and kićićaǧa (second dative), as in wowapi kićaǧa, to write a letter to another, and wowapi kićićaǧa, to write a letter for or instead of another (or by request). In some cases the first dative is not differentiated from the possessive. See note on § 54.—J. O. D.

NOUNS.

FORMS OF NOUNS.

§ 60. Dakota nouns, like those of other languages, may be divided into two classes, *primitive* and *derivative.*

§ 61. Primitive nouns are those whose origin can not be deduced from any other word; as, maka, *earth,* peta, *fire,* pa, *head,* ista, *eye,* ate, *father,* ina, *mother.*

§ 62. Derivative nouns are those which are formed in various ways from other words, chiefly from verbs, adjectives, and other nouns. The principal classes of derivatives are as follows:

1. Nouns of the *instrument* are formed from active verbs by prefixing 'i;' as, yumdu, *to plough,* iyumdu, *a plough;* kasdeċa, *to split,* iċasdeċe, *a wedge;* kahiŋta, *to rake* or *sweep,* iċahiŋte, *a rake* or *broom* These again are frequently compounded with other nouns. (See § 68.)

2. Nouns of the *person* or *agent* are formed from active verbs by prefixing 'wa;' as, ihaŋgya, *to destroy,* waihaŋgye, *a destroyer;* yawaste, *to bless,* wayawaste, *one who blesses, a blesser.*

3. Many abstract nouns are formed from verbs and adjectives by prefixing 'wo;' as, ihaŋgya, *to destroy,* woihaŋgye, *destruction;* wayazaŋ, *to be sick,* wowayazaŋ, *sickness;* waoŋsida, *merciful,* wowaoŋsida, *mercy;* waste, *good,* wowaste, *goodness.*

4. Some nouns are formed from verbs and adjectives by prefixing 'o;' as, waŋka, *to lie down,* owaŋka, *a floor;* apa, *to strike,* oape, *a stroke;* owa, *to mark* or *write,* oowa, *a mark* or *letter* of the alphabet; sni, *cold,* as an adjective, osni, *cold,* a noun; maste, *hot,* omaste, *heat.*

5. *a.* 'Wiċa,' prefixed to neuter and intransitive verbs and adjectives sometimes forms of them abstract nouns; as, yazaŋ, *to be sick,* wiċayazaŋ and wawiċayazaŋ, *sickness;* waste, *good,* wiċawaste, *goodness.*

b. It sometimes forms nouns of the agent; as, yasiċa, *to speak evil of, curse,* wiċayasiċe, *a curser.*

c. Some nouns, by prefixing 'wiċa' or its contraction 'wiċ,' have their signification limited to the human species; as, wiċaċaŋte, *the human heart;* wiċanape, *the human hand;* wiċoie, *human words;* wiċohaŋ, *human actions.* We also have wiċaatkuku, *a father* or *one's father;* wiċahuŋku, *one's mother;* wiċaċiŋċa, *one's children.*

In like manner 'ta' (not the possessive pronoun, but the generic name of ruminating animals, and particularly applied to *the moose*) is prefixed to the names of various members of the body, and limits the signification to such animals; as, taċaŋte, *a buffalo* or *deer's heart;* tapa, *a deer's head;* taćeźi, *a buffalo's tongue;* taha, *a deer's skin;* taćesdi, *the 'bois de vache'* of the prairie.

When to such nouns is prefixed 'wa' (from waliaŋksića, *a bear*), their signification is limited to the *bear species;* as, **wapa,** *a bear's head;* waha, *a bear's skin;* waśuŋ, *a bear's den.*

In like manner, 'ho,' from hoġaŋ, *a fish,* prefixed to a few nouns, limits their signification to that genus; as, hoape, *fish-fins;* hoaśke, *the bunch on the head of a fish.*

6. Abstract nouns are formed from adjectives by prefixing 'wićo,' which may be regarded as compounded of 'wića' and 'wo;' as waśte, *good,* wićowaśte, *goodness,* waoŋśida, *merciful;* wićowaoŋśida, *mercy.*

7. *a.* Nouns are formed from verbs in the intransitive or absolute state by suffixing 'pi;' as, wowa, *to paint* or *write,* wowapi, (*they wrote* something) *something written, a writing* or *book;* wayawa, *to count,* wayawapi, *figures* or *arithmetic.*

b. Any verb may be used with the plural ending as a verbal noun or gerund, sometimes without, but more commonly with, the definite article; as, ićazo, *to take credit,* ićazopi, *credit;* wayawaśte, *to bless,* wayawaśtepi, *blessing;* waihaŋgya, *to destroy,* waihaŋgyapi, *destroying;* ećoŋ, *to do,* ećoŋpi kiŋ, *the doing* of a thing.

8. When 's'a' is used after verbs, it denotes *frequency of action,* and gives them the force of nouns of the person; as, kaġe s'a, *a maker;* ećoŋpi s'a, *doers;* yakoŋpi s'a, *dwellers.*

Diminutives.

§ 63. 'Daŋ' or 'na' is suffixed to nouns, pronouns, adjectives, and verbs, and has sometimes a diminutive and sometimes a restrictive signification.

1. Suffixed to nouns, 'daŋ' is generally diminutive; as, mde, *lake,* mdedaŋ, *little lake;* wakpa, *river,* wakpadaŋ, *little river* or *rivulet;* apa, *some,* apadaŋ, *a small part.*

2. Some nouns now appear only with the diminutive ending, although they may formerly have been used without it; as, hokśidaŋ, *boy;* śuŋhpadaŋ, *little dog, puppy;* śuŋġidaŋ, *fox.*

3. Nouns ending with this diminutive take the plural termination before the daŋ; as, hokśidaŋ, *boy,* hokśipidaŋ, *boys.*

4. Some nouns ending in 'na,' when they take the plural form, change 'na' into 'daŋ;' as, wićiŋyaŋna, *girl,* wićiŋyaŋpidaŋ, *girls;* wanistiŋna, *a few,* plur. wanistiŋpidaŋ. In some cases 'daŋ' is used only in the plural form; as, tonana, *a few,* plur. tonanaŋpidaŋ.

The Ihaŋktoŋwaŋ and Sisitoŋwaŋ commonly use 'na,' and the Titoŋwaŋ 'la,' instead of 'daŋ,' for the diminutive ending; as, hokśina and hokśila, for hokśidaŋ.

§ 64. 1. 'Daŋ' is often joined to adjectives and verbs, as the last principal word in the clause, although it properly belongs to the noun; as, śuktaŋka waŋ waśte-daŋ (*horse a good-little*), *a good little horse*, not *a horse a little good;* nićiŋkśi ćeye-daŋ (*thy-son cries-little*), *thy little son cries.*

2. When used with a transitive verb, 'daŋ' may belong either to the subject or the object of the verb; as, nisuŋka śuŋka kiktedaŋ (*thy-brother dog his-killed-little*), *thy little brother killed his dog,* or *thy brother killed his little dog.*

Gender.

§ 65. 1. Gender is sometimes distinguished by different names for the masculine and feminine; as, wićaśta, *man,* winohiŋća, *woman;* tataŋka, *buffalo bull,* pte, *buffalo cow;* hehaka, *the male elk,* upaŋ, *the female elk.*

2. But more commonly the distinction is made by means of adjectives. 'Wića' and 'wiŋyaŋ' denote the male and female of the *human species;* as, hokśiyoķopa wića, *a male child,* hokśiyoķopa wiŋyaŋ, *a female child.* 'Mdoka' and 'wiye' distinguish the sex of *animals;* as, tamdoka, *a buck;* tawiyedaŋ, *a doe,* the 'daŋ' being diminutive. These words, however, are often written separately; as, paġoŋta mdoka, *a drake;* zitkadaŋ wiye, *a hen bird.* In some instances contraction takes place; as, śuŋg mdoka, *a horse;* śuŋg wiye, *a mare,* from śuŋka.

3. Proper names of females of the human species frequently have 'wiŋ,' an abbreviation of 'wiŋyaŋ,' *female,* for their termination; as, Totidutawiŋ (*Woman of her red house);* Wakaŋkaźuźuwiŋ (*Female spirit that pays debts*). Sometimes the diminutive 'wiŋna' is used for 'wiŋ;' as, Mahpiwiŋna (*Cloud woman*).

Number.

§ 66. To nouns belong two numbers, the *singular* and *plural.*

1. The plural of animate objects is denoted by the termination 'pi,' which is attached either to the noun itself; as, śuŋka, *a dog,* śuŋkapi, *dogs;* or, as is more commonly the case, to the adjective or verb which follows it in the same phrase; as, śuŋka ksapapi, *wise dogs;* śuŋka ećoŋpi, *dogs did it.*

2. (a) Names of inanimate objects seldom take the plural termination, even when used with a plural meaning; as, ćaŋ, *a tree* or *trees;* máġa, *a field* or *fields.*

(b) On the other hand, some nouns formed from verbs by adding the plural termination 'pi' (§ 62. 7. *a.*) are used with a singular as well as a plural meaning; as, tipi, *a house* or *houses;* wowapi, *a book* or *books.*

Case.

§ 67. Dakota nouns may be said to have two principal cases, the *subjective* and *objective*.[1]

The subjective and objective cases are usually known by the place which they occupy in the sentence. When two nouns are used, the one the subject and the other the object of the action, the subject is placed first, the object next, and the verb last; as, wićaśta waŋ wowapi waŋ kaġa (*man a book a made*), *a man made a book;* Dawid Sopiya waśtedaka (*David Sophia loves*), *David loves Sophia;* Dakota Beśdeke wićaktepi (*Dakota Fox-Indian them-they-killed*), *the Dakotas killed the Fox Indians.*

When, from some consideration, it is manifest which must be the nominative, the arrangement may be different; as, wićaśta Wakaŋtaŋka kaġa (*man God made*), *God made man.*

As this distinction of case is rather syntactical than etymological, see further in the Syntax.

Possession.

§ 68. The relation of two nouns to each other, as *possessor* and *possessed*, is sometimes indicated by placing them in juxtaposition, the name of the possessor coming first; as, wahukeza ihupa, *spear-handle;* tipi tiyopa, *house-door;* wićaśta oie, *man's word.*

Sometimes the first noun suffers contraction; as, malićiŋća, *a gosling,* for maġá ćiŋća (*goose child*); maliiyumdu, *a plough,* for mága iyumdu (*field-plough*); maliićahiŋte, *a rake,* for mága ićahiŋte (*field-rake*).

§ 69. But the relation is pointed out more definitely by adding to the last term a possessive pronoun, either separate or incorporated.

1. Sometimes the pronouns 'tawa' and 'tawapi' are used after the second noun; as, tataŋka woyute tawa (*buffalo food his*), *buffalo's food;* woyute śuktaŋka tawapi (*food horse theirs*), *horses' food;* wićaśtayatapi tipi tawa (*chief house his*), *the chief's house.*

2. (*a*) But generally the possessive pronouns are prefixed to the name of the thing possessed; as, tataŋka tawote (*buffalo his-food*), *buffalo's food;* Dawid taaŋpetu (*David his-day*), *the days of David.*

Sometimes 'ti' is prefixed instead of 'ta;' as, waŋhiŋkpe, *an arrow;* Dawid tiwaŋhiŋkpe, *David's arrow.*

Nouns commencing with 'i' or 'o' prefix 't' only; as, ipahiŋ, *a pillow;* Hake tipahiŋ, *Hake's pillow;* owiŋźa, *a bed;* Hake towiŋźe, *Hake's bed.*

Abstract nouns which commence with 'wo' drop the 'w' and prefix 't;' as, wowaśte, *goodness;* Wakaŋtaŋka towaśte, *God's goodness.* (See § 23, 2. *b*.)

---

[1] A. L. Riggs thinks a better arrangement would include the *genitive* case with the *subjective* and *objective*. The rule of position would then be: A noun in the genitive case qualifying another noun is placed before the noun it qualifies. See § 68.

(*b*) Nouns expressing relationship form their genitive by means of the suffix pronouns 'ku,' ' ću,' 'tku;' as, suŋka, *younger brother*, Dawid suŋkaku, *David's younger brother;* ćiŋye, *the elder brother* of a man, Tomas ćinću, *Thomas's elder brother;* ćiŋkśi, *a daughter*, wićaśta ćiŋkśitku, *man's daughter.*

Proper and Family Names.[1]

§ 70. The proper names of the Dakotas are words, simple and compounded, which are in common use in the language. They are usually given to children by the father, grandfather, or some other influential relative. When young men have distinguished themselves in battle, they frequently take to themselves new names, as the names of distinguished ancestors of warriors now dead. The son of a chief, when he comes to the chieftainship, generally takes the name of his father or grandfather; so that the same names, as in other more powerful dynasties, are handed down along the royal lines.

1. (*a*) Dakota proper names sometimes consist of a single noun; as, Maḣpiya, *Cloud;* Hokśidaŋ, *Boy;* Wamdenića, *Orphan;* Wowaćiŋyaŋ, *Faith.*

(*b*) Sometimes they consist of a single adjective; as, Śakpe, (*Six*) *Little-six*, the chief at Prairieville.

2. (*a*) But more frequently they are composed of a noun and adjective; as Iśtaḣba (*eyes-sleepy*), *Sleepy-eyes;* Tataŋka-haŋska (*buffalo-long*), *Long buffalo;* Matohota, *Grizzly-bear;* Wamdi-duta, *Scarlet-eagle;* Matotamaheća, *Lean-bear;* Mazaḣota, *Grey-iron;* Maza-ś'a, *Sounding-metal;* Wapaha-śa, *Red-flag-staff*, called now *Wabashaw.*

(*b*) Sometimes they are formed of two nouns; as, Maḣpiya-wićaśta, *Cloud-man;* Peźihuta-wićaśta, *Medicine-man;* Ite-wakiŋyaŋ, *Thunder-face.*

3. Sometimes a possessive pronoun is prefixed; as, Ta-makoće, *His country;* Ta-peta-taŋka, *His-great-fire;* Ta-oyate-duta, *His-red-people.*

4. (*a*) Sometimes they consist of verbs in the intransitive form, which may be rendered by nouns; as, Wakute, *Shooter;* Wanapeya, *One-who-causes-flight.*

(*b*) Sometimes they are compounded of a noun and verb; as, Akićita-naźiŋ, *Standing-soldier* or *Sentinel;* Tataŋka-naźiŋ, *Standing-buffalo;* Maḣpiya-mani, *Walking-cloud;* Waŋmdi-okiya, *One-who-talks-with-the-eagle;* Maḣpiya-hdinape, *Cloud-that-appears-again.*

[1] A classification of personal names of the Omaha, Ponka, Kansa, Osage, Iowa, Oto, and Missouri tribes will be found on pp. 393–399, Proc. A. A. A. S., xxxiv, 1885. See also "Indian personal names," pp. 263–268, Amer. Anthropologist, July, 1890.—J. O. D.

(c) Sometimes they are formed of two verbs; as, Iŋyaŋg-mani, *One-who-walks-running*. In some instance a preposition is prefixed; as, Anawaŋg-mani, *One-who-walks-as-he-gallops-on*.

§ 71. The names of the women are formed in the same way, but generally have 'wiŋ' or 'wiŋna,' *female*, added; as, Aŋpetu-sapa-wiŋ, *Black-day-woman ;* Mahpi-wiŋna, *Cloud-woman*.

§ 72. The Dakotas have no family or surnames. But the children of a family have particular names which belong to them, in the order of their birth, up to the fifth child. These names are, for boys, Ćaské, Hepáŋ, Hepí, Ćatáŋ, and Haké. For girls, they are, Winóna, Hápaŋ, Hápistiŋna, Wáŋske, and Wiháke. Thus the first child, if a boy, is called Ćaské, if a girl, Winóna; the second, if a boy, is called Hepáŋ, and if a girl, Hápaŋ, etc. If there are more than five children in the family, the others have no names of this kind. Several of these names are not used by the Titoŋwaŋ and Ihaŋktoŋwaŋ.

§ 73. The names of certain family relations, both male and female, are presented in the following table:

	A Man's.	*A Woman's.*
elder brother	ćiŋyé	timdó
elder sister	taŋké	ćuŋ
younger brother	suŋká	suŋká
younger sister	taŋkśí	taŋká
male cousin	taháŋśi	ićéśi
female cousin	haŋkáśi	ićépaŋśi
brother-in-law	taháŋ	śićé
sister-in-law	haŋká	ićépaŋ

The other relations, as, father, mother, uncle, aunt, grandfather, grandmother, etc., are designated, both by men and women, by the same names.

ADJECTIVES.

§ 74. 1. Most adjectives in Dakota may be considered as primitive; as, ska, *white*, taŋka, *large*, waśte, *good*.

2. A few are formed from verbs by prefixing 'wa;' as, oŋśida, *to have mercy on* one, waoŋśida, *merciful;* ćaŋtekiya, *to love*, waćaŋtkiya, *benevolent*.

§ 75. Final ' a' or ' aŋ' of many adjectives is changed into ' e' when followed by certain particles, as, hiŋća, do, kiŋ or ćiŋ, etc.: śića, *bad*, śićé hiŋća, *very bad;* wićaśta śićé ćiŋ, *the bad man*.

§ 76. Adjectives have three numbers, the *singular, dual,* and *plural.*

§ 77. The *dual* is formed from the singular by prefixing or inserting 'uŋ,' the pronoun of the first person plural; as, ksapa, *wise;* wićaśta uŋksapa, *we two wise men;* waoŋśida, *merciful;* waoŋśiuŋda, *we two merciful ones.*

§ 78. 1. The *plural* is formed by the addition of 'pi' to the singular; as, waśte, *good;* wićaśta waśtepi, *good men.*

2. Another form of the plural which frequently occurs, especially in connection with animals and inanimate objects, is made by a reduplication of one of the syllables.

(*a*) Sometimes the first syllable reduplicates; as, ksapa, *wise,* plur., ksaksapa; taŋka, *great,* plur. taŋktaŋka.

(*b*) In some cases the last syllable reduplicates; as, waśte, *good,* plur., waśteśte.

(*c*) And sometimes a middle syllable is reduplicated; as, taŋkiŋyaŋ, *great* or *large,* plur., taŋkiŋkiŋyaŋ.

§ 79. Adjectives are not inflected to denote degrees of comparison, but are increased or diminished in signification by means of adverbs.

1. (*a*) What may be called the *comparative* degree is formed by saŋpa, *more;* as, waśte, *good,* saŋpa waśte, *more good* or *better.* When the name of the person or thing, with which the comparison is made, immediately precedes, the preposition 'i' is employed to indicate the relation, and is prefixed to saŋpa; as, wićaśta kiŋ de isaŋpa waśte, *this man is better than that.* Sometimes 'sam iyeya,' which may be translated *more advanced,* is used; as, sam iyeya waśte, *more advanced good* or *better.*

It is difficult to translate 'iyeya' in this connection, but it seems to convey the idea of *passing on* from one degree to another.

(*b*) Often, too, comparison is made by saying that one is good and another is bad; as, de śića, he waśte, *this is bad, that is good,* i. e. *that is better than this.*

(*c*) To diminish the signification of adjectives, 'kitaŋna' is often used; as, taŋka, *large,* kitaŋna taŋka, *somewhat large,* that is, *not very large.*

2. What may be called the *superlative* degree is formed by the use of 'nina,' 'hiŋća,' and 'iyotaŋ;' as, nina waśte, or waśte hiŋća, *very good;* iyotaŋ waśte, *best.*

NUMERAL ADJECTIVES.

Cardinals.

§ 80. The cardinal numerals are as follows:

waŋća, waŋźi, or waŋźidaŋ,	*one.*	wikćemna,	*ten.*
noŋpa,	*two.*	wikćemna noŋpa,	*twenty*
yamni,	*three.*	wikćemna yamni,	*thirty.*
topa,	*four.*	wikćemna topa,	*forty.*
zaptaŋ,	*five.*	opawiŋǵe,	*a hundred.*
śakpe,	*six.*	opawiŋǵe noŋpa,	*two hundred.*
śakowiŋ,	*seven.*	kektopawiŋǵe,[1]	*a thousand.*
śahdoǵaŋ,	*eight.*	woyawa taŋka,	*the great count,*
napćiŋwaŋka,	*nine.*		*or a million.*

1. The numbers from eleven to eighteen inclusive, are formed in two ways:

(*a*) By ake, *again;* as, ake waŋźidaŋ, *eleven;* ake noŋpa, *twelve;* ake yamni, *thirteen,* etc. Written in full, these would be wikćemna ake waŋźidaŋ, *ten again one;* wikćemna ake noŋpa, *ten again two,* etc.

In counting, the Dakotas use their fingers, bending them down as they pass on, until they reach ten. They then turn down a little finger, to remind them that one ten is laid away, and commence again. When the second ten is counted, another finger goes down, and so on.

(*b*) By saŋpa, *more;* as, wikćemna saŋpa waŋźidaŋ, *ten more one,* $(10 + 1)$ or *eleven;* wikćemna saŋpa topa $(10 + 4)$, *fourteen;* wikćemna saŋpa śahdoǵaŋ $(10 + 8)$, *eighteen.*

2. *Nineteen* is formed by uŋma, *the other;* as, uŋma napćiŋwaŋka, *the other nine.*

3. (*a*) Wikćemna noŋpa is (10×2) twenty, and so with *thirty, forty,* etc. The numbers between these are formed in the same way as between *eleven* and *eighteen;* as, wikćemna noŋpa saŋpa waŋźidaŋ, or, wikćemna noŋpa ake waŋźidaŋ $(10 \times 2 + 1)$, *twenty-one;* wikćemna noŋpa saŋpa napćiŋwaŋka $(10 \times 2 + 9)$, *twenty-nine;* wikćemna yamni saŋpa topa, $(10 \times 3 + 4)$, *thirty-four;* wikćemna zaptaŋ saŋpa napćiŋwaŋka $(10 \times 5 + 9)$, *fifty-nine.* Over *one hundred,* numbers are still formed in the same way; as, opawiŋǵe saŋpa wikćemna śakpe saŋpa śakowiŋ $(100 + [10 \times 6] + 7)$, *one hundred and sixty-seven;* kektopawiŋǵe noŋpa saŋpa opawiŋǵe zaptaŋ saŋpa wikćemna yamni saŋpa śakpe $([1000 \times 2] + [100 \times 5] + [10 \times 3] + 6)$, *two thousand five hundred and thirty-six.*

---

[1] Also koktopawiŋǵe.

(b) The numbers between *twenty* and *thirty*, *thirty* and *forty*, etc., are occasionally expressed by placing an ordinal before the cardinal, which denotes that it is *so many* in *such a ten;* as, iyamni topa, *four of the third (ten)*, i. e., *twenty-four;* itopa yamni, *three of the fourth (ten)*, i. e., *thirty-three.*

It is an interesting study to analyze these numerals. It has been stated above, that the Dakota, in common with all Indians, it is believed, are in the habit of using the hands in counting. It might be supposed then that the names indicating numbers would be drawn largely from the hand. The following derivations and explanations, it is believed, will be found in the main reliable.

1. Waŋċa, etc. from waŋ! interjection—calling attention—perhaps, at the same time, *holding up a finger.*

2. Noŋpa, from en aoŋpa, *to bend down on*, or *place on*, as the second finger is laid down over the small one; or perhaps of nape oŋpa, nape being used for *finger* as well as *hand.* The Ponka and Omaha is naŋba, and the Winnabago nuŋp.[1]

3. Yamni, from mni (*root*) signifying either *turning over* or *laying up ;* the 'ya' perhaps indicating that it is done with the mouth. (See § 34.*f.*)

It is suggested, as a further solution of yamni, that the 'mni' may be an old root, meaning *together* or *flow together*, as we have it in the reduplicate amnimni, e. g., mini amnimni, *to sprinkle water upon.* The Ponka and Omaha is dha-bdhiŋ.[2]

4. Topa, from opa, *to follow;* (perhaps ti, *a house*, and opa, *follow with*) as we say, 'in the same box,' with the rest. The three have banded together and made a 'ti' or 'tidaŋ,' as we would say *a family*, and the fourth joins them. The Ponka and Omaha is duba.

5. Zaptaŋ, from za, (root) *holding* (or perhaps *whole*, as in zani), and ptaŋyaŋ or ptaya, *together.* In this case the thumb is bent down over the fingers of the hand, and *holds them together.*

6. Śakpe, from śake, *nail*, and kpa or kpe, (root) *lasting* as some kinds of food which go a good ways, or *filled*, as a plump grain. This is the second thumb, and the reference may be to the other hand being *completed.* Possibly from the idea of bending down as in nakpa, *the ear.*

7. Śakowiŋ, from śake, *nail*, and owiŋ, perhaps from owiŋġa, *to bend down ;* but possibly from oiŋ, *to wear*, as jewelry, this being the *fore finger* of the second hand; that is, the *ring finger.*

---

[1] *Two* takes the form ¢aⁿba (dhaŋ-ba) in the Omaha name Ӽaxe ¢aⁿba, Two Crows and de¢aⁿba, seven (+2?). *Two* in Winnebago is expressed variously, even by the same speaker. Thus, we find noŋp, noŋpa, noŋpi, and nuŋp.—J. O. D.

[2] ℂa-b¢iⁿ in the notation of the Bureau of Ethnology.—J. O. D.

8. Śahdoġaŋ, from śake, *nail* probably, and hdoġaŋ, possessive of yuġaŋ, *to open ;* but perhaps it is oġaŋ or oġe, *to cover, to wear ; the nail covers itself.* Two fingers now cover the thumb.[1]

9. Napćiŋwaŋka, from nape, *hand,* ćistiŋna, *small,* and waŋka, *lies—hand-small-lies ;* that is, the remainder of the hand is very small, or perhaps, the hand now lies in a small compass.

Eli Abraham explains 'napćiŋwaŋka' as from napćupe. All *fingers* are napćupe, in the original sense; that is they are *marrow bones of the hand.* Now this finger of the second hand lies down alone. Two fingers have covered the thumb and this has to take a bed by itself. Rather the finger lies in the napćoka, *inside of the hand.*

10. Wikćemna, from wikće or ikće, *common,* and mnayaŋ, *gathering,* or from mna, *to rip,* that is *let loose.* It would then mean either that the *common* or *first gathering* of the hands was *completed,* or that being completed, the whole are loosed, and the ten thrown up, as is their custom; the hands in the *common position.*

100. Opawiŋge, from pawiŋga, *to bend down with the hand,* the prefixed 'o' indicating *perfectness* or *roundedness ;* that is, the process has been gone over as many times as there are fingers and thumbs.

1000. Kektopawiŋge or koktopawiŋge, from opawiŋge and ake or kokta, meaning *again* or *also.* This would indicate that the *hundred* had been counted over as many times as there are hand digits.[2]

§ 81. Numeral adjectives by reduplicating a syllable express the idea of *two and two* or *by twos, three and three* or *by threes,* etc.; as, nomnoŋpa, *by twos;* yamnimni, *by threes;* toptopa, *by fours,* etc.

(1) Waŋźikźi, the reduplicate of waŋźi, properly means *by ones,* but is used to signify *a few.*

(2) Noŋpa and topa are often contracted into nom and tom, and are generally reduplicated in this form; as, nomnom, *by twos;* tomtom, *by fours.*

(3) Yamni, zaptaŋ, śakowiŋ, and wikćemna, reduplicate the last syllable; as, yamnimni, zaptaŋptaŋ, śakowiŋwiŋ, and wikćemnamna. The same is true of opawiŋge and kektopawiŋge; as, opawiŋgege, *by hundreds.*

(4) Napćiŋwaŋka and śahdoġaŋ reduplicate a middle syllable, as napćiŋwaŋgwaŋka, *by nines,* śahdohdoġaŋ, *by eights.*

§ 82. Waŋća, noŋpa, yamni, etc., are also used for *once, twice, thrice,* etc. Noŋpa noŋpa hećen topa, *twice two so four,* that is, *twice two are four.*

---

[1] The author gives, in the Dictionary, oġaŋ and oġe, *clothes, covering, a sheath;* but not as a verb.—J. O. D.

[2] Can there be a satisfactory analysis of the Dakota numerals without a full comparison with those of the cognate languages of the Siouan family? I think not.—J. O. D.

And 'akihde' is sometimes used for this purpose; as, noŋpa akihde noŋpa, *two times two.*

§ 83. 1. 'Daŋ' or 'na,' suffixed to numeral adjectives, is restrictive; as, yamni, *three,* yamnina, *only three;* zaptaŋ, *five,* zaptaŋna, *only five.*

2. With monosyllabic words 'na' is doubled; as, nom, *two,* nomňana, *only two;* tom, *four,* tomnana, *only four;* huŋȟ, *a part,* huŋȟnana, *only a part.*

Ordinals.

§ 84. 1. The ordinal numbers, after tokaheya, *first,* are formed from cardinals by prefixing 'i,' 'ići,' and 'wići;' as, inoŋpa, ićinoŋpa, and wići-noŋpa, *second;* iyamni, ićiyamni, and wićiyamni, *third;* itopa, ićitopa, and wićitopa, *fourth;* iwikćemna, *tenth,* etc.

2. In like manner we have iake waŋźi, *eleventh;* iake noŋpa, *twelfth;* iake yamni, *thirteenth,* etc.; iwikćemna noŋpa, *twentieth;* iopawiŋge, *one hundredth,* etc.

§ 85. When several numbers are used together, the last only has the ordinal form; as, wikćemna noŋpa saŋpa iyamni, *twenty-third;* opawiŋge saŋpa iake noŋpa, *one hundred and twelfth.*

ADVERBS.

§ 86. There are some adverbs, in very common use, whose derivation from other parts of speech is not now apparent, and which may therefore be considered as primitives; as, eća, *when;* kuya and kun, *under, below;* kitaŋna, *a little, not much;* nina and hiŋća, *very;* ohiŋni, *always;* saŋpa, *more;* taŋkan, *without, out of doors;* waŋna, *now,* etc.[1]

§ 87. But adverbs in Dakota are, for the most part, derived from *demonstrative pronouns, adjectives, verbs,* and other *adverbs;* and in some instances from other parts of speech.

1. Adverbs are formed from *demonstrative pronouns,* by adding 'han' and 'haŋ,' 'ken' and 'ćen,' 'ketu' and 'ćetu,' 'en,' 'ki' and 'kiya,' 'ći' and 'ćiya.'

(a) By adding 'han' and 'haŋ;' as, de, *this,* dehan, *here, now;* he, *that;* hehan, *there, then;* ka, *that,* kahan and kahaŋ, *then, there, so far.* The forms dehaŋ and hehaŋ are used with a slight difference of signification from dehan and hehan; the first indicating place and the latter time.[2]

(b) By adding 'ken' and 'ćen;' as, kaken, *in this manner;* eća, *when;* ećaken, *whenever, always;* dećen, *thus;* hećen, *in that way.*

---

[1] A. L. Riggs suggests that eća has the force of *when* only by position, and that eća and eće, ća and će are frequentative particles, akin, in radical meaning, and perhaps in origin, to 'ake,' *again.*

[2] In the cognate languages, time words and space words are not fully differentiated. Thus in Çegiha, ataⁿ ȟ, *how long? how far? when?*—J. O. D.

(c) By adding 'ketu' and 'ćetu;' as, kaketu, *in that manner;* dećetu, *in this way;* hećetu, *so, thus.*

(d) By adding 'en,' *in,* in a contracted form; as, de, *this,* den, *here;* he, *that;* hen, *there;* ka, *that,* kaŋ, *yonder;* tukte, *which?* tukten, *where?*

(e) By adding 'ki' and 'ći,' 'kiya' and 'ćiya;' as, ka, *that,* kaki and kakiya, *there;* de, *this,* deći and dećiya, *here.*

2. Adverbs are formed from *adjectives,* by adding 'ya;' as, waśte, *good,* waśteya, *well;* śića, *bad,* śićaya, *badly;* taŋka, *great,* taŋkaya, *greatly, extensively.*

3. (a) Adverbs are formed from *verbs,* by adding 'yaŋ;' as, iyuśkiŋ, *to rejoice,* iyuśkiŋyaŋ, *rejoicingly, gladly;* taŋyaŋ, *well,* may be from the obsolete verb 'taŋ' (as they still use ataŋ, *to regard, take care of*); itoŋśni, *to tell a lie,* itoŋśniyaŋ, *falsely.*

(b) Some are formed by adding 'ya' alone; as, aokaǵa, *to tell a falsehood about* one, aokaḣya, *falsely.*

(c) In a few instances adverbs are formed from verbs by adding 'na;' as, inaḣni, *to be in haste,* inaḣnina, *hastily, temporarily.*

4. Adverbs are formed from other *adverbs.*

(a) By adding 'tu;' as, dehan, *now,* dehantu, *at this time;* hehan, *then,* hehantu, *at that time;* tohan, *when?* tohantu, *at what time?*

(b) Other forms are made by adding 'ya' to the preceding; as, dehantuya, *thus, here;* hehantuya, *there;* dećetuya, *so;* toketuya, *in whatever way.*

(c) Others still are made by the further addition of 'ken;' as, dehantuyaken, toketuyaken. The meaning appears to be substantially the same after the addition of 'ken' as before.

(d) Adverbs are formed from other adverbs by adding 'yaŋ;' as, dehan, *now, here,* dehaŋyaŋ, *to this time* or *place, so far;* tohan, *when?* tohaŋyaŋ, *as long as, how long?* ohiŋni, *always,* ohiŋniyaŋ, *for ever.*

(e) Adverbs are formed from other adverbs by adding 'tkiya;' as, kun, *below,* kuŋtkiya, *downwards;* waŋkan, *above,* waŋkaŋtkiya, *upwards.*

5. Some adverbs are formed from *nouns.*

(a) By prefixing 'a' and taking the adverbial termination 'ya;' as, paha, *a hill,* apahaya, *hill-like, convexly;* wanića, *none,* awaniŋ and awaninya, *in a destroying way.*

(b) By suffixing 'ata' or 'yata,' etc.; as, ḣe, *a hill* or *ridge,* ḣeyata, *back at the hill.*

Words so formed may be called *prepositional nouns.* See § 91.

6. Adverbs are derived from *prepositions*.

(*a*) By adding 'tu' or 'tuya;' as, mahen, *in* or *within*, mahentu or mahetu and mahetuya, *inwardly*.

(*b*) By adding 'wapa;' as, ako, *beyond*, akowapa, *onward;* mahen, *in*, mahenwapa, *inwardly*.

PREPOSITIONS.

§ 88. (*a*) What are named prepositions in other languages are in Dakota properly post-positions, as they *follow* the nouns which they govern. (See § 186.)   (*b*) Prepositions may be divided into *separate* and *incorporated*.

SEPARATE PREPOSITIONS.

§ 89. The separate prepositions in Dakota follow the nouns which they govern; as, ćaŋ akan nawaźiŋ (*wood upon I-stand*), *I stand upon wood;* he maza oŋ kaġapi (*that iron of is-made*), *that is made of iron.*   The following are the principal separate prepositions, viz:

ahna, *with*	etkiya, *towards*	om, *with them*
akan, *on* or *upon*	etu, *at*	oŋ, *of* or *from, with, for*
ako, *beyond*	kahda, *by, near to*	opta, *through*
ehna, *amongst*	kići, *with him, her,* or *it*	saŋpa, *beyond*
ekta, *at, to*	mahen, *within*	taŋhaŋ, *from*
en, *in*	ohna, *in*	yata, *at.*
etaŋhaŋ, *from*	ohomni, *around*	

Some of these are quite as often used as *adverbs* as *prepositions*.

INCORPORATED PREPOSITIONS, OR PREPOSITIONAL PARTICLES.

§ 90. These are suffixed to nouns, prefixed to or inserted into verbs, and prefixed to adverbs, etc.

§ 91. The prepositions suffixed to nouns are 'ta,' and 'ata' or 'yata,' *at* or *on;* as, tíŋta, *prairie*, tiŋtáta, *at* or *on the prairie;* máġa, *a field*, maġáta, *at the field;* ćaŋ, *wood* or *woods*, ćaŋyáta, *at the woods.*   The preposition en, *in*, contracted, is suffixed to a few nouns; as, ti, *a house*, tin, *in the house.* These formations may also be regarded as adverbs; as, he, *a hill* or *ridge*, heyáta, *at the hill* or *back from.*

T. L. Riggs suggests that this class of words should be denominated *prepositional nouns* or *adverbial nouns.*

§ 92. The prepositions 'a,' 'e,' 'i,' 'o,' instead of being suffixed to the noun, are prefixed to the verb.

1. (*a*) The preposition 'a,' *on* or *upon*, is probably a contraction of

'akan,' and is prefixed to a very large number of verbs; as, mani, *to walk*, amani, *to walk on*, ćaŋkaġa amawani, *I walk on a log.*

(*b*) The preposition 'e,' *to* or *at*, is probably from 'ekta,' and is prefixed to some verbs; as, yuħpa, *to lay down* anything one is carrying, eyuħpa, *to lay down at* a place.

(*c*) The preposition 'i' prefixed to verbs means *with, for, on account of;* as, ćekiya, *to pray*, ićekiya, *to pray for* a thing.

(*d*) The preposition 'o,' *in*, is a contraction of 'ohna,' and is found in a large class of verbs; as, hnaka, *to place* or *lay down*, ohnaka, *to place* a thing *in* something else.

2. The prepositions which are either prefixed to or inserted into verbs, in the pronouns' place, are 'ki' and 'kići.'

(*a*) 'Ki,' as a preposition incorporated in verbs, means *to* or *for;* as, kaġa, *to make*, kićaġa, *to make to* one; huwe ya, *to go to bring* anything, kihuwe ya, *to go to bring* a thing *for* one.

(*b*) 'Kići' incorporated into verbs, means *for;* as, kaksa, *to chop off*, as a stick; kićićaksa, *to chop off for* one.

§ 93. The preposition 'i' is prefixed to a class of adverbs giving them the force of prepositions. In these cases it expresses *relation to* or *connexion with* the preceding noun; as, tehaŋ, *far*, itehaŋ, *far from* any time or place; heyata, *behind*, iheyata, *back of* something. These adverbial prepositions are such as:

iako, *beyond*	ihukuya, *under*	itehaŋ, *far from*
iakan, *upon*	ilieyata, *behind, back of*	itokam, *before*
iaśkadaŋ, *near to*	ikaŋyeta, *down from*	iwaŋkam, *above*
ićahda, *by, near to*	ikiyedaŋ, *near to*	iyohakam, *after*
ihakam, *behind*	isaŋpa, *beyond*	iyotahedaŋ, *between*
ihdukśaŋ, *round about*	itakasaŋpa, *over from*	iyotahepi, *between*
ihektam, *behind*	itaŋkan, *without*	iyotakoŋs, *opposite to.*

CONJUNCTIONS.

§ 94. Conjunctions in Dakota, as in other languages, are used to connect words and sentences; as, waśte ķa ksapa, *good and wise;* wićaśta śićeća koya, *men and children:* "Uŋkaŋ Wakaŋtaŋka, Oźaŋźaŋ kta, eya: uŋkaŋ oźaŋźaŋ," *And God said, 'Let light be:' and light was.*

§ 95. The following is a list of the principal conjunctions, viz: uŋkaŋ, ķa and ća, *and;* ko and koya, *also, and;* uŋkaŋś, kiŋhaŋ and ćiŋhaŋ, kinahaŋ and ćinahaŋ, *if;* eśta and śta, keś and ćeś, ķeś and ćeś, *although;* ķaeś and ćaeś, ķeyaś and ćeyaś, *even if;* ķa iś, *or;* tuka, *but.* For uŋkaŋ and uŋkaŋś the Titonwaŋ say yuŋkaŋ and yuŋkaŋś, for 'ķa' and 'ća' they use 'na,' and for 'ķa iś,' 'na iś.'

INTERJECTIONS.

§ 96. It is very difficult to translate, or even to classify, Dakota interjections. Those in common use may be arranged under the following heads, according to the emotions they express:

Pain: yuŋ! wiŋświ! *ah! oh!*

Regret: hehe! hehehe! huŋhe! huŋhuŋhe! *oh! alas!*

Surprise: hopidaŋ! hopidaŋniye! hopidaŋśni! iŋah! inama! iŋyuŋ! iyanaka! *wonderful! surprising! astonishing! truly! indeed!*

Attention: a! e! beś! hiwo! iho! ito! mah! toko! waŋ! *hark! look! see! behold! halloo!*

Self-praise: ihdataŋ! ihdataŋh! *boast!*[1]

Affirmation: ećahe! ećaś! ećaeś! eeś! ehaeś! ehtakaeś! eyakeś! eyaḳeś! nakaś! nakaeś! *indeed! truly! yes!*

Disbelief: eze! hes! hiŋte! ho! hoećah! iyeśnića! oho! taze! or tase! (Yankton) *fie! fudge! you don't say so!*

'Eya,' when used at the beginning of a phrase or sentence, is an interjection, and seems to mean nothing.

---

[1] "Boast" does not appear as an interjection in Webster's dictionary, nor in that of the Century Company. As ihdataŋ means *he praises himself, he boasts,* a better translation is, *O how he boasts!*— J. O. D.

CHAPTER III.

SYNTAX.

PRONOUNS.

PERSONAL PRONOUNS.

Incorporated Pronouns.

§ 97. The *incorporated* pronouns are either *prefixed to* or *inserted into* verbs, adjectives, and nouns.

1. POSITION IN VERBS.

§ 98. 1. (*a*) Monosyllabic verbs, such as, ba, *to blame*, da, *to ask for*, etc., necessarily prefix the pronouns; as mayaba (*me-thou-blamest*), **thou** *blamest me.*

(*b*) Those verbs which are formed by adding the prefixes ' ka ' and ' pa,' and also the possessive forms in ' kpa ' or ' tpa,' ' hda,' and ' hdu,' have the pronouns prefixed ; as, kaksa, *to cut off with an axe*, wakaksa, *I cut off ;* paġaŋ, *to part with* anything, wapaġaŋ, *I part with ;* kpaġaŋ, and tpaġaŋ, *to part with one's own*, wakpaġaŋ, *I part with my own ;* hduta, *to eat one's own*, wahduta, *I eat my own.*

(*c*) Other verbs, whose initial letter is ' d ' or ' k,' have the pronouns prefixed ; as, daka, *to esteem so*, wadaka, *I esteem so ;* kaġa, *to make*, yakaġa, *thou makest.*

(*d*) For the forms of the subjective pronouns of the first person singular and the second person singular and plural of verbs in ' ya ' and ' yu,' see §§ 39. (*b*), 50.

2. (*a*) All verbs commencing with a vowel which is not a prefix, insert the pronouns immediately after the vowel ; as, opa, *to follow*, owapa, *I follow ;* excepting the first person plural, ' uŋk,' which is prefixed ; as, uŋkopapi, *we follow.* But ouŋpapi is also used.

(*b*) The prefixing of the prepositions ' a,' ' e,' ' i,' ' o,' does not alter the place of the pronouns ; as, kaśtaŋ, *to pour out*, wakaśtaŋ, *I pour out ;* okaśtaŋ, *to pour out in*, owakaśtaŋ, *I pour out in ;* pahta, *to bind*, pawahta, *I bind ;* apahta, *to bind on*, apawahta, *I bind on.*

(*c*) Verbs formed from verbal roots and adjectives by prefixing 'ba,' 'bo,' and 'na,' take the pronouns after the prefix; as, baksa, *to cut off with a knife*, bawaksa, *I cut off;* boksa, *to shoot off*, as a limb, boyaksa, *thou shootest off;* naksa, *to break off with the foot*, nawaksa, *I break off with the foot*.

(*d*) Other verbs whose initial letter is 'ć,' 'ś,' 'm,' or 'n,' have the pronouns inserted after the first syllable; as, ćapá, *to stab*, ćawápa, *I stab ;* máni, *to walk*, mawáni, *I walk*. Pahta, *to bind* or *tie*, also inserts the pronouns after the first syllable.

(*e*) Verbs that insert or prefix the prepositions 'ki' and 'kíći,' take the pronouns immediately before the prepositions. (See § 40. 5. *a. b.*)

(*f*) Active verbs formed from other verbs, adjectives, or nouns, by adding the causative 'kiya' or 'ya,' take the pronouns immediately before the causative; as, waŋyagkiya, *to cause to see*, waŋyagmakiya, *he causes me to see;* samkiya, *to blacken*, samwakiya, *I blacken;* ćaŋtekiya, *to love*, ćaŋtewakiya, *I love* any one.

(*g*) The compound personal and reflexive pronouns (§ 24) occupy the same place in verbs as do the ordinary incorporated pronouns; as, waśtedaka, *to love*, waśtewadaka, *I love* anything, waśtemićidaka, *I love myself*.

2. Position in Adjectives.

§ 99. 1. (*a*) The pronouns are prefixed to what may be called adjective verbs and adjectives; as, yazaŋ, *to be sick;* taŋćaŋ mayazaŋ, (*body me-sick*) *my body is sick;* waśte, *good*, niwaśte, (*thee-good*) *thou art good*.

(*b*) The pronouns 'ma,' ' ni,' and 'un' are prefixed to the simple numerals; as, mawaŋźidaŋ, *I am one;* ninoŋpapi, *you are two;* uŋyamnipi, *we are three*.

2. (*a*) But if the adjective verb has assumed the absolute form by prefixing ' wa,' or if it commences with a vowel, the pronouns are inserted; as, wayazaŋka, *to be sick*, wamayazaŋka, *I am sick;* asni, *to get well*, amasni, *I have recovered*.

(*b*) Waoŋśida and waćaŋtkiya, and perhaps some others, which we are accustomed to call adjectives, insert the pronouns; as, waoŋśiwada, *I am merciful*.

3. Position in Nouns.

§ 100. 1. (*a*) The possessive pronouns are always prefixed to the noun. (See §§ 21, 22, and 23.)

(*b*) When a noun and pronoun are joined together, with the substantive verb understood, the incorporated pronoun is prefixed to some nouns and inserted in others; as, niśuŋka, (*thee-dog*) *thou art a dog;* winićaśta, (*thee-man*) *thou art a man;* Damakota, (*me-Dakota*) *I am a Dakota.*

In some nouns the pronoun may be placed either after the first or second sylla-ble, according to the taste of the speaker; as, wićaḣiiŋća, *an old man*, wimaćaḣiiŋća or wićamaḣiiŋća, *I am an old man.*

(*c*) When a noun is used with an adjective or adjective verb, and a pronoun is required, it may be prefixed either to the noun or to the adjec-tive; as, nape masuta (*hand me-hard*), or minape suta, (*my-hand hard*) *my hand is hard.*

2. In nouns compounded of a noun and adjective, the place of the pro-noun is between them; as, Isaŋtaŋka, (*knife-big*) *an American*, Isaŋmataŋka, *I am an American.*

4. Position with Respect to Each Other.

§ 101. 1. When one personal pronoun is the subject and another the object of the same verb, the first person, whether nominative or objective, is placed before the second; as, mayaduhapi, (*me-you-have*) *you have me;* uŋniyuhapi (*we-thee-have* or *we-you-have*) *we have thee* or *we have you.*

2. Wića, the objective plural of the third person, when used in a verb with other pronouns, is placed first; as, wićawakaśka (*them-I-bound*), *I bound them.*

Number.

§ 102. Incorporated pronouns, when intended to express plurality, have the plural termination *pi* attached to the end of the word, whether verb, noun, or adjective; as, wayazaŋ, *he is sick*, wauŋyazaŋpi, *we are sick;* wakaġa, *I make* any thing, uŋkaġapi, *we make;* nitaśuŋke, *thy dog*, nita-śuŋkepi, *thy dogs* or *your dog* or *dogs;* niwaśte, *thou art good*, niwaśtepi, *you are good.*

Separate Pronouns.

§ 103. The *separate* personal pronouns stand first in the clauses to which they belong.

(*a*) They stand first in propositions composed of a pronoun and noun, or of a pronuon and adjective; as, miye Isaŋmataŋka, *I am an American;* uŋkiye uŋćuwitapi, *we are cold.*

(*b*) In a proposition composed of a pronoun and verb, whether the pronoun be the subject or object of the verb; as, uŋkiye uŋyaŋpi kta, *we will go;* miye makaśka (*me he-bound*), *he bound me.*

The separate pronouns are not needed for the purpose of showing the person and number of the verb, those being indicated by the incorporated or article pronouns, or inflexion of the verb; but they are frequently used for the sake of emphasis; as, nisuŋka he ķupi he; hiya, he miye maķupi (*thy-brother that was-given? no, that me me-was-given*), *was that given to thy brother? no, it was given to me;* ye maśi wo; hiya, miye mde kta (*to-go me-command; no, me I-go will*), *send me; no, I will go myself.*

(*c*) When a separate pronoun is used with a noun, one being the subject and the other the object of the same verb, the pronoun stands first; as, miye mini waćiŋ (*me water I-want*), *I want water;* niye tóka kiŋ niyuzapi (*you enemy the you-took*), *the enemies took you.* But when the pronoun is the object, as in this last example, it may stand after the noun; as, tóka kiŋ niye niyuzapi (*enemy the you you-took*), *the enemies took you.*

(*d*) In relative clauses, the separate pronoun is placed last; as, wićaśta hi ķoŋ he miye (*man came that me*), *I am the man who came;* ónićiyapi kiŋ hena uŋkiyepi (*you-help the those we*), *we are they who help you.*

(*e*) The adverb 'hiŋća' is often used with the separate pronouns to render them more emphatic; as, miye hiŋća (*me very*), *my very self's* niye nitawa hiŋća (*thee thine very*), *truly thine own.*

(*f*) In answering questions, the separate pronouns are sometimes used alone; as, tuwe hećoŋ he; miye, *who did that? I;* tuwe yaka he; niye, *whom dost thou mean? thee;* tuwe he kaġa he; iye, *who made that? he.* But more frequently the verb is repeated in the answer with the pronouns; as, he tuwe kaġa he; he miye wakaġa (*that who made? that me I-made*), *who made that? I made it;* tuwe yaka he; niye ćića (*whom meanest-thou? thee, I-thee-mean*), *whom dost thou mean? I mean thee.*

§ 104. When the separate pronouns are used with verbs or adjectives the plural termination is attached to the last word.

(*a*) When the pronoun stands first, it is attached to the verb or adjective; as, uŋkiye ećoŋkupi, *we did it;* niye yakaġapi, *you made it;* niye niwaśtepi, *you are good.*

(*b*) When the pronoun stands last, it is attached also to the pronoun; as, tona waoŋśidapi kiŋ hena niyepi (*as-many merciful the those you*), *you are they who are merciful.*

Agreement of Pronouns.

§ 105. Personal pronouns, and the relative and interrogative tuwe, *who*, refer only to animate objects, and agree in person with their antecedents, which are either expressed or understood; as, he tuwe, *who is that?* de miye, *this is I;* he Dawid tawa, *that is David's;* he miye mitawa, *that is mine;* he tuwe tawa, *whose is that?*

Omission of Pronouns.

§ 106. The third person, being the form of expression which most commonly occurs, is seldom distinguished by the use of pronouns.

1. (*a*) There is no incorporated or article pronoun of the third person, either singular or plural, except 'wića' and 'ta.' (See §§ 18. 6, 19. 4, 23. 1.)

(*b*) The separate pronoun 'iye' of the third person, and its plural 'iyepi,' are frequently used in the subjective and sometimes in the objective case.

2. But ordinarily, and always except in the above cases, no pronoun of the third person is used in Dakota; as, śiyo waŋ kute ķa o (*grouse a shot and killed*), *he shot a grouse and killed it;* śuktaŋka kiŋ yuzapi ķa kaśka hdepi (*horse the caught and tied placed*), *they caught the horse and tied him.*

Repetition of Pronouns.

§ 107. 1. In the case of verbs connected by conjunctions, the incorporated subjective pronouns of the first and second persons must be repeated, as in other languages, in each verb; as, wahi, ķa waŋmdake, ća ohiwaya, *I came, and I saw, and I conquered.*

2. (*a*) 'Wića' and other objective incorporated pronouns follow the same rule; as, tataŋka kiŋ waŋwićamda ke ća wićawakte (*buffalo the, them-I-saw, and them-I-killed*), *I saw the buffalo and killed them.*

(*b*) So, too, in adjective verbs; as, oŋniśike ća niśiħtiŋ (*thee-poor and thee-feeble*), *thou art poor and feeble.*

3. Two or more nouns connected by conjunctions require the possessive pronoun to be used with each; as, nitaśuŋke ķa nitamazakaŋ, *thy-dog and thy-gun.*

DEMONSTRATIVE PRONOUNS.

§ 108. Demonstrative pronouns may generally be used in Dakota wherever they would be required in English.

1. When a demonstrative pronoun forms with a noun, pronoun, adjective, or verb a proposition of which it is the subject or object, it is placed first; as, hena tataŋkapi, *those are oxen;* de miye, *this is I;* dena waśteśte, *these are good;* he mayaķu (*that me-thou-gavest*), *thou gavest me that.*

2. But when used as a qualificative of a noun, or noun and adjective, it is placed last; as, wićaśta kiŋ hena (*man the those*), *those men;* wićaśta waśte kiŋ dena (*man good the these*), *these good men.*

§ 109. The demonstrative pronouns 'he' and 'hena' are often used where personal pronouns would be in English; as, ate umaśi kiŋ he wićayadapi śni (*father me-sent the that ye-believe not*), *my father who sent me, him ye believe not;* ate umaśi kiŋ he mahdaotaŋiŋ (*father me-sent the that me-declareth*), *my father who sent me he beareth witness of me.*

§ 110. Demonstrative pronouns are often used in Dakota when they would not be required in English; as, isaŋ kiŋ he iwaću (*knife the that I-took*), *I took the knife.*

RELATIVE PRONOUNS.

§ 111. 1. Tuwe, *who*, and taku, *what*, are used, both as interrogative and relative pronouns, and in both cases they stand at the beginning of the phrase or sentence; as, tuwe yaka he, *whom dost thou mean?* taku odake ćiŋ, *what thou relatest.*

2. (*a*) In affirmative sentences, 'tuwe' and 'taku' are often used as nouns, the former meaning *some person*, and the latter, *some thing;* as, tuwe he manoŋ, *someone has stolen that;* taku iyewaya, *I have found something.*

(*b*) In negative sentences with 'daŋ' suffixed, tuwe may be rendered *no one*, and taku *nothing;* as, tuwedaŋ hi śni, *no one came* (lit. *some-little-person came not*); takudaŋ duhe śni (*some-little-thing thou-hast not*), *thou hast nothing.* See § 25. 3.

§ 112. It has been shown (§ 25. 1) that compound relative pronouns are formed by joining 'kaśta' or 'kakeś' to 'tuwe' and 'taku;' as, tuwe kaśta hi kiŋhaŋ he waku kta (*whoever comes if, that I-give will*), *if anyone comes I will give it to him;* taku kaśta waŋmdake ćiŋhaŋ wakute kta (*whatever I-see if, I-shoot will*), *if I see anything I will shoot it,* or *I will shoot whatever I see.*

ARTICLES.

Definite Article.

POSITION.

§ 113. 1. When a noun is used without any qualificative, the definite article immediately follows the noun; as, maka kiŋ (*earth the*), *the earth;* wićaśta kiŋ waśte (*man the good*), *the man is good.*

2. When a noun is used with an adjective as a qualifying term, the article follows the adjective; as, wićaśta waśte kiŋ (*man good the*), *the good man.*

3. When the noun is followed by a verb, an adverb and verb, or an adjective, adverb, and verb, the definite article follows at the end of the phrase, and is generally rendered into English by a demonstrative or relative pronoun and article; as, taku ećamoŋ kiŋ (*what I-did the*), *that which I did;* wićaśta śićaya ohaŋyaŋpi kiŋ (*men badly do the*), *the men who do badly;*

wićaśta śića śićaya ohaŋyaŋpi kiŋ (*meͧn bad badly do the*), *the bad men who do badly.*

§ 114. The signs of the past tense, 'ḳoŋ' and 'ćiḳoŋ,' are used in the place of the definite article, and are rendered by the article and relative; as, wićaśta waŋmdake ćiḳoŋ, *the man whom I saw.*

USE.

§ 115. In general, the definite article in Dakota is used where it would be in English. But it also occurs in many places where in English it is not admissible.

(*a*) It is used with nouns that denote a class; as, wićaśta kiŋ bosdan naźiŋpi (*men the upright stand*), *men stand upright;* śuktaŋka kiŋ duzahaŋpi (*horses the swift*), *horses are swift* or *run fast.*

(*b*) It is often used, as in Greek, French, etc., with abstract nouns; as, wowaśte kiŋ (*goodness the*), *goodness;* woaḣtani kiŋ awihnuniwićaya (*sin the destroys-them*), *sin destroys them.*

(*c*) It is used with a noun in the vocative case; as, maka kiŋ naḣoŋ wo (*earth the hear-thou*), *O earth, hear!*

(*d*) As in Greek and Italian, it is used with nouns which are qualified by possessive or demonstrative pronouns; as, ninape kiŋ (*thy-hand the*), *thy hand;* wićaśta kiŋ de (*man the this*), *this man.*

(*e*) It is often used with finite verbs, giving to them the force of gerunds or vebal nouns; as, kaġapi kiŋ, *the making;* mauŋnipi kiŋ (*we walk the*), *our walking;* yahi kiŋ iyomakipi (*thou-come the me-pleases*), *thy coming pleases me.*

§ 116. In Dakota the definite article is sometimes omitted where it would be required in English.

(*a*) Nouns governed by prepositions are generally used without the article; as, ćoŋkaśke ekta mda (*garrison to I-go*), *I am going to the garrison;* ćaŋ mahen wai (*wood into I-went*), *I went into the woods;* tiŋta akan muŋka (*prairie upon I-lie*), *I lie upon the prairie.*

(*b*) Proper names and names of rivers and lakes are commonly used without the article; as, Tataŋka-naźiŋ (*buffalo-stands*), *The-standing-buffalo;* Wakpa-minisota, *the Minnesota river;* Mdeiyedaŋ, *Lac-qui-parle.*

(*c*) When two nouns come together in the relation of possessor and possessed (§ 68), the last only takes the article, or rather the entire expression is rendered definite by a single article placed after it; as, ćaŋpahmihma ihupa kiŋ, *the thill of the cart;* Waśićuŋ wićaśtayatapi kiŋ, *the King of the French.*

Indefinite Article.

§ 117. The indefinite article is more limited in its use than the definite, but so far as its use extends it follows the same rules; as, hokśidaŋ waŋ (*boy a*), *a boy;* hokśidaŋ waśte waŋ (*boy good a*), *a good boy.*

§ 118. Sometimes both articles are used in the same phrase, in which case the definite is rendered by the relative (see § 113. 3); as, wićaśta waŋ waśte kiŋ he kaġa (*man a good the that made*), *he was a good man who made that.*

VERBS.

Position.

§ 119. 1. Dakota verbs are usually placed after the nouns with which they are used, whether subject or object; as, hokśidaŋ kiŋ mani (*boy the walks*), *the boy walks;* wowapi waŋ duha (*book a thou-hast*), *thou hast a book.*

2. Verbs also are usually placed after the adjectives which qualify their subjects or objects, and after the adverbs which qualify the verbs; as, Waanataŋ wićaśta wayapike ćiŋ he taŋyaŋ waŋmdaka (*Waanatan man eloquent the that well I-saw*), *I saw Waanatan the eloquent man very plainly.*

For the relative position of verbs and personal pronouns, see § 98.

Number.

PLURAL.

§ 120. A verb, by its form, designates the number of its subject or object, or both; that is to say, the verb, being the last principal word in the sentence, usually takes the plural ending 'pi' when the subject or object is plural in signification.

1. (*a*) When the subject represents animate objects, the verb takes the plural termination; as, manipi, *they walk;* wićaśta kiŋ hipi (*man the came*), *the men came.*

(*b*) But when the subject of a verb denotes inanimate objects, the verb does not take a plural form for its nominitive's sake; as, ćaŋ topa ićaġa (*tree four grows*), *four trees grow.*

2. (*a*) A verb also takes the plural termination when it has a plural object of the first or second persons; as, Wakaŋtaŋka uŋkaġapi (*God us-made*), *God made us;* Dakota niye Wakaŋtaŋka ćaŋtenićiyapi (*Dakota you God you-loves*), *God loves you Dakotas.*

(*b*) When the plural object is of the third person, this plurality is pointed out by wića, *them*, incorporated in the verb; as, waŋwićayaka, *he saw them;* Hake waȟaŋksića yamni wićakte (*Hake bear three them-killed*), *Hake killed three bears.*

§ 121. As there is but one termination to signify plurality both of the subject and object, ambiguity is sometimes the result.

(*a*) When the subject is of the first, and the object is of the second person, the plural termination may refer either to the subject or to the subject and object; as, wašteuŋnidakapi, *we love thee,* or *we love you.*

(b) When the subject is of the third, and the object of the second person, the plural termination may refer either to the subject or the object, or to both; as, waštenidakapi, *they love thee, he loves you,* or *they love you.*

§ 122. Nouns of multitude commonly require verbs in the plural number; as, oyate hećoŋpi, *the people did that.*

§ 123. The verb 'yukaŋ' is often used in its singular form with a plural meaning; as, wakiyedaŋ ota yukaŋ, *there are many pigeons.*

§ 124. The verb 'yeya' and its derivatives 'iyeya,' 'hiyeya,' etc., have rarely a plural termination though used with a plural subject; as, wićota hen hiyeya, *many persons are there.*

DUAL.

§ 125. 1. The dual is used only as the subject of the verb and to denote the person speaking and the person spoken to. It has the same form as the plural pronoun of the first person, excepting that it does not take the termination 'pi.'

2. Hence, as this pronoun is, in meaning, a combination of the first and second persons, it can be used only with an object of the third person, except when, the agent and patient being the same persons, it assumes the reflexive form (§ 24); as, wašteuŋdaka, *we two* (meaning *thou* and *I*) *love him;* waštewićuŋdaka, *we two love them.* See § 42. 1.

Government.

§ 126. Active transitive verbs govern the objective case; as, makaška (*me binds*), *he binds me;* wićašta waŋ waŋmdaka (*man a I-saw*), *I saw a man.*

§ 127. Active verbs may govern two objectives.

1. A verb may govern two direct objects or so-called accusatives. When an action on a part of the person is spoken of, the whole person is represented by an incorporated pronoun, and the part by a noun in apposition with the pronoun; as, nape mayaduza (*hand me-thou-takest*), *thou takest me by the hand,* or *thou takest my hand.* Compare the French, '*me prendre la main.*'

2. A verb may govern a direct object or accusative and an indirect object answering to a dative.

(*a*) When one of the objects is a pronoun, it must be attached to the verb; as, wowapi kiŋ he mayaku kta (*book the that me-thou-give wilt*), *thou wilt give me that book.*

(*b*) But when both the objects are nouns, the indirect is usually placed before the direct object; as, Hepaŋ wowapi yaku kta (*Hepan book thou-give wilt*), *thou wilt give Hepan a book;* Hepi taspaŋtaŋka waŋ hiyukiya wo (*Hepi apple a toss*), *toss Hepi an apple.*

§ 128. Transitive verbs with the prepositions 'a' or 'o' prefixed may govern two objectives, and even three when two of them refer to the same person or thing; as, śina kiŋ aniċaḣpapi (*blanket the on-thee-laid*), *they covered thee with a blanket;* mini pa amakaśtaŋ (*water head on-me-poured*), *he poured water on my head.*

§ 129. Intransitive verbs, with the prepositions 'a' or 'o' prefixed, govern an objective case; as, mani, *to walk*, ċaŋku kiŋ omani (*road the in-walks*), *he walks in the road;* haŋ, *to stand*, maka kiŋ awahaŋ (*earth the on I-stand*), *I stand on the earth.*

Possessive Form.

§ 130. This form of the verb is used whenever possession or property is indicated, and is very important in the Dakota language. For the ways in which the possessive form is made, see § 39. 3.

The use of this form of the verb does not necessarily exclude the possessive pronoun, but renders it superfluous; as, nape yahduźaźa (*hand thou-washest-thine-own*), *thou dost wash thy hands;* ninape yahduźaźa is also correct. The occurrence of the possessive pronoun does not render the possessive form of the verb the less necessary.

MODES.

Imperative.

§ 131. 1. In prohibitions the imperative mode is often indicated by the adverb 'ihnuhaŋ' placed before the verb, with 'kiŋ' or 'kiŋhaŋ,' 'ċiŋ' or 'ċiŋhaŋ,' following; as, ihnuhaŋ heċanoŋ kiŋ, *do not do that;* ihnuhaŋ wiċayadapi kiŋhaŋ, *do not believe it.* This is a stronger form than the common imperative.

2. When two verbs in the imperative mode are connected by conjunctions, the first is used without the sign; as, owiŋźa kiŋ ehdaku ka mani wo, *take up thy bed and walk.*

Infinitive.

§ 132. 1. Verbs in the infinitive mode immediately precede those by which they are governed; as, ćaŋ kakse yahi (*wood to-cut thou-hast-come*), *thou hast come to cut wood;* he ećoŋ ćiśipi, *I told you to do that.*

2. The use of the infinitive mode in Dakota is limited, the finite verb being often used where the infinitive would be in English; as, mda waćiŋ (*I-go I-desire*), *I desire to go.*

3. The infinitive mode can not be used as a noun, as it sometimes is in English; that is, it can not have anything predicated of it, as in the phrases, "to see the sun is pleasant," "to walk is fatiguing." In such cases verbal nouns or gerunds are used; as, wi waŋyakapi kiŋ he oiyokipi (*sun seeing the that pleasant*), *the seeing of the sun is pleasant.*

Subjunctive.

§ 133. What may be called the subjunctive mode is formed by the aid of conjunctions which follow the verb. (See § 42.)

1. (*a*) Kiŋhaŋ and its derivatives, ćiŋhaŋ, kinahaŋ, and ćinahaŋ, usually refer to future time, future events only being considered as uncertain and contingent; as, yahi kiŋhaŋ mde kta, *if thou come, I will go.*

But 'kiŋhaŋ' does not always render the sense subjunctive, it being sometimes used as an adverb of time, especially when preceded by tohan; as, tohan yahi kiŋhaŋ mde kta, *when thou comest, I will go.*

(*b*) When anything past is spoken of as uncertain, 'hećiŋhaŋ' is commonly used; as, hećanoŋ hećiŋhaŋ ećen ohdaka wo, *if thou didst that, confess it.*

2. The conjunctions eśta, śta, ķeyaś, and ķeś, signifying *though, although,* are also used to form the subjunctive mood; as, oćićiyaka eśta wićayada śni, *although I tell thee, thou dost not believe;* hi ķeyaś kići mde kte śni, *though he come, I will not go with him;* amapa ķeś en ewaćaŋmi śni, *though he struck me, I paid no attention to it.*

3. Uŋkaŋś, *if,* usually relates to past time or to something already known, and is used to state what would have been the case if the thing mentioned had been different from what it is. It is usually followed by tuka, *but;* as, miyećićaźuźu uŋkaŋś ćiću kta tuka (*me-thou-hadst-paid if, I-thee-give would but*), *if thou hadst paid me, I would have given it to thee;* śuktaŋka mduha uŋkaŋś mde kta tuka (*horse I-had if, I-go would but*), *if I had a horse I would go.*

Optative, Potential, etc.

§ 134. The adverb tokiŋ, *oh that!* is used with verbs to express strong desire; in which case an ' n ' is suffixed to the verb; as, tokiŋ mduhen, *oh that I had it!*

§ 135. The Dakotas have no way of expressing fully and forcibly the ideas of necessity and obligation. The place of the English words *ought* and *must* is partially supplied by the word iyeċeċa, *fit, proper;* as, eċanoŋ kta iyeċeċa, *it is fit that thou shouldst do it.*

§ 136. 1. The idea of ability or power is expressed by the help of the verb okihi, *to be able*, used after other verbs, which are either in the form of the infinitive or gerund; as, eċoŋ owakihi (*to do I-able*), *I am able to do it*, or *I can do it;* maŋipi kiŋ owakihi (*walking the I-able*), *I can walk.* Or they are put in a finite form; as, śuktaŋka mduza owakhi (*horse I-catch I-able*), *I can catch a horse.*

2. Inability is expressed either by 'okihi' with the negative 'śni,' or 'okitpani;' as, mawaŋi kta owakihi śni (*I-walk will I-can not*), or, mawani kta owakitpani (*I-walk will I-unable*), *I cannot walk.* 'Tóka' or 'tókadaŋ, followed by the negative 'śni,' is often used for the same purpose; as, tókadaŋ mawani śni (*any-way I-walk not*), *I cannot possibly walk.*

3. The word 'piċa' is suffixed to verbs to denote *possibility* or that the thing *can be done;* as, eċoŋpiċa, *it can be done;* waŋyagpiċa, *it can be seen.* But it more frequently occurs with the negative 'śni;' as, kaħpiċa śni, *it cannot be made.*

TENSES.

§ 137. Notwithstanding the Dakota verb has but two distinct forms of tense, there is no difficulty in expressing, by the help of adverbs, etc., all the varieties of time found in other languages.

Aorist.

§ 138. 1. The aorist is used to denote *present* time, and generally needs no mark to show that the present is referred to, that being usually determined by attendant circumstances or by the context; as, tiyata yaŋka, nakaha waŋmdaka, *he is at the house, I have just seen him.*

2. When necessary the adverb dehan, *now*, or hinahiŋ, *yet*, is used to indicate present time; as, dehan tiyata yaŋka, *he is now at the house;* hinahiŋ den uŋ, *he is here yet.*

3. The aorist is used in general propositions, which apply equally to present, past, and future; as, śiċeċa waskuyeċa waśtedapi, *children love fruit.*

§ 139. 1. The predominant use of the aorist is to denote *past* time, it being always used in the narration of past events; as, ećamoŋ, *I have done it;* he mdustaŋ, *I have finished that.*

2. (*a*) By the help of the adverb waŋna, *now,* the aorist expresses *perfect* or *finished* time; as, waŋna yustaŋpi, *they have now finished it;* waŋna oćićiyaka, *I have now told thee.*

(*b*) In a narrative of past events, 'waŋna,' together with the aorist, makes what is called the pluperfect tense; as, waŋna yustaŋpi hehan wai, *they had finished it when I arrived.*

3. The aorist used with tuka, *but,* expresses what is sometimes called the imperfect tense; as, hen wauŋ tuka (*there I was, but* am not now), *I was there.*

§ 140. Before naćeća, *perhaps,* the aorist tense is sometimes used for the *future;* as, hećoŋ masipi kiŋhaŋ, ećamoŋ naćeća, *if they tell me to do that, I shall probably do it.*

Future.

§ 141. 1. The sign of the future tense is usually 'kta.' It may be used with verbs, adjectives, nouns, or pronouns; as, mani kta, *he will walk;* he waste kta, *that will be good;* he tiŋta kta, *that will be prairie;* he miye kta, *that will be I.*

2. The future tense is often used in narrating past events respecting something that was future at the time mentioned; as, waŋna upi kta hehan wai, *they were about to come when I arrived there.*

3. The future tense is used to denote that a thing would have taken place if something had not prevented. In this case it is commonly followed by 'tuka,' whether the reason is stated or not; as, waŋ kta tuka, *I would have come;* upi kta tuka wićawakisića, *they would have come, but I forbade them.*

4. The future tense with the adverb 'hiŋća,' is used to indicate a desire, purpose, or determination to do a thing; as, mde kte hiŋća (*I-go will very*), *I want to go;* ećoŋ kte hiŋća ećoŋ (*do will very did*), *he did it because he wished to do it,* or *he did it intentionally.*

5. The future tense is often used where the infinitive mode would be in English; as, wau kta owakitpani (*I-come shall, I-unable*), *I am unable to come;* ṭeyapi kta akitapi, *they sought to kill him.*

6. The future tense is sometimes used for the aorist, as in German, when there is uncertainty about the thing spoken of; as, tinwićakte kiŋ hee kta (*murderer the that-be will*), *that is the murderer,* the idea being, that he will be found to be the murderer.

7. When two verbs in the future tense are connected by a conjunction, the first may be either with or without the sign; as, nihiŋnićiyapi kta ķa yaćeyapi kta, or nihiŋnićiyapi ķa yaćeyapi kta, *you will be troubled and weep.*

§ 142. 'Nuŋ' or 'noŋ' is sometimes used instead of 'kta,' as the sign of the future tense, in interrogative sentences, and also when something future is spoken of as uncertain; as, mda nuŋ he, *shall I go?* token ećoŋpi nuŋ taŋiŋ śni, *they knew not what they should do.*

§ 143. Before the verbs 'ećiŋ' and 'epća,' 'ke' sometimes marks the future tense of the first person; as, mda ke epća, *I will go, thought I.*

§ 144. In interrogative sentences 'hiŋ' is sometimes used for 'kta he,' denoting the future tense; as, wau hiŋ, *shall I come?*

AUXILIARY VERBS.

§ 145. There are several verbs which are used with others as auxiliaries; such as, 'iyeya,' 'kiya,' and 'ya' or 'yaŋ.'

§ 146. 1. 'Iyeya,' when used with other verbs, expresses the additional ideas of *completion* and *suddenness;* as, yuśtaŋ iyeya, *he made a finish of it;* kaksa iyeya, *he cut it off suddenly.* In this way 'iyeya' is often used to give force and animation to the style.

2. Verbs used with 'iyeya,' if capable of contraction, are contracted; as, kaptuźa, *to split,* kaptuś iyeya, *he split it open.*

3. 'Iyeya' is often used with prepositions and adverbs, sometimes with and sometimes without their taking the verbal prefixes; as, pamahen iyeya, *to push into;* yuhukun iyeya, *to put down;* ohna iyeya and mahen iyeya, *to put into* anything.

§ 147. 'Kiya' is used with verbs as a causative suffix; as, ećoŋkiya, *to cause to do;* kahkiya, *to cause to make;* naźiŋkiya, *to cause to stand.* The pronouns are inserted before the causative.

§ 148. 'Ya' or 'yaŋ' is a suffix which occurs so frequently, and whose use is sometimes so different from that of any English verb, that it demands a special notice.

1. (*a*) It is used as a causative suffix; as, ećoŋya, *to cause to do;* maniya, *to cause to walk.* In this case it always has a noun or pronoun for its object expressed or understood; as, mani mayayapi, *you cause me to walk.*

(*b*) 'Ya' used with adjectives makes of them active verbs; as, śaya, *to dye* or *paint red;* samya, *to blacken.*

2. (*a*) It is used with words denoting relationship, where in English we should employ a possessive pronoun, and seems to have the force of *to*

have, or *have for;* as, he atewaya (*that father-I-have*), *that is my father;* Ateuŋyaŋpi maḣpiya ekta naŋke ćiŋ (*father-we-have heaven in thou-art the*), *our Father who art in heaven.*

(*b*) 'Ya' with nouns shows what use a thing is put to; as, de iśaŋwaya, *this I have for a knife;* he tiyopayaya, *that thou usest for a door.*

3. When the pronouns 'ma,' 'ni,' and 'uŋ' are used without the pronoun 'ya' following, 'ya' becomes 'yaŋ;' as, atemayaŋ, *he has me for father;* ateuŋyaŋpi, *our father.* But when 'ya,' *thou* or *you*, follows, the vowel is not nasalized; as, atemayaya, *thou hast me for father;* ateuŋyayapi, *you call us father.*

VERBS OF REPETITION.

Reduplicated Verbs.

§ 149. 1. The reduplication of a syllable in Dakota verbs is very common. In intransitive verbs it simply indicates a *repetition* of the action; as, ipsića, *to jump,* ipsipsića, *to hop* or *jump repeatedly;* iḣa, *to laugh,* iḣaḣa, *to laugh often.* In transitive verbs it either indicates that the action is repeated on the same object, or that it is performed upon several objects; as, yaḣtaka, *to bite,* yaḣtaḣtaka, *to bite often;* baksa, *to cut* a stick *in two;* baksaksa, *to cut* a stick *in two often*, or *to cut several* sticks *in two.* Verbs of one syllable are rarely reduplicated.

2. There are some verbs whose meaning almost necessarily implies a repetition of the action and which therefore are generally used in their reduplicated form; as, yuhuhuza, *to shake;* panini, *to jog;* kapsiŋpsiŋta, *to whip;* yuśiŋśiŋ, *to tickle;* nasuŋsuŋ, *to struggle*, etc.

3. Verbs signifying *to be* are repeated to denote continuance; as, den maŋka maŋke, *I continue to stay here;* hen dukaŋ dukaŋpi, *you reside there.*

§ 150. The use of a reduplicated form of a verb in its proper place is very important. It is as much a violation of the rules of the Dakota language to use a simple for the reduplicated form as to use the singular for the plural number.

Verbs with the Suffixes ' s'a' *and* ' ka.'

§ 151. 'S'a' is suffixed to verbs to denote *frequency of action* or *habit;* as, yahi s'a, *thou comest often;* iyatoŋśni s'a, *thou dost tell lies habitually*, i. e., *thou art a liar;* wamanoŋ s'a, *one who steals often*, i. e., *a thief.*

§ 152. 'Ka' has sometimes the same signification with 's'a;' as, waoka, *a good hunter.* But sometimes it does not produce any perceptible difference in the meaning of the verb; as, waśteda and waśtedaka, *to love* anything.

§ 153. When the verb, to which 'ka' or 's'a' is suffixed, takes the plural form, the suffix usually follows the plural termination; as, waopika, *marksmen;* ećoŋpi s'a, *doers.* But in the verb 'da,' *to esteem,* 'ka' may either precede or follow the plural termination; as, waśtedakapi and waśtedapika.

SUBSTANTIVE VERBS.

§ 154. The verbs 'uŋ,' 'ouŋyaŋ,' 'yaŋka,' 'yukaŋ,' and 'hiyeya,' all signify *to be,* but when used, they are accompanied by other verbs, adverbs, participles, or prepositions, descriptive of the place or manner of being; as, mani wauŋ, *I am walking;* ti mahen maŋka, *I am in the house;* héćiya yakoŋpi, *they are there;* en mauŋ, *it is in me.*

§ 155. The verb 'e' or 'ee' occurs without a word descriptive of the mode or place of existence; but it is confined to the third person, and is used rather to declare the *identity* than the *existence* of a thing. This verb combines with the pronouns, as, 'hee,' 'dee,' etc. 'Yukaŋ' is used to declare that *there is,* and wanića, that *there is none;* as, Wakaŋtaŋka yukaŋ, *there is a God;* Wakaŋtaŋka wanića, *there is no God.*

§ 156. The bringing of two words together in the Dakota language answers all the purposes of such a copula as our substantive verb; as, Wakaŋtaŋka waśte (*God good*), *God is good;* wi kiŋ kata (*sun the hot*), *the sun is hot;* de miye (*this I*), *this is I;* hena iŋyaŋ (*those stones*), *those are stones;* Danikota (*Dakota-thou*), *thou art a Dakota.*

§ 157. From these examples it appears that there is no real necessity for such a connecting link between words; and accordingly we do not find any single verb in the Dakota language which simply predicates being. The Dakotas can not say abstractly, *I am, thou art, he is;* but they can express all the modes and places of existence. And the verb of existence is understood in pronouns, nouns, and adjectives.[1]

PARTICIPLES.

Active.

§ 158. 1. Active participles follow the nouns and precede the verbs with which they are used; as, mazakaŋ hduha yahi (*gun having thou-come*), *thou hast come having thy gun.*

---

[1] A. L. Riggs makes the following classification of substantive verbs:

1. Of *being* or *existence,* as uŋ, yukaŋ, yaŋka, etc.

2. Of *condition;* with participles and adverbs of manner; as, ni uŋ, *living is;* taŋyaŋ yaŋka, (*well is*), *is comfortable.*

3. Of *place;* with prepositions and adverbs of place; as, akan uŋ, *is on;* timahen yaŋka, *within is.*

4. Of *identity;* e or ee, with the forms hee, dee. See § 155.

5. Of *classification;* heća, is such, as, hokśidaŋ waśte heća, *he is a good boy;* he śuŋktokeća heća, *that is a wolf.*

2. The objective pronouns are used with and governed by active participles, in the same way as by verbs; as, mayuha yukaŋpi (*me-having they remain*), *they still retain me;* niyuha yapi kta (*thee-having they-go will*), *they will take thee along.*

3. Active participles are used to denote prolonged or continued action; as, kiksuya uŋ, *he is remembering;* Wakaŋtaŋka ćekiya uŋ, *he is in the habit of praying to God;* iahaŋ ićuŋhaŋ, *whilst he was speaking.*

4. A few participles are used with the verbs from which they are derived; as, manihaŋ mani (*walking walks*), that is, *he walks* and does not ride; naźiŋhaŋ naźiŋ (*standing he stands*), *he gets up and stands.*

5. Two verbs together may be used as participles without a conjunction; as, ćeya patuś inaźiŋ (*weeping stooping stands*), *he stands stooping and weeping.*

Passive.

§ 159. 1. A verb used as a passive participle follows the noun to which it relates; as, tahiŋća kiŋ opi, *the deer is shot.*

2. Passive participles are used to make what may be called the passive form of the verb; as, ktepi, *killed,* niktepi kta, *thou wilt be killed.*

3. They are sometimes used independently as nouns; as, ktepi kiŋ, *the slain.*

NOUNS.

POSITION.

§ 160. The place of the noun, whether subject or object, is before the verb; as, wamnaheza ićaga, *corn grows;* mini waćiŋ (*water I-want*), *I want water.*

Occasionally the subject comes after the verb; as, eya Wakaŋtaŋka, *said God.*

§ 161. When two nouns are used together, one the subject and the other the object of the same verb, the subject is usually placed first (§ 67); as, tataŋka peźi yutapi (*oxen grass eat*), *oxen eat grass;* Dakota Padani kiŋ wićaktepi (*Dakota Pawnee the them-killed*), *the Dakotas killed the Pawnees.*

§ 162. 1. Of two nouns in composition or combination the noun sustaining the relation of possessor always precedes the name of the thing possessed. See § 68.

2. There are cases where two nouns are brought together in which the latter may be regarded as in *apposition:* as, aguyapi wićoni, *bread of life,* or more properly, *the bread that is life.*—A. L. RIGGS.

§ 163. The principle on which the plural termination is employed is that of placing it as near the end of the sentence as possible. The order in a Dakota sentence is, first the noun, next the adjective, and lastly the verb. Hence, if a noun or pronoun is used alone or has no word following it in the phrase, it may take the plural ending; if an adjective follows, it is attached to the adjective; and if a verb is used, it is attached to the verb.

1. When nouns are used to convey a plural idea, without qualificatives or predicates, they have the plural termination; as, ninapepi, *thy hands;* hena Dakotapi, *those are Dakotas.*

2. When a noun which represents an animate object is to be made plural, and is followed by a qualificative or predicate, the sign of the plural is joined, not to the noun, but to the qualificative or predicate; as, wićaśta waśtepi, *good men;* kośka kiŋ hipi, *the young men have arrived;* wićaśta waśte kiŋ hipi, *the good men have arrived.*

§ 164. The plural of nouns representing animate objects in the objective case, whether they are governed by active verbs or prepositions, is designated by 'wića' following, which is prefixed to or inserted in the governing word; as, tahiŋća wićaktepi (*deer them-they-kill*), *they kill deer;* Dakota ewićataŋhaŋ (*Dakota them-from*), *he is from the Dakotas.*

ADJECTIVES.

§ 165. When the adjective is used simply as a qualifying term, it is placed immediately after its noun; as, wićaśta waśte, *good man;* ćaŋ śića, *bad wood.*

The adjective ikće, *common,* is placed *before* the noun which it qualifies, but its derivative ikćeka comes *after;* as, ikće haŋpa and haŋpikćeka, *common moccasins;* ikće wićaśta, *a common man, an Indian.* The numeral adjectives, when used with ćaŋ, *a day,* are placed before; as, noŋpa ćaŋ, *two days,* etc.

§ 166. When the adjective forms the predicate of a proposition, it is placed after the article, and after the demonstrative pronoun, if either or both are used; as, wićaśta kiŋ waśte, *the man is good;* wićaśta kiŋ he waśte, *that man is good;* taku ećanoŋ kiŋ he śića, *that which thou didst is bad.*

§ 167. Adjectives, whether qualificative or predicative, indicate the number of the nouns or pronouns to which they belong; as, iŋyaŋ sapa waŋ, *a black stone;* inyaŋ sapsapa, *black stones;* tataŋka kiŋ waś'aka, *the ox is strong ;* tataŋka kiŋ waś'akapi, *the oxen are strong.*

2. Adjectives do not take the plural form when that can be pointed out by the verb of which the noun is either the subject or object (see §§ 163, 164); as, wićaśta waśte he kaġapi (*man good that they-made*), *good men made that;* Wakaŋtaŋka wićaśta waśte nom wićakaġa (*Great-Spirit men good two them-made*), *God made two good men.*

3. As the numeral adjectives after waŋźi denote plurality by virtue of their meaning, they may be used either with or without the plural termination; as, wićaśta yamni, or wićaśta yamnipi, *three men.*

NUMERAL ADJECTIVES.

§ 168. 1. Numeral adjectives used distributively take the reduplicated form; as, yamni,. *three,* yamnimni, *three and three,* yamnimni ićupi, *they each took three,* or *they took three of each.*

2. Numeral adjectives are used alone to express the number of times an event occurs; as, yamni yahi, *thou camest three times.* When a succession of acts is spoken of, the word 'akihde' is often used; as, topa akihde yakutepi, *you shot four times successively.*

§ 169. To supply the want of words like *place* and *ways* in English, the adverbial termination 'kiya' is added to the numeral; as, noŋpakiya yakoŋpi, *they are in two different places;* he topakiya oyakapi, *that is told in four different ways.*

§ 170. The Dakotas use the term haŋke, *one-half;* but when a thing is divided into more than two aliquot parts they have no names for them; that is, they have no expressions corresponding to *one-third, one-fourth, one-fifth,* etc. By those who have made some progress in arithmetic, this want is supplied by the use of 'oŋśpa' and the ordinal numbers; as, oŋśpa iyamni (*piece third*) *one-third;* oŋśpa itopa (*piece fourth*), *one-fourth.*

The language more recently adopted is kiyuśpapi, *divided.* So that one-fourth is topa kiyuśpapi waŋźi.—A. L. R.

PRONOMINAL ADJECTIVES.

§ 171. Owasiŋ and iyuȟpa, *all,* sakim and napin, *both,* apa and huŋȟ, *some* or *a part,* tonana and wanistiŋna, *few, a small quantity,* uŋma, *the other, one of two,* ota, *many, much,* and some others, are sometimes used as adjectives qualifying nouns, and sometimes stand in the place of nouns.

§ 172. 1. As the adjective 'ota,' *many, much,* conveys a plural idea, its reduplicated form ' onota' or ' odota,' is not used when speaking of inanimate objects, except when different quantities or parcels are referred to; as, ota awahdi, *I have brought home many* or *much;* odota awahdi, *I have brought home much of different kinds.*

2. When 'ota' relates to animate objects, it may have the plural termination, but is generally used without it. When it relates to the human species, and no noun precedes, it has 'wića' prefixed; as, wićota hipi, *many persons came,* or *a multitude of persons came.*

3. When 'ota' relates to a number of different companies of persons, it has what may be called a double plural form, made by prefixing 'wića' and by reduplication; as, wićokćota ahi, *companies of persons have arrived.*

§ 173. 1. When the same thing is predicated of two or more nouns connected by conjunctions, the adjective is commonly repeated with each noun; as, śuktaŋka kiŋ waśte ķa ćaŋpahmihma kiŋ waśte, *the horse is good, and the wagon is good.*

2. But sometimes a single adjective is made to apply to all nouns by using a pronominal adjective or demonstrative pronoun; as, śuktaŋka kiŋ ķa ćaŋpahmihma kiŋ napin waśte, *the horse and the wagon are both good;* wićaśta ķa winohinća kiŋ hena waśteśte, *man and woman, they are beautiful;* Hepaŋ ķa Hepi ķa Hake, hena iyuḣpa haŋskapi, *Hepan, and Hepi, and Hake, they are all tall.*

3. When two nouns are connected by the conjunction 'ko' or 'koya,' *also,* the adjective is only used once; as, śuktaŋka ćaŋpahmihma ko śića (*horse wagon also bad*), *the horse and the wagon also are bad.*

ADVERBS.

§ 174. Adverbs are used to qualify verbs, participles, adjectives, and other adverbs; and some of them may, in particular cases, be used with nouns and pronouns; as, iwaśtedaŋ mani, *he walks slowly;* śićaya hduha uŋ, *he is keeping it badly;* nina waśte, *very good;* kitaŋna taŋyaŋ, *tolerably well;* he ćaŋ śni (*that wood not*), *that is not wood;* tonitaŋhaŋ he (*whence-thou*), *whence art thou?*

§ 175. 1. Adverbs are commonly placed before the words which they qualify; as, taŋyaŋ wauŋ, *I am well;* śićaya ohaŋyaŋpi, *they do badly;* nina waśte, *very good.*

2. (*a*) The adverbs 'hinća' and 'śni' follow the words which they

qualify; as, waśte hiŋća, *very good;* ećoŋ kte hiŋća, *he wishes very much to do it;* ećoŋpi śni, *they did not do it.*

(*b*) The adverbs of time, 'kiŋhaŋ,' 'ća' or 'ića,' 'ķehaŋ,' and 'ćoh,' are placed after the words to which they relate; as, yahi kiŋhaŋ, *when thou comest;* waŋyaka ića, *when he sees it.*

3. (*a*) Interrogative adverbs commonly stand at the beginning of the clause or sentence; as, tokeća wowapi dawa śni he, *why dost thou not read?*

(*b*) But 'to,' a contracted form of 'tokeća' and 'he,' the common sign of interrogation, stand at the end; as, duhe śni to, *why dost thou not have it?* yahi he, *hast thou arrived?*

§ 176. Interrogative adverbs and others often prefix or insert personal pronouns; as, nitonakapi he, *how many are there of you?* tonitaŋhaŋ he, *whence art thou?* hemataŋhaŋ, *I am from that place.*

REDUPLICATION.

§ 177. 1. Most adverbs may make a plural form by doubling a syllable, in which case they may refer either to the subject or the object of the verb, and are used with verbs both in the singular and plural number; as, taŋyaŋ ećoŋ, *he does it well;* taŋtaŋyaŋ ećoŋ, *he has done several things well;* taŋtaŋyaŋ ećoŋpi, *they have done well.*

2. If the verb relates to the united action of individuals, the adverb is not reduplicated; but if the individuals are viewed as acting independently, the reduplicated form must be used; as, śuktaŋka kiŋ tketkeya ķiŋpi, *the horses carry each a heavy load.*

3. The reduplicated form of the adverb is used when reference is had to different times, places, distances, etc.; as, wićaśta kiŋ tehaŋ ni, *the man lived long;* wićaśta kiŋ tehaŋhaŋ nipi ee, *men live long;* ećadaŋ wahi, *I came soon;* ećaćadaŋ wahi, *I come frequently;* he haŋskaya baksa wo, *cut that long;* hena haŋskaskaya baksa wo, *cut those long;* aśkadaŋ euŋtipi, *we encamped at a short distance;* aśkaśkadaŋ euŋtipi, *we encamped at short distances.*

USE OF CERTAIN ADVERBS.

§ 178. 1. In general propositions, 'eća' or 'ća,' *when,* is used with 'eće' or 'će' at the end of the clause or sentence; as, waniyetu ća wapa će, *when it is winter it snows.*

2. The particles 'eće' and 'ećee,' used at the end of clauses or sentences, signify *frequency* or *habit,* as; ećamoŋ ećee, *I am accustomed to do.*

3. The particle 'će,' in most cases, indicates the close of a direct quotation of the words of oneself or of another; as, dećen ećanoŋ kiŋhaŋ yani kta će, Wakaŋtaŋka eya će, *if thou dost thus, thou shalt live, God said.*

4. The free adverbial particle 'do' is used for emphasis, at the end of a clause or sentence, as, wahi kte do, *I will come.* It is used generally by young men, and not considered necessary by good speakers.[1] 'Ye' is sometimes used in the same way by women and others.

5. Among the free adverbial particles may be mentioned 'wo,' 'we,' 'yo' and 'ye' with 'po,' 'pi' and 'miye,' the signs of the imperative; and 'kta' and 'kte' signs of the future. These all follow the verb. See §§ 42 and 43.

§ 179. In reply to questions which have the negative form, assent to the negative proposition contained in the question is expressed by haŋ, *yes,* and dissent by hiya, *no;* as, yahi kte śni he; haŋ, wahi kte śni, *thou wilt not come, wilt thou? yes, I will not come;* yahi kte śni he; hiya, wahi kta, *thou wilt not come, wilt thou? no, I will come.* If the question be put affirmatively, the answer is the same as in English.

§ 180. 'Tohan' and 'kiŋhaŋ' are often used together with the same verb, in which case 'tohan' precedes the verb and 'kiŋhaŋ' follows it; as, tohan yahi kiŋhaŋ mde kta, *when thou comest I will go.*

§ 181. When 'itokam' is used in reference to time, it is often preceded by the adverb of negation; as, yahi śni itokam (*thou-comest not before*), *before thou comest.*

NEGATIVE.

§ 182. 1. Negation is expressed by placing after the verb, adjective, noun, or pronoun, the adverb 'śni;' as, mde śni (*I-go not*), *I did not go;* he ćaŋ śni (*that wood not*), *that is not wood.*

2. An emphatic negation is sometimes indicated by 'kaća,' which, however, is seldom used except in contradicting what has been previously said; as, yao kaća, *thou didst not hit it.*

3. A negative used interrogatively often implies permission; as, iyaću śni to (*dost thou not take it?*), may signify, *thou mayest take it.*

§ 183. 1. In Dakota two negatives make an affirmative; as, wanića, *there is none;* waniće śni (*there-is-none not*), i. e., *there is some.*

---

[1] 'Do' in Isaŋyati and Ihaŋktoŋwaŋ, and 'lo' in Titoŋwaŋ, seem to be equivalent to the masculine oral period hă of the Omaha and Ponka, au of the Kansa, Osage, and Kwapa, ke of the Iowa, ke-i of the Oto, sh of the Mandan, ts of the Hidatsa, and k of the Crow. Hă is seldom used by the Ponka, but is common among the Omaha.—J. O. D.

2. When two negative verbs are connected by a conjunction, the first *may* be without the sign of negation; as, kakipe ça iyotaŋ taŋka śni (*he-surpassed and more great not*) *he neither surpassed nor was the greatest.*

INTERROGATIVE.

§ 184. 1. 'He' is the common interrogative particle, and is placed at the end of the sentence; as, wićayada he, *dost thou believe ?*

2. When the person spoken to is at a distance, 'hwo,' compounded of 'he' and 'wo,' is used; as, toki da hwo, *whither art thou going?* This last is not used by females.

3. Sometimes 'ka' is employed instead of 'he,' as the sign of interrogation; as, he taku hoġaŋ ka, *what kind of fish is that?*

4. Sometimes, however, the interrogation is distinguished only by the tone of voice. Unlike the English, the voice falls at the close of all interrogative sentences.

ADVERBIAL INCORPORATED PARTICLES.

§ 185. As has been stated (§ 34), by means of adverbial particles, large classes of active verbs are formed from verbal roots and adjectives. There are 'ba,' 'bo,' 'ka,' 'na,' 'pa,' 'ya,' and 'yu,' with the possessive forms 'hd,' 'kd,' and 'gl,' which are prefixed or agglutinated. See the Verb Paradigm.

PREPOSITIONS.

§ 186. Prepositions are placed after the *nouns* which they govern, and so are properly *post-positions.*

(*a*) Some are written as separate words (§ 89); as, maka kiŋ akan, *on the earth;* tipi ićahda, *by the house;* ćoŋkaśke ekta, *at the garrison.* In this ease plurality of the noun is expressed by 'wica' incorporated into the preposition; as, tataŋka kiŋ wićikiyedaŋ (*ox the them-near-to*), *near to the oxen;* Dakota ewićataŋhaŋ, *from the Dakotas.*

(*b*) Other prepositions are suffixed to nouns (§ 91); as, tiŋtata, *on the prairie;* maġata *at the field;* ćaŋyata, *at the woods.*

(*c*) And others are prefixed to the following verb (§ 92); as, amani, *to walk on;* ićekiya, *to pray for.*

2. (*a*) *Pronouns* governed by a preposition are sometimes prefixed to it, in which case those prepositions which have 'i' for their initial letter cause an elision of the last vowel of the pronoun; as ikiyedaŋ, *near to;* mikiyedaŋ, *near to me;* itehaŋ, *far from;* nitehaŋ, *far from thee.* If the pro-

noun is plural, the plural termination is attached to the preposition; as, uŋketaŋhaŋpi, *from us.*

(*b*) Sometimes the pronoun is inserted in the preposition, if the latter consists of more than two syllables; as, enitaŋhaŋ, *from thee.*

(*c*) And sometimes it is contained in the following verb; as, en mau, *he is coming to me;* ekta niipi, *they went to you.*

§ 187. Of the two prepositions 'kiói' and 'om,' both meaning *with*, the former governs singular and the latter plural nouns; as, he kiói mde kta, *I will go with him;* hena om mde kta, *I will go with them.*

§ 188. 1. The names of the natural divisions of time, when they refer to the past, terminate in 'haŋ,' and when to the future, in 'tu;' as, wehaŋ, *last spring;* wetu, *next spring.*

The termination 'tu' or 'etu,' in waniyetu, mdoketu, ptaŋyetu, wetu, haŋyetu, aŋpetu, litayetu, etc., may have been orignally a preposition, signifying, as it still does in other cases, *at* or *in;* and the termination 'haŋ,' in wanihaŋ, wehaŋ, mdoke-haŋ, ptiŋhaŋ, etc., is probably the adverbial ending.

2. The preposition 'i' prefixed to the natural divisions of time signifies *the next after;* as, iwetu, *the spring following;* imdoketu, *the next summer;* ihaŋhaŋna, *the next morning.*

CONJUNCTIONS.

§ 189. 1. Conjunctions commonly stand *between* the words or sentences which they connect; as, mahpiya ḳa maka, *heaven and earth;* waŋóiyaka tuka iyeóióiye śni, *I saw thee but I did not recognize thee;* eóoŋ yaśi eśta eóoŋ kte śni (*do thou-told although, do will not*), *although thou told him to do it, he will not.*

2. But the conjunctions 'ko' or 'koya' and 'ahna' are placed *after* the words they connect; as, óaŋka waŋhi ko mduha (*fire-steel flint also I have*), *I-have flint and steel;* mahpiya maka ahna kaġa, *he made heaven and earth.*

§ 190. 'Uŋkaŋ' and 'ḳa' both signify *and*, but they are used somewhat differently, 'ka' denoting a closer connection than 'uŋkaŋ.'

1. When two or more verbs having the same nominative are connected by a copulative conjunction, 'ḳa' is commonly used; as, ekta wai ḳa waŋmdaka, *I went and saw.* But if a new nominative is introduced, 'uŋkaŋ' will be required; as, ekta wai uŋkaŋ waŋmayakapi, *I went there and they saw me.*

2. When after a period the sentence begins with a conjunction, 'ḳa' is not used unless the sentence is closely connected with the preceding one.

3. 'Uŋkaŋ' never connects single nouns or adjectives, 'ka' and 'ko' being used for that purpose; as, waśte ka ksapa, *good and wise;* ćaŋ mini ko, *wood and water.*

For the use of the conjunctions kiŋhaŋ, uŋkaŋś, and tuká, see § 133.

§ 191. The words 'ećiŋ' and 'nakaeś,' although more properly adverbs, often supply the place of conjunctions; as, he waku, ećiŋ makida, *I gave that to him because he asked me for it;* he tewahiŋda, nakaeś hećedaŋ mduha, *I refused that because it was the only one I had.*

§ 192. The idea conveyed by the conjunction *than* can not be expressed in Dakota directly. Such a phrase as, "It is better for me to die than to live," may indeed be rendered by an awkward periphrasis in several ways; as, maṭe ćiŋ he waśte ka wani kiŋ he śića, *for me to die is good, and to live is bad;* wani kiŋ he waśte eśta maṭe ćiŋ he iyotaŋ waśte, *although it is good for me to live, it is more good for me to die;* or, maṭe kte ćiŋ he waśte ka wani kte ćiŋ he śića, *that I should die is good, and that I should live is bad.*

§ 193. The conjunction *or* is represented by 'ka iś;' but the sentences in which it is introduced have not the same brevity as in English; as, *I do not know whether he is there or not,* hen uŋ iś ka iś hen uŋ śni, uŋma tukte iyećetu sdonwaye śni (*there is or there is not, which of the two I know not*); *Is that a horse or an ox?* he śuktaŋka ka iś tataŋka uŋma tukte hećetu he (*that horse or ox, which of the two*)?

INTERJECTIONS.

§ 194. Some interjections have no connexion with other words, while others are used only as a part of a sentence. When connected with other words, interjections usually stand at the beginning of the phrase. Considerable knowledge of their use is necessary to enable one to understand the language well, as the interjections not only serve to indicate the feelings of the speaker, but often materially modify the meaning of a sentence; as, hehehe, didita oŋ maṭe kta, *oh! I shall die of heat;* "Wićoni kiŋ iho hee; wićoni kiŋ he wićaśta iyoźaŋźaŋ kiŋ iho hee" (*Life the lo! that is; life the that man light the lo! that is*), John i, 4.

DAKOTA GRAMMAR, TEXTS, AND ETHNOGRAPHY.

PART SECOND.

TEXTS.

TEXTS.

WIĆAŊHPI HIŊHPAYA; OR, THE FALLEN STAR.

WRITTEN IN DAKOTA BY MICHEL RENVILLE.

Oyate waŋ kakeŋ tipi; uŋkaŋ winohiŋća nom taŋkaŋ waŋkapi; uŋkaŋ
People one so lived; and women two out-doors lay; and

wićaŋhpi kiŋ iyeǧa waŋyakapi. Uŋkaŋ iŋyuŋ uŋmaŋ heya: Ićepaŋśi, ito
stars the shining saw. And behold the-one this said: Cousin lo

wićaŋhpi waŋ iyeǧe hća e yaŋke ćiŋ he hihnawaya ćeś, eya. Uŋkaŋ
star one shines very afore- is the that husband I-have oh- she And
  said that! said.

uŋma kiŋ iś; Miś ito ka wićaŋhpi waŋ kitaŋna iyehya yaŋke ćiŋ he
other the she; I lo that star one little shining is the that

hihnawaye ćeś, eya. Uŋkaŋ ihnuhaŋna napin ekta awićakipi, keyapi.
husband I-have oh she And suddenly both thither they were taken they say.
  that! said.

Makoće waŋ waśte hiŋća hokśićekpa ożużuya namdaye waśte waŋka
Country one good very twin-flowers full blooming beautiful were

e ekta uŋpi. Uŋkaŋ wićaŋhpi waŋ nina iyeǧe ćiḳoŋ he wićaśta taŋka;
that in they-were. And star one much shining the that man large,

ḳa uŋma ḳoŋ he kośka, keyapi. Hećen kinukaŋyaŋ hihna wićayapi.
and other the that young-man, they say. So one-and-the-other husband them-had.
  [aforesaid]

Uŋkaŋ uŋma waŋna ihduśaka. Makoće kiŋ tipsiŋna ota hu waśteśte.
And one now with-child. Country the Pomme blanche many stalks beautiful.

Hećen winyaŋ ḳoŋ waŋźi bopte kta keś hiknaku kiŋ tehiŋda: Ustaŋ wo,
So woman the one dig would although husband-has the forbid: Stop

tuwedaŋ deći hećoŋ śni će, eya eće. Uŋkaŋ ihdaka aye ḳa etipi. Uŋkaŋ
no-one here that does not he-said always. And moving went and camped. And

winyaŋ ihduśake wakeya itićaǧe ḳa timahen piye kta e timahen hiyu, uŋkaŋ
woman with child tent pitched and inside fix-up would house-inside came, and

tipsiŋna waŋ hu taŋka waśte e aitićaǧa; uŋkaŋ, Ito de waḳa ke, ećiŋ,
Pomme blanche one stalk large beautiful that over it tent and Lo this I dig will, she
  pitched: thought;

etaŋhaŋ tuwe waŋmayake ća, ećiŋ, ḳa hoŋpe iću ḳa bopte ća iyupta iću;
for who me-see will ? she thought, and digger took and dug-it and pulled-it-out;

ićuŋhaŋ makoće yuohdog iyeya ḳa ohna hiyu, ḳa maka kiŋ ekta tezi kamdas
in the country opened out and from came, and earth the to belly burst
meantime

hiŋhpaya keyapi.   Hećen winohiŋća ḳoŋ e ṭa, tuka hokśiyoḳopa e ṭe śni
she-fell they say. So woman the that died, but child that died not
            [aforesaid]

naġaŋgata waŋka.   Wićahiŋća waŋ en hi; hokśiyopa kiŋ ićn ḳa itpihnake
kicking lay. Old-man one there came; child the took and placed in bosom

ća tiyataki, ḳa heya: Wakaŋka, taku waŋ waŋmdaka uŋkaŋ ćaŋte maśiće
and came home, and this said: Old woman, something one I saw and heart me-bad

do, eya.   Uŋkaŋ tawićn kiŋ, He taku he, eya.   Uŋkaŋ winohinća waŋ tezi
. he said. And his wife the, That what ? she said. And woman one belly

kamdas ṭa waŋka; uŋkaŋ hokśiyopa waŋ naġaŋgata waŋke, ahna wićana
bursted died lay; and child one kicking lay also boy

tuka će, eya.   Wićahinća, tokeća ayaku śni he, eya.   Uŋkaŋ, Dee do, eya
but he said. Old man, why you bring not ? she said. And, This is it . he said
          home

ća itpi taŋhaŋ ićn.   Uŋkaŋ tawićn kiŋ heya: Wićahiŋća, ito de ićahuŋye
and bosom from took. And his wife the this said: Old man, now this we-raise

ćeś, eya.   Uŋkaŋ wićahiŋća ḳoŋ heya: Wakaŋka, ti ahmihbeuŋye kta će,
oh-that! she-said. And old man the this said: Old woman, house around-we-roll will ,
       [aforesaid]

eye, ća tićeśka kiŋ ohna kohoya iyeya.   Uŋkaŋ ahmihmaŋ-hiyaye ća
he said, and tent-top the through he tossed it up. And whirling around he went and

hiŋhpaya.   Uŋkaŋ sdohaŋhaŋ tin hiyu.   Tuka ake ićn ḳa tiće ohna kahoya
fell down. And creeping house-in he But again he and smoke through he tossed
          came. took hole

iyeya.   Uŋkaŋ hehan mani tin hiyu.   Tuka ake ićn ḳa ećen iyeya.   Uŋkaŋ
it up. And then walking house in came. But again he took and so threw it. And

hehan hokśina waŋ ćaŋsakana ḳeya yuha tin hiyu ḳa, Tuŋkaŋśina, dena
then boy one green sticks even having house in came and, Grandfather, these

waŋhiŋkpe mićaġa ye, eya.   Tuka ake ićn ḳa ećen iyeya, uŋkaŋ hehan
arrows make-me, he said. But again he took and so threw, and then

toki iyaya taŋiŋ śni; uŋkaŋ kośka waŋ ćaŋsaka ḳeya yuha tin hiyu; ḳa,
where he went manifest not; and young man one green sticks even having house in came; and,

Dena, tuŋkaŋśina, mićaġa wo, eya.   Hećen waŋhiŋkpe ota kićaġa.   Hećen
These, grandfather, make me, he said. So arrows many made for him. So

pte ota wićao ća wakeya waŋ taŋka ićićaġapi, ḳa ćatku kin en waŋkan
buffalo many them-shot when tent one large made for and back-part the in high
           themselves,

ohehdekiyapi, nina waśećapi.
bed-they-placed, very rich-were.

Uŋkaŋ wićahiŋća kiŋ heye: Wakaŋka, taŋyaŋ uŋyakoŋ e imduśkiŋ
And old man the this said: Old woman, well we-are that I-glad-am

će, ito eyaŋwapaha kte do, eye, ća haŋhaŋna hiŋ tiće iŋkpata iyotaŋka ća
, lo! I proclaim will , he said, and morning very house top-at he sat and
           comb

heya: Miye taźu watoŋ, taśiyaka śiŋ mdadopa, eya.   Uŋkaŋ he Taśiya-
this said: I laid-up I have, big-gut fat I chew, he-said. And this meadow

kapopo hee keyapi : Zitkana waŋ taśiyakapopo ećiyapi kiŋ hee; maku zi
lark that-is they say: bird one meadow lark named the that is; breast yel-
                    low

ḳa ćokaya sape ćiŋ he aŋpao zi kiŋ he tataŋka he śduśduta e inapiŋ
and middle black the that morning yellow the that buffalo horn smooth that collar-has

keyapi.
they say.

Hehan kośka ḳoŋ heye : Tuŋkaŋśina, ito omawanini kta će, eya.
Then young man the this said: Grandfather, lo! I walking will , he said.
    [aforesaid]

Uŋkaŋ wićahiŋća kiŋ heya: Ho, takoźa, kośka eća oyate ećen wawaŋyag
And   old-man   the   this said: Yes, grandchild, young man when people   so   to see

omani će, eya keyapi.
walks always, he said, they say.

Uŋkaŋ hećen kośka ķoŋ iyaye ça oyate waŋ tipi en i; uŋkaŋ iŋyuŋ
And   so young man the   went and people   one living there came;   and   behold
                 [aforesaid]

ćaŋhdeśka kutepi en i. Uŋkaŋ kośkana waŋ en wawaŋyaka, keyapi.
hoop   shooting there came. And   young man   one thither   looking-on,   they said.

Hećen en inaźiŋ, ķa, Ito kićuwa kići wawaŋmdake kta, eya. Hećen kići
So   there he stood, and, Lo! my friend with   I-look-on   will he said.   So   with

naźiŋ. Uŋkaŋ heye: Kićuwa, yati ekta uŋhde kta, eya. Hećen kići hda
he-stood.   And   this said: Friend, your home to   we go home will, he said.   So   with   went-
                          (dual)   home

ķa kići ki. Uŋkaŋ he kuŋśitku ićaĥya heća, hećen kuŋkiśitku kići ti en
and with arrived. And   that grandmother his raised   such,   so   grandmother his with lived there

i, keyapi.
came, they say.

Uŋkaŋ, Uŋci, kićuwa kići wahdi će, taku yute kta ikihni ye, eya.
And,   Grand- my friend with I come home , what   eat   will   that [please], he
         mother   provide   said.

Uŋkaŋ kuŋkiśitku kiŋ heya: Takoźa, token wahaŋ kta he, eya. Uŋkaŋ
And grandmother his the this said: Grandchild how   I do   will ? she said.   And

kośka uŋma ķoŋ heya: Toketu hwo uŋćina, eya. Uŋkaŋ, Oyate kiŋ de
young man other   the this said· How is it   ? grandmother, he said.   And, People the this
              [aforesaid]

waŋna ipuza wićate kta će, eya; tuwe mini huwe-i keś hdi śni ećee, eya.
now   thirsty they die will , she said; who water goes-for although come not always, she
                                           home   said.

Uŋkaŋ, Kićuwa ćeĝa iću wo, mini huwe uŋye kta će, eya. Uŋkaŋ, Takoźa
And   Friend   kettle take thou water   for   we go will , he said.   And   My grand-
                                                     child

kitaŋ ićaĥwaye ćiķoŋ! eya. Taku śni-śni ikoyapa, eye, ça hećen kići ye ça
hardly I raised   in the past! she said. What not-not   you fear, he said, and so   with went and ça

mde kahda inaźiŋpi. Uŋkaŋ mini kiŋ kahda wakiśkokpa mini oźugźudaŋ
lake   by   they stood.   And   water the   by   troughs   water   each full

hiyeya. Uŋkaŋ tuwe mini huwe hi ća taku e yakte eće keyapi ķoŋ
stood.   And   who   water to get comes when what that you kill always they say the
                              [comes for]   [afore-
                                                                   said]

toki idada hwo, de mini huwe wahi do, eya.
where have you ? this water   to get I come . he said.
gone   [I come for]

Uŋkaŋ ihnuhaŋna toki iyayapi taŋiŋ śni; hećen iŋyuŋ ti haŋska waŋ
And   suddenly   whither they went manifest not;   so   behold! house long   one

kakiyotaŋna iyeya, ohna kośka ķa wikośka oźuna hiyeya: waŋna apa ţapi
in this direction lay,   in   young and maidens full   were: now some dead
                               men

ķa apa ţe ićakiśya hiyeya, en opeya ipi. Uŋkaŋ, Dena token dukaŋpi he,
and some to   suffering   were,   in together they And,   These how are-you-here ?
    die   came.

eya. Uŋkaŋ, Taku yaka he; dena mini huwe uŋhipi heś, taku waŋ
he said. And,   What you mean ? these water to bring we came although, some- one
                                                              thing

nauŋpćapi ećee će, eyapi, keyapi.
us-swallowed always , they said, they say.

Uŋkaŋ kośka ķoŋ pa kiŋ en taku iyapapa yaŋka. Uŋkaŋ, De taku he,
And   young men the   head the   in some-   striking   was   And,   This what ?
       [aforesaid]   thing   [sitting].

eya. Uŋkaŋ, Haŋta, he ćaŋte ee će, eyapi. Uŋkaŋ he hećen isaŋ ehdaku
he said.   And   Get-away   that   heart   is   ,   they said.   And   he   so   knife   his-took

ka baśpuśpu yaŋka. Uŋkaŋ ihnuhaŋna taku nina ham hiŋhda; uŋkaŋ he
and   cut-to-pieces was [sitting].   And   suddenly   what   very   made a noise;   and   that

taŋmahen taŋka e hena nawićapće, tuka ćaŋte kiŋ baśpupi nakaeś ohna ta
body inside   large   that those   them-swallowed,   but   heart   the   cut-up   indeed   in   dead

kiŋ ekta hi ta, keyapi. Hećen ćuwi kiŋ pahdoke ća kośka wikośka ko
the   at   come dead, they say.   Hence   side   the   punched   and young men   maidens   also

om hdićupi.
with came out.
them

     Uŋkaŋ oyate kiŋ nina pidawićaya e hećen wikośka nom kupi. Tuka,
     And   people   the   much   glad-them-he-made that   hence   maidens   two   gave him.   But,

Ohiŋni omaniyaŋ wauŋ e hećen kicuwa iye wićayuze kta će, eya, ka
Always   journeying   I am that   so   my friend   he   them take   will   ,   he said, and

kośkana koŋ napin ku. Uŋkaŋ hećen hoćokam wakeya waŋ itićaġapi ka
young man   the   both   gave.   And   so   in-the-court   tent   one   pitched-for,   and
[aforesaid]

hokśina koŋ kuŋkśitku kići akiyuha en awićakipi. Wikośka noŋpa koŋ hena
boy   the   grandmother his with   bearing   there them brought.   Young women   two   the   those
[aforesaid]   [aforesaid]

om en ahitipi.
with in they moved.

     Hećen kośka koŋ ake itoopteya iyaya keyapi. Uŋkaŋ waŋna ake
     Then   young man the   again   onward   went   they say.   And   now   again

kośkana waŋ manin naźiŋ ćaŋhdeśka kutepi. Uŋkaŋ wawaŋyaka haŋ
young man   a   outside   stood   hoop   shooting.   And   looking-on   standing

en i ka heya: Ito, kićuwa kići wawaŋmdake kta eye, ća kići naźiŋ. Uŋkaŋ
in he and this-said: Lo,   friend   with   I-look-on   will he said, and with   stood.   And
came

heye: Kićuwa, uŋhde kta će, eye ća kići ki. Ka, Uŋćina, kićuwa kići wahdi
this-he-   Friend,   we-go home will   he-said, and with came.   And, Grandmother, my friend   with   I come
said: (dual)   home.   home,

će, takuŋ ikihni naŋka wo, eya. Tuka kuŋkśitkuna kiŋ, Token wahaŋ kte
something hunting up   be thou   he-said.   But   grandmother his   the,   How   I-do   will

e heha he, eya. Uŋkaŋ, toketu he, eya. Uŋkaŋ, Oyate kiŋ de waŋna
this you say ?   she said.   And,   How is it   !   he said.   And,   People   the   this   now

ćaŋ oŋ wićatakuniśni će, eya; tuwe ćaŋ kiŋ i keś tohiŋni hdi śni, eya.
wood for   they perish   she-said;   who   wood-to-carry goes if   at any time   come home not,   she
                                                                                    said.

Uŋkaŋ, Kićuwa, hiŋśka ićú wo, ćaŋ kiŋ uŋye kta će, eya. Uŋkaŋ
And,   Friend,   strap   take,   wood to-carry we-go   will   ,   he said.   And

wakaŋkana kiŋ, Takuś kitaŋna ićahwaye ćikoŋ, eya. Tuka, Wakaŋka iś
old woman   the,   Grandchild   hardly   I-raised   in the past, she said.   But,   Old woman   that

de takuśniśni ikoyapića: heye ća kośkana koŋ kići iyaye ća heye: Ćaŋ
this   trifles   you afraid-of: this said and young man   the   with   went   and this said: Wood
                                                            aforesaid

kiŋ mda će, tuwe yaćiŋpi kiŋhaŋ u po. Eyaya uŋkaŋ, Kośka waŋ tokiya-
to-carry I-go,   who   you wish   if   come ye.   They went   and,   young man   a   somewhere

taŋhaŋ hi ka heya će eyapi, ka ihakamya eyaye. Waŋna ćaŋ kiŋ en ipi,
from   come and this said   they said, and   after   they went.   Now   wood   the   in   they
                                                                              came,

uŋkaŋ ćaŋ kiŋ ikaŋtoŋ hiyeya e hećen oyate koŋ hetaŋhaŋ ahdiyakupi
and   wood the   tied-up   lay,   that   so   people   the   that from   started home with

tuka, iye en naźiŋ ka, Tuwe ćaŋ kiŋ den hi ća, taku yakte keyapi koŋ
but.   he there stood and,   Who   wood   the   here comes when, what   you-kill   they say   the
                                                                                 aforesaid

toki idada hwo, eya. Uŋkaŋ ihnuhaŋna toki iyaya taŋiŋ śni. Hećen
where you have gone ? he said. And suddenly where he had gone manifest not. So

iŋyuŋ, wakeya waŋ ohna dećen kośka wikośka ko, apa wotapi ḳa apa ni
behold tent a in thus young men maidens also, some eating and some alive

hiyeya e apeya yaŋka. Uŋkaŋ, Dena token dukaŋpi he, eya. Uŋkaŋ,
were waiting were. And, These how are you ? he said. And,

Taku yaka he; dena ćaŋ ḳiŋ uŋhipi keś taku dećen uŋkahdipi ećee; niś
What you mean ? these wood to carry we came although some- thus us brought home always; you
thing

eya nitakuniśni će, eyapi. Uŋkaŋ heyata etoŋwaŋ uŋkaŋ iŋyuŋ, ohdoka
also you-are-destroyed , they said. And behind looked and behold hole

waŋ dećen hiyeya. Uŋkaŋ, De taku he, eya. Uŋkaŋ, Uśtaŋ, he taku kiŋ
a so was. And, This what ? he said. And, Stop, that what the

hee će, eyapi. Tuka waŋhiŋkpe ikikću ḳa okatkataŋyaŋ. Uŋkaŋ wakeya kiŋ
that is, they said. But arrow his-took and transfixed it. And tent the

ihnuhaŋna kazamni iyaya. Uŋkaŋ he hiŋyaŋkaġa e noġe awićayuhmuza
suddenly opened went. And that owl's that ear them shut up

keyapi. Hećen kte nakaeś noġe kiŋ namdaya iyaya. Hećen, Kośka
they say. Thus killed indeed ear the opened out went. So, Young men

wikośka kiŋ owasiŋ taŋkan ku po, eye, ća om hdiću, keyapi.
maidens the all out come ye, he said, and with started out, they say.
them

Uŋkaŋ ake witaŋśna uŋ nom ḳupi. Tuka ake, Kicuwa iye napin
And again maidens were two gave him. But again, My-friend he both

wićayuze kta će, eya. Hećen hokśina ḳoŋ kuŋkśitkuna kići ḳa wiŋyaŋ kiŋ
them take will he said. So boy the grandmother his with and women the
aforesaid

napin om hoćokam wakeya waŋ ohna ewićahnakapi.
both together in the middle tent a in they placed them.

Hećen ake itoopta iyaya. Ake oyate waŋ tipi waŋ en i, uŋkaŋ ake
So again forward he went. Again people a dwelling a in came, and again

ćaŋhdeśka kutepi, uŋkaŋ kośkana wawaŋyaka haŋ e en inaźiŋ. Ḳa, Ito,
hoop shooting, and young man looking on standing there stood. And, Lo,

kićuwa kići wawaŋmdake kta, eye ća kići inaźiŋ. Uŋkaŋ heye: Kićuwa,
my friend with I look-on will, he said and with he stood. And this-said: My friend,

uŋhde kta će, eya, uŋkaŋ kići ki. Uŋkaŋ ake he kuŋkiśitku ićahya heća.
we-go- will he-said, and with he- And again that grandmother his raised such.
home went-home.

Uŋkaŋ, Uŋćina, kićuwa kići wahdi će, takuŋ ikihni naka wo, eya. Uŋkaŋ,
And, Grandmother, my friend with I come home, something hunt thou for him, he said. And,

Taku tukten iwaću kta e heha he, eya. Uŋkaŋ, Uŋćina toka e heha he,
What whence I-take will that you say ? she said. And, Grandmother why that you say ?

eya. Uŋkaŋ, Waziya waŋ de oyate kiŋ tehiya wićakuwa će, pte opi
he said. And, Waziya a this people the hardly them treats , buffalo kill

keś owasiŋ iću, ḳa waŋna akihaŋ wićaṭe kta, eya. Uŋkaŋ, Uŋćina ekta ye
although all he-takes, and now starving they die will, she said. And, Grandmother there go

ća, Mitakoźa ićimani hi tuka takuna yute śni e umaśi će, eya wo, eya.
and, My grandchild travelling has but nothing eats not so me sent say thou, he said.
come,

Hećen wakaŋka iyaye ća itehaŋyaŋ inaźiŋ, ḳa, Waziya, mitakoźa ićimani
So old woman went and afar off stood, and, Waziya, my grandchild travelling

hi, tuka takuna yute śni e umaśi ye, eya. Tuka, Wakaŋka śića ekta
has but nothing eats not so me-sent she said. But, Old woman bad to
come

kihda wo, de taku yaka he, eya. Hećen wakaŋka ćeya hdi, ḳa takuya ke
go-home, this what you mean ? he said. So old woman crying came and friends meant,
home

ça, Waziya makaṭe kta, keya će, eya   Uŋkaŋ, Kićuwa, ikaŋ iću wo, ekta
and,   Waziya kill for me would, he said she said.   And,   My friend   strap   take,   thither

uŋye kta će, eya.   Uŋkaŋ, Takuś kitaŋ ićahwaye ćikoŋ!   Uŋćina de
we go   will , he said.   And,   My-grand- hardly I have raised in the past   Grand   this
(dual)   child   mother

wikopapake, eye ça hećen iyayapi; ḳa Waziya ti on ipi ḳa waćonića
much afraid,   he said, and   so   they went;   and Waziya house to they and   dried meat
came,

taŋkan hiyeya e hećen takodaku kiŋ tona okihi ḳiŋ kiye ça ahdiyakukiye
without   hung that so   friend his   the many as able to carry caused and sent him home with it

ça iye e Waziya ti kiŋ en i, ḳa, Waziya he tokae uŋćina den uwaśi uŋkaŋ
and he him- Waziya house the in went, and, Waziya this why   grand-   here I sent   and
self   mother

heha eya.   Tuka Waziya ite tokeća yanke.   Uŋkaŋ ćaġa itazipa waŋ
this you he said.   But   Waziya face different   was.   And   ice   bow   a
said,

otkeya yanke.   Uŋkaŋ, Waziya, de token yahnakeća he, eya.   Uŋkaŋ,
hanging up   was.   And,   Waziya,   this how   you place away ? he said.   And,

Uśtaŋ wo, he tuwe yutaŋ ça isto ayuweġa će, eya.   Uŋkaŋ, Ito, isto
Stop thou   that who   touches when arm   on-it-breaks , he said.   And,   Lo! arm

amduweġa ke eye ça ćaġa itazipe ḳoŋ snayeh yumden iyeya, ḳa, hećen
I-break-on-it, will he said, and ice   bow   the   snapping   broke   went, and,   so

hdiću.
he came home.

    Ḳa haŋhaŋna uŋkaŋ waŋna ake oyate kiŋ wanase aye ça waŋna pte
    And   morning   then   now   again people the buffalo hunting went and   now   buffalo

kiŋ ota opi.   Uŋkaŋ waŋna ake owonase kiŋ iyaza tona opi kiŋ owasiŋ
the many shot.   And   now   again surrou.d the through many killed the   all

pahi ećee ḳa ikpihnaka au.   Uŋkaŋ kośka waŋ he hi ḳoŋ pte waŋ ćepa
gathered-up   and placed in blanket brought.   And young man a that came the   cow a fat

apata.   Uŋkaŋ Waziya pte kiŋ ikpihnag u ḳoŋ en hinaźiŋ, ḳa heya: De
dressed.   And   Waziya cows the putting in belt came the there coming stood, and this said: This

tuwe pata he, eya.   Uŋkaŋ, Miye wapata do, eya.   Uŋkaŋ Waziya heye:
who   dressed ? he said.   And,   I   I-dressed , he said.   And   Waziya this said:

Kośka ḳoŋ he ke ça, Wićaŋhpi hiŋhpaya, de tokiyataŋhaŋ wanićaġe ça e
Young man   the that meant and, Star   Fallen,   this   from whence have you grown ? that

dećehiŋ wahaŋnićida he, eya.   Uŋkaŋ iś, Waziya, niś de tokiyataŋhaŋ
so that thus   you boast yourself ? he said.   And he,   Waziya, you this   from whence

wanićaġe ça e wahaŋnićida he, eya.   Uŋkaŋ Waziya heya: Wićaŋhpi
you-grow-up ? that you boast yourself ? he said.   And   Waziya this said: Star

hiŋhpaya, tuwe napamapazo eća ṭa ećee do, eya.   Uŋkaŋ, Ito, napawapazo
Fallen,   who finger me points to when dies always , he said.   And   Well, finger I point

ke eća maṭe ça, eye ça napapazo, tuka tokeća śni.   Uŋkaŋ hehaŋ iś heya:
will when I-die, ? he said and hand showed,   but   different   not.   And   then   he this said:

Waziya, tuwe napamapazo eća nape kiŋ naiheyaya iyeya ećee do, eya.
Waziya,   who finger me points to when hand the paralyzed becomes always , he said.

Uŋkaŋ, Ito, napawapazo ke, ito eća naiheyaya iyemayića, eye, ça ećoŋ,
And,   Well,   I point finger will, lo there paralyzed   make me.   he said, and did it.

tuka nape ḳoŋ iśpa kiŋ hehaŋyaŋ naiheyaya iyeya.   Uŋkaŋ ake uŋma
but   hand   the lower arm the   so far   paralyzed   was.   And again   other

ećiyataŋhaŋ ećoŋ tuka ake iśpa kiŋ hehaŋyaŋ naiheyaya iyeya.   Hećen
from   did-it, but again lower arm the so-far   destroyed   was.   So

Wićaŋhpi hiŋhpaya isaŋ ehdaku ḳa Waziya śina abapote; hećen pte
Star   Fallen   knife his-took and Waziya blanket cut up;   hence buffalo

ikpihnag uŋ kiŋ owasiŋ kadada.   Hećen oyate kiŋ hewićakiye: Detaŋhaŋ
in-blanket was the   all   fell out.   So that people the this-them-said to: Henceforth

patapi ḳa aḣda po, eye.   Hećen oyate kiŋ wapatapi ḳa tado iḣaŋpi ḳa tiyata
dress   and carry ye home, he said.   So   people   the   dressed   and meat prepared and houses to

aḣdi.   Ḳa haŋḣaŋna uŋkaŋ heyapi: Waziya śina abapotapi ḳoŋ waŋna
brought   And next morning   and   this was said: Waziya blanket cut-up-was   the   now
home.   aforesaid

tawiću kiŋ kaġeġe yuśtaŋ e hdatata kta će, eyapi.   Waziyata itoḣe inaźiŋ
wife-his   the   sewing up   finished that he shake   will.   they said.   North-to   facing   standing
                                                      his own

katata e hećen waziyata taŋhaŋ tate uye ća wa kiŋ wakeya kiŋ hiŋskokeća
he shook that so   north   from   wind came and snow the   tents   the   so far around

hiŋḣpaye ća oyate kiŋ owasiŋ wa mahen eyaye, ća wićanihiŋćiye ća heyapi:
fell   and people the   all   snow under   went,   and they were troubled and this said:

Toketuya kećaś ni uŋyakoŋpi ḳoŋ; kośka waŋ token ḣaŋ ḳa waŋna
In some way   even living we were   in the past; young man a   how   does   and   now

uŋtakuŋipi śni, eyapi.
we perish,   they said.

Uŋkaŋ, Uŋćina, ićadu waŋźi omakide wo, eya.   Uŋkaŋ hećen wa mahen
And, Grandmother, wing   one   hunt thou for me   he said.   And   so   snow under

ćaŋkuyapi: Mitakoźa heya će, ićadu waŋźi da će, eya e hećen iho toketu
road made: My grand child this says ,   wing   one   he asks ,   she that   so   behold how is it
                                                                                        said,

keye ća će, eyapi; ḳa waŋźi ḳupi.   Uŋkaŋ tiće kiŋ iwaŋkam wa kiŋ iyaye
he says that? ,   they said; and one they gave.   And tent top the   above   snow the   went

nakaeś, wa paḣdogye ća tićeśka kiŋ akan iyotaŋke ća itokah itoheya iyotaŋ
indeed,   snow   punched   and tent-top the   on   he-sat   and   south   towards   most

ićadu ḳoŋ, heoŋ ihdadu yaŋka, uŋkaŋ itokaġa taŋhaŋ tatahiyuye ća odidita
blowed the,   therefore fanning   was,   and   south   from   wind-brought   and   heat
                           himself

taŋka, ḳa wa kiŋ mini ipiġa akaśtaŋpi kiŋ hećen iyaya, ḳa skaŋ iyaye ća
great,   and snow the   water boiling thrown-on the   so   went,   and melted   went,   and

maka kiŋ owaŋća po iću, ḳa hećen Waziya tawiću ćiŋća ko om didita ṭapi.
earth   the   all over   fog took, and   so   Waziya   wife his   children also together heat of   died.

Tuka Waziya ćinća hakaktana niġe śdana he tośu huta opaḣdi kiŋ ohna
But   Waziya   child   youngest   belly   bare   that tent pole bottom   hole   the   in

oḣewaŋke ćiŋ heći oŋapena ḳa he nina oŋ etaŋhaŋ dehaŋ Waziya yuke ćiŋ
frost   the   there   took refuge   and that little   wherefore   now   Waziya   is   the
                                              one lived

hećeća, keyapi.   Hećen ohuŋkakaŋ kiŋ de, Wićaŋḣpi Hiŋḣpaya ećiyapi.
that sort,   they say.   So   myth   the   this.   Star   Fallen   is called.

NOTES.

1. The use of the definite article "kiŋ" or "ćiŋ" with the demonstratives "he"
and "de" with their plurals is noticeable. "Kiŋ he" and "kiŋ de" have been rendered "the that" and "the this." Sometimes they are equivalent to only "that" and
"this," as, wićaśta kiŋ de, *this man;* at other times they are equivalent to "that
which" or "what;" as, Wićaŋḣpi yaŋke ćiŋ he, *that star which is.*

2. Attention is called to the almost uniform repeating of the verb "say" in dia-
logues; that is, both before and after the thing said. Before the words said, the form
is "heya," which is compounded of "he" and "eya," *that said.* It might be "hećen
eya," *thus said.* Then at the close of the words spoken comes in "eya" again, which
to us seems superfluous. But it serves to close up and finish off the expression, and
is helpful to a good understanding of the matter.

3. It is commonly affirmed, and admitted in good part, that Indian languages
have no substantive verbs; that is, there is no one which corresponds exactly with the

verb "to be." But in the Dakota language there are several ways of expressing it. One that appears frequently in these myths is in, dee, hee, ee, ćee, and ećee; the last "e" is the verb of existence; "this is it," or, more properly, "this is," "that is,"[1] "it is." In ćee and ećee the idea is that of continuance. Heya ećee, he was saying that; that is, he repeated it; he kept on saying it. So also the verb "uŋ," when it can be used, corresponds to our verb "to be." But the use of "uŋ" is limited. Then we have "yaŋke" and "waŋke," which have reference to *place* as well as *being*. But still it remains true that in many cases the Dakotas do not need a substantive verb; *I am good* they can express by the pronoun and adjective alone, "ma-waśte."

4. The study of these Dakota myths has greatly strengthened my former impressions of the necessity of the supernatural. In this myth the deliverer of the people is "star-born." In the Badger and Bear myth the deliverer is created by mysterious power. But everywhere and always the supernatural is recognized. The bad forces, whether the nameless, shapeless thing that swallowed them all up that went for water, or the mythic owl's ear that covered them all in when they went for wood, are more powerful and tangible force, the north-god, all these and others must be met and conquered by the supernatural. So the incarnation of selfishness and meanness, impersonated in Gray Bear, must be overcome and killed by the mysterious born.

TRANSLATION.

A people had this camp; and there were two women lying out of doors and looking up to the shining stars. One of them said to the other, " I wish that very large and bright shining star was my husband." The other said, " I wish that star that shines less brightly were my husband." Whereupon they say both were immediately taken up. They found themselves in a beautiful country, which was full of beautiful twin flowers. They found that the star which shone most brightly was a large man, while the other was only a young man. So they each had a husband; and one became with child. In that country the teepsinna,[2] with large, beautiful stalks, were abundant. The wife of the large star wanted to dig them, but her husband forbade it, saying " No one does so here."

Then the encampment moved; and the woman with child, when she had pitched her tent and came inside to lay the mats, etc., saw there a beautiful teepsinna, and she said to herself, " I will dig this—no one will see it." So she took her digging stick and dug the teepsinna. When she pulled it out immediately the country opened out and she came through, and falling down to the earth, they say, her belly burst open. And so the woman died; but the child did not die, but lay there stretched out.

An old man came that way, and seeing the child alive took it up, put it in his blanket, and went home. When he arrived he said, " Old woman, I saw something to-day that made my heart feel badly." " What was it?" said his wife. And he replied, "A woman lay dead with her belly bursted, and a little boy child lay there kicking." " Why did you not bring it home, old man?" she said. He answered, " Here it is," and took it out of his blanket. His wife said, " Old man, let us raise

---

[1] As the author has said in another part of this volume, "e" predicates identity rather than existence. And this is the case in the cognate languages: e in Ȼegiha, are in J̣oiwere, and hére or ére in Winnebago, should be rendered "the aforesaid," "the foregoing." etc.—J. O. D.

[2] Tipsiŋna, the *Psoralea esculenta* (Pursh), the *Pomme blanche* of the French Canadians.—J. O. D.

this child." "We will swing it around the tent," the old man said, and whirled it up through the smoke hole. It went whirling around and fell down, and then came creeping into the tent. But again he took it and threw it up through the top of the tent. Then it got up and came into the tent walking. Again the old man whirled him out, and then he came in a boy with some green sticks, and said, "Grandfather, I wish you would make me arrows." But again the old man whirled him out, and where he went was not manifest. This time he came into the tent a young man, and having green sticks. "Grandfather, make me arrows of these," he said. So the old man made him arrows, and he killed a great many buffalo, and they made a large tepee and built up a high sleeping place in the back part, and they were very rich in dried meat.

Then the old man said, "Old woman, I am glad we are well off; I will proclaim it abroad." And so when the morning came he went up to the top of the house and sat, and said, "I, I have abundance laid up. The fat of the big guts I chew." And they say that was the origin of the meadow lark, a bird which is called tašiyakapopo.[1] It has a yellow breast and black in the middle, which is the yellow of the morning, and they say the black stripe is made by a smooth buffalo horn worn for a necklace.

Then the young man said, "Grandfather, I want to go traveling." "Yes," the old man replied, "when one is young is the time to go and visit other people." The young man went, and came to where people lived, and lo! they were engaged in shooting arrows through a hoop. And there was a young man who was simply looking on, and so he stood beside him and looked on. By and by he said, "My friend, let us go to your house." So he went home with him and came to his house. This young man also had been raised by his grandmother, and lived with her, they say. Then he said, "Grandmother, I have brought my friend home with me; get him something to eat." But the grandmother said, "Grandchild, what shall I do?" The other young man then said, "How is it, grandmother?" She replied, "The people are about to die of thirst. All who go for water come not back again." The star-born said, "My friend, take a kettle; we will go for water." The old woman interposed, "With difficulty I have raised my grandchild." But he said, "You are afraid of trifles," and so went with the Star-born. By and by they reached the side of the lake, and by the water of the lake stood troughs full of water. And he called out, "You who they say have killed every one who came for water, whither have you gone? I have come for water."

Then immediately whither they went was not manifest. Behold there was a long house which was extended, and it was full of young men and young women. Some of them were dead and some were in the agonies of death. "How did you come here?" he said. They replied, "What do you mean? We came for water and something swallowed us up."

Then on the head of the young man something kept striking. "What is this?" he said. "Get away," they replied, "that is the heart." So he drew out his knife and cut it to pieces. Suddenly something made a great noise. In the great body these were swallowed up, but when the heart was cut to pieces and died death came to the body. So he punched a hole in the side and came out, bringing the young men and the young women. So the people were very thankful and gave him two maidens.

---

[1] Tašiyaka is the name of the large intestine, the *colon;* sometimes applied to the pylorus. Dr. Riggs gives another form of the name of the bird in the dictionary, tašiyakapopopa.—J. O. D.

But he said, "I am journeying; my friend here will marry them," and so he gave them both to him. Then in the middle of the camp they put up a tent, and the young man with his grandmother and the two young women were brought to it.

Then the young man—the Star-born—proceeded on his journey, they say. And again he found a young man standing without where they were shooting through a hoop. And so, saying he would look on with his friend, he went and stood by him. Then he said, "My friend, let us go home," and so he went with him to his tepee. "Grandmother, I have brought my friend home with me," he said, "hunt up something for him to eat." But the grandmother replied, "How shall I do as you say?" "How is it?" he said. "This people are perishing for wood; when any one goes for wood he never comes home again," was the reply.

Then he said, "My friend, take the packing strap; we will go for wood." But the old woman protested, "This one my grandchild I have raised with difficulty." But, "Old woman, what you are afraid of are trifles," he said, and went with the young man. "I am going to bring wood," he said; "if any of you wish to go, come along."

"The young man who came from somewhere says this," they said, and so followed after him.

They had now reached the wood, and they found it tied up in bundles, which he had the people carry home, but he himself stood and said, "You who have killed every one who came to this wood, whatever you are, whither have you gone?" Then suddenly where he went was not manifest. And lo! a tent, and in it were young men and young women; some were eating and some were alive waiting. He said to them, "How came you here?" And they answered, "What do you mean? We came for wood and something brought us home. Now, you also are lost."

He looked behind him, and lo! there was a hole; and, "What is this?" he said. "Stop," they said, "that is the thing itself." He drew out an arrow and transfixed it. Then suddenly it opened out, and it was the ear of an owl that had thus shut them up. When it was killed it opened out. Then he said, "Young men and young women, come out," and with them he came home.

Then again they gave him two maidens; but he said again, "My friend will marry them." And so the young man with his grandmother and the two women were placed in a tent in the middle of the camp.

And now again he proceeded on his journey. And he came to the dwelling place of a people, and again he found them "shooting the hoop." And there stood a young man looking on, to whom he joined himself as special friend. While they stood together he said, "Friend, let us go to your home," and so he went with him to his tent. Then the young man said, "Grandmother, I have brought my friend home with me; get him something to eat." For this young man also had been raised by his grandmother. She says, "Where shall I get it from, that you say that?" "Grandmother, how is it that you say so?" interposed the stranger. To which she replied, "Waziya[1] treats this people very badly; when they go out and kill buffalo he takes it all, and now they are starving to death."

---

[1] The weather spirit, a mythical giant, who caused cold weather, blizzards, etc.

See Amer. Anthropologist for April, 1889, p. 155. Waziya resembles a giant slain by the Rabbit, according to Omaha mythology. (See Contr. N. A. Ethn., VI, pt 1, 22, 25.)—J. O. D.

Then he said, "Grandmother, go to him and say, 'My grandchild has come on a journey and has nothing to eat, and so he has sent me to you.'" So the old woman went and standing afar off, called, "Waziya, my grandchild has come on a journey and has nothing to eat, and so has sent me here." But he replied, "Bad old woman, get you home; what do you mean to come here?" The old woman came home crying, and saying that Waziya threatened to kill some of her relations. Then the Star-born said, "My friend, take your strap, we will go there." The old woman interposed with, "I have with difficulty raised my grandchild." The grandchild replied to this by saying, "Grandmother is very much afraid," and so they two went together. When they came to the house of Waziya they found a great deal of dried meat outside. He put as much on his friend as he could carry, and sent him home with it, and then he himself entered the tepee of Waziya, and said to him, "Waziya, why did you answer my grandmother as you did when I sent her?" But Waziya only looked angry.

Hanging there was a bow of ice. "Waziya, why do you keep this?" he said. To which he replied, "Hands off; whoever touches that gets a broken arm." So he thought, "I will see if my arm is broken," and taking the ice bow he made it snap into pieces, and then started home.

The next morning all the people went on the chase and killed many buffaloes. But, as he had done before, the Waziya went all over the field of slaughter and gathered up the meat and put it in his blanket. The "Star-born" that had come to them was cutting up a fat cow. Waziya, on his round of filling his blanket with meat, came and stood and said, "Who cuts up this?" "I am dressing that," he answered. Waziya said, addressing himself to the young man, Fallen Star, "From whence have you sprung that you act so haughtily?" "And whence have you sprung from Waziya that you act so proudly?" he retorted. Then Waziya said, "Fallen Star, whoever points his finger at me dies." So he said to himself, "I will point my finger at him and see if I die." He did so, but it was no whit different.

Then he on his part said, "Waziya, whoever points his finger at me, his hand becomes paralyzed." So Waziya thought, "I will point my finger and see if I am paralyzed." This he did and his forearm was rendered entirely useless. He did so with the other hand, and it too was destroyed even to the elbow. Then Fallen Star drew out his knife and cut up Waziya's blanket, and all the buffalo meat he had gathered there fell out. Fallen Star called to the people, "Henceforth kill and carry home." So the people dressed this meat and carried it to their tents.

The next morning it was reported that the blanket of Waziya, which had been cut to pieces, was sewed up by his wife, and he was about to shake it. He stood with his face toward the north and shook his blanket, and the wind blew from the north, and the snow fell all around about the camp so that the people were all snowed in and very much troubled, and they said: "We did live in some fashion before, but a young man has acted so that now we are undone." But he said, "Grandmother, find me a fan." So, a road being made under the snow, she went and said to the people, "My grandchild says he wants a fan." "Whatever he may mean by saying this?" they said, and gave him one.

The snow reached up to the top of the lodges, and so he punched a hole up through and sat on the ridge of the lodge, and while the wind was blowing to the south he sat and fanned himself and made the wind come from the south, and the heat became great, and the snow went as if boiling water had been poured on it, and it melted away, and all over the ground there was a mist, and Waziya with his wife and children all died of the heat. But the little, youngest child of Waziya, with the smooth belly, took refuge in the hole made by a tent-pole, where there was frost, and so lived. And so they say he is all that there is of Waziya now. So also this myth is called the Fallen Star.

WOTANIĆE HOKŚINA OHAŊ KIŊ.
BLOOD-CLOT   BOY   DOINGS THE.

WRITTEN IN DAKOTA BY DAVID GREY CLOUD.

Iŋyuŋ kaked: Ḣoka waŋ waśed ti keyapi. Ḣoka ćiŋća ota hiŋća.
Behold thus: Badger a rich lived they-say. Badger children many very.

Ḣoka waŋhiŋkpe waŋźidaŋ yuha, tuka haŋska hiŋća yuha. Ḣoka hoćoka waŋ
Badger arrow one had, but long very had. Badger surround a

kaḣmiŋ e yuha. Uŋkaŋ he ohaŋhaŋna otoiyohi pte optaye oźudaŋ ećee.
river-bend that had. And that morning each buffalo herd full always.

Tohan hećeća eća owasiŋ ḣamwićaye, ća owasiŋ ćaŋkuye waŋźidaŋ ahda
When so then all drove-he them, and all path one went home

eća wićihektapataŋhaŋ inaźiŋ, ḳa tukte ehakedaŋ uŋ eća, waŋhiŋkpe waŋ
then them-behind-from he-stood, and which the-last was when, arrow a

haŋska yuhe ćiḳoŋ, he oŋ owasiŋ ićiyaza wićao ećee. Ḣoka hećoŋ yaŋke
long had that, that by all one-after- them-shot always. Badger this-doing was,
another

ća waŋna waśeća hiŋća.
and now rich very.

Uŋkaŋ ihnuhaŋna Mato waŋ en hi, ḳa Mato kiŋ heya: Huŋhuŋhe!
And suddenly Gray-Bear a in came, and Gray-Bear the this-said: Wonderful!

suŋg, niye ḳe dećen waśed yati naŋka he, eya. Miye ḳeś mićiŋća om
brother, you even thus rich you-live are-you ? he-said. I even my-children with

akiḣaŋ mate kte do, suŋg, eya. Ḣećen, suŋg, iyonićipi kiŋhaŋ den ahi wati
starve I-die will , brother, he-said. So brother, please-you if here move I-live

kte do, eya. Uŋkaŋ Ḣoka, Ho, eya; iyokosaŋs ićimaġaġayaken sakim
will , he-said. And Badger, Yes, said; moreover amusing-ourselves-thus both

uŋti kte do, eya. Waŋna Mato kiŋ hde kta, uŋkaŋ Ḣoka woheyuŋ waŋ
we-live will , he-said. Now Gray-Bear the go-home would, then Badger bundle one

ikikću ḳa Mato ḳu, ḳa ḳiŋ akiyahda.
took and Gray-Bear gave, and carrying he-took-home.

Ihaŋhaŋna hehan Ḣoka ti kiŋ en Mato ahiti. Ḣoka ti kiŋ en Mato
The-next-morning then Badger house the in Gray-Bear moved. Badger house the in Gray-Bear

hi kiŋ hećehnana Ḣoka taŋkan iyeyapi; ḳa Mato iye ohna iyotaŋka,
came the immediately Badger out-doors was-turn d; and Gray-Bear himself in sat-down,

ḳa Ḣoka woyute tawa koya owasiŋ kipi; hećen Ḣoka taŋkan eti, ḳa nina
and Badger provisions his also all were-taken; so Badger out-doors dwelt, and very-much

akiḣaŋ. Mato en hiyotaŋke ćiŋ ihaŋhaŋna uŋkaŋ Mato haŋhaŋna hiŋ
starved. Gray-Bear in came-sat-down the next-morning then Gray-Bear morning very

kikta, ḳa taŋkan hinaźiŋ ḳa heya: Ḣoka nuksi śićamnana kiŋ taŋkan hinaŋpa
waked-up, and outside came-stood and this-said: Badger ears stinking the outside come

95

wo, nitahoćoka kiŋ pte oźudaŋ do, eya.   Uŋkaŋ Ḣoka waŋhiŋkpe ehdaku;
imper. your-surround   the buffalo   full-is   ,   he said.   And   Badger   arrow   his took;
sing.

ḳa Ḣoka hećoŋ ećee kiŋ ake iyećen ećoŋ, ḳa owasiŋ ićiyaza wićao.   Tuka
and Badger that-doing always the again   so   he-did,   and   all   one-after- them-hit.   But
                                                                 another

owasiŋ Mato iću, ḳa waŋźina kaeś Ḣoka kićupi śni.   Haŋḣaŋna otoiyohi
all   Gray-Bear took, and one   even   Badger was-given not.   Morning   each

hećoŋ, tuka tohiŋni Ḣoka waŋźidaŋ ahdi śni ećee: ḳa ećen waŋna Ḣoka
that-he-did, but never Badger one brought not always: and   so   now   Badger
                                              home

ćiŋća om akihaŋ ṭe kte hiŋća.   Tuka Mato ćiŋćadaŋ waŋźi hakaktadaŋ ḣća,
children with starve die will very.   But Gray-Bear children   one   youngest   very,

uŋkaŋ hee haŋḣaŋna otoiyohi tasićoǵaŋ waŋźi yuha śkata ećee, ḳa tohan
and   that-one   morning every buffalo-leg one   had played always, and when

waŋna hde kta ećá Ḣoka ti kiŋ en tiyokahmihma iyewićakiya ećee, ḳa
now go-home will then Badger house the in rolling-houseward[1] caused-them to-go always, and

heoŋ ni yukaŋpi.
by-that living they-were.

Hanḣaŋna waŋ ake Mato taŋkan hinapa ḳa heya: Ḣoka nuksi
Morning one again Gray-Bear outside came and this said: Badger ears

sićamnana kiŋ, waŋhiŋkpe ahiyu wo, nitahoćoka kiŋ pte oźudaŋ do, eya.
stinking   the,   arrow   bring out, your-surround the buffalo full-is . he said.

Mato heya tka Ḣoka ye śni.   Uŋkaŋ Mato heya: Ećiŋ yau śni kiŋhaŋ
Gray- this-said but Badger go not.   And Gray-Bear this-said: Now you-come not if
Bear

inaćibdaska kte do, eya.
I-smash-you will he said.

Uŋkaŋ Ḣoka tawićú heya: Wićahiŋća, eyaḳeś tokiki ewaćiŋ we, waŋna
Then   Badger wife-his this-said: Old-man,   at-any-rate somehow think of it (female now
                                                                           sp.)

ećen mićiŋća om akihaŋ maṭe kte, eya.   Uŋkaŋ Ḣoka heya: Ho, ekta mde ća
so my-children will starve I-die will, she said.   And Badger this-said: Yes, there I-go and

owasiŋ wićawao, ḳa ećiŋ tukte iyotaŋ ćepe ćiŋhaŋ he wahdohdi kte do;
all them-I-kill, and then which most fat if that I-bring-home will ;

ḳa naḳuŋ en makte eśta kte do, Ḣoka eya, ća Mato kići ya.   Uŋkaŋ Ḣoka
and also thus me-he-kill even will Badger said, and Gray-Bear with went.   And   Badger

hećoŋ ećee ake owasiŋ ićiyaza wićao.   Uŋkaŋ Mato heya: Pte tom ćepapi
that-did always again all one-after them-killed.   And Gray-Bear this-said: Buffalo four fat ones
                                       another

kiŋ hena niś pate ća ahdi wo, eya.   Uŋkaŋ Ḣoka, Ho, eya; ḳa waŋźi
the those you cut-up and bring-home, he said.   And Badger, Yes, said; and one

iyotaŋ ćepe hca, uŋkaŋ hećeedaŋ pata, ḳa waŋna yuśtaŋ, uŋkaŋ Mato heya:
more fat very, and that-only he-dressed, and now finished, then Gray-Bear this-said:

Tokeća ake waŋźi yapate śni, eya.   Tuka Ḣoka wićada śni.   Dećeedaŋ
Why again one you-cut-up not. he said.   But Badger would not.   This-alone

keś hokśiyopa wićawakahde kta, eya.   Hehaŋyaŋ hinaḣ Mato wapata
even children them-to-I-take-home will, he said.   So-long as-yet Gray-Bear cutting-up

hduśtaŋ śni.   Tuka waŋna Ḣoka tado kin ikaŋ kitoŋ ḳa ḳiŋ kta, uŋkaŋ
finished his own not.   But now Badger meat the string tied and carry would, then

Mato heya: Ḣoka nuksi śicamnana kiŋ, tokaŋ iyaya wo, we namayakiḣdi
Gray-Bear this-said: Badger ears stinking the, away go, (male blood you-for-me-tread-in
                                                                 sp.)

---

[1] Tiyokahmihma is not in the dictionary; but it is probably derived from ti, *tent*, and okahmi-
hma, which latter is from kahmihma, *to roll along, make roll by striking.*—J. O. D.

kte do, eya. Tuka Ĥoka iś heya: Hoĥo, miś haṇtuḳe de wahdohdi kte
will,   he·said.   Ĵut   Badger   he   this·said: No, no;   I   indeed   this   I·carry·home   will

do, eyạ. Mato ake eya, tka Ĥoka wićada śni. Uṇkaṇ Mato hiyu, ḳa
, he·said.   Gray·Bear again said·it,   but   Badger   would   not.   Then   Gray·Bear came,   and

Ĥoka we kiṇ ehna paha eĥpeyapi.
Badger blood the   in   pushed   was·thrown.

Uṇkaṇ wotanićе waṇ aputag iĥpaya, uṇkaṇ we kiṇ he oṇśpa napoĥmus
Then   blood·clot   one   kissing he·fell·down,   and   blood the   that a·piece   in·shut·hand

iću, ḳa yuha ćeya hda, ḳa peźi oṇǵe yuśda ḳa we kiṇ opemni ahde ća
he·took, and 'having   crying went·home, and   grass   some   ' pulled   and blood   the   wrapped·in   carried- and
                                                                                                                     home

ćatku kiṇ en akiĥnaka; ḳa hehan iṇyaṇ ḳa initośu ḳa peźiĥota ko huwe i
back·of-   the   in   placed·at·home;   and   then   stones   and sweat·poles and   *Artemisia*   also   to·get went
tent

ḳa ini kaǵa. Ḳa initipi ćatku kiṇ en peźiĥota kiṇ hena owiṇźe ća akan
and sweating made.   And   sweat lodge back·part the   in   *Artemisia*   the   them   made·bed·of and   upon

we kiṇ he ehnaka, ḳa hehan initi kiṇ he akantaṇhaṇ kiṇ he taṇyeĥ nataka.
blood   the   that   placed,   and   then   sweat-   the   that   the·outside   the   that   very·well   fastened.
                                           lodge

Hehan mini iću ḳa timahen ehde, ḳa iṇyaṇ kadye ća waṇna kate ćehaṇ
Then   water he·took and   within·house   placed,   and   stones   heated   and   now   hot   when

initi kiṇ mahen ewićahnaka, hehan tiyopa kiṇ ećen nataka. Hehan isto
sweat-   the   within   them·he·placed   then   'door   the   so   he·fastened.   Then   arm
lodge

ećeedaṇ timahen iyeye ća mini kiṇ oṇ iṇyaṇ kiṇ akaśtaṇ yaṇka.
alone   house·within he·thrust and   water   the   with   stones   the   pouring·on   was.

Uṇkaṇ ihnuhaṇna tuwe mahen ćomnihdazi niya Ĥoka nahoṇ. Ake
And   suddenly   some·one within   sighing   breathe   Badger   heard.   Again

ećoṇ, mini oṇ iṇyaṇ kiṇ akaśtaṇ yaṇka. Uṇkaṇ tuwe timahen heya niya:
he·did,   water with stones   the   pouring·on   was.   And   some·one within·house this·said breathing:

De tuwe akśa pidamayaye ća waṇna makiyuĥdoka wo, eya. Hećen tiyopa
This   who   again   glad·you·me·make   and   now   open for me (male sp.),   he·said.   So   'door

yuĥdoka, uṇkaṇ kośka waṇ wićaśta waśte ĥća hinaṇpa: hećen Ĥoka
' he·opened,   and   young·man   a   man   beautiful   very   came·out: so   Badger

Wotanićе Hokśidaṇ eya caźe yata, ḳa he Ĥoka ćiṇkśiya.
Blood·clot·Boy   saying name   called,   and that   Badger   son·had.'

Uṇkaṇ hehan Wotanićе Hokśidaṇ heya: Ito, ate, heya wo, Ito, mićiṇkśi
And   then   Blood·clot   Boy   this·said: Now father   this·say;   Now   my·son

heyake waśte ĥće ćeś, eya wo, eya. Uṇkaṇ eya, uṇkaṇ ećetu. Uṇkaṇ
clothes   good   very oh·that,   say thou,   he·said.   And   he·said,   and   it·was·so.   And

ake heya: Ito, mićiṇkśi ptaṇha waṇźu waṇ waṇhiṇkpe oźudaṇĥ yuhe ćeś,
again this·say: Now   my·son   otter·skin   quiver   a   arrows   full·very   ' have oh·that

eya wo, eya. Uṇkaṇ eya, uṇkaṇ ake ećetu. Uṇkaṇ hehan Wotanićе
'say thou.   he said.   And   he·said,   and   again   it·was·so.   And   then   Blood·clot

Hokśidaṇ pa hiṇ kiṇ waṇźi hduźuṇ iću, ḳa tiyopa kiṇ en ehde ḳa waṇhiṇkpe
Boy   head hair the   one   pulling   took, and   'door   the   in   placed and   arrow

oṇ kute, uṇkaṇ kasden iheya. Hehan Wotanićе Hokśidaṇ heya: Ate togća
with shot,   and   splitting   hit·it.   Then   Blood·clot   Boy   this·said: Father   why

wo mayaḳupi śni he. Uṇkaṇ Ĥoka heya: Hehehe, ćiṇś, taku yaka hwo:
food   me·you·give   not   ?   And   Badger this·said: Alas!   son   what   you·mean   ?

waṇna akiĥaṇ uṇṭapi kte do, wamaśeća ĥća, uṇkaṇ Mato den hi ḳa owasiṇ
now   starving   we·die   will   ,   I·was·rich   very,   and   Gray·bear here came and   all

maki ḳa taṇkaṇ hiyu maye ća owasiṇ iću, ḳa waṇna akiĥaṇ uṇṭapi kte do,
took-   and outdoors   come   made·me and   all   took,   and   now   starving   we·die   will   ,
from·me

eya.
he·said.

Uŋkaŋ Wotaniće Hokśidaŋ heya: Hena, ate, sdonwaye ćа heoŋ
And   Blood-clot   Boy   this said: These, father, I-know,   and therefore

imaćaġa će, eya.   Ate, tokeŋh' ećoŋ ćiśi kiŋhaŋ ećen ećoŋ wo, eya. Uŋkaŋ
I-have-grown he-said. Father, just-as to-do I-you- if   so   do   , he-said.   And
                                         command   (male sp.)

Hoka, Ho, eya.   Haŋhaŋna Mato taŋkan hinaźiŋ ḳa nićipaŋ eśta yau kte
Badger, Yes, said. In-the-morning Gray-Bear without stands and you-call although you-come shall

śni; tuka inoŋpa eye ćiŋhaŋ hehan yahinaŋpe kta ḳa kići de kta, tuka
not; but second-time he-says if   then you-come out will and with you-go will, but

miye he itokam waŋna ekta inawahbe kta, eya. Waŋna haŋhaŋna hiŋ
I-myself this before already at I-hide will, he-said. Now morning very

Mato taŋkan hinape ćа heya: Hoka nuksi śićamnana kiŋ waŋhiŋkpe kiŋ
Gray-Bear outside came and this said: Badger ears stinking the arrow the

ahiyu wo, nitahoćoka kiŋ pte oźudaŋ do, eya. Tuka ye śni, ḳa inoŋpa
bring out, your-surround the buffalo full-is , he-said. But he-go not, and second-time

eye ćiŋ hehan waŋhiŋkpe ehdaku ḳa kići ya ḳa ake owasiŋ hamwićaya, ḳa
he-said the then arrow his-took and with went, and again all   them-scared, and

ćaŋku waŋzidaŋ ahda, hehan Hoka waŋhiŋkpe oŋ owasiŋ ićiyaza wićao, ḳa
path   one   they went, then   Badger arrow with all in-a line them-shot, and

waŋźi ćepa he Hoka pata
one   fat that Badger dressed.

Uŋkaŋ Mato heya: Kohaŋna pata wo, eya. Waŋna Hoka pata yuśtaŋ
And Gray Bear this said: Soon cut up, he said. Now Badger cut-up finished

ḳehaŋ ḳiŋ hdićuu kta; uŋkaŋ Mato heya: Hoka nuksi śićamnana hiŋ tokan
then carry come would; and Gray Bear this said: Badger ears stinking the away
      home

hiyaya wo, we namayakihdi kte do, eya. Tka iyowiŋye śni kiŋ kta śkaŋ.
go thou   blood you-trample-in-for-me will , he said. But stopping not carry would worked.

Uŋkaŋ Mato hiyu ḳa iyahpaya ḳa we kiŋ ehna ehpeya. Tuka ake naźiŋ
Then Gray Bear came and fell-upon and blood the in threw him. But again rising

hiyaye ćа iću kta tka. Ake we kiŋ ehna ehpeya. Hehan Hoka ćeya
went and take would but. Again blood the in he-threw-him. Then Badger cried
śkaŋ.
working.

Uŋkaŋ hehan Wotaniće Hokśidaŋ naźiŋ hiyaye, ćа en ya, ḳa keya:
And then Blood-Clot Boy rising started, and there went, and this said:

Tokeća ate hećen yakuwa hwo, eya. Uŋkaŋ Mato heya: He iś, ćiŋś,
Why my-father so you treat ? he said. And Gray Bear this said: This that son

hepe do; Sung, kohaŋna niś nićiŋća tado wicakahda wo, epe do, eya.
this I said; Brother, soon you your children meat take home to them. I-said , he said.

Tuka Wotaniće Hokśidaŋ heya: Hiya, ate kahoya iyeyaye ćiŋ he
But   Blood Clot   Boy this said: No, my father throwing you shoved the that

waŋmdaka ce, eya; ḳa waŋhiŋhpe ehdaku, uŋkaŋ Mato nakipa, tuka kute
I saw   , he said; and arrow he-took, and Gray Bear fled, but he-shot

uŋkaŋ śastedaŋ kiŋ he okataŋyaŋ ḳa kte.
and little finger the that transfixed and killed.

Hehan Hoka deya: Ćiŋś, Mato ćiŋća waŋ hakaktadaŋ kiŋ tezi śdaśdadaŋ
Then Badger this said: Son, Gray Bear child a youngest the belly smooth

he kte śni wo, he tasicoġaŋ nahmana uŋkahipi ećee, ḳa heoŋ dehaŋyaŋ ni
that kill not, that leg-bone secretly us brought always, and by that to this time alive

uŋyakoŋpi će, eya.
we-are,   he said.

Uŋkaŋ hehan Wotaniće Hokśidaŋ tiyatakiya hda ḳa Mato tawićuu
And then Blood Clot Boy homeward went and Gray Bear wife his
                                            home

kipaŋ ḳa heya: Mato okpe u wo, eya. Uŋkaŋ Mato tawiću wikaŋi ću
called to and this said: Gray Bear to help come thou, he said. And Gray Bear wife his strap took
carry the meat

ḳa u ḳa heya: Optaye tonakeća he, eya. Uŋkaŋ Wotaniće Hokśidaŋ
and came and this said: Herd how many ? she said. And Blood Clot Boy

heya: Optaye waŋźi do, eya. Uŋkaŋ, Hena henakeća eća takukiye śni
this said: Herd one , he said. And, Those so many when something count not

ecee ḳoŋ, eya. Waŋna kiyedaŋ u uŋkaŋ ake heya: Optaye tonakeća he,
always in the she said. Now near came and again this said: Herd how many?
past

eya. Uŋkaŋ Wotaniće Hokśidaŋ heya: Optaye waŋźi će epe do, eye ća
she said. And Blood Clot Boy this said: Herd one, I said , he said and

waŋhiŋkpe ehdaku. Uŋkaŋ, Taŋni hećeće kte ćiḳoŋ eye ća naźića, tuka
arrow his took. And, Of old so would be, I she said and fled, but
thought

śastedaŋ kiŋ en okataŋyaŋ ḳa kte. Hehan Mato ti kiŋ en timahen
little finger the in drove it and killed. Then Gray house the in within
Bear

iyaya, uŋkaŋ owasiŋ pamahdidaŋ hiyeya. Wotaniće Hokśidaŋ heya:
went. and all heads-down were. Blood Clot Boy this said:

Waŋźi tukte de ate woyakupi eće he, eya iwićawaŋġa; uŋkaŋ owasiŋ ho
One which this my father food always ? he said, them asking; and all voice
you gave

waŋźidaŋ heyapi; Miye, miye, eyapi. Tuka waŋźidaŋ eye śni. Uŋkaŋ
one this said; I, I, they said. But one said not. And

hehan heya: Miye, miye, eyapi, uŋkaŋ etaŋhaŋ wićani kteća, eya; uŋkaŋ
then this said: I, I, they say, and for that they live shall? he said; and

Wotaniće Hokśidaŋ itazipe ehdaku ḳa owasiŋ wićakata ḳa hećeedaŋ okapta.
Blood Clot Boy bow his took and all them killed and that alone spared him.

Hećen he Hoka ti kiŋ en aki ḳa he mini aku ḳa nakuŋ cahod yuġe
So that Badger house the in he and that water bring and also ashes take up
brought,

kiyapi.
they made him.

Hehan ake Hoka nina waśeća hćą. Uŋkaŋ hehan Wotaniće Hokśidaŋ
Then again Badger very rich much. And then Blood-Clot Boy

ićomni ḳa heya: Ate, ićimani mde kte do, tukte oyate waŋźi ikiyedaŋ tipi
tired and this said: Father, traveling I go will , which people one near-by live
staying

sdoŋyaye ćiŋhaŋ ekta mde kte do, eya.
you know if there I go will , he said.

Uŋkaŋ Hoka heya: Dećiya oyate waŋ wićota tipi će, eya; hećen, ćiŋś,
And Badger this said: Here people a many dwell, he said; so son

ekta de kta; tuka wićahća waŋ nitkokim u kta, uŋkaŋ he nihnaye waćiŋ
there you go will; but old-man a you meeting come will, and he you deceive desire

kte do; tuka ihnuhaŋ taku eye ćiŋhaŋ ećanoŋ kte śni do, eya. Uŋkaŋ
will ; but take care what he says if you do will not , he said. And

Wotaniće Hokśidaŋ, Ho, eya.
Blood-Clot Boy, Yes, he said.

Wotaniće Hokśidaŋ waŋna iyaya, uŋkaŋ iŋyuŋ! wićahća waŋ sagye-
Blood-Clot Boy now had gone, and lo! old man a staff

kitoŋ u waŋka, ḳa heya: Takoźa, tokiya da he, eya. He iś, Hećegćen
holding coming was, and this said: Grandchild, where you ? he said. This he, In this way
go

omawaninake, eya. He ićuŋhaŋ śiyo ḳeya iwaŋkam hiyahaŋpi. Uŋkaŋ
I am walking truly (?) he said. This in the meantime grouse many above alighted. And

wićahća heya: Takoźa waŋźi makio wo, waŋna akihaŋ mațe kte do, eya.
old man this said: Grandchild one for me shoot, now starving I die will he said.

Tuka, Hiya dećiya mde ća inawahni do, eya, ķa iyoopta iyeya.   Waŋna
But,   No, thitberward I-go and I hasten , he said, and onward   went.   Now

htayetu uŋkaŋ ake nakuŋ wićahća waŋ sagyekitoŋ itkokim u ķa waŋna
evening and again also old-man a   staff baving to meet came and now

ehaŋ i kta uŋkaŋ iyotaŋka, hećen en inaźiŋ.   Uŋkaŋ wićahća heya:
there go would, and   sat down,   so there came-stood. And old man this said:

Takoźa, eya ito inayahni ešta owapaġi kte do, eya.   Uŋkaŋ Wotanići
Grandchild, even if you hasten although I fill pipe will , he said.   And   Blood-Clot

Hokśidaŋ hećiŋ, Ito ešta kići ćaŋnoŋmuŋpe ća hehan imdamde kta, eciŋ, ķa,
Boy   this thought, Lo if with I smoke   and then I go on will, he thought, and,

Ho, eya.   Hećen kići ćaŋnoŋpa yaŋke ća ećen akpaza.   Haŋyetu kiŋ he
Yes, said.   So with he smoking was and so night on.   Night the that

ihuŋniyaŋ kići yaŋka, ķa Wotanići Hokśidaŋ ištiŋbe śni uŋ, tuka waŋna
all through with was, and Blood-Clot Boy   sleep not was, but now

wićahća kiŋ ećen ištiŋma waŋka.   He ićuŋhaŋ waŋna aŋpa kamdes aya,
old man the even asleep lay.   That whilst now morning brightened went,

uŋkaŋ hećen, ito ešta miś waŋna mištinma ke, waŋnaś etaŋhaŋ aŋpa kta
and   so,   lo! even I now I sleep will, now from daylight will,

ećiŋ, ķa iwaŋka.
he and lay down.
thought,

    Uŋkaŋ tohiŋni ehaŋķoŋ Uŋktomi hee tka sdoŋye śni.   Wotanići
    And aforetime indeed Uŋktomi this was but he knew not.   Blood Clot

Hokśidaŋ ištiŋbeh iyaye ćiŋ hehan wićahća kiŋ hee naźiŋ hiyaye ća
Boy   asleep fast went the then old man the who was standing went and

heya: Tuwe iś tokenken ţenićiyena, eyaya naźiŋ hiyaye ća akamdaś
this said: Who this howsoever killing you, he said often standing went and astride

inaźiŋ, ķa ćaŋkaku kiŋ paweh iyeya, ķa huha kiŋ owasiŋ yuzigziŋ iyeya,
stood, and backbone the broke turned, and limbs the all stretched he made,

ķa nakpe kiŋ napin yuzića, ķa hećen śuŋka waŋ śići hća kaġa.   Uŋkaŋ
and ears the both he stretched, and this dog a bad very made.   And

wokoyake wašteśte kiŋ hena ićų ķa iye uŋ ķa tawokoyake wizi ećee uŋ
clothes beautiful the those he took and he wore, and his-clothes old only wore
                                                                    clouts those

kiŋ hena en ehpeya, ķa hetaŋhaŋ iyoopta kići ya.   Hećen Wotanići
the those there he-left, and thence forward with went.   So Blood Clot

Hokśidaŋ hee śuŋka kaġapi.   Uŋktomi hee hnaye ća hećen ećakićoŋ.
Boy   that was dog made.   Uŋktomi it was deceived and so did to him.

Hetaŋhaŋ Uŋktomi iyoopta ya ķa śuŋka kiŋ he kići ya kićoćo aya,
Thence Uŋktomi forward went and dog the that with went calling to led
                                                                   him often him

Wotanići Hokśidaŋ, wohwo, wohwo, eya aya.   Wotanići Hokśidaŋ oyate
Blood Clot Boy,   "wohwo, wohwo" saying led him. Blood Clot Boy   people

waŋ ekta ye ćiķoŋ hee waŋna Uŋktomi ehaŋ i, uŋkaŋ śuŋka kiŋ he išteća
a to went the that-is now Uŋktomi to come, and dog the that ashamed

ķa manin ihdonića, ķa Uŋktomi iśnana oyate kiŋ ehna iyaya.   Uŋkaŋ
and outside kept himself, and Uŋktomi he alone people the among went.   And

oyate kiŋ heyapi keyapi: Wotanići Hokśidaŋ hee u do, eyapi, ķa nina
people the this said they say: Blood Clot Boy that was comes, they said, and much

wićiyuśkiŋ hća, keyapi.
they rejoiced very they say.

NOTES.

1. The use of ¢eś, which is "ḳeś" frequently, is to be noted as indicating *wish* or *strong desire.* "Father, say this, 'Oh that my son might have good clothes.'" This is used at the end of the phrase or sentence, and is accompanied by the verbs *think* or *say,* in some form. Like to these is "tokiŋ," used at the beginning of the wish.[1]

2. The life-giving qualities of the sweating process are strongly brought out in this myth. There may be two objects or thoughts in the mind of the Dakota when he makes a "sweat lodge." It is sometimes resorted to for curing disease. That good quality Dr. Williamson always commended. No doubt it often afforded relief to a congested condition of the system. But it was resorted to more frequently for the purpose of getting into communication with the spirit world. This is the object here. From the blood of the buffalo, "which is the life thereof," is, by this process, created a man. Is this evolution? The sweat lodge was usually made, as described here, by taking willow boughs, bending them over, making their tops meet and interlacing or tying them together, and thus making a booth, which was large enough for one to sit naked inside and pour water on the heated stones. The whole was covered over tightly with blankets or robes. This is the initipi (eneteepee). The sweater sang as well as sweated. But in this case the object was to have the "mysterious power" do its work alone.

3. This myth ends abruptly. It would hardly be true to the thought of an Indian to leave the god-born in the shape of a dog, and that an ugly dog. There must be a sequel to it.[2]

TRANSLATION.

Once upon a time there was a Badger who was rich and had many children. He had one arrow, but it was a very long one. And in the bend of a river he had a buffalo surround, which was full of buffalo every morning. When it was so and all started out on one path, he stood behind them and shot his long arrow into the hindermost, and it went from one to another through the whole herd. So the Badger became very rich in dried meat.

Then suddenly there came a Gray Bear to his tent. And the Gray Bear said,

---

[1] The Titoŋwaŋ use tokiŋ only in soliloquies. When it is used it must be followed by ni or niŋ at the end of the clause expressing the wish; as, tokiŋ he bluha niŋ, *Oh that I had it!*—J. O. D.

[2] There is more of this myth in the Ȼegiha versions. The hero, there called "The Rabbit's Son," was caused to adhere to a tree, which he had climbed at the request of the deceiver, Ictinike. This latter character corresponds to Uŋktomi of the Santee Dakota, whom the Teton call Ikto and Iktomi. It seems better to leave these mythical names untranslated. While the Omaha and Ponka now apply the name Ictinike to the monkey, ape, etc., it is plain that this is a recent use of the term. Ictinike was one of the creators, according to the Omaha myths. After causing the Rabbit's son to adhere to the tree, he donned the magic clothing of the latter, went to a village near by, and married the elder daughter of the chief. The younger daughter, becoming jealous of her sister, fled to the forest, where she found the Rabbit's son, whom she released. At this point the Omaha version differs from the Ponka. The girl married the Rabbit's son and took him to her home. After several exhibitions of the skill of the young man, a dance was proclaimed. Thither went Ictinike, who was compelled to jump upward every time that the Rabbit's son hit the drum. The fourth time that he beat it his adversary jumped so high that when he struck the ground he was killed.

See Contr. to N. A. Ethnol., vol. VI, pt. I, pp. 43–57, and pt. II, pp. 586–609.—J. O. D.

"Wonderful! my brother, that you should live here in such abundance, while I and my children are starving. If it please you I will come here and live with you." The Badger said, "Yes;" and added, "So we will amuse ourselves." And when the Gray Bear was starting home, he took a bundle of buffalo meat and gave to the Gray Bear to carry home.

The next morning Gray Bear came with his household, and as soon as he moved in Mr. Badger was turned out and Gray Bear took possession of all his meat. The Badger lived out doors and starved. The next morning after he took possession, Gray Bear awoke very early in the morning and standing outside said, "You Badger with the stinking ears, come out, your surround is full of buffalo." So the Badger took his long arrow and as he was accustomed to do shot it through the whole line of buffalo. But the Gray Bear took them all and did not let the Badger have one. This he did morning by morning, but never did the Badger bring home one; and so he and his children were about to die of hunger. But the youngest of Gray Bear's children every morning played with a buffalo leg, and when he was tired playing he tossed them over to the Badger's tent. Thus they maintained an existence.

One morning again Gray Bear came out and called, "You Badger with the stinking ears, bring out your long arrow, your surround is full of buffalo." But the Badger did not go; when the Gray Bear said, "I will crush you if you don't come."

And the Badger's wife said, "Old man, in some way consider, for I and my children are starving to death." To this the Badger replied, "Yes, I will go and kill them all, and I will dress and bring home the fattest one, even if he kills me." So he went with the Gray Bear and did as he was accustomed to do, killing them all. Then the Gray Bear said, "You skin and carry home some of the fattest." To this the Badger said "Yes," and went to work to dress one of the fattest. When he was finishing that Gray Bear said, "Why don't you dress another?" But the Badger would not, and said, "This alone will be sufficient for my children."

As yet Gray Bear had not finished cutting up his meat, but when the Badger had tied up his meat and was about to pack it home, Gray Bear said, "You stinking-eared Badger, get away, you will trample in this blood." But the Badger replied, "No, I am going to carry this home." Gray Bear ordered him away again, but the Badger would not go. Then Gray Bear came and pushed Badger down in the blood. Thus, as he fell down in the clotted blood he kissed it, and taking a piece up in his hand he went home crying. By the way he pulled some grass and wrapped it around the blood and laid it away in the back part of his tent. Then he went and brought stones and sticks for a sweat-house, and *Artemisia* or wild sage, and made a steaming. In the back part of the sweat-house he made a bed of the *Artemisia* and upon it placed the blood, and then he covered the lodge well on the outside. Then he took a dish of water and placed it within, and when the stones were well heated he rolled them in also and fastened the door. Then he thrust his arm alone inside and poured water on the stones.

Suddenly the Badger heard some one inside sighing. He continued to pour water on the stones. And then some one breathing within said, "Again you have made me glad, and now open for me." So he opened the door and a very beautiful young man came out. Badger at once named him Blood-Clot Boy, and had him for his son.

Then Blood-Clot Boy said, "Now, father, say this: 'Oh that my son might have good clothes.'" So he said it, and it was so. Then he said again, "Say this: 'Oh that my son might have an otter-skin quiver filled with arrows.'" This he said also, and it was so. Then Blood-Clot Boy pulled a hair out of his head and placed it on the door, and, shooting it with an arrow, split it. And then he said, "Father, why don't you give me something to eat?" But the Badger answered, "Alas! my son, what do you mean? We are all starving to death. I was very rich in food, but Gray Bear came and took it all from me and drove me out, and now we are starving and will die."

Then Blood-Clot Boy said, "Father, I know these things, and therefore I grew. Now, father, do just as I tell you to do." To this the Badger said "Yes." Then Blood-Clot Boy continued: "In the morning when Gray Bear comes out and calls you, you will not go; but the second time he calls then go with him, for I shall then have hidden myself." So very early in the morning Gray Bear stood without and called: "Stinking-eared Badger, take your arrow and come, your surround is full." He did not go; but when he called the second time he took his arrow and went with him. And when they had scared the buffalo, and all had started home on one line, Badger shot his arrow through them all, and dressed the fattest one.

Then Gray Bear said, "Dress it quickly." And when the Badger had finished dressing and was about to start home with it, Gray Bear said, "Badger with the stinking ears, get away, you will trample in my blood." To this Badger paid no attention but continued to prepare to carry. Then Gray Bear came and fell upon him and threw him down in the blood. He arose and went to take up his pack, but again he threw him down in the blood. Then the Badger burst into tears.

But then Blood-Clot Boy appeared, and said, "Why do you treat my father so?" To which Gray Bear replied, "My son, this I said, 'My brother, take home meat to your children without delay.'" But Blood-Clot Boy said, "No, I saw you throw my father down." Saying that he pulled out an arrow, and as Gray Bear fled, he hit him in the little finger and killed him.

Then Badger said, "Do not kill Gray Bear's youngest child, the smooth-bellied boy, for he it was who brought us leg bones and so kept us alive until this time." Blood-Clot Boy then went towards home and called to Gray Bear's wife, "Come out and help Gray Bear." So she took her packing strap and said as she approached him, "How many herds were there?" Blood-Clot Boy said, "One herd." "When there are only that many he has never counted it anything," she said. And as she came near she asked again, "How many herds are there?" Blood Clot Boy again replied, "I have told you there was one," and he took out an arrow. She said, "I apprehended this before," and fled; but he shot her in the little finger and killed her. Then he went into Gray Bear's lodge and all bowed their heads. Blood-Clot Boy said, "Which one of you brought food to my father?" And all but one with one voice said, "It was I, it was I." Then he said, "You who said 'I, I,' shall you live?" And Blood-Clot Boy took his bow and killed all but the one who said nothing. And him he brought into Badger's lodge where he brought water and took up the ashes.

Then the Badger became very rich again. Blood-Clot Boy was discontented and said, "Father I want to take a journey; I want to go to the people that you know live near by." And the Badger answered, "My son, there is a people living just here, to them you will go. But an old man will come to meet you with the intent of deceiving you. You must not do anything he tells you to do." To this Blood-Clot Boy assented.

Blood-Clot Boy was now gone, and behold an old man with a staff came to meet him and said, "Whither do you go, my grandchild?" But he replied, "I am just walking." In the meantime a flock of grouse came and alighted. "My grandchild, shoot one for me, for I am starving," the old man said. But he answered, "No, I am going in haste in this direction," and so he passed on.

It was now evening, and again an old man with a staff was coming to meet him, who sat down just before their meeting, and so he came and stood. The old man said, "Grandchild, although you are in haste, I will fill my pipe." Then Blood-Clot Boy thought, "I will smoke with him and then go on;" so he said, "Yes." While they smoked together the darkness came on, and Blood-Clot Boy passed the night without sleeping. In the meantime the old man had fallen asleep; and the day was breaking. Then the young man thought, "I will sleep a little for it will soon be morning," and so he lay down.

This old man was the mythic being Uŋktomi, but the young man knew it not. While Blood-Clot Boy was sleeping very soundly, the old man that was got up and said, "What if in some way you are killed?" Saying which he arose and stood astride of him and bent his back and pulled out his limbs and stretched his ears, and so made him into a very ugly looking dog. The good clothes of the young man he took and put on himself, and his own old clothes he threw away, and so went on with him.

In this way Blood-Clot Boy was made into a dog. It was Uŋktomi who deceived him and did this to him. Then Uŋktomi took the dog with him calling to him, "O Blood-Clot Boy; wo-hwo! wo-hwo!" as he went along. And now when Uŋktomi had come to the people whither Blood-Clot Boy had been going, the dog was ashamed and kept himself outside of the camp, and Uŋktomi alone went among the people. Then the people said, "The famous Blood-Clot Boy is coming," and so they rejoiced greatly.

LEGEND OF THE HEAD OF GOLD.

WRITTEN IN DAKOTA BY WALKING ELK.

Wićaśa waŋ ćiŋća topapi, tka owasiŋ kośkapi; tka wahpanićapi, ka
Man   a   children were four,   but   all   were young   but   were poor,   and

onśika oŋ ṭa nuŋ se uŋpi. Uŋkaŋ wićahća kiŋ heya: Iho wo, wakaŋka,
poor   for dead would be   were.   Then   old-man   the this-said: Come,   old-woman,

mićiŋća hakakta kiŋ de iyotaŋ oŋśiwakida, tka oŋśika oŋ ṭiŋ kte
my-child   youngest   the this   most   I-have-mercy-on,   but   poor because-of die   will

ćiŋ wahtewada śni. E ito, Wakaŋtaŋka uŋkode ka iyeuŋye ćiŋhaŋ, ito waku,
the   I dislike.   Behold,   Great Spirit   we-two-seek, and we-two-find   if,   lo,   I-give

ka ito, taŋyaŋ ićahmićićiyiŋ kte do, eya.
and, lo,   well   he-rain-for-me   will   ,   he-said.

Uŋkaŋ wakaŋka kiŋ heya: Iho, wićahća, taŋyaŋ eha e ito hećoŋkoŋ
And   old-woman   the this said: Come,   old-man,   well   you-say, that lo,   that-we-do

kta, eya.
will, she-said.

Hećen iho waŋnaka wiyohpeyatakiya Wakaŋtaŋka ode yapi, ka
So   behold   now   to-the-westward   Spirit-Great   to-seek they-went, and

paha waŋ taŋka hća e en iyahaŋpi; uŋkaŋ iho wićaśa waŋ hiyahaŋ e hećen
hill   a   large   very that on 'they-stood;   and   behold   man   a   coming-stood that as

en ipi. Uŋkaŋ wićaśa koŋ heya: De taku oyadepi he, eya. Uŋkaŋ
into they came. And   man   that this-said: This   what   you seek   ?   he said.   And

wićahća iś heya: Hehehe! koda, mićinća kiŋ de oŋśiwakida e Wakaŋtaŋka
old-man   he this said: Alas!   friend,   my child   the this I-have-mercy-on that   Spirit-Great

waku kta e owade ye do, eya. Uŋkaŋ, Ho, koda, de Wakaŋtaŋka miye do.
I give   will that I seek   .   he-said.   And,   Yes,   friend, this   Spirit Great   me   .

Koda maku wo, kići wakde kta će, eya.
Friend give thou to me with I-go-home will   ,   he-said.

Hećen iho, ku ćaŋkeŋ waŋnaka kići kda, uŋkaŋ tipi waŋ mahpiya
So   behold, gave   when   now   with went-   and   house   a   heaven

ekta se haŋ e en kići ki, ka heya: Tipi kiŋ owasiŋ tokećiŋyaŋ waŋyag
to almost stood that in   with came- and this said: House the   all   as much as you please observing

uŋ wo. Hehan śuŋkawakaŋ kiŋ de taŋyaŋ wićakuwa yo, ka tipi waŋ de
be thou.   Then   horses   the this   well   them-care-thou for, and house   a   this

ćikana e den he ćiŋ de waŋyake śni yo, eye ća tiyopa iyuhdoke kiŋ owasiŋ
little that here stands the this   look-at   not,   he said and   door   keys   the   all

105

ḳu, ḳa hehan heya: Ho, en etoŋwaŋ yo; ito, omani mde kta će, eye ća
gave- and   then   this-said: Yes, to   look thou;   lo, walking I-go will , he-said and
him,

iyaya.
went.

Uŋkaŋ htayetu, uŋkaŋ wićaśa ota om kdi, ḳa tipi kiŋ ożuna ahiyotaŋka;
Now   night,   then   men   many with he came and house the full   they-sat-down;
                                                       home,

uŋkaŋ waŋnaka tehaŋ yaŋkapi oŋ wićaśa kiŋ waŋżi heya: Koda, hokśina
and   now   long-time were, therefore men the   one   this-said: Friend,   boy

kiŋ waśte e heceknana kte do, eye ća kinaŋpa.   Uŋkaŋ wićaśta kiŋ owasiŋ
the good that that-enough will , he said and went-out. And   men   the   all

iś eya kinaŋpapi.
they likewise went out.

Uŋkaŋ ake wićaśa kiŋ heya: Iho wo, ake omani mde kta ce; owanżina
Then   again man   the this-said: Come, again traveling I-go will; staying-at-home

en etoŋwaŋ yo, eye ća ake iyaya.
look thou after it,   he-said and again he went.

E hećen iho en etoŋwaŋ, uŋkaŋ śuŋkawakaŋ kiŋ uŋmaŋ heya: Koda,
Thus behold he looked after it, uŋkaŋ horses   the   one   this-said: Friend,

tipi waŋ ćikana e waŋyake śni niśi ḳoŋ ito en ye ća timahen ćaŋ owinża
house a little that look-at not thee-com- that lo in go and within wood bed
                                        manded

ćokaya taku waŋ zi en haŋ će, he en paha kiŋ oputkaŋ yo, ḳa koyahaŋ yo,
in-the-middle some- a yellow in stands , that in head the dip thou, and be-thou-in-haste,
thing

nauŋpiŋ kta će.   De wicaśa ota awićakdi kiŋhaŋ hena niyatapi kte e miś
we-together will be. This man many them-bring- if   they you-eat will that me
                                        home

hen mayutapi kta tka tawaṭeŋwaye śni, e nauŋpiŋ kta će, eya.
there me-eat will, but   I willing   not, we both together will be, he said.

Hećen hokśina ḳoŋ tipi waŋ ćikana ḳoŋ en i; uŋkaŋ ćaŋ owiŋża kiŋ
So   boy   that house a little that in went; and   wood bed the

ćokaya taku waŋ zi e mibeya haŋ e en paha kiŋ oputkaŋ, unkaŋ paha kiŋ
in-the- something a yellow in-a-circle stood in head the he dipped, and   head the
middle

zi, ḳa tipi kiŋ ataya ożaŋżaŋ ḳa iyoyaŋpa.   Hećen iho heyata kdićU ḳa
yellow, and house the all-over shone and was-light. So behold back he-returned and

śuŋkawakaŋ waŋ wokiyake ćiḳoŋ he akaŋyotaŋke ća nakipapi. Keyaś
horse   a   told-him the-that that he-sat-upon and they-fled. Nevertheless

nina iyayapi.
fast they went.

Uŋkaŋ tehaŋ ipi uŋkaŋ iho hektataŋhaŋ Wakaŋtaŋka keićiye ćiḳoŋ
When   far they went then behold from-behind Spirit-Great called-himself the-that

śuŋkawakaŋ uŋma ḳoŋ he akan yaŋke ća kuwa awićau, ḳa heya: Wahteśni
horse   other the that upon was and following to them came, and this said: Worthless

śica, inażiŋ po, yanipi kte śni ye do; makoće waŋ niskoyena waŋke ćiŋ
bad,   stop ye, ye-live shall not   country a so-large lies the

tukte en dapi kta hwo, eyaya en wićau, ćaŋken nihiŋćiyapi. Uŋkaŋ ake
where to you-go will ? saying to them came, whilst they-trembled. Then   again

heya: Wahteśni śića, inażiŋ po, yanipi kte śni ye do, ake eya. Ćaŋken
this said: Worthless bad, stop ye, ye-live shall not   again he said. Meanwhile

nipi kte śni seećeća.
they live would not   it-seemed.

Uŋkaŋ śuŋkawakaŋ kiŋ heya: Witka waŋ duha ḳoŋ he hektakiya
Then   horse   the this-said: Egg a thou-hast the that backwards

kaȟona iyeya yo, eya; e hećen iho iyećen ećoŋ. Uŋkaŋ maka kiŋ
throwing ʼsend thou ʼit, he ʼsaid; that so behold in-like-manner he-did. Then earth the

hdakiŋyaŋ miniwaŋća waŋ ićaǵa; ćaŋkeŋ kuwa au ḳoŋ eŋna hinaźiŋ ḳa
the-breadth of ocean a grew; meanwhile following came the there stopped and

heya: Hehehe, śuŋkawakaŋ, oŋśimada ḳa akasam eȟpemayaŋ yo; ećiŋ
this ʼsaid: Alas. O horse. pity-me and across throw-ʼthou-me; indeed

hećanoŋ kiŋhaŋ tećiȟiŋda kte do, eya. Hećen śuŋkawakaŋ kiŋ heya:
that-thou-doest if, I-you-value-much will ʼ he ʼsaid. Thus horse the this ʼsaid:

Hehehe, tawaṭenwaye śni ye do, eya. Tka nina kitaŋ e hećen iho mini kiŋ
Alas. I willing not , he ʼsaid. But much he-urged so-that behold water the

iwaŋkam hiyuićiya, tka hećen mini kiŋ ćokaya hi kiŋ hehan hiŋȟpaye ća
above he threw himself, but thus water the midst came the then he-fell-down and

hećen mahen iyaya ḳa miniṭapi. Hećen hetaŋhaŋ hokśina ḳoŋ zaniyaŋ
so within went and were-drowned. Thus from-thence boy the safely

iyoopta iyayapi.
beyond went.

Uŋkaŋ oyate waŋ wićoti e en ipi ḳa hen uŋpi. Uŋkaŋ hektataŋhaŋ
Then people a dwellings in came and there they were. Then from behind

nataŋ ahi ḳa wicakizapi, tka hokśina ḳoŋ paha kiŋ kaobeŋ iyeye ća paha
to attack they- and them fought, but boy the head-hair the around turned and head-
came hair

kiŋ mazaskazi ayuwiŋtapi, ćaŋkeŋ ziyena śuŋkawakaŋ akan iyotaŋke,
the gold was-rubbed-over, meanwhile goldenly horse on he-sat,

ḳa watakpe ahi ḳoŋ kaȟpa iyewićaya ḳa tonana owićakapte ḳa awićayuśtaŋ.
and to-attack they- those fall-off he-made-them and few them-spared and them-left.
came

Uŋkaŋ ake takpe ahi tka ake wićakasota. Hokśina ćaŋkeŋ hetaŋhaŋ
And again to-attack they-came but again he-destroyed-them. Boy therefore from-that

oyate kiŋ teȟiŋdapi.
people the much-thought-of.

Iho mitakuyepi, taku oŋ hokśina hena hećoŋ he. Toki ni kta ćiŋ, ḳa
Well my-friends, what for boy these this-did ? Somewhere live would wished, and

Wakaŋtaŋka ikpi iyonape kta ćiŋ ḳa ode naćeća. Iho iyeya uŋkaŋ
Spirit-Great bosom in-take-refuge should wished, and sought-him, perhaps. Well he found and

Wakaŋśića temye wićakiye kta ćiŋ. E hećen toki napa naćeća, he ake ni
Spirit-Bad to eat up them-cause would desired. And so somewhere he fled perhaps, that again live

kta ćiŋ ḳa napa naćeća. Tka ake takpe ipi e hećen ake wićakize, ḳa
might he- and fled perhaps. But again to attack they that so again them-he-fought, and
desired came

owasiŋ wićakte naćeća. He iye tawiyukćaŋ oŋ hećoŋ śni naćeća. Tuwena
all them-killed perhaps. This he his ʼpurpose for this-did not perhaps. No one

en ayepića śni, seećeća, ḳa tuwena iyaoŋpepića śni. Tka iś paha kiŋ
can be laid to not, as it seems, and no one can-be-blamed not. But they head the
his charge (or-hill)

mazaskazi ayuwiŋtapi kiŋ he ćiŋpi, ḳa hećoŋpi naćeća.
gold ʼcovered over the that they desired, and this did perhaps.

Tataŋka Iyotaŋke he iyećeća wadake.
Bull Sitting this is-like I-think.

NOTES.

The writer of this is a Yankton Dakota, and this appears in a very marked way throughout the story. Notice the "yo," sign of the imperative, used in various instances instead of "wo;" and also the form "yiŋ," as in "ićalimićićiyiŋ kta," for "ićalimićićiye kta." And also the form "kd" for "hd," as in "kda," *to go home;* "kdiću," *to*

start home, etc. Another thing noticable is the abundant use of free adverbial particles, as, "e" at the beginning of sentences and "ye do" at the end, which can not be
translated, and are only used for emphasis or for rounding off the speech.[1]

In the dialogue between the old man and old woman in the beginning of the
fable there are a number of examples of the use of the Dakota dual, as, "uŋkode,"
"iyeuŋye," and "hećoŋkoŋ."

TRANSLATION.

A man had four children. And they were all young men, but they were poor
and seemed as if they would die of thriftlessness. And the old man said, "Behold,
old woman, my youngest child I have greatest pity for, and I dislike to have him die
of poverty. See here; let us seek the Great Spirit, and if we find him, lo, I will give
him to him to train up well for me."

The old woman replied, "Yes, old man, you say well; we will do so," she said.
And so immediately they went to the westward, seeking the Great Spirit, and they
came on to a very high hill; and as they came to it, behold, another man came there
also.

And this man said, "For what are you seeking?" And the old man said,
"Alas, my friend, my child whom I pity I want to give to the Great Spirit, and so I
am seeking him." And he said, "Yes, friend, I am the Great Spirit. My friend,
give him to me, I will go home with him." (That is, "I will take him to my home.")

And so when he (the father) had given him, he (the Great Spirit) took him home
with him to a house that seemed to stand up to the clouds. Then he said, "Examine
all this house as much as you like; and take good care of these horses; but do not
look into the little house that stands here." Having said this, he gave him all the
keys, and he added, "Yes, have a watch of this. Lo, I am going on a journey." He
said this, and went away.

It was evening, and he had come home with a great many men, who sat down,
filling the house. When they had been there a good while, one of the men said: "The
boy is good; that is enough." And saying this he went out. In like manner all the
men went home.

Then again, the man said: "Behold, I go again on a journey. Do you stay and
keep watch." So again he departed.

While he was watching, it happened that one of the horses said, "Friend, go
into the small house into which you are commanded not to look, and within, in the
middle of the floor, stands something yellow, dip your head into that, and make
haste—we two are together. When he brings home a great many men, they will eat
you, as they will eat me, but I am unwilling—we two shall share the same," he said.

So the boy went into the little house, and in the middle of the floor stood a round
yellow thing, into which he dipped his head, and his head became golden, and the
house was full of shining and light.

Then he came out and jumped on the horse that had talked with him and they
fled.

---

[1] "Ye do" of the Isaŋyati ("ye lo" of the Titoŋwaŋ), as an emphatic ending, seems equivalent
to the Osage "e¢au," Kansa "eyau," and Çegiha "a¢a." The last means "indeed;" but "e¢au" and
"eyau" contain the oral period "au" (= Dakota do, lo) as well as "indeed."—J. O. D.

Now when they had gone a long way—they went very fast—behold, there came, following them, the one who called himself the Great Spirit. And he said, "You bad rascals, stop; you shall not live; whither will you go in such a small country as this?" Saying this he came toward them, when they were much frightened. And again he said, "You are bad rascals, stop; you shall not live." And indeed it seemed as if they should not live.

Then the horse said, "Take the egg you have and throw it rearward." And he did so, whereupon the whole breadth of the country became a sea, so that he who followed them came to a standstill, and said, "Alas, my horse, have mercy on me and take me to the other side; if you do I will value you very much." And the horse replied, "Ah, I am not willing to do that." But he continued to urge him; whereupon he threw himself above the water, and so that, when he came to the middle, he went down and both were drowned. By this means the boy passed safely on.

So it was they came to the dwellings of a people and remained there. But from behind they came to attack, and fought with them; but the boy turned his head around, and his head was covered with gold, the horse also that he sat upon was golden, and those who came against them, he caused to be thrown off, and only a few remained when he left them. Again, when they returned to the attack he destroyed them all. And so the boy was much thought of by the people.

Now, my friends, why did the boy do these things? He wanted to live somewhere, and he desired to take refuge in the bosom[1] of the Great Spirit, perhaps, and so he sought him. When he had found him, then the Bad Spirit sought to make him (the Great Spirit) eat them up. So he fled—again he desired to live, perhaps, and fled. But they followed him, so that he again fought with them and killed them all, it seems. It appears that he did not do this of his own purpose. It seems as if no one was chargeable with it, and no one was to be blamed for it. But they wanted the head (hill) of gold, perhaps, and so they did it. I think that this is like Sitting Bull.

---

[1] Ikpi generally means *belly, abdomen.* Sometimes it may mean the *thorax* also; but that is more properly called "maku." So says the author in his Dakota Dictionary, p 195.—J. O. D.

ODOWAN ŚIGŚIĆE.[1]
SONGS BAD.

WRITTEN IN DAKOTA BY DAVID GREY CLOUD.

Hituŋkaŋkaŋpi waŋ hećen oyakapi.   Uŋktomi waŋ kaken ya waŋka;[2]
Myths   a   thus is-told.   Uŋktomi one   so   going was;

mde waŋ kahda ya waŋka, uŋkaŋ mde kiŋ ćaŋnan maġaksića, ḳa maġa,
lake one by-the- going was, and   lake the   out-in   ducks,   and geese,
         side-of

ḳa maġataŋka koya ota hiyeya.   Uŋktomi waŋwićayaka ća ićićawiŋ
and swans   also many were.   Uŋktomi them-saw   and backward

pustagstag isiŋyaŋ kihde; ća peźi yuśda, ḳa owasiŋ yuskiskite ća ḳiŋ, ḳa
crawling out-of-sight went-home; and grass plucked, and   all   bound-up and carried ard
                                                                              on his back

ake mde kiŋ kahda ya.
again lake the by-the- went.
             side-of

Uŋkaŋ maġaksića ḳa maġa ḳa maġataŋka kiŋ hena heyapi: Uŋktomi,
And   ducks   and geese and swans   the they this said: Uŋktomi,

hena taku e yaḳiŋ hwo, eyapi.   Uŋkaŋ Uŋktomi heya: Hena iś odowaŋ
these what that you-carry ? they said.   And   Uŋktomi this-said: These they   Songs

śigśićedaŋka e he waḳiŋ do, eya.   Uŋkaŋ maġaksića heyapi: Eća Uŋktomi,
bad-little ones that I-carry on , said.   And   ducks   this said: Now   Uŋktomi,
             my back

uŋkidowaŋ miye, eyapi.   Tka Uŋktomi heya: Hoho! tka eća odowaŋ kiŋ
us-for-sing,   they said.   But Uŋktomi this-said: Indeed! but now   songs   the

śigśiće se eya.   Tuka maġaksića kiŋ nina kitaŋpi hiŋća.   Uŋkaŋ, Iho po,
bad-ones like, he said.   But ducks   the   much insisted-on very.   And, Come-on (ye)

eća peźi wokeya waŋźi kaġa po, eya.   Uŋkaŋ waŋźi taŋka kaġapi ḳa
now   grass   booth   one   make ye, said.   And   one   large they-made and

yuśtaŋpi.
they finished.

Uŋkaŋ Uŋktomi heya: Waŋna, maġaksića, ḳa maġa, ḳa maġataŋka
And   Uŋktomi this-said: Now,   ducks,   and geese, and   swans

owasiŋ peźi wokeya kiŋ timahen iyaya po, ćićidowaŋpi kta će, eya.
all   grass   lodge   the   within go ye , I-for-you (pl.) sing   will , said.

Uŋkaŋ maġaksića ḳa maġa, ka maġataŋka owasiŋ timahen iyayapi, ka
And   ducks   and geese, and   swans   all   within   they went, and

---

[1] For the corresponding Omaha and Ponka myth, see Contr. N. A. Eth., VI, pt. 2, pp. 66–69.—J. O. D.
[2] Ya waŋka, he was going; literally, going he-reclined. Waŋka, originally a classifier of attitude (the reclining object), is used here as haŋka (hañka) is in Winnebago.—J. O. D.

peźi wokeya kiŋ oźudaŋ iyotaŋkapi. Uŋkaŋ Uŋktomi peźi wokeya tiyopa
grass lodge the full they sat-down. And Uŋktomi grass lodge door

kiŋ ohna iyotaŋka, ḳa heya: Ćićidowaŋpi kiŋhaŋ, ićuŋhaŋ tuwedaŋ toŋwe
the in he sat-down, and this-said: I-for-you (pl.) sing if, whilst no-one look

kte śni, odowaŋ kiŋ he hećen kapi će, eya: ḳa waŋna heya ahiyaya:
shall not, song the that thus means , said: and now this-said sang:

"Iśtohmus waći po; Tuwe yatoŋwe ćiŋ, Iśta niśapi kta; Iśta niśapi kta."
"Eye-shut dance ye; Who you look the, Eyes you-red shall; Eyes you-red shall."

Heya ahiyaye ćiŋ he ićuŋhaŋ, maĝaksića, ḳa maĝa, ḳa maĝataŋka owasiŋ
This- he-sung the that whilst ducks, and geese, and swans all
saying

iśtohmus waćipi, keyapi.
eyes-shut they danced, they-say.

Uŋkaŋ Uŋktomi naźiŋ hiyaye ća heya ahiyaya: "Miye keśkeś
And Uŋktomi to-stand went and this-saying sang: "I even-even

owakipa; Miye keśkeś owakipa," heya opeya waći kiŋ he ićuŋhaŋ owasiŋ
I follow-in-my- I even-even I follow-in- this- with danced the that whilst all
own; my-own," saying

hotoŋ waćipi kiŋ, hehan Uŋktomi wićiyotahedaŋ waći uŋ; ḳa maĝaksića,
gabbling danced the, then Uŋktomi them-among dancing was; and ducks,

ḳa maĝa, ḳa maĝataŋka tona ćemćepa owaŋyag waśtepi kiŋ hena tahu
and geese, and swans as-many fat ones to-look-at they good the those necks

yuksa awićaya. Uŋkaŋ maĝataŋka waŋ tahu yukse kta tka okihi śni, ḳa
twisted-off took-them. And swan one neck twist-off would but able not, and

yuhotoŋtoŋ. Uŋkaŋ maĝaksića waŋ, Skiska ećiyapi, kiŋ heća waŋ iśtoĝiŋ-
made-squall-often. And duck one, Ski-ska by name, the such one eye-half

kiya toŋwe kta, uŋkaŋ Uŋktomi hee maĝataŋka waŋ tahu yukse kta, tka
open look would, and Uŋktomi himself swan a neck break-off would, but

okihi śni he waŋyaka: uŋkaŋ Skiska kiŋ heya: Tonwaŋ po, toŋwaŋ po,
able not that saw: and Ski-ska the this-said: Look ye! look ye!

waŋna Uŋktomi uŋkasotapi kta će, toŋwaŋ po, eya.
now Uŋktomi us-use-up will , look ye! said.

Uŋkaŋ hećehnana owasiŋ toŋwaŋpi, ḳa taŋkan akiyahde kta; uŋkaŋ
And without delay all they looked, and out-doors go-home would; and

Uŋktomi tiyopa kiŋ ohna ehpeićiye ća tiyopa kiŋ aniće waćiŋ; ḳa hećoŋ,
Uŋktomi door the in threw-itself and door the forbid intended; and this-did,

tka hupahu ḳa·siha koya oŋ apapi, ḳa ećen kaṭapi, ḳa siha kiŋ oŋ tezi kiŋ
but wings and feet also with they-smote, and thus knocked-dead, and feet the with stomach the

eŋ amanipi, ḳa tezi owasiŋ kinaksaksapi, ḳa en ṭa waŋka; kitaŋh ni,
on they-walked, and stomach all they-cut-up-with- and there dead he lay; by-a-little lived,
their-feet,

uŋkaŋ inaźiŋ ḳa ohomni etoŋwaŋ, tuka waŋna tokiya akiyahda. Uŋkaŋ
and he-arose and around looked, but now somewhere gone-home. And

Skiska waŋ tokaheya toŋwe ćiŋ heoŋ iśta śa keyapi.
Ski-ska one first looked the therefore eyes red, they-say.

Hehan Uŋktomi maĝaksića, ḳa maĝa, ḳa maĝataŋka tona tahu
Then Uŋktomi ducks, and geese, and swans, many-as necks

wićayukse ćiḳoŋ hena wićapahi ḳa ḳiŋ ḳa iyoopta ya waŋka; ḳa wakpa
them-twisted-off had been those them-gathered and carried and thence going was; and river

waŋ iyohpaya ḳa kahda ya, wakpa oha waŋ tehaŋ kiŋ iyokopeya yeya;
a came-to, and by-the-side went, river reach a long very in-sight stretched;

uŋkaŋ hen e wohaŋ. Maĝaksića, maĝa ḳa maĝataŋka, tona tahu wićayukse
and there he-boiled. Ducks, geese and swans, many-as necks them-twisted-off

ćiŋ hena ohaŋ ehde: ḳa hehan iśtiŋma iwaŋka; wakpa kiŋ ohnayaŋ paptus
the those to-boil placed: and then to-sleep lay-down; river the upon squatting

iwaŋka, ḳa heya: Mioŋze ećiŋ tuwe u kiŋhaŋ mayuhića wo, eya ḳa
he-lay, and this-said: My oŋze, now who comes if wake thou me up, said, and
iśtiŋma waŋka.
asleep lay.

Uŋkaŋ Dokśinća hee wakpohna watom u waŋka, uŋkaŋ iŋvuŋ,
And Mink it-was river-on paddling coming was, and behold,
Uŋktomi hee wohaŋ hde, ḳa en iyapeya paptus iśtiŋma waŋka waŋyaka.
Uŋktomi it-was boiling had-placed, and in close-by squatted asleep lying he-saw.
Hećen etkiya ya, uŋkaŋ Uŋktomi hee oŋsyuhmuze kta, tka ikiyowiŋ[1]
So thither went, and Uŋktomi it-was close up his oŋze would, but he-mouth-motion
iyekiya, uŋkaŋ kićuŋni, tka ićan u, dus ye ća en i, ḳa Uŋktomi
made suddenly, and he-stopped, but just com- swiftly went and there ar- and Uŋktomi
then ing, rived,
iśtiŋma waŋka, tka wohe ćiḳoŋ he iću ḳa owasiŋ temye ća huhu kiŋ owasiŋ
sleeping lay, but boiled had that took and all devoured and bones the all
ićićawiŋ ćeġa kiŋ en okada, ḳa tokiya iyaya. Waŋna isiŋyaŋ iyaya,
back-again kettle the in he-put, and somewhere went. Now out-of-sight had-gone,
uŋkaŋ hehan Uŋktomi oŋze waawaŋyag kiye ćiḳoŋ he oyaka, ḳa kitata
and then Uŋktomi oŋze to-watch caused had that told, and shook
oŋsyuhmuza. Uŋkaŋ Uŋktomi heya: Iya, mioŋze iś kakećadaŋ ye,
the oŋze closed. And Uŋktomi this-said: Well, my-oŋze he (acted) indeed (?)
in that manner
eya hiŋhda iyotaŋg hiyaya, ḳa ohomni etoŋwaŋ, tka tuwedaŋ waŋyake śni
saying suddenly sitting up went, and around looked, but no one saw not
uŋkaŋ heya: Okiŋni ećaś waŋna wowahe ćiŋ mićispaŋ, oŋ mayuhiće,
and this-said: Perhaps indeed now my-boiling the for-me-cooked. on ac- me-waked,
count of
eye ća kun ehde, ḳa ćaŋwiyuze oŋ patata, tuka huhu ećee oźudaŋ. Uŋkaŋ
said and down set, and holding-wood with stirred, but bones alone full. And
akeś heya: Ehaeś owasiŋ onahba do, eye ća tukiha oŋ kaze, tka huhu
again this-said: Indeed all fallen-off , said and spoon with dipped-out, but bones
ećedaŋ ohna uŋ. Uŋkaŋ heya: Mioŋze, tokeća tuwe u kiŋhaŋ omakiyaka
only in were. And this-said: My-oŋze, why who comes if me-tell-thou
wo, epe seće ćiḳoŋ; ihomića kakiśćiye kta, eye ća ćaŋ ota pahi ḳa
I-said I-thought in the past surely I you-punish will, said and wood much gathered and
aoŋ, ḳa waŋna peta nina ide, uŋkaŋ iwaŋkam oŋze hdúġaŋ inaźiŋ, ḳa
put-on, and now fire much burn, and over-it oŋze opened his own stood, and
oŋze kiŋ ġaġahaŋ, tka hećen naźiŋ, ḳa waŋna ṭe-hnaśkiŋyaŋ, uŋkaŋ hehan
oŋze the squirmed, but so he-stood, and now death-struggle, and then
yuktaŋyaŋ iŋyaŋke, ća ećen kasamyedaŋ ihpaye ća en ta waŋka, keyapi.
to-turn-over he-ran, and so a-blackened-mass it-fell-down and there dead lay, they-say.
Hećen hituŋkaŋkaŋpi kiŋ de Odowaŋ Śigśićedaŋka ećiyapi.
So myth the this Songs Bad-little-ones is-called.
Homakśidaŋ maćistiŋna kiŋ heehaŋ de nina nawahoŋ s'a, tuka
Me-boy me-little the then this much I-heard habitually, but
waŋna ehaŋtaŋhaŋ waniyetu wikćemna nom aktoŋ nawahoŋ śni.
now from years ten two more-than I-hear not.

---

[1] Riggs gives in his Dakota Dictionary iyokiwiŋ, *to gesture to one with the mouth.* If ikiyowiŋ
be an alternative form, it is a case of metathesis.—J. O. D.

NOTES.

These Dakota myths, with interlinear translations, are all written out by
Dakota men, and hence are pure specimens of the language.   This one of the
Bad Songs is by Rev. David Grey Cloud, one of our native pastors, and, as he is a
Santee, the peculiarities are of that dialect, in which our books are generally written.
The rhythmic quality of the language comes out very fairly in Uŋktomi's songs:

> Iśtohmus waći po;
> Tuwe yatoŋwe ćiŋ,
> Iśta niśapi kta;
> Iśta niśapi kta.

And in this, reduplication and repetition are finely illustrated:

> Miye keśkeś, owakipa:
> Miye keśkeś, owakipa.

TRANSLATION.

There is a myth which is told in this way: Uŋktomi was going along; his way
lay along by the side of a lake.   Out on the lake were a great many ducks, geese,
and swans swimming.   When Uŋktomi saw them he went backward out of sight,
and plucking some grass bound it up in a bundle, which he placed on his back and
so went again along by the side of the lake.

Then the ducks and the geese and the swans said, " Uŋktomi, what is that you
are carrying?"   And Uŋktomi said, "These are bad songs which I am carrying."
Then the ducks said, "Now, Uŋktomi, sing for us."   But Uŋktomi replied, "But
indeed the songs are very bad."   Nevertheless the ducks insisted upon it.   Then
Uŋktomi said, "Make a large grass lodge."   So they went to work and made a large
inclosure.

Then Uŋktomi said, "Now, let all of you ducks, geese, and swans gather inside
the lodge, and I will sing for you."   Whereupon the ducks, the geese, and the swans
gathered inside and filled the grass lodge.   Then Uŋktomi took his place at the door
of the grass lodge and said, "If I sing for you, no one must look, for that is the meaning of the song."   So saying, he commenced to sing:

> "Dance with your eyes shut;
> If you open your eyes
> Your eyes shall be red!
> Your eyes shall be red!"

While he said and sung this the ducks, geese, and swans danced with their
eyes shut.   Then Uŋktomi rose up and said as he sang:

> "I even, even I,
> Follow in my own;
> I even, even I,
> Follow in my own."

So they all gabbled as they danced, and Uŋktomi, dancing among them, commenced twisting off the necks of the fattest and the best looking of the ducks, geese,

and swans. But when he tried to twist off the neck of a large swan, and could not, he made him squall. Then a small duck, which is called Skiska, partly opening its eyes, saw Uŋktomi attempt to break off the neck of the swan, and immediately made an outcry:

"Look ye, look ye,
Uŋktomi will destroy us all,
Look ye, look ye."

Whereupon they all immediately opened their eyes and started to go out; but Uŋktomi threw himself in the doorway and attempted to stop them. But with feet and wings they smote him and knocked him over, walking over his stomach and cutting it all up, leaving him lying there for dead. But coming to life he got up and looked around. All were gone. But they say that the Wood duck, which first looked, had his eyes made red.

Then Uŋktomi gathered up the ducks and geese and swans whose necks he had twisted off, and carried them on his back. He came to a river, and traveled along by the side of it till he came to a long straight place or "reach," where he stopped to boil his kettle. When he had put all the ducks, geese, and swans, whose necks he had twisted off, into the kettle and set it on the fire to boil, then he lay down to sleep. And as he lay there curled up on the bank of the river, he said, Now, my oŋze, if any one comes you wake me up. So he slept. Meanwhile a mink came paddling on the river, and coming to Uŋktomi's boiling place saw him lying close by fast asleep. Thither he went, and although the oŋze of Uŋktomi should have given the alarm by closing up, it made a mouth at the mink, at which he stopped only for a moment (till he felt all was safe). Then he pressed on swiftly, and, while Uŋktomi slept, took out all his boiling and ate it up, putting back the bones into the kettle. Now, when the mink was gone out of sight, the oŋze of Uŋktomi which he had set to watch told of it. Uŋktomi commended the faithfulness of his guard, and sitting up looked around, but saw no one. "Perhaps my boiling is cooked for me. and that is the reason he has waked me," he said, and set down his kettle, and taking a stick he found it full of bones only. Then he said, "Indeed the meat has all fallen off," and so he took a spoon and dipped it out, but there was nothing but bones. Then said he, "Why, my oŋze, I thought that I told you to inform me if any one came. I will surely punish you." So saying he gathered much wood and put on the fire, and when the fire burned fiercely he turned his oŋze to it, and there stood holding it open, although it squirmed even in the death struggle, and then turned it over, so that finally, they say, it fell down a blackened mass and lay there dead.

This is the myth of Uŋktomi and the Bad Songs.[1]

---

[1] This is a very free rendering of the original. See p. 112, l. 20: "So this myth is called, 'The Bad Little Songs.'" Lines 21, 22 should have been translated: "When I was a little boy I used to hear this (myth) very often; but it has been more than twenty years since I have heard it."—J. O. D.

TASIŊTA–YUKIKIPI.

WRITTEN IN DAKOTA BY M. RENVILLE.

Iŋvuŋ kakeħ: Kośka eće topapi, ḳa waŋźi Hakekena ećiyapi; hena
Behold thus: Young-men alone were four, and one Hakaykayna was-called; these
tipi keyapi. Hećen tohan wotihni yapi kta eća waŋźi hakakta kiŋ he ti
dwelt they say. So when to-hunt they-go would when one youngest the that house
awaŋhdagkiyapi ḳa hećiyapi ećee: Misuŋ, tokiya ye śni, owaŋźi yaŋka wo,
to-watch-they-caused-him and this-said-to always: My-brother nowhere go not, in-one-place be thou
eyapi, ḳa hećen wotihni iyayapi eće. Hećen taŋyaŋ ti awaŋhdaka ećee.
they said, and so hunting they-went always. Thus well house his-own-watched always.
Hećen ti haŋska waŋ nina haŋska otipi, tuka waḳiŋ kiŋ ti-wihdukśaŋ
Thus house long a much long in they dwelt, but packs the house around
ićiyahdaskiŋ hiyeya keyapi. Ḳa nakuŋ taŋkata kiŋ iś woćaŋahde kiŋ
piled-on-each were they say. And also without the it scaffolds the
hiyeya keyapi; taku woteća oćaźe kiŋ aŋpetu eća ahdi yuke nakaeś nina
were they say; what animals kinds the day when brought- wore indeed, very
home
waśećapi keyapi.
rich-they-were they say.
Uŋkaŋ ake wotihni iyayapi ḳa Hakekena ti awaŋhdaka tuka ićomni
Then again hunting they-went and Hakaykayna house his-own-watched but weary
ḳehaŋ waŋ sag bakse i; tuka siha taku ićapa, ḳa nina yazaŋ ḳehaŋ hdićiu,
when arrow green to cut went; but foot something stuck in, and very sore when started-
home,
ḳa hdi ḳehaŋ hdaśdoka: uŋkaŋ iŋyuŋ hokśiyopa waŋ wiŋyaŋ e kaśdog
and come home when pulled-out-his: and behold baby a girl that pulling-out
iću keyapi. Uŋkaŋ Hakekena nina ićaŋte śića yaŋka. Śina waŋ iyapemni
he took they say. And Hakaykayna very heart bad was. Blanket a he-wrapped
around
ḳa heyata ehnaka. Hećen inina yaŋka. Tokiŋ ićage ćeś, ećiŋ; hećen
and behind placed. Thus quiet was. Oh that grow may, he-thought; so
ćaŋte śića yaŋka, ećen ćiŋćɯ kiŋ owasiŋ wotihni hdipi. Hećen hdipi eća
heart bad was, until his brothers the all hunting came home. So they-come- when
home
nina wiyuśkiŋ eće, tuka ećeće śni, heoŋ ćiŋćɯ kiŋ taku ićan sića iyukćaŋpi,
very he rejoiced always, but like-that not, therefore brothers- the something heart bad they-judged,
his
ḳa hećiyapi: Misuŋ, tokeća taku ićaŋte niśića; tuwe taku ećanićoŋ hećiŋhaŋ
and this said to: My-brother. why what heart you-bad: who what has-done-to-you if
uŋkokiyaka po, eyapi. Uŋkaŋ, Hiya, tuwena taku ećamićoŋ śni, tuka
us-tell, they-said. And, No, no one something has-done-me not, but
taku waŋmdaka, uŋkaŋ iyomakiśiće ća inina maŋke. Uŋkaŋ, He taku he,
something I-have-seen, and I-am-sad and silent I-am, And, That what ?
eyapi.
they said.

115

Uŋkaŋ, Ćiŋye, owasiŋ idadapi ķehaŋ ićomamni ećen waŋ sag yukse
And,   Brothers,   all   you were gone when   I-was-weary so-that arrows green   cut

wai, tuka siha ćamape, ķa nina mayazaŋ ķehaŋ wahdićn; ķa wahdi ķehaŋ
I went, but foot me-pierced, and very me-sore   when I-started-home; and I-came-home when

wahdaśdoka, uŋkaŋ hokśiyopa waŋ wakaśdoka, uŋkaŋ wiŋyaŋ naće;
I-pulled-off-my-own. and   child   a   I-pulled-out,   and   girl   may-be;

uŋkaŋ, Tokiŋ ićaġe ćeś, epća; uŋkaŋ heoŋ iyomakiśića će, eya.   Uŋkaŋ
and,   Oh that grow may, I thought; and therefore I-sad-am   , he said.   And

ćinću kiŋ, Misuŋ, tukte e he, eyapi ķehaŋ ićn ķa wićakipazo.
brothers-his the, My brother, which is it ? they said when, he-took and showed-it-to-them.

Uŋkaŋ ićiyaza kiciću yekiyapi ķa, E, tokiŋ ićaġe ćeś, eyapi.   Uŋkaŋ
Then   one-to-other gave each they caused and, E, oh that it grow may, they said.   And

ake Hakekena heya heyapi: Hopo, ćiŋye, ti ahmihbe uŋyaŋpi kta će,
again Hakaykayna this said, they say: Come ye, brothers, house whirl around we cause will ,

eya, keyapi. Hećen ićupi ķa tićeśka kiŋ ohna kaħoya iyeyapi.   Uŋkaŋ
he said, they say. Then they took and house-top the through whirling they sent it.   And

ohmihmaŋ hiyaye ća iħpaya.   Uŋkaŋ hokśiyopa waŋ sdohaŋhaŋ ćeya tin
whirling   it went and fell down.   And   baby   a   creeping   crying house-
                                                                                       in

hiyu keyapi. Tuka ake ićupi ķa ećen iyeyapi; uŋkaŋ hehan wićiŋyaŋna
it came, they say. But again they took and so threw it;   and   then   girl

waŋ mani tin hiyu. Tuka ake ićupi ķa ećen iyeyapi.   Uŋkaŋ wićiŋyaŋna
a walking house in came.   But again they took and so threw her.   Then   girl

ćaŋ ade yuha tin hiyu ķa aoŋpa. Tuka ake ićupi ķa ećen iyeyapi—
wood-to-burn having house in she came and laid-on.   But again they took and so threw—

itopa iyeyapi; uŋkaŋ hehan wikośka waŋ ćaŋ ķiŋ hdi, ķa hiŋśka hduśke
the fourth time they   and   then young woman a wood carrying came, and strap   unbound
threw;   home   her own

ća tin hiyu ķa hiyotaŋka.
and house in came and   sat down.

Uŋkaŋ, Iho, taku uŋyaŋpi kta hwo, eyapi.   Uŋkaŋ waŋźi heya:
Then,   Come, what we-have-her shall ? they said.   And   one this-said:

Misuŋka iye he iyeya e hduze kta će, eya.   Tuka Hakekena heya: Hiya,
My-brother he this found he take-her shall ? , he said.   But Hakaykayna this said: No

hećetu kte śni će, eya. Uŋkaŋ eća taku uŋyaŋpi kta hwo, eyapi, ķa
that-so shall not , he said. And   then what we-have-for shall ? they said, and

wowahećoŋ waŋźikśi kapi; tuka Hakekena wićada śni.   Eća misuŋ, taku
relationships several meant; but Hakaykayna willing not. Then my brother, what

uŋyaŋpi kta yaćiŋ he, eyapi.   Uŋkaŋ, De uŋkiyohakam ićaġa, heoŋ
we have her will you want ? they said.   Then, This us-after   grew, therefore

taŋkśiuŋyaŋpi kta će, eya.   Uŋkaŋ, He hećetu će, eyapi, ķa ćatku kiŋ en
younger sister we have will , he said.   And,   That is fitting , they said, and back part the in

ohehdepi kićaġapi ķa ohna ehnakapi. Hećen wipata wayupika, nakaeś
bed   for-her-made and, on   placed her.   And-so embroidering skillful,   indeed

waŋźu ķa haŋpa ķa isaŋ ożuha wićiŋ ko ipata wićakićaġe nakaeś
quivers and moccasins and knife sheaths, straps also embroidered them for she made indeed

nina iyuśkiŋpi, ķa wotihni yapi kta ća hehan, E, misuŋ, taŋkśi taŋyaŋ
much   rejoiced, and hunting they go would when then, See, my brother, sister   well

awaŋyaka wo, eyapi ķa iyayapi ećee, keyapi.
look thou after her, they said and they went always, they say.

Uŋkaŋ ake heyapi ķa iyayapi: tuka ićomni ķehaŋ, Taŋkśi, ito awaŋ-
Then again this they said and they went: but he-tired when, Sister, to   keep

yaka wo, waŋ saka waŋźi bakse mde kta će, eya; ķa hećen iyaya; ķa
thou watch, arrow green one to cut I go will , he said; and so   he-went; and

ećana hdi tuka taŋkśitku en yaŋke śni.   Hdi tuka inahnina toki iyaya
soon came back but sister-his in was not.   He-came- but hurriedly somewhere gone
home

hećiŋ: ḳa hdi ape yaŋka.   Tuka tehaŋ hdi śni ḳehaŋ ode i ḳa kipaŋ uŋ,
he thought: and to come wait- was.   But long time come not when to went and calling was,
home ing home hunt

taku iyeye śni; hećen hdi ḳa akipe yaŋka.   Tuka hdi śni ećen ćinću kiŋ
but found not; so came and waiting for was.   But come not even brothers his the
home home

hdipi, ḳa, Misuŋ, taŋkśi toki iyaya he, eyapi ḳehaŋ ećen owićakiyaka.
came home and, My brother, sister whither gone ? they said when even so them he told.

Uŋkaŋ, Hehehe taŋkśi toki iyaya kta hwo, eyapi, ḳa ape yukaŋpi; tuka
Then, Alas, alas! sister whither go will ? they said, and waiting were; but

ećen okpaza e hećen Hakekena ćeya; hećen ćinću ḳoŋ owasiŋ om ćeya.
so dark was so-that Hakaykayna cried; so brothers his the all with he-cried.

Tuka tokapa kiŋ heya: Misuŋ, ayaśtaŋ po, tokeśta aŋpa kta će, eya: maka
But eldest the this said: My brothers, stop ye crying presently light will be , he said: earth

wita ćistiyena će, he taku kae uŋyućeyapi hećiŋhaŋ waŋuŋyakapi kta će,
island small , that what ever us make cry if we-see will ,

eya, keyapi.
he said, they say.

Hećen waŋna aŋpa ḳehaŋ tate ouye topa kiŋ hena otoiyohi ećen ipi,
Thus now morning when winds source four the those each thus went-to,

ḳa nakuŋ maka kiŋ owaŋćaya uŋpi tuka; hećen iyekiyapi śni nakaeś nina
and also earth the all-over were but; so-that finding their own not indeed very

ćaŋte śićapi ḳa baićismismi ćeya yakoŋpi; ećen okide ayuśtaŋpi. Uŋkaŋ
heart bad, and cutting themselves crying were; until to hunt they ceased. Then
their own

kaketu: Hakekena aŋpetu ećä manin ćeya okawiŋġa uŋ ećé, ake manin
thus it was: Hakaykayna day when abroad crying going around was always, again abroad

ćeya uŋ ećen iśtiŋma; uŋkaŋ iŋyuŋ oġuŋġa uŋkaŋ toki tuwe ćeya nahoŋ,
crying was until he slept; and behold he waked and somewhere someone crying he heard,

tuka taŋyaŋ nahoŋ śni ḳehaŋ paha waŋ tehaŋwaŋkaŋtuya kiŋ akan inaźiŋ,
but well heard not when hill a very-high the upon he stood,

uŋkaŋ iŋyuŋ winohiŋća waŋ toki ćeya wiwakoŋza niyaŋ nahoŋ: Timdo,
and behold woman a somewhere crying wailing out breathed he heard: Brothers,

Tasiŋtayukikipi ewićakiyapi ḳoŋ, timdo, wasasmayapi ḳoŋ, maka tom
Tasintayookeekeepee them called that were, brothers, you-thought-much-of-me the, seasons four

iyotaŋ iyewakiye, eyaniyaŋ, nahoŋ.   Uŋkaŋ, E toke taŋkśi hee se, eye, ća
hard I find it, she cried out, he heard.   And, Well indeed sister this-is it he said, and
seems,

hećen ćeya ku, ḳa ećen hdi nakaeś ake ćiŋću ḳoŋ om ćeyaya. Uŋkaŋ,
so crying return, and so he came indeed again brothers his the with cried often. And,
back

Ćiŋye, ayaśtaŋpi ḳa wohaŋ po, wahaŋpi uŋyatkaŋpi kta će, eya.   Hećen
Brothers, stop ye and cook ye broth we drink will , he said. So

wohaŋpi ḳa wotapi, uŋkaŋ hehan Hakekena, heya: Ćiŋye, tuwe Tasinta
they cooked and ate, and then Hakaykayna this said: Brothers, who Tasinta

yukikipi ewićakiyapi he eye.   Uŋkaŋ tokapa kiŋ he heya: Oyate hiyeye
yookeekeepee them-called ? he said. Then eldest the that this said: People all

ćiŋ uŋkiśnana wića ećé uŋkićaġapi e heuŋkićiyapi do, eya.   Uŋkaŋ,
the we alone men only we-grew therefore this-to-us-they-say , he said. And,

Tokeća heha he, eyapi.   Uŋkaŋ, Winohiŋća waŋ ćeya wiwakoŋze ća
Why this you say ? they said. And, Woman a crying wailed and

heya niyaŋ nawahoŋ će, eya.   Uŋkaŋ, Hehehe taŋkśi hee sećé do, eyapi,
saying aloud I heard , he said. Then, Alas, alas! sister that-is it seems , they said,
that

ḳa peta enen inaźiŋpi.   Tuka Hakekena, Ćiŋye, ayaśtaŋ po, tokeśta taŋkśi
and fire in in they stood.   But Hakaykayna, Brothers, cease ye crying presently   sister

hee e nahaŋḳiŋ ni hećiŋhaŋ waŋna waŋuŋhdakapi kta naćeća će, eya.
that-is until-now lives if   now   we-see-ours   will perhaps , he said.

Hećeŋ waŋna aŋpa ḳehaŋ yapi ḳa etaŋhaŋ nahoŋ ḳoŋ en om inaźiŋ. Ho,
So   now morning when they went and whence he-heard the in with he stood.   Yes,

detaŋhaŋ nawahoŋ će, eya.   Uŋkaŋ ake eya niyaŋ: Timdo, Tasiŋta
from here I-heard it . he said.   And again said it aloud: Brothers, Tasinta

yukikipi ewićakiyapi ḳoŋ, Timdo wasasmayayapi ḳoŋ, maka tom iyotaŋ-
yookeekeepee who were called, Brothers you-who-cared-for-me seasons four very hard

iyewakiye, eya niyaŋ nahoŋpi.   Uŋkaŋ, E, taŋkśi hee seće do, eyapi ḳa
I find it, she cried out they heard.   Then, Well sister that is it seems , they said and

ćeyapi.   Tuka, Ayaśtaŋ po, tokeśta aŋpetu haŋkeya taŋkśi waŋuŋhdakapi
they cried.   But, Stop ye crying, presently day half sister we-see-ours

kta će, Hakekena eye ća, Miye tokaheya waŋwahdake kta će, eye ća,
shall , Hakaykayna eye ća, I first I see her my own will , he said, and

wiyuśkiŋśkiŋna ićićage ća en i, ḳa taŋkśitku ḳoŋ huha topa kiŋ owasiŋ
chickadeedee made himself and in went, and sister his the limbs four the all

okataŋ waŋka en i; uŋkaŋ ite kiŋ haŋahohoya waŋka e waŋhdaka e
fastened lay to [or he and face the broken out [she lay] thus he saw her, then
          there] came;   was   his own

hecen en iyahaŋ tuka timdoku waŋźi hee kećiŋ śni nakaeś heye:
so (there) he alighted but her brothers one that was she not indeed this said:
    in   thought that

Wiyuśkiŋśkiŋna, timdo waŋwićawahdaka uŋkaŋś ćekpa [lit: navel] ićipate
Chickadeedee, my brothers I could see them, my own if breast   I-you-
                                                                      embroider

kta tuka, eya.   Uŋkaŋ wiyuśkiŋśkiŋ ḳoŋ, Taŋkśi, de miye do, eya.
would but, she said.   And chickadeedee the. Sister, this is I , he said.

Uŋkaŋ, Timdo, uŋkiyahde kta, eya.   Tuka, Tokeśta taŋkśi; waŋna
And, Brother, we-go-home will she said.   But, Presently sister; now

iyeuŋniyaŋpi će, eya, keyapi.   Taŋkśi, taŋyaŋ wohdaka wo, eya. Uŋkaŋ,
we-you-have-found he said, they say.   Sister, well tell-your-story, he-said.   Then,

Timdo de ptaŋpi e amahdipi će, eya keyapi.   Maka kiŋ mahen taŋhaŋ
Brother the otters they brought-me-home, she said, they say.   Earth the within from

ḳa ayapi ḳa ećen maŋka ćiŋ etoopta yahdogyapi ḳa ohna yumahen-imaćupi
dig- they came and even I was the towards they gnawed a hole, and through dragged-me inside
ging

ḳa maka kiŋ ećen paohduta iyeyapi nakaeś, heoŋ iyemayayapi śni će eye
and earth the like hole stopped they made indeed, therefore me-you-find not she said

ća ćiŋću en wićahdi, keyapi.   Taŋkśi hee će, eye ća om en ya.   Uŋkaŋ
and brothers his to them he came they say.   Sister that is, he said and with to went.   And
home,

tihaŋska kakiyotaŋna iyeya haŋ e en itaŋkan taŋkśitkupi ḳoŋ huha topa
house long in that direction extending stood that there outside sister-theirs the limbs four

kiŋ owasiŋ okataŋ oŋpapi e en ipi.   Uŋkaŋ heya: Timdo, waŋna maka
the all fastened placed that there came.   Then she this said: Brothers, now seasons

tom den iyotaŋ iyekiya maŋka, tuka ni waŋmayahdakapi kiŋ he taku
four here experiencing difficulty I-am, but alive you (pl.) see me, your own the that some-
                                                                                        thing

waŋźi oŋ hećeće ćiŋ he oćićiyakapi kta će, eya keyapi.   Ptaŋ kiŋ de oćaźe
one for that-so the that I-you-tell will , she-said they say.   Otters the this kinds

zaptaŋpi će; waŋźi śa, waŋźi to, waŋźi źi, ḳa waŋźi ska ḳa waŋźi sapa he
are five one red, one blue, one yellow, and one white and one black this

oŋ timdo dehaŋ ni maŋka će.   Tohan hogaŋ ohaŋpi huhu kiŋ kadapi ća
by brothers now alive I-am.   When fish they boiled bones the threw out when

wahaŋpi kate ćiŋ huhu ko akada akaśtaŋ-iyemayaŋpi eće; hećen kate ćiŋ
broth   hot the bones also emptied on   they-poured out on me   always; so-that hot the

oŋ maśpaŋ, ḳa huhu kiŋ iś omakasdate ćiŋ oŋ ite kiŋ mahdi kiŋ demaćeća
by I-was-burnt, and bones the that me stuck in the by face the me-sore, the this me such:

 će: tuka tohaŋ ptaŋ sapa kiŋ u ḳa hoġaŋ hu kiŋ kada kta ća ćonića ḳa
but when otter black the came and fish bones the throw out would then   meat and

haŋpi ko oŋġe iyohnagmakiya eće ḳoŋ oŋ ni waŋmayadakapi; heoŋ ptaŋ
broth also some put in my mouth always that for alive you see me, your own   therefore otter

waŋ sape ćiŋ he ni waćiŋ će, eya, keyapi. Tohan htayetu ća hehan waŋna
a black the that alive I want , she said, they say. When night when then now

wihni aku eće eća śa kiŋ he ku ća wakaŋhdi śa e tiyoboġaġa eće, ḳa to
hunting come always then red the that comes then lightning red it is house shines always, and blue
home   through

kiŋ he ku eća wakaŋhdi kiŋ to e tiyoboġaġa eće; ḳa zi kiŋ ku ća
the that comes when lightning the blue that house glints through always and yellow the comes when

wakaŋhdi zi e tiyoboġaġa eće, ḳa ska kiŋ ku ća wakanhdi ska e tiyo-
lightning yellow that house shines in always, and white the comes when lightning white that house

boġaġa eće, eya.
illumes always, she-said.

Uŋkaŋ waŋna timdoku kiŋ ćaŋhpi ićićaġapi tihaŋska kiŋ tiyopa
And   now.   brothers hers the war clubs made for themselves house long the door

anokataŋhaŋ inaźiŋpi: uŋkaŋ waŋna wakaŋhdi śa kiŋ e tiyoboġaġa, uŋkaŋ
both sides stood: and now lightning red the that house illumed, and

ptaŋ śa ḳoŋ hee pa tin uye ća, Wati takumna, eya, tuka kaṭa ehpeyapi ḳa
otter red the that is head house pushed and, My house smells, he said, but they beat him to death and
                                                                        in

tiyoyusdohaŋ ićupi. Tuka ake wakanhdi to e tiyoboġaġa, ḳa to kiŋ, Wati
house into they dragged him. But again lightning blue that house lighted, and blue the, My house

takumna, eya hiŋhda pa tin uya, tuka kaṭa ehpeyapi ḳa tiyoyusdohaŋ
smells, saying suddenly head house in thrust, but they beat him to death and dragged him in-

ićupi. Tuka ake wakaŋhdi zi e tiyoboġaġa, uŋkaŋ ptaŋ zi e, Wati takumna,
to the But again lightning yellow that house illumed, and otter yellow that, My smells
house.   house

eya pa tin uya, tuka kaṭa ehpeyapi ḳa tiyoyusdohaŋ ićupi. Ake wakaŋhdi
saying head house in thrust, but they beat him to death and dragged him into the house. Again lightning

waŋ ska e tiyoboġaġa, uŋkaŋ ptaŋ waŋ ska pa tin uya, tuka kaṭa ehpeyapi
one white that house shined in, then otter one white head house thrust, but they beat him to death
is   in

ḳa tiyoyusdohaŋ ićupi. Hehaŋ ptaŋ sape ćiŋ hee ku, uŋkaŋ, Timdo he
and house in dragging took him. Then otter black the that is came, and, Brothers that

ećoŋ eya e. hećen niyake yuzapi. Hehan taŋkśitkupi ḳoŋ okataŋ he ćiḳoŋ
did it she said that so that alive they took it. Then sister theirs the fastened that was

ikaŋ kiŋ owasiŋ bapsakapi ḳa ite kiŋ hdi ḳoŋ owasiŋ kiyuźaźa ḳa hdokupi.
thongs the all they cut and face the sores the all for washed and brought home.

Ḳa ptaŋ kiŋ nakuŋ. Hećen hdipi hehan iyotaŋ taŋkśitkupi kiŋ taŋyaŋ
And otter the also. So came home then. most sister theirs the well

awaŋhdakapi; ḳa nakuŋ ptaŋ kiŋ niyake taŋyaŋ yuhapi. Tuka ohiŋni
watched over theirs; and also otter the alive well they kept. But always

iyokiśića ḳa ićidowaŋ ća heya eće keyapi: Hepaŋ ćiŋye, Hepaŋ ćiŋye,
sad and sang-himself when this said always, they say: Haypaŋ brothers, Haypaŋ brothers.

oiyakapte tokeća uŋkoŋpi kte epe ćiŋ anamayaġoptaŋpi śni ḳa miye hiŋ
ladle another we use should I said the me you listened to not aud me hair

śića omakaptapi ye, Hepaŋ ćiŋye, Hepaŋ ćiŋye, eya ićidowaŋ ećee.
bad me they have spared, Haypaŋ brothers,. Haypaŋ brothers, saying he sung to himself always.

Uŋkaŋ hećiyapi, keyapi: Taŋyaŋ ećauŋyećonpi e oŋ taŋyaŋ uŋniyuhapi
And this they said to, they say: Well to us you did therefore well we-you-have

uŋćiŋpi, tuka ohiŋni iyonićiśiće kta e hećen niye taku iyonićipi kiŋhaŋ ećen
we wish,   but   always   you sad   will be that 'so   you   what   'please you   if   so

ećanoŋ kta će, ećiyapi; iś tokećiŋ yauŋ kta yaćiŋ kiŋhaŋ ećen yauŋ
you do   shall ,   they said to whether as you   you be will you want   if   so   you-be
                him;   please

kta će, ećiyapi.   Uŋkaŋ, Ho, tokećiŋ wauŋ waćiŋ će, eya keyapi.   Uŋkaŋ,
shall [usu- they said to   And,   Yes, anywhere   I be   I want   ,   he said, they say.   Then,
ally?]   him.

Ho, huŋktiya wo, Wiyohpeyata Wakaŋheźa Ptaŋ enićiyapi kta će, ećiyapi
Yes,   go thou forth,   westward   child   otter   you called   shall [usu- they said
                                                                            ally?]   to him

ka hiyuyapi.   Uŋkaŋ heoŋ dehaŋ ptaŋ sapa ećeedaŋ yuke ćiŋ heoŋ hećetu
and sent him forth.   And   therefore now   otter black   alone   are   the therefore so it is

keyapi.
they say.

NOTES.

1. The name of the myth: Tasiŋta means *Deer's tail*, and from that is applied to
the tail of any ruminating animal. Tasiŋt-ośtaŋ is the name of the upper joint of the
tail where it joins the backbone, and is regarded as a peculiarly nice little piece to
roast. As for yukikipi, it is said to belong to the old language, and they do not
know what it means. One old woman suggests that yukiki means to twist or rub
off. It would then mean deer's-tail-twisted-off. That appears to correspond with the
reason given by the eldest of the brothers. In reply to Hakaykayna's question, Who
were called Tasiŋta yukikipi? he replied, "Of all people we only are males, and hence
are so called."

2. At first one would think that the four young men constituted the household,
and that the youngest of those four was called Hakaykayna. But that is not so.
Hakaykayna was only a boy and is not counted in the *four*. He was the *fifth*, as the
name Hakay would necessarily require.

3. It is opportune to note the use of " misuŋ," *my younger brother*, used by the
brothers in their collective capacity, both in a direct address to, and also in speaking
of, Hakaykayna. Also he uses " ćiŋye," *older brother*, in speaking of and to one or
all of them together. In like manner they use " taŋkśi," *younger sister* (of a man), in
speaking of or to the girl, and she uses " timdo," *older brother* (of a woman), in her
addresses to one or all of them. It is like our use of " brother" and " sister" without
the pronoun " my." But the Dakotas always say " misuŋ " or " misuŋka," and a woman
always says " mićuŋ " and " mitaŋka," *my older sister* and *my younger sister*. The
peculiarities of the language in the uses of brother and sister, whether older or
younger, and whether of a man or woman, are well illustrated in this myth; but in
the translation I have not thought it needful to add the *older* and the *younger*.

4. Everything is possible in a myth, as illustrated by Hakaykayna's suddenly
changing himself into a chickadeedee. Animals always have the gift of speech in
myths.

5. The *wail* of the captive girl in her affliction is very affecting: " Brothers who
are called Tasiŋta yukikipi—brothers who once cared for me tenderly." The word
" wasasya " here used is a very peculiar one, expressing great care and love. The
same is true of the *song* or *wail* of the black caged otter—"Hepaŋ ćiŋye! Hepaŋ
ćiŋye!—Brothers Haypaŋ! Brothers Haypaŋ! You did not listen to me; now I, the

bad-furred one, alone am saved!" Hepaŋ, which means the *second son*, is the sacred name for the otter.—S. R. R.

In the Omaha myth of "The Brothers, Sister, and the Red Bird" (Contr. N. A. Eth., VI, Pt. I, pp. 219–226), the youngest brother finds a sister in the manner described in the Dakota myth. In the myth of "Ictinike, the Brothers, and Sister" (Contr. N. A. Eth., VI, Pt. I, pp. 79–83), the youngest brother finds the sister who had been carried underground by an elk.—J. O. D.

TRANSLATION.

Behold, thus it was: There were four young men and one who was called Hakay-kayna. These lived together. And so it was that when they went hunting they made the youngest one the keeper of the house, and said to him, "My youngest brother, don't go anywhere, stay at home." Saying this they went to hunt, and he watched the house. Now the house they lived in was a very long one, but all around the inside the packs were piled up on each other, and also there were scaffolds on the outside, for every day they brought home all kinds of wild animals, and so they had a great abundance of meat.

And so, on a time, they went out to hunt and Hakaykayna watched the house, but when he was lonesome he went out to cut arrow sticks, and when something pierced his foot that it was very sore he started home. When he reached the house he opened the sore place, and, lo! he took out a girl baby.

And on account of this Hakaykayna, sad of heart, wrapped a blanket around it and laid it back and so was silent. "Oh that it might grow up!" he thought, and so was sad of heart until all his brothers came home from the hunt. He had always been glad when they came home, but it was not so now. They judged something had made him sad, and so they said to him, "My brother, what makes you sad of heart? If anyone has done anything to you, tell us." But he said, "No one has done anything to me, but I have seen what makes me heart-sore and silent." And they said, "What is it?" And he said, "Brothers, when you went away I was lonesome and went out to cut arrow sticks, and something stabbed my foot and it was very sore, so that I came home. When I reached home and took it out, it was a baby that I pulled out; and it was a girl baby, perhaps. 'Oh, that it might grow up!' I thought, and on that account I am heart-sore."

And his brothers said, "Where is it?" So he took it up and showed it to them, and they passed it from one to another, and said, "Oh, that it might grow up!" Then Hakaykayna said, "My brothers, come, let us whirl it around the house." So they took it up and threw it out of the roof hole and it whirled around and fell down. But now it was a creeping baby and came in crying. Again they took it up and whirled it as before, and then she came in walking, a little girl. But again they took her up and threw her, and she came in a girl bringing sticks of wood, which she placed on the fire. But again they took her up and threw her as before. This was the fourth time they whirled her, and then she came with a back-load of wood. She untied the strap and came in the house and sat down.

Then they asked, "What relation shall she be to us?" And one said, "My youngest brother found her, let him take her for his wife." But Hakaykayna said, "No, that shall not be so." And they said, "What then shall be her relation to us?"

and mentioned several terms of relationship. But Hakaykayna did not consent. "What then," they said, "shall we have her for? What do you want?" And he said, "This one came after us, let us have her for younger sister." They all said, "That is the proper thing." So they made her a bed and placed her in the back part of the house.

Now she was very skillful in needle and quill work. She embroidered quivers, moccasins, knife sheaths, and carrying-straps for them, so that they greatly rejoiced.

When they were to go out hunting they said, "Now, my brother, watch over sister well." But when he grew tired, he said, "Now sister, do you watch, I will go and cut a green arrow stick." He went and soon came back, but his sister was not there. He thought she had gone for a little while, and so waited for her to come home. But when she came not for a long while, he went to hunt her. Not finding her, he came in and waited until his brothers came home and said to him, "My brother, where is sister?" When he told them about it, they said, "Alas, alas! where has our sister gone?" And they waited and it became dark, and Hakaykayna cried and the brothers all cried with him.

Then the oldest one said, "My brothers, stop crying, soon it will be morning; this island earth is small; we will then see what has made us cry." So now when the morning came they started out to each of the four winds, and they went all over the earth. And when they found her not, they were very sad and cut off their hair as they wept.

When they had ceased to hunt for her Hakaykayna every day went abroad and walked around crying. One day, after crying around, he fell asleep, and lo! on waking up, he heard someone crying somewhere. But not hearing it distinctly he went to a high hill and stood on it. Then, lo! somewhere he heard a woman wail out in her crying, "Brothers, who are called Tasintayookeekeepee; brothers, who once cared for me tenderly, for four seasons I have had a hard time." This he heard and said, "Well! that seems to be sister somewhere;" and so he started home crying. When he arrived his brothers cried too; but he said, "My brothers, cease and boil the kettle; we will drink some soup." So they cooked and ate. Then Hakaykayna said, "My brothers, who are they who are called Tasintayookeekeepee?" The eldest one answered, "Of all people we only are all males, and hence are so called. But why do you ask that?" And he said, "I heard a woman wail out that as she cried." "Alas, alas! that is probably our sister," they said, and they stood in the fire. But Hakaykayna said, "Brothers, cease; if indeed this is our sister she is alive and we shall perhaps see her again," and he cried.

Now when the morning came they went and stood with him where he had heard the voice. He said, "Yes, this is where I heard it." Then they heard her again saying, "My brothers who are called Tasintayookeekeepee, brothers who cared for me tenderly, for four seasons I have had a hard time." They heard this cry and said, "Yes, this is our sister," and they all cried. But Hakaykayna said, "Stop, we shall indeed see our sister in a part of a day, and I will see her first." So saying he changed himself into a chickadeedee and went in and saw his sister lying with her limbs fastened and her face covered with sores. He alighted by her, but she did not think it was one of her brothers; and so she said, "Chickadeedee, if I could only see my brothers I would embroider your breast around." And the chickadeedee said,

"My sister, it is I." She said, " Brother, let us go home." But he said, "Presently, my sister. We have now found you. Tell all about it." And she said, "Brother, the otters brought me home. They dug from within the earth, and made a hole up to where I was and dragged me in. Then they closed up the hole in the earth so that you could not find me."

When she had said this, he said, "Yes, I will go for my brothers." When he came home to his brothers, he said, "It is our sister." And they went with him. And they came to a house that was stretched out very long, outside of which their sister was placed with her four limbs fastened. Then she said, "My brothers, I have been now four seasons in this suffering state, but I am still alive, as you see me. That is owing to one thing, of which I will tell you. There are five kinds of otters here; one is red, one is blue, one is yellow, one is white, and one is black. It is because of the last one that I am alive, brothers. When they boiled fish and threw out the bones they emptied the bones and the hot soup upon me, so that I am burned by the heat, and the bones pierced me so that my face is all sore. That is the reason of my being so. But when the black otter came to empty out the bones he would put into my mouth some of the meat and of the soup also. On account of that you see me alive. Therefore my desire is that the black otter may live."

"When the evening comes then they return from their hunts. When the red one comes he makes red lightning shimmer through the house; when the blue one comes he lights up the house with blue lightning ; when the yellow one comes he makes yellow lightning shoot through the house; when the white one comes he make white lightning shine through the house."

Now, when her brothers had made themselves war clubs they took their stations at each side of the door of the long house. Now it came to pass when the red lightning gleamed through the house and the red otter put his head in at the door and said, "My house smells of something," then they killed him and drew him inside the house. Then, again, the blue lightning gleamed through the house, and as he said, "My house smells of something," he put in his head, but they killed him and drew him into the house. The yellow lightning gleamed through the house, and the yellow otter, saying, "My house smells of something," pushed in his head, but they killed him and pulled him into the house. By and by a white lightning gleamed through the house and a white otter pushed in his head, but they killed him also and drew him into the house. Then the black otter came home, and the sister said, "That is the one that did it." So they took him alive. Then they cut all the cords that bound their sister and washed the sores on her face, after which they took her and the otter to their home. Now, when they had come home they watched over their sister better, and they took good care of the otter that they saved alive. But he was always sad of heart, and as he sung to himself, he said, "Brothers Haypan! Brothers Haypan! I said we ought to use a different ladle; you did not listen to me, and I, the bad-furred one, alone am saved. Brothers Haypan! Brothers Haypan!"

And they said this to him, " You did well to us, and therefore we want to treat you well, but if you are going to be always sad of heart, you shall do what pleases you; if you want to go where you please, so you shall do." And he said, "Yes, I want to be free to go where I please." And they said to him, "Go, you shall be called the Western Child Otter." And they let him go.

Therefore they say it is that now there are only black otters.

CHEE-ZHON, THE THIEF.[1]

WRITTEN IN DAKOTA BY JAMES GARVIE.

Iŋyuŋ kaken wiwazića waŋ ćiŋhiŋtku kići ti, keyapi. Waŋna
Lo! thus widow one son-hers with dwelt, they say. Now

hokśidaŋ kitaŋna taŋka hehan huŋku kiŋ heya iwaŋġa: Ćiŋś, waŋna
boy little large then mother-his the this said inquiring: My-son now

wićohaŋ duhe kta iyehaŋtu, hećen tukte wićohaŋ iyonićipi kta iyećeca he,
work you-have should it-is-time, so which work please-you will is-like ?

eya. Hehan hokśidaŋ kiŋ iś, Wamanoŋpi s'a, eya. Hehan huŋku kiŋ
she-said. Then boy the he, Thieves, he-said. Then mother-his the

heya: Ćiŋś, wicohaŋ kiŋ he iyotaŋ tehike wada ḳoŋ, eya. Tuka ake
this said: Son, work the that most difficult I esteem that, she said. But again

nakuŋ yuhe kta keya; ḳa heya: Howo eća ina, wanaġi tipi ekta ye ḳa
also have would he-said; and this said: Come now mother, ghosts house to go and

tukte wićohaŋ mduhe kta hećiŋhaŋ iwićawaŋġa wo, eya.
which work I shall if of them inquire thou, he said.

Hehan huŋku kiŋ iyaya. Tuka Ćiźaŋ duzahaŋ nakaeś ohomni iŋyaŋg
Then mother-his the went thither. But Chee-zhon swift indeed around running

iyaye ća iye tokaheya ekta i, ḳa wanaġi kiŋ hewićakiya: Ećiŋ ina den hi
went and he first there ar- and ghosts the this-to-them-said: To-day mother here comes
rived,

ḳa wićohaŋ tukte mduhe kta iniwaŋġapi kiŋhaŋ, wamanoŋpi s'a eya po;
and work which I-have shall inquires of you if, stealing regularly say-ye;

eye ća hdićú ḳa hdi. Hehan itehaŋ hehan huŋku kiŋ ćeya hdi. Hehan
he-said and started and came Then long-after then mother-his the crying came Then
home. home. home.

Ćiźaŋ heya: Ina, taku wićohaŋ maḳupi he, eya. Hehan huŋku kiŋ iś
Chee-zhon this said: Mother, what work me-they-give ? he said. Then mother-his the she

heya: Ćiŋś, wićohaŋ kiŋ he nina tehike wada ḳoŋ, eya. Tuka heya:
this said: Son, work . the that very hard I-esteemed that, she said. But this-he-said:

Howo, ina, inina yanka wo, tokeśta waŋna ećadaŋ wiuŋźiće kta će, eya.
Well, mother, silent be thou, presently now soon we-rich will , he said.

Ḳa hehan tokiya iyaya. Uŋkaŋ ećiyataŋhaŋ śugtaŋka[2] waŋźi ahdi. Ake
And then somewhere he went. And from-thence horse one he-brought- Again
home.

---

[1] Though stories resembling this are found in many countries of the Old World, it has been thought best to retain the story of Cheezhon to show how the Dakota adopt stories of foreign origin. A version of Jack the Giant-killer has been adopted by the Omaha—J. O. D.

[2] Śuktaŋka or Śuŋktaŋka is the usual Santee form of this word.—J. O. D.

tokiya iyaya eća ećiyataŋ pte, ḳaiś tahiŋća ska, ḳaiś taku wanuŋyanpi
somewhere went then from-thence cow, or deer white, or some cattle
hećekćen awićahdi ećee.
thus them-brought- always.
home

Ihnuhaŋnaḣ huŋku otoŋwe ećiyataŋ hdi, uŋkaŋ heya: Ćiŋś, haŋyetu
Suddenly mother-his village from came home, and this said: Son, night
kiŋ de wićaśtayatapi tawićn mazanapćupe tawa kiŋ iyaću śni kiŋhaŋ
the this chief wife-his finger-ring hers the you take not if
haŋḣaŋna wiyotaŋhaŋ kiŋhaŋ pa niyuksapi kta, keyapi, tka eye, ḳa ćeya.
tomorrow noon if head they break off will, they-say, but she said, and cried.
for you

Tuka iyoki śni ḳa heya: Ina, inina yaŋka wo, he takuśni će. Ḳa waŋna
But permitted not and this said: Mother quiet be [sit thou], that nothing-is . And now
ḣtayetu tuka iye wokoyake tawa ḳeya wićaśta iyećen opugitoŋ eća hehaŋ
evening but he clothes his even man like stuffed when then
ćaŋiyamanipi waŋźi kaġa; ḳa hehan waŋna haŋyetu tuka wićaśta kaġe ćiŋ
ladder one made; and then now night but man made the
he ćaŋiyamanipi iyahna iću ḳa ekta i. Hehan ćaŋiyamanipi ećen ehde ća
that ladder with took and there went. Then ladder so placed when
wakaŋtkiya ye ća owaŋye ohena timahen etoŋwaŋ; uŋkaŋ wićaśtayatapi
upward went and window through house-within looked; and chief
kiŋ mazakaŋ ptećedaŋ napanuŋkataŋhaŋ yuha iśtiŋma waŋka. Tuka
the gun short hands-both-with had sleeping lay. But
owaŋye pakokog pawaŋkaŋ-iyeya eća peźi wićaśta kaġe ćiŋ he owaŋye
window rattling shoved-up when grass man made the that window
ohna yuza. Hehan wićaśtayatapi oġuŋġa ḳa kute. Tuka peźi wićaśta
in held. Then chief waked and shot. But grass man
kaġe ćiḳoŋ kiŋ he o, nakaeś kun yuḣpa eḣpeya; ḳa hehan tin iyaya.
made had the that hit, indeed down threw it threw it and then house-in he went.
down away;
Tuka ićuŋhaŋ wićaśtayatapi kte kećiŋ heoŋ kun iyaya. Tuka ićuŋhaŋ
But whilst chief killed he thought therefore down he-went. But in-the-meantime
Ćiźaŋ wićaśtayatapi tawićn kiŋ hećiya: Mazanapćupe kiŋ he hiyu
Chee-zhon chief wife-his the this-said-to: Finger-ring the that to-come
makiya wo, Ćiźaŋ hee śni, tuka wakte će, eya. Uŋkaŋ ḳu; tuka ićn eća
to-me-cause, Chee-zhon that was not, but I-killed , he said. And she-gave; but took when
kun hdićn.
down he-came.
Hehan wićaśtayatapi tin hdićn ḳa tawićn hećiya: Mazanapćupe kiŋ
Then chief house-in came and wife-his this-said-to: Finger-ring the
hiyu makiya wo, Ćiźaŋ hee śni tuka wakte će, eya. Tuka iś heya: Naka
to-come to-me-cause, Chee-zhon that was not but I-killed , he said. But she this-said: But-just
waŋna heha ćeś ćiću sece ćiḳoŋ, eya. E, he Ćiźaŋ ee tka yaḳu do, eya.
now that-you- since I-gave- it seems in the she said. Well, that Chee-zhon was but you-gave- , he said.
said to-you past, it-to-him.
Tuka ićuŋhaŋ waŋna Ćiźaŋ ki, ḳa huŋku kiŋ hećiya: Iho! deće-
But in-the-meantime now Chee-zhon reached- and mother-his the this-said-to: Lo! this-
home
hnana tuka he taku oŋ ćeya yauŋ he eya, ḳa hehan mazanapćupe kiŋ ḳu.
is-all but that some- for crying you were ? he-said, and then finger-ring the gave-
thing her.
Hehan waŋna ake kitaŋna tehaŋ hehan huŋku otoŋwe ekta i, uŋkaŋ
Then now again little long then mother-his town to went and
nakuŋ ake ćeya hdi. Uŋkaŋ Ćiźaŋ heya: Ina, de taku yaka he; de
also again crying came home. And Cheezhon this said: Mother this what you mean ? this

winiziće śni kiŋ heehaŋ kaeś yaceye śni; de winiźića uŋkaŋ ećaŋ ćeya
you rich   not   the   then   even   you-cry not, this you-rich   and   now   crying

vauŋ he, eya.   Hehan huŋku kiŋ heya: Ćiŋś, haŋtuķe wićaśtayatapi kiŋ
you-are ? he-said.   Then mother-his the   this said: Son, now-indeed   chief   the

iye hiŋća wihuwe hi kta keya tuka, eya.   Hehan Ćiźaŋ heya: Ina, iś he
he very to-take-you come will he-said but, she said. Then Cheezhon this said: Mother.this that

taku śni do, eya: ķa hećehnana ćotaŋka ćistiŋna waŋ kaġa yaŋka ća yuśtaŋ.
something not , he said: and that alone   whistle small   one   making was (sat?) whenhe-finished.

Hehan heya: Ina, taśupa waŋźi we okaśtaŋ ķa oŋhohda imahentaŋhaŋ uŋ
Then this said: Mother. gut   one blood pour-in and clothes underneath from wear

wo; hećen tohan hi kiŋhaŋ isaŋ kiŋ de oŋ ćapa ihećiye kta, tokeśta taśupa
thou; so   when he-come if   knife the this with stabbing I-strike-you will, indeed   gut

kiŋ he cawape kta, hećen he we kiŋhaŋ ćikte kećiŋ kta će: eśta hehan
the that I-stab   will. so   that bleed if I-you-kill he-think will : but   then

tohan ćotaŋka kiŋ de mdaźoźo kiŋhaŋ naźiŋ yahidade kta će, eya.   Hehan
when whistle the this I-blow often if   you rise to your feet will , he said.   Then

waŋna wiyotaŋhaŋ hehan wićaśtayatapi kiŋ tin hiyu, tuka huŋku ćapa
now   noon   then   chief   the   the house in came, but mother-his stab

iheya waŋyaka.   Hehan wićaśtayatapi kiŋ heya: Hoeća Ćiźaŋ, winitkotkoka
he-thrust saw.   Then   chief   the   this said: Astonishing Cheezhon, you-fool

ećee śta ake nakahake seećeća, eya.
always although again this-time it seems, he said.

Uŋkaŋ Ćiźaŋ iś heya: De taku yaka he; de miś ina niwakiye kta
And Cheezhon iś heya: This what you mean ?   this I mother I-bring-to-life will

hećamoŋ, eya; ķa ćotaŋkadaŋ kiŋ ehdaku eća ayaźoźo, uŋkaŋ huŋku kiŋ
this-I-do, he said; and whistle (-small) the   took-up his when whistled-on, and   mother-his the

naźiŋ hivaya.   Hehan wićaśtayatapi kiŋ heya: Ćiźaŋ, he mazaska tona
she rose to her feet.   Then   chief   the   this said: Cheezhon. that money how many

ivahdawa he, eya.   Hehan Ćiźaŋ iś heya: Hehe de ota iyopewaye hećen
you count your ? he said.   Then Cheezhon he this said: Alas? this much I-pay-for so
own

wiyopewaya waćiŋ śni će eya.   Ećiŋ miś tohan tuwe ţa eśta niye maśipi
I-sell I-want not , he said. For   I when any-one dead although make command
live   me

kiŋhaŋ de oŋ niwaye kta nakaeś heoŋ tewahiŋda će, eya.   Tuka tona
if   this with I make live will indeed, therefore I-prize-it , he said. But many-as

hiŋća ihdawa eśta iyena ku kta keya.   Hećen mazaska opawiŋge zaptaŋ
very he-counts although so many he-give would, he said.   So   money   hundred   five
his own

kta, keya.   Uŋkaŋ, Ho, eye, ķa ivena ķu ķa akiyahda.
will, he said.   And,   Yes, he said, and so many gave. and took it home.

Hehan oyate owasiŋ wićakićo eća taku waŋźi ećoŋ kta, keya.   Hećen
Then people all them-he-called when something one he-do would, he said.   So

wićaśta itaŋćaŋ ota en hipi.   Hehan waŋna ećoŋ kta keye ćiŋ waŋna
men   chief many there came.   Then   now   do would he-said the   now

iyehaŋtu, hehan tawićiu en hinaźiŋ śi eća he ćape ķa kte eśta ake kiniye
it-was-time,   then wife-his then to-stand com- when that stab and kill although again make live
manded

kta keya, eća ćape ķa kte.   Hehan ćotaŋkadaŋ kiŋ ayaźoźo yaŋka, tuka
would, he said.   then he-stabbed and killed.   Then (small?) whistle the he-blew-on-it (sat) was, but

hećen ţa waŋka waŋke.   Hehan nina ćaŋze hiŋća.
so   dead lying (lay) was.   Then   much heart-hurt very.

Hehan Ćiźaŋ huŋku ećiyataŋhaŋ hdi, ķa, Ćiŋś, haŋhaŋna waŋna,
Then Cheezhon mother-his from-there came-home, and, Son, in-the-morning then

woźuha ohna minin ehpeniyaŋpi kta, keyapi tuka, eya.   Tuka Ćiźaŋ, Ha!
bag   in in-water they-you-throw will, they say but, she said.   But Cheezhon, Ha!

ha! ina, iś he taku śni do eya. Hehan waŋna haŋhaŋna wiyotaŋhaŋ uŋkaŋ
ha! mother, this that some-   not . he said.   Then   now   morning   noon   and
thing

wićaśtayatapi kiŋ hi ećʼa akiyahda. Hehan waŋna kići ki, hehan akićita
chief   the come when took-him home.   Then   now   with went then soldiers
home,

woźuha waŋźi mahen ohnag wićaśi, ķa minin ehpeya wićaśi: ķa waŋna
bag   one   within place them com- and water-in throw-him them com- and now
manded.   manded:

Ćiźaŋ woźuha en ohnaka ķa ayapi ķa ikiyedaŋ aipi, hehan wićaśtayatapi
Cheezhon bag in placed and took and near-to carried him, then   chief

kiŋ, Ito wićakićo ķa akiyahda. Hehan tuwe tahiŋća ska iyaśaśa
the, Hold, them call and take him home.   Then   some one deer white shouting to

nahoŋ. Hehan Ćiźaŋ heya hiŋhda: Wićaśtayatapi ćuŋwiŋtku kići uŋpi
he heard.   Then Cheezhon said this suddenly: Chief   daughter-his with being

waćiŋ śni! Wićaśtayatapi ćuŋwiŋtku kići uŋpi waćiŋ śni! eya yaŋka.
I-want not!   Chief   daughter-his with being I-want not! he-saying (sat) was.

Hehan tahiŋća ska awaŋyake ćiŋ en hi ķa heya: De taku yaka he.
Then   deer   white watched-over the there came and this said: This what you mean ?

Uŋkaŋ heya: He de wićaśtayatapi ćuŋwiŋtku waŋ kići wauŋ kta keyapi,
And this he said: That this   chief   daughter-his one with I-be shall they say,

ķa wićawada śni tuka ekta amayaŋpi će, eya. Uŋkaŋ hećehnana wićaśta
and I-willing not but there me-they-take . he said.   And   immediately   man

kiŋ heya: Howo, miye e mde kta će, eya. Hehan, Koyahaŋna wo ećʼa, eya.
the this said: Well, I that I-go will , he said. Then,   Hurry thou   now, he said.

Hehan wićaśta kiŋ woźuha kohaŋna yuśka iveya, ķa Ćiźaŋ naźiŋ
Then   men   the bag   quickly ʼuntied tore it,[1] and Cheezhon standing

hiyaya; ķa wićaśta kiŋ iśto ohna pahta ehpeya, ećʼa tahiŋća ska wanuŋyaŋpi
ʼwent; and man   the him-now in tied they put him, then deer white tame animals

owasiŋ ćaŋmahen kaham ewićayaya, ķa hećiya un yaŋka.
all   wood-into driving them took. and there was (sat) continued.

Hehan waŋna kitaŋna tehaŋ hehan tahiŋća wanuŋyaŋpi optaye kiŋ
Then   now   little   long   then   deer   tame animals flock the

owasiŋ wićaśtayatapi ti kiŋ en awićahdi, ķa heya: Ho, ćaŋnaŋwapa
all   chief   house the to them-brought-home, and this said: Yes, far-out-in-the-water

ehpemayayapi uŋkaŋś hećiya śugtaŋka totopi ķa tataŋka kiŋ iś he kiŋ
you-me-had-thrown if   there   horse blue-ones and oxen   the they horns the

mazaskazizipi tuka će, eya. Hehan wićaśtayatapi kiŋ heya: Ćiźaŋ, hećeya
golden-ones   but he said.   Then   chief   the this said: Cheezhon, so

wićayaka he, eya. Hehan Ćiźaŋ; Ho, hećeya wićawaka će, eya. Hehan
are you true ? he said. Then Cheezhon. Yes, so   I-am-true   he said. Then

akićita tuwe token okihi minin ehpeićiyapi waŋka. Hehan ećen wićaśtaya-
soldiers whoever so was-able into-water threw themselves (lay) were. Then so   chief

tapi iś eya minin ehpeićiya ķa minin ta, keyapi. Hećen Ćiźaŋ iye ni
he also in the water threw himself and in water died, they say.   So   Cheezhon himself lived

naćeća.
probably.

TRANSLATION.

There was once a widow who had a son. When the boy was well grown his
mother inquired what trade or business would suit him. The boy replied that he
would like to be a robber. The mother said she very much disliked that business.
But the boy repeated that he would have that, and then proposed to his mother to go

---

[1] Iyeya does not mean "to tear," but conveys the idea of forcible or sudden action.—J. O. D.

and ask the spirits. While she was going on this errand he went around and reached the house of spirits first, and he instructed them how to answer his mother.

The mother came home crying. When the boy asked her what employment had been assigned to him, she had to reply, "The work that I think difficult." But the boy said, "Never mind, mother, soon we will be rich." Then he went away and brought home a horse; and again he brought home cows, sheep, and all kinds of domestic animals.

One day his mother came home from the village crying, and told her son of a plan to take off his head the next day at noon if he did not get possession of the chief's wife's finger ring. He told her to be quiet, and said, "That is nothing." Then in the evening he took his own clothes and stuffed them. He made a ladder, and taking the stuffed man and the ladder he went to the chief's house. The ladder he placed upright and looked in at a window. The chief was lying asleep with a pistol in his hands. As the young man shoved up the window he held in it the grass man. The chief was waked by the noise and fired his pistol. Cheezhon, which was the young man's name, let fall the grass man, and while the chief went to seek the man he supposed he had killed, Cheezhon made his way to the chamber, and said to the chief's wife, "Hand me the finger ring; that was not Cheezhon, but I have killed him." Whereupon she gave it, and he took it home. Afterwards the chief came in and said to his wife, "Hand me the finger ring; that was not Cheezhon, but I have killed him." To which she replied, "It was but just now you said that, and I gave up the ring." To which he said, "Really, that was Cheezhon, and you gave it to him after all!"

In the meantime Cheezhon reached his home, and saying to his mother, "See, this is what you cried for," he handed her the ring.

Sometime after this his mother came home from the village again crying, when Cheezhon said, "Mother, what do you mean? When we were not rich you did not cry, but now we are rich you are always crying." On which the mother said, "My son, the chief said that he himself would come and take you." But Cheezhon made light of this also, and said, "Mother, that is nothing." In the meantime he went on making a small whistle, which he finished. Then he told his mother to fill a large entrail with blood and put it under her clothes. "When he comes," said he, "I will stab you with this knife, but I will only run it into the entrail, but as there will be blood he will think I have killed you; and when I blow on this whistle you will stand up again."

On the morrow at noon the chief came and saw Cheezhon stab his mother. He was much astonished, and said, "Cheezhon, you were always a fool, but this beats all the rest." But Cheezhon replied, "What do you mean by saying that? I have done this that I may bring my mother to life again." So he took up his whistle and blew upon it, and his mother stood up. The chief then offered him any sum he might name for the whistle. But Cheezhon said, "I have paid a great sum for the whistle, and I do not want to sell it. When anyone asks me to bring back to life one who is dead, I can do it by means of this, so I value it very highly." But the chief repeated that he would give him any sum, and Cheezhon named five hundred dollars.

This was given and the whistle taken home. Then the chief called all the people together, and said he would do a thing. Then all the principal men came, and the chief proposed to stab his wife, kill her, and then restore her to life. When he had stabbed her and killed her he blew his whistle over her to bring her to life, but she lay there dead.

He was thereupon much enraged. Then Cheezhon's mother came home and told him that in the morning they planned to put him in a bag and cast him in the water. But he laughed and said, "Mother, that is nothing."

It came to pass the next day at noon the chief came and took Cheezhon home with him, and commanded his soldiers to put him into a bag and cast him into the water. And when they had placed him in the bag and carried him along and were now near to the place, the chief said, "Call them and take him home."

Just then Cheezhon heard some one calling sheep, whereupon he cried out, "I do not want to live with the chief's daughter! I do not want to live with the chief's daughter!" So the shepherd came and said, "What do you mean?" Said Cheezhon, "They say I must live with a daughter of the chief, and I am not willing; nevertheless, they are taking me there." The shepherd replied, "I will go." So they tore open the bag, released Cheezhon, and bound the other man whom they put in the bag.

In the meantime the flock of sheep was scattered, and Cheezhon, having his liberty, drove them to the woods and there kept them.

After some time he brought the whole flock back to the chief's house and said, "If you had thrown me far out into the water there would have been blue horses and oxen with horns of gold." Then the chief said, "Are you indeed telling the truth?" And Cheezhon said, "I am indeed telling the truth." Then the soldiers, as fast as they were able, cast themselves into the water (to find the blue horses and the oxen with horns of gold). And the chief also, they say, threw himself into the water and was drowned. Thus Cheezhon saved himself.

THE YOUNGER BROTHER; OR, THE UNVISITED ISLAND.

WRITTEN IN DAKOTA BY M. RENVILLE.

Oyate waŋ kaken tipi. Uŋkaŋ en wićaśtayatapi waŋ ćiŋća yamni,
People one so lived. And then chief one children three,

hena hokśinćaŋtkiyapi. Nom wićapi ķa waŋźi wiŋyaŋ. Uŋkaŋ tokapa kiŋ
these boys beloved. Two males and one female. Then eldest the

he tawićutoŋ, hećen suŋkaku kiŋ hduha. Uŋkaŋ haŋkaku kiŋ ena sićeću
that wife-his-took, so that younger-brother-his the he-had his own. Then sister-in-law-his the then brother-in-law-hers

kiŋ nagiyeya: Uŋwaŋke kte, eya keś, Hoȟo, ćiŋyewaye ćiŋ miśnana
the troubled: We-two-lie-together will, she-said although, No indeed, older-brother-mine the me-alone

temahiŋda, tokeŋ iwakiȟaȟa kta he, eya ećee, keyapi.
thinks-much-of-me, how I-make-him-ashamed shall ? he said always, they say.

Uŋkaŋ kaketu: Winyaŋ ķoŋ ćaŋ ķiŋ i tin hdiću ķa heya; Śiće, ito
And thus-it-was: Woman the wood carry went house came home in and this said; Brother-in-law lo

śiyo ķeya kaŋ yukaŋpi će, waŋźi makio· ye, eya. Tuka, Ho, miye
grouse many yonder are , one shoot-for-me, she said. But, Not-so, I

nahaȟiŋ wićaśta waoka hemaća śni, tuwe tokeća kute yaśi śni, eya. Tuka
as-yet man good-shooter such-me not, some one else shoot you-com-mand not, he said. But

ćiŋću kiŋ, Waŋźi kio wo, eye, e hećen waŋhiŋkpe ikikću ķa iyaye ça waŋźi
brother-for-her the, One for-her-kill. said, that so that arrows he took and went and one

kio, ķa, Hee će, iću wo, eye, ça ićuŋom iyaya. Uŋkaŋ winyaŋ ķoŋ ku ķa
for-her-killed, and, That is it, take it, he said, and to another-place went. Then woman the is re-turning and

ćeya hdi, ķa hihnaku hećiya: Nisuŋka waćiŋtaŋka ća ohiŋni nagiyemayaŋ
crying has come home, and husband-her this-said-to him: Your younger brother persistent when always troubles me

će, epa ća, ćeţuŋmayahda ķoŋ, dena ećamaoŋ će, eye ça śiyo siha kiŋ oŋ
, I say when, you-me-disbelieve the, these he-has-done-to-me, she said and grouse claws the with

ćaŋna kiŋ owaŋćaya hduȟdaȟdate ça kipazo. Uŋkaŋ hećen wićada, ķa
thighs the all over she-scratched-herself. and showed-him. And so he-believed-her, and

heya: Uŋktomi kićo ya po,[1] eya. Hećen Uŋktomi hi. Uŋkaŋ, Uŋktomi,
this said: Uŋktomi to-call-him go ye, he said. So Uŋktomi came. Then, Uŋktomi,

misuŋka wita-ipi-śni ekta eeȟpeya wo, hećen taŋkśi duze kta će, eya.
my-younger-brother island they-go-to-not at there-take-and-leave, so sister-mine you have shall , he said.

---

[1] This use of the plural for the singular (ya wo, *go thou*) occurs now and then in myths.—J. O. D.

130

Hećen waŋna kośka ķoŋ hdi, uŋkaŋ hećen Uŋktomi heye: Suŋg,
So now young man the came home, and thus Uŋktomi this said: Brother,

ito wiŋtka pahi uŋye śni, eya. Tuka, Hiya, miye-na-hiŋ, tuwe kaśta
come eggs to gather we-two-go not, he said. But, No, I-am-alone, some one else

kići de śni, eya. Uŋkaŋ ćinćú kiŋ, Kići ya wo, eya. Uŋkaŋ hećen
with you-go not, he said. And brother-his the, With him go thou, he said. Then thus

kići iyaya. Wata waŋ en opapi ķa wita kin ekta ipi, ķa wiŋtka pahipi:
with he-went. Boat one in they-followed and island the to they came, and eggs gathered:
him

ķa waŋna wata kiŋ ożuyapi, uŋkaŋ kośka kiŋ heya; Waŋna uŋhde
and now boat the they filled, then young-man the this said; Now we-go-home

kte, eya e hećen waŋna wata kiŋ en okipapi. Uŋkan Uŋktomi heya:
will, he said that so now boat the in they went. Then Uŋktomi this said:

Suŋg, kana eeś waśteśte će, ehake ićú ye, eya. Tuka, Hi, waŋna de ota kiŋ,
Brother, those there are-very-good, the last take, he said. But, Why, now this much the,

eya. Tuka Uŋktomi kitaŋ, uŋkaŋ iyaye ća ićú, tuka Uŋktomi wata kiŋ
he said. But Uŋktomi persisted, and he-went and got them, but Uŋktomi boat the

paćaŋnaŋ iyeye ća hdićú. Uŋkaŋ, Hi, Uŋktomi, wata he au ye, eya.
head-out turned and started Then, Fie, Uŋktomi, boat that bring please, he said.
home.

Tuka, Tuwe, tokenken ţenićiya he, eya. Hi, au ye, eya. Tuka wićada
But, Who, in-some-ways you kill ? he said. Fie, bring please, he said. But he was
yourself willing

śni. Uŋkaŋ, Uŋktomi, wata kiŋ he au wo, uŋki kiŋhaŋ taŋkśi duze kte do,
not. Then, Uŋktomi, boat the that bring, we-reach- if sister-mine you shall .
home have

eya. Uŋkaŋ, De iś he iyape makiyapi oŋ hećamoŋ se, eya. Tuka
he said. And, That is it that wait-for-they-cause-me for this-I-do as if, he said. But

keya yaŋka; uŋkaŋ taku śića hdute śi, uŋkaŋ ećoŋ. Hehaŋ Uŋktomi
this he-was; then what bad his-own- com- and he did it. Then Uŋktomi
saying [or, he sat] to-eat manded,

iha. Uŋkaŋ, Waḣte-śni śića mayahnaye do, eye ća ake ośtehda. Uŋkaŋ,
laughed. Then, Good-not bad you-have-deceived , he said and again he cursed him. Then,

Huŋktiya wo, Ćapoŋg taŋka waŋdake kte do, eya. Tuka ake ośtehda.
Go thou away Musquito-large you-see will , he said. But again he cursed him.

Uŋkaŋ, Huŋktiya wo, Mato waŋdake kte do, eya. Ake eya, uŋkaŋ,
Then, Go thou away Gray-bear you-see will , he said. Again he said it, when,

Huŋktiya wo, Iśpa-tahiŋśpa waŋwićadake kte do, eya. Tuka ake eya:
Go thou away Arm-awls them-you-see will , he said. But again he said it:

Uŋkaŋ, Huŋktiya wo, Taśuŋke-ota waŋdake kte do, eya. Tuka ake
Then, Go thou along His-dogs-many you see will , he said. But again

eya. Uŋkaŋ, Huŋktiya wo, Wiŋyaŋ-noŋpapika waŋwićadake kte do, eya,
he said it. Then, Go thou away Women-two them you see will , he said,

ķa hećen kihda.
and so went home.

Uŋkaŋ kośka kiŋ iś hećen iyaye, uŋkaŋ waŋkan taku ḣmuŋyaŋ u
Then young man the he so went, and from above something whizzing coming

nahoŋ ķehaŋ ćapoŋpa¹ waŋ minin iḣpaye ća oḣtateya eḣpeićiya. Uŋkaŋ
he heard when mosquito one in water fell, and underneath it he-threw-himself. And

iŋyuŋ taku waŋ pehaŋgina se hinaźiŋ ķa heya: Taku den ośkaŋśkaŋ e
behold something one crane-brown like coming stood and this said: What hen moving often that

en hibu ķoŋ toki iyaye se eye ća, Kozaŋ den uŋ kiŋhaŋ kaken ećamoŋ
to[or I come the [in some- has gone as if he said and, Indeed here was if so [in that I do
there] the past] where manner]

---
¹Ćapoŋka is the usual form. Ćapoŋg is a contraction of this.—J. O. D.

kta tuka, eye, ćą ćapoŋpa ḳoŋ pasu oŋ apa.   Tuka pasu oyatake, hećen
would but, he said, and mosquito the   bill with struck.   But   bill   he stuck in,   so-that
                            [aforesaid]

iye itkom kte, ḳa pasu bakse ćą yųha iyaya.   Ake taku nahoŋ; uŋkaŋ
he in-turn killed him, and bill cut-off and having went on.   Again something he heard;   and

mato waŋ hoyeya u.   Tuka ake wakanaṭeca ićićage ćą mini en waŋka.
gray-bear one sending-his-voice came.   But again mysterious-dead made-himself and. water in lay.

Uŋkaŋ, Taku den ośkaŋśkaŋ uŋ e wau ḳoŋ, eyaya.   Mato ḳoŋ hinaźiŋ ća
Then,   What here moving often was when I was coming, he repeated. Gray bear the came and when
                                                                              [aforesaid] stood

heya; Kae kakeś wate kta, eya; ḳa hoġaŋ ṭeća ḳoŋ iyohnag iveya: tuka
this said; Yonder whatever I-eat will. he said; and fish dead the into-his-mouth-took: but

mdaska nakaeś iyoha uŋma en itokto ekta iyaye ćą ećen otosa napća.
flat   indeed jaws each in time-about to it-went and thus whole swallowed.

Tuka tezi ekta isaŋ ićų ḳa ćaŋte kiŋ baśpuśpu, ḳa kte, ḳa ćuwi kiŋ bahdoke
But belly in knife he-took and heart the cut-to-pieces, and killed, and side the cut-hole-in

ćą etaŋhaŋ hdićų ḳa nape napin bakse ćą yuha iyaye.   Uŋkaŋ ćaŋku ohn̄a
and from came forth and fore-feet both cut-off and having went.   And   road   in

ćaŋha wokeya waŋ śota izita haŋ e ya ḳehaŋ, Iśpa-tahiŋśpa eye ćiḳoŋ deepi
bark lodge one smoke burning stood to went when, Arm-awls he said that [in these-are
                                                                        the past]

će ećiŋ, ḳa śina yupśuŋka adoksohaŋ ḳa tiyonaśdog iyaye ćą ćatku
he thought, and blanket rolled-up under-arm and tent-went-into and back-part

iyotaŋke ćą heya; Ito uŋćina tipi en wahi kta, eya.   Tuka wakaŋka nom
sat-down and this said; Lo, grandmother house in I-come will, he said.   But old-woman two

tianoŋg yukaŋpi, ḳa tiyopata takitih iyotaŋg heyayapi.   Uŋkaŋ ake naźiŋ
house-each-side were,   and door-at fussing sitting they kept saying.   Then again rose-to

hiyaye ćą, Uŋćina, tipi wahi tuka iyokipipi śni e wahde kta, eya, ćą nasa-
his-feet and, Grandmother house I-came, but they-pleased not when I-go-home will, he said, when blanket-

yupśuŋka yus kihde koŋze ćą tiyopa en ehpeya.   Uŋkaŋ iśpa oŋ napin
bundle holding go-home pretended and door in he-threw it.   And   arm with both

ćapa-iheyapi, tuka śina ećena ćapapi nakaeś saŋpa ćakićipapi ḳa heyapi;
they stabbed-through, but blanket only they stabbed indeed beyond stabbed-each-other and this said;

Ićepaŋśi, mayakte ye, eyapi.   Tuka, Taku denićeća makte waćaŋnipi he;
Cousin,   me you have killed, they said.   But, What like you [you are me-kill you thought ?
                                                           such as this]

eye, ćą napin wićakaṭe ćą iyoopta-iyaya.
he said, and both them-killed and went-onward.

Uŋkaŋ tuwe tokata, Mitaśuŋke wo-wo, eya u niyaŋ.[1]   Suŋg kićoćo u
And some-one ahead, My-dogs come come, saying was calling.   Dog calling was
                                  coming   often com-
                                                                             ing

ḳehaŋ poġe ihduwewe ḳa waŋhiŋkpe kiŋ owasiŋ wekiye ćą ćaŋku kiŋ ohn̄a
when nose made bleed often and arrows the all made-bloody and road the in

yumden-ehpeya ḳa ituŋkam iwaŋka.   Uŋkaŋ mnaźa ḳa inmutaŋka henaos
scattered them and on-his-back lay down.   Then lion and great-lynx these-two

tokaheya en hipi ḳa we kiŋ sdipapi.   Tuka, Uśtaŋ, iyoopta-iyaya po,
first there came and blood the they licked.   But, Stop, go-ye-on-beyond,

wakaŋheźa tuwe oŋśihaŋ ee, eya.   Uŋkaŋ iyoopta iyayapi.   Uŋkaŋ en u
child   who poor is, he said.   And on they went.   And to was
                                                                   coming

ḳa, E, mitakoźa, wita-ipi-śni ekta eehpeyapi keyapi-ḳoŋ he niye he, eya,
and, "See, my-grandchild, island-go-to-not at was-left they-have-told-about that you ? he said,

keyapi.   Huŋktiya wo, mitaśuŋke nom hekta upi će, henaos kaṭe ća
they say.   Go thou along, my-dogs two behind they are , those two kill and
                                        coming

---

[1] Dr. Riggs gives niyaŋ in the dictionary as *audibly, with a loud voice,* and eya niyaŋ as *to say
audibly,* or *with a loud voice.*—J. O. D.

wićayuta wo, eya.　　He Taśuŋke-ota ee: taku maka aśkaŋśkaŋ uŋ kiŋ
them eat thou,.　he said.　This　His-many-dogs　is:　what　earth　on-moving　is　the

iyuḣpa taśuŋkeya keyapi.
all　he-has-it-for-a-dog　they say.

Hećen naźiŋ ḳa iyaya.　　Uŋkaŋ wića nom wohdag upi, tuka napin
So　he-arose　and　went.　　And , raccoons　two　talking　were　but　both
coming.

wićakaṭe ća ḳiŋ iyaya.　　Uŋkaŋ ćaŋḱu ohna ćaŋha wokeya waŋ haŋ e en
them-killed　and carrying went on.　And　road　in　bark　lodge　one　stood that to

ya, ḳa taŋkan wića ḳoŋ napin ehnake ća tin iyaya.　　Uŋkaŋ wakaŋka nom
he and　outside raccoons the　both　he laid　and house- he went.　And　old-women　two
went,　　　　　　　　　　　　　　　　　　　　　　in

tianog yukaŋpi, ḳehaŋ ćatku kiŋ en iyotaŋka.　　Uŋkaŋ heyapi : Takoźa,
house　were,　when　back part the　in　he-sat-down.　And　this-they-said: Grand-son,
each side

wita-ipi-śni ekta eeḣpeyapi ḳoŋ he niye he, eyapi.　　Hena eḳe wakaŋka
island-go-to-not　at　they left　the　that　you　?　they said.　Those　ones　old-woman

waśte hećapi.　　Uŋkaŋ uŋma heya : Taku ṭa noŋ keś wota će, wokihaŋ ye,
good　such-were.　And　one　this said: What　die　as although eats　, boil thou for　him,

eya.　　Uŋkaŋ hećen wokihaŋpi, ḳa wo ḳupi, ḳa heyapi : Takoźa, taku
she said.　And　so　they boiled for him, and　food　gave,　and thus said:　Grandchild,　what

teḣika ota ehna yau tuka iyotaŋ kiŋ he tokata haŋ će, eyapi, ḳehaŋ,
hard　much through you have but　most　the　that　ahead　stands　,　they said,　when,
been coming

Uŋćina, wića nom den taŋkan ahiwahnaka će, iću po, eya.　　Hećen
Grandmother, raccoons two　here　outside　I brought-laid　, take ye them, he said.　So

ićupi ḳa ake owićahaŋpi; uŋkaŋ uŋma heya: Eyaḳeś, mitakoźa tak ećiya ye,
they took and again　them boiled;　and　the other this said:　Indeed　my-grandchild some- say to him
thing (female sp.)

eya.　　Uŋkaŋ heya : Takoźa, Wiŋyaŋ-noŋpapika de tipi en yai kta, tuka
she said.　Then　this-she-said: Grandchild,　Woman-two　this house there you- will,　but
reach

taŋyaŋ nićuwapi kta; tuka haŋyetu kiŋ he hehan niktepi kta će; tuka
well　they you treat will;　but　night　the　that　then　you kill　will　;　but

tokeśta en uŋyakoŋpi kta će, eye ća hi kiŋ wanźi yupśuŋ ḳu keyapi.
presently　then　we-be　will　, she said and tooth the　one　pulling out gave,　they say.

Uŋkaŋ uŋma iś wapaḣta waŋ ḳu keyapi.　　Uŋma hi yupśuŋ ḳu kiŋ he
And　the other she　bundle　one　gave　they say.　The one　tooth pulled out gave　the　that

manića ee.　　Uŋma wapaḣta waŋ ḳu kiŋ he ḣoka ee; noŋksi kiŋ he apaḣte
gopher　was.　The other　bundle　a　gave the that badger was;　ear　the　that tied up

ća ḳu, keyapi.　　Tohaŋ uŋma kići inuŋke ćiŋhaŋ śina waŋ anićaḣpe ća toka
and gave,　they say.　When　the one with　you lie　if　blanket a　with you-cover and no way

yaniya śni kiŋhaŋ hi kiŋ de oŋ śina kiŋ pahdog-iyeye ća oniya nuŋke
you breathe not　if　tooth the　this with blanket the　pierce-through　and breathing you lie

kta će; ḳa wapaḣta kiŋ de duśke kta će, eya keyapi.　　Ḳa wo nićupi kiŋhaŋ
will　;　and　bundle　this you-untie will　, she said they say.　And food they give you　if

makata eyatoŋwe ća, Uŋćina, toki idada hwo, ehe kta će, eyapi.　　Tokeśta
earth-to　you look　and, Grandmother, where have you　?　you say will　, they said.　Presently
gone

hen uŋyakoŋpi kta će, eyapi.
there　we-be　will　, they said.

Hećen waŋna ekta iyaya.　　Uŋkaŋ wakeya waŋ taŋka e haŋ.　　Uŋkaŋ
So　now　thither he went.　And　tent　one　large there stood.　And

itaŋkan ćaŋha wokeya waŋ he en ye ća wakeya kiŋ en tin iyaye ća
outside　bark　lodge　one　the to went and　tent　the　in house-in he went　and

ćatku kiŋ en iyotaŋke, tuka tuwena en yaŋke śni.　　Uŋkaŋ ḣtayetu hehan
back-part the　in　sat down,　but　no-one　in　was　not.　And　evening　then

toki wikośka iħa niyaŋpi.   Uŋkaŋ ćaŋha wokeya waŋ taŋkan he ćiķoŋ hen
some- girls laughed aloud.   And   bark lodge one outside it the the
where   stood [aforesaid]

wakaŋka waŋyaka hee heya: Wihomni iśta taŋka inina kum, eya.   Hećen
old-woman · he-saw she-it-was this-said: Courtezan eyes large silently come, she said.   So that

uŋma tin hdićn kta, tuka en yaŋka waŋyaka, uŋkaŋ, Wati takumna, eye ća
the one house- start would, but in he-was she-saw, and, My-house smells of she-said and
in   home   something

ićićawiŋ iyaya.   Ake uŋma eye ća iyaya.   Uŋkaŋ waŋna napin tin hdipi
back   went.   Again the other said and went.   And   now both came home

hehan uŋma waŋna wokihaŋ; uŋkaŋ wićaśta kamdapi okihe ća ķu, wakśića
then the-one now boiled-for-him; and   man   cut-up boiled for and gave, dish
him

waŋ ohna ahikíhde ķehaŋ, pamahdena iyotaŋke ća, Uŋćina, toki idada hwo,
one in placed-for-him, when head-bowed he-sat and, Grandmother where have you ?
gone

eye ća makata etoŋwaŋ, uŋkaŋ iŋyuŋ maka mahentaŋhaŋ iskaya ićam
he said and earthward he looked, and behold earth within-from white-mouth pushing

hiyotaŋka e, hećen owas en okihnake ća wakśića kiŋ kićn.   Uŋkaŋ, Mitaŋ,
sat down there, so all in placed for him and dish the gave back.   Then, My younger
sister

naka wićadote wakaŋ uŋke ye, eye.   Uŋkaŋ uŋma kiŋ iś ake wo ķu: ake
now man-food mysterious we-two-have, she said.   Then other the she again food gave: again

iś eya wićaśta-ćonića eće ķu; tuka ićn ķa ake; Uŋćina, toki idada hwo,
she also man-flesh alone gave; but he-took and again; Grandmother where have you gone ?

eya.   Uŋkaŋ maka mahentaŋhaŋ iskaya hiyotaŋka.   Hećen, owas en
he said. And earth within-from white mouth coming sat down.   So-that all in

okihnake ća wakśića kiŋ kićn.   Uŋkaŋ, Mićuŋ, naka wićadote wakaŋ
placed for him and dish the returned.   Then, My elder sister, now man-food holy

uŋke ye, eya.
we-have, she said.

Hećen waŋna okpaza, uŋma tokaheya kići iwaŋke; uŋkaŋ śina waŋ
So now dark, the one first with him she-lay-down; and blanket one

akaħpa, tuka nina tke hiŋća e oŋ toka niya śni, ķehaŋ manića hi ķoŋ he oŋ
she-threw- but much heavy very, so that in no breathe not, when gopher tooth the that with
over,   way   [aforesaid]

paħdog-iyeye ća poģe ohna niya waŋka.   Uŋkaŋ tak ećiŋ ķa yutaŋ:
pushed-a-hole-through and nose through breathing lay.   And some- thought and ·touched:
thing

wiŋyaŋ kiŋ he hećoŋ.   Tuka hehan wapaħte ćiķoŋ he yuśke, uŋkaŋ wiŋyaŋ
woman the that did it.   But then bundle the that ·he loosed, and woman
[aforesaid]

ķoŋ śina kiŋ kazamni-iyeye ća, Mitaŋ naka wića okoye, eye ća iyaye.   He
the blanket the threw off and, My-side now man hole-made, she and went.   That
[aforesaid]   said

śina kiŋ kasota śina, keyapi.   Hehan uŋma kiŋ iś ake kići iwaŋke, uŋkaŋ
blanket the clear sky blanket, they say.   Then other the she again with him she lay down, and

taku waŋ akaħpa, tuka nina tke e akaħpe ća waŋna ake toka niya śni ķehaŋ
what one covered, but very heavy that covered and now again in no way breathe not when

manića hi ķoŋ he oŋ paħdog-iheye ća oniya waŋka.   Uŋkaŋ ake yutaŋ,
gopher tooth the that with pushed-a-hole-in and through- lay.   And again he touched,
[aforesaid]   breathing

tuka tokeća śni, he ţa kećiŋ ķa hećoŋ; tuka ake wapaħte ķoŋ hee yuśke.
but different not, that he she and she did it; but again bundle the that unloosed
died thought   [aforesaid]   he.

Uŋkaŋ, Mitaŋ naka wića okoye, eya hiŋhda śina kazamni-iyeya.   He
And, My side now man hole-made, she said suddenly blanket she threw off.   That

maḣpiya sapa śina keyapi. Hećen napin wićayuwaśte keyapi; ḳa napin
cloud   black blanket they say.   So that   both   them-he-made-good they say; and both

wićayuze.
them he took.

Uŋkaŋ hewićakiye; Taku yatapi kiŋ de eḣpeya po, eya. Uŋkaŋ,
Then this-to-them-he-said; What you-eat the this throw ye away, he said. And,

Taku uŋtapi kta he, eyapi. Ećiŋ tuwe wićaśta yute kta he, he śića će,
What we-eat shall ? they said. Indeed who men eat would ? that bad ,

eya. Tokeśta taku yutapi tokeća waśte ota će, eya. Uŋkaŋ wićadapi, ḳa
he said. Presently what is-eaten different good much he said. And they-believed, and

hećen wićaśta yutapi ḳoŋ ayuśtaŋpi. Hehan waŋna napin ćiŋća toŋpi;
so men they ate the [in the past] they stopped. Then now both children had;

uŋkaŋ sakim wića wićayuhapi. Uŋkaŋ ihnuhaŋna tiyata ewaćiŋ ḳa
and both male them-had. . And suddenly at-his-home he-thought and

iyokiśiće ċa inina yaŋka. Uŋkaŋ heyapi; Tokeća inina yauŋ he, ećiyapi.
was sad and silent was [sitting]. And this they said: Why silent you are ? they said to him.

Uŋkaŋ, Iyomakiśića će, eya. Uŋkaŋ, He etaŋhaŋ tehaŋtu he, tokeśta ekta
And, I am sad , he said. And, That from far is ? presently to

uŋhdapi hta će, eyapi, ḳa hoŋkupina kiŋ hećiyapi; Ina, ćeguka aćeti, de
we-go-home will , they said, and their mother the this said to: Mother, soft-stone burn, this

iyokiśića e ekta uŋkayapi kta će, eyapi. Hećen wakaŋkana kiŋ ćeguka
is-sad there to we-take-him will , they said. Thus old woman the soft-stone

aćeti ḳa yuśtaŋ. Uŋkaŋ hehan, Ate kipaŋ, eyapi. Uŋkaŋ mini kahda
burnt and finished. And then, Father call, they said. And water by the side of

inaźiŋ, ḳa, Wićaḣiŋća, kuwa, mićuŋkśi hutata yapi kta ye, eya. Uŋkaŋ
she stood, and, Old man, come, my daughters to-main-land go will indeed she said. And
(?)

ihnuhaŋna taku waŋ mini kiŋ etaŋhaŋ okapote ċa u ḳa hihuŋni; uŋkaŋ
suddenly what one water the from floated and was and came to land; and
coming

hihnakupi kiŋ woźuha waŋ en okihnakapi. Taku ḳoŋ he wakaŋkana kiŋ
husband-theirs the bag one in they placed. What the that [aforesaid] old woman the

hihnaku ḳa wikośka kiŋ heŋaos ćiŋća he Uŋktehi keyapi. Hećen waŋna
husband-hers and young woman the those-two children that Uŋktehi they say. Thus now

Uŋktehi ḳoŋ u ḳa hihuŋni; uŋkaŋ ćeguka aćetipi ḳoŋ hena iśta kiŋ napin
Uŋktehi the was and arrived; and soft-stones burned the those eyes the both
[aforesaid] coming   [aforesaid]

oźuna okadapi, ḳa he kiŋ ota hena waḣpaya kiŋ ekikśupi, ḳa hihnakupi
full they-sprinkled, and horns the many those baggage the they-piled-on, and husband-theirs

waḣpaya ićihnuni ekihnakapi. Uŋkaŋ heya: Ćuŋś, taku nimna se, eya.
baggage among they placed. And this he said: Daughter, something alive it seems, he said.
                                            smells

Tuka; Wićaḣiŋća śića, taku omnapi kta he, eyapi. Uŋkaŋ, O, eya keyapi.
But; Old-man bad, what be-smelled will ? they said. And, O, he said they say.

Hećen waŋna iyayapi. Uŋkaŋ, Ćuŋś, mitakoźa ćaŋna etaŋhaŋ yuke-
So now they-went. And, Daughter, my grandchildren sticks from [rather, some] have-

wićayakiyapi, ḳa uwaśtena mda ća he kiŋ makakokokapi kta će, eya; ḳa
them-you-cause, and slowly I-go when horns the me-they-drum-on will , he said; and

nakun, Ćuŋś, nina wakitapi, eya. He Wakiŋyaŋ aku kte ćiŋ he ka. Ećiŋ
also, Daughter, much look out for, he said. That Thunder come will the that he ka. For
                                                              meant.

kići tokakićiya uŋpi. Waŋna mini kiŋ opta huta kiŋ ekta hdapi, uŋkaŋ
with foes to each other they-are. Now water the across show the to they go home, and

iŋyuŋ heya; Ćuŋś, taku ahaŋzimayaŋ će, eya.   He waŋna mahpiya
behold   this he said: Daughter, something   shades·me   ,   he said.   That   now   clouds
ahdinaŋpa, uŋkaŋ sdoŋye ća heya.   Tuka, Taku ahaŋźiniye kta he, de
had·come·over,   and   he·knew   and this said.   But,   What   shade·you   should   ?   this
kasota ye, eyapi.   He hnayaŋpi, waŋna mahpiya ahdinaŋpa tuka heyapi.
sky·clear indeed they said.   This they·deceived,   already   clouds   had come over   but they·said·that.
(?)
Hećen waŋna huta kiŋ dehaŋna, tuka Wakiŋyaŋ kiŋ iś kiyena aku.   Tuka
So   now   shore   the   near·by,   but   Thunder   the   he   near   comes.   But
huta kiŋ en kihuŋnipi ķehaŋ hihnakupi e tokaheya heyata ehpeyapi: hehan
shore   the there they·reached   when   husband theirs that   first   ashore   they carried: then
wahpaya kiŋ owasin ićupi, ķa hehan, Huŋktiya, ate, Wakiŋyaŋ kiyena aku
baggage   the   all   they took, and   then,   Go·along,   father,   Thunder   near   comes
će, eyapi.   Uŋkaŋ, Hehe! ćuŋś, taŋni hećeće kta ćiķoŋ, eye ća kihda; tuka
*,   they said.   And,   Alas!   daughter, long ago   so be   would   the [in   he said and started home;   but
the past]*
ećen Wakiŋyaŋ kiŋ kutepi ķa mini kiŋ owaŋćaya we hiŋhda, oŋ wićaśta
so   Thunder   the   shoot·him and   water   the   all over   blood   became,   therefore   man
kiŋ, Ho! tuŋkaŋśi ķoŋ, eya.   Tuka heyapi: Hetaŋhaŋ țe kte śni, hećoŋpi
*the,   Alas! my·father·in·law the [in   he said.   But   this they said: From·that   die will   not,   this·they·do
the past]*
keś țe śni ećee, eyapi, keyapi.
though dies not,   always,   they said,   they say.
Hećen waŋna hetaŋ ye ćiķoŋ en wahdi, tuka oyate kiŋ toki eyaya
*Thus   now   whence he·went the [in   there all·come·   but   people   the   when   had·gone
the past]   home,*
taŋiŋ śni ķehaŋ heye; Den wakeya tikićaġa po, ito, ekta mde kta će, eye
manifest not   when   this said;   Here   tent   put·ye·up   lo,   there   I·go   will   ,   he said
ća ekta ye ća miniyowe kiŋ en ya; uŋkaŋ iŋyuŋ winohiŋća pa nisko u
*and   to   went and   spring   the   to   went;   and   behold   woman   head so·large was
coming*
waŋyake.   Uŋkaŋ taŋkśitku ķoŋ hee keya, pa nisko, ite kiŋ iś owas hdi
*he saw.   And   sister·his   the   it is she he said,   head so large,   face   the   it   all   sores
[aforesaid]*
ķa u waŋka.   E, hećen taŋkśi ķoŋ, eya; uŋkaŋ, Timdo ķoŋ, 'eye, ća
*and was   was [she   Indeed   so   my sister   that   he said;   and,   My brother   that   she said, and
coming lay]   [aforesaid]*
poskiŋ kiyahpaya ķehaŋ, Taŋkśi, toketu hwo, eya.   Uŋkaŋ, Timdo,
he·embraced·her   when,   My sister,   how·is·it   ?   he said.   And,   My brother,
Uŋktomi oyate kiŋ owasiŋ wićakasote ća miśnana omakapte; tuka nakuŋ
Uŋktomi   people   the   all   them destroyed and   me alone   me·has·left;   but   also
tehiya mayuha će, eya keyapi: dećen mini huwe wahi ķa waki ća waŋna
*hardly   me·he·has   ,   she said they say: thus   water   to bring I·come   and I·reach· when   then
home*
ake, Tuwe onićiya naće, eye ća ćahota kata ite kiŋ amakada ećee, oŋ ite
*again,   Who   has courted perhaps, he·says and   ashes   hot   face   the   sprinkles on me   always there· face
you   fore*
kiŋ owasiŋ mahdi će, eya.   Uŋkaŋ, Huŋktiya wo, mini kiŋ ahde, ća ake
the   all   me·sore   ,   she said.   And,   Go·thou·along,   water   the take home, and   again
eye ćiŋhaŋ, Oyate waŋ owasiŋ wićayakasote, tuwe ni uŋ ķa omakiye kta
he·say   if,   People   one   all   them·you·destroyed,   who   alive   is   and   court·me   would
he, eye ća mini kiŋ apapsoŋ ķa hiyu wo, den ahdi wati će, eya.   Uŋkaŋ
*?   say and   water   the   throw on him and   come thou,   here   I·have·come·   ,   he said.   And
home·to·dwell*
hećen mini kiŋ ahde ća tin kihda.   Uŋkaŋ waŋna ake Uŋktomi ite ećeće
so   water   the took home and house in she went.   And   now   again   Uŋktomi   face   like
śni yaŋke ća waŋna ake, Tuwe onićiya naće eś, eya.   Tuka, Na ye oyate
*not   was   and   now   again, Some one has courted perhaps , he said.   But,   See ·!   people
[sitting]   you*

waŋ owasiŋ wićayakasote ćiḳoŋ, tuwe ni uŋ ća omakiye kta he, eya; ḳa
one all them you have the [in the who alive is when court-me will ? she said; and destroyed past]

mini kiŋ apapsoŋ-iyeya. Uŋkaŋ iha, ḳa, Wiŋyaŋ, tahaŋ hdi he, eya. Niś
water the threw-on-him-suddenly. And he and, Woman, Brother- he has ? said. You laughed, in-law come home

wita ipi śni ekta eelipeniyaŋpi ḳeś yahdi ka, eye ća hećen hiyu keyapi, ḳa
island go-to not at you-were-taken if you come ? she-said and so came they say, and home towards

timdoku ti kiŋ en hdićú. Uŋkaŋ heye; Taŋkśi koyakiháŋ po, eye, ća
brother-her house the there she started And he said: Sister be-ye-in-haste-for, he said, and home.

hećen mini kanyapi ḳa oŋ yuźaźapi ḳa kićakćapi, ḳa heyake waśte uŋkiyapi
so water they-heated and with washed-her and combed-her, and clothes beautiful put-on-her

ḳa ćatku kiŋ en ekihnakapi. Hehan ćiŋća hokśina kiŋ napin, Huŋktiya
and back-part the in they placed her Then children boys the both, Go ye a-their own.

po, Uŋktomi kićo ya po, ewićakiya. Uŋkaŋ yapi ḳa; Uŋktomi, uŋnićopi
long, Uŋktomi to call go ye, to them he said. And they went and; Uŋktomi, we-you-invite

do, eyapi. Uŋkaŋ, E, mitoŋśkapina taku waśtepi ye, eye ća wićiyahna u
they said. And, Well, my little nephews what good ! he-said and them-behind was coming

ḳa tin hiyu. Uŋkaŋ tawićú ḳoŋ taŋyehiŋ ihduze ća ćatku en yaŋka waŋyag
and tent came. And wife-his the well-very dressed and back-part in was to see her into [aforesaid] herself [sitting]

hiyu. Tuka, Tiyopa kiŋ hen hiyotanka wo, eya. Uŋkaŋ, Haŋ, tahaŋ,
he came But, Door the there sit thou down, he said. And, Yes brother-towards. in-law,

token ehe ćiŋ ećen ećamoŋ kta, eya. Ḳa en iyotaŋke ćehaŋ, Uŋktomi
how thou- the so I-do will, he said. And there he-sat-down when, Uŋktomi sayest

(taku śića waŋ ćaźeyata ḳa) he hduta wo, eya. Uŋkaŋ ećen ećoŋ keyapi.
(what bad one he named and) that eat-thou-thy- he said. And so he-did they say. own,

Iś eya hećoŋ śi nakaeś tokićoŋ. Hehan Makaŋ yaŋ'-ka wo, ḳa iihduta
He also that-do com- indeed he avenged. Then Tamarack- weave thou it, and your-own-manded roots size

yaŋ'-ka wo, ḳa tahu kiŋ en yuotiŋs ićupi kta hećen yaŋ'-ka wo, eya.
weave-thou-it, and neck the in tightly drawn will so weave-thou-it, he said.

Uŋkaŋ owasiŋ ećen yuśtaŋ. Uŋkaŋ, Ohna iyotaŋka wo, eya. Uŋkaŋ
And all so he-finished. And, In-it sit-thou-down, he said. And

ohna iyotaŋka, tuka yuotiŋs-ićú ḳa petá iwaŋkam otkeya. Nihiŋćiya, tuka,
in-it he sat down, but he-pressed it-in and fire above he-hung. Affrighted-was, but,

Ćaŋ ota aoŋ po, eye, ća Uŋktomi śota ṭeye, ća ćaŋte kiŋ ićú ḳa pusye ća
Wood much pile-on ye, he said, and Uŋktomi smoke killed, anu heart the he-took and dried and

kapaŋ ḳa peźihuta ićahiye ća ćiŋćana kiŋ napin wićaḳu, ḳa, Otiwota kiŋ
pounded- and medicine mixed and children the both them-gave, and, Village ruins the fine

owaŋća okada po, eya. Uŋkaŋ ećoŋpi.
all over scatter ye it, he said. And they did it.

Haŋhaŋna ḳehaŋ, Ho po, peźihuta oyakadapi ḳoŋ waŋyaka po, eya.
Morning when, Come ye, medicine you scattered that look-ye-after, he said. [aforesaid]

Ekta ipi ḳa heyapi: Ate, taku wamdudaŋ se owaŋćaya śkaŋśkaŋpi do,
Thither they and this said: Father, what worms like all over they are moving about . went

eyapi. Ake ihaŋhaŋna ḳehaŋ ye-wića-śi. Uŋkaŋ, Ate taku kiŋ waŋná
they said. Again morning next when them he sent. And, Father what the now

taŋkiŋkiŋyaŋpi do, eya hdipi. Ake haŋhaŋna ḳehaŋ ekta yewićaśi.
they are very large saying they returned. Again morning when to he-sent-them.

Uŋkaŋ hdipi, ķa, Ate, hena wićaśtapi-na do: naźiŋ wo nipakśa, eyapi,
And   they returned, and, Father, those   they are little men   .   stand thou up thou art-crooked, they said,

ķa pasto-iħpayapina ećee do, eyapi. Itopa ćaŋ hehan oyate kiŋ ekićetu, ķa
and brushing   they fell down always . they said. Fourth day   then people the perfected, and
along   [little ones]

aŋpao tuka ćeġapapi ķa paŋpaŋpi ķa eyaŋpahapi, ķa owodutatoŋ, ķa kośka
daylight but kettle beating and yelling and crying the news, and great noise, and young
man

ķoŋ ti kiŋ ihdukśaŋ hoćokatoŋ ahitipi, ķa Itaŋćaŋ kićaġapi, keyapi.
the house the around in a circle they-put-their- and Chief they made him, they say.
[afore-   tents,
said]

Uŋktomi ćaŋte kiŋ oŋ oyate kiŋ ekićetu, keyapi. Henana.
Uŋktomi heart the by people the were- they say. That is all.
resurrected,

NOTES.

1. On furnishing this myth Mr. Renville remarked, "It is another Joseph." By
which he did not mean that the Dakota legend had received anything from the Bible
story; but that the impure desires of a wicked woman had worked out similar results.
In the whole structure of it there is evidence that this is a genuine Dakota myth.

2. It will be noticed that the language of the Dakotas has simple words to express *younger brother*, (suŋka), *elder-brother*, (ćiŋye), *a man's sister-in-law*, (haŋka),
a woman's brother-in-law, (śiće), *a man's brother-in-law*, (tahaŋ), *a man's father-in-law*,
(tuŋkaŋ), etc. These all are found in the myth, and others like them exist in the
language. However they may have been formed in the first place, these words are
now beyond analysis. Now it is claimed that the existence in a language of such radical words expressing relationships is evidence of descent from a higher civilization.
Whence came the Dakotas?

3. In all Dakota myths Uŋktomi is represented as the incarnation of evil. Here
it overreaches itself and is properly punished. But the annihilation of it is only local
and temporary.

4. This myth gives the best characterization of this great water god, Uŋktelii,
which answers to the Neptune and Poseidon of the Greeks and Romans. Also it
portrays vividly the eternal enmity that exists between him and their Jupiter
Tonans—the Wakiŋyaŋ.

5. The word ćeġuka, translated *soft-stone*, is of somewhat uncertain signification.
What was it the old woman burned and sprinkled in the eyes of Uŋktelii to enable
him to swim so long in the light? The analysis would seem to be *the skin of a kettle*.
The word ćeġa is now applied to all iron kettles as well as wooden buckets. But the
original ćeġa was undoubtedly *earthen*. Then the uka, *the skin*, would mean the
glazing. This, too, would point back to a higher civilization.

6. The element of the supernatural is prominent in all the Dakota myths. Here
in answer to his prayer the earth opens and the gopher comes to his assistance, while
the aid of the badger is no less needed for his deliverance and victory. And not only
is deliverance secured by supernatural help, but the race is elevated by a mixture
with the gods.

7. It is significant that, after this miraculous passage across the water, they find
the mainland uninhabited. The spirit of Evil has destroyed the race. But, as
Deucalion and Pyrrha repeopled the world by casting "the bones of the earth" behind

them, so here the Younger Brother repeoples his fatherland by burning up the Evil One and sowing the ashes.

8. The use of śni in the following phrases is peculiar:

Tuwe tokeća kute yaśi śni, *Why do you not tell some one else to shoot?*
<u>Who different to shoot you not</u>
at command

Tuwe kaśta kići de śni, *Why do you not go with someone else?*
<u>Who soever with him you go not</u>

In these two, śni has the force of *why not?*

Suŋg, ito wiŋtka pahi uŋye śni, *Younger brother, come, we have not (yet) gathered*
<u>Younger come egg to gather we two not</u>
<u>brother go</u>

eggs. But this last implies a request, *Come, let us gather eggs.*—J. O. D.

P. 134, line 1. He, from haŋ, *to stand on end,* as an inanimate object. See p. 7, §6, *c.*—J. O. D.

TRANSLATION.

Once there was a people, the chief among whom had three beloved children, two boys and one girl. The eldest son married a wife and the younger brother lived with him. But the sister-in-law troubled her brother-in-law, "Let us lie together," often saying to him. But he always answered, "How can I make my older brother ashamed, seeing he sets such store by me?"

One day, when the woman had brought home some wood, she said, "Brother-in-law, yonder are many prairie chickens; shoot one for me." To which he replied, "No; I am not a hunter; send some one else to shoot them." But his brother said, "Shoot them for her." So he took his arrows and shot one for her, and said, "There it is, take it," and so went away. After awhile the woman came home crying, and said to her husband, "Your younger brother persists in troubling me. But when I tell you of it you do not believe me. See, this is what he has done to me," and she showed him where she had scratched her thighs all over with the prairie chicken's claws.

Then he believed her, and said, "Go call Uŋktomi." And Uŋktomi came. Then he said, "Uŋktomi, you take my younger brother to the Unvisited Island and leave him there, and you shall have my sister for your wife."

The young man came home and Uŋktomi said to him, "My younger brother, come, we will go and hunt eggs." But he said, "No, I can not. Go with some one else." But the elder brother said, "Go with him," and he went with him.

They entered a canoe and went to the island and gathered eggs. And when they had filled the canoe the young man said, "Let us go home." And so they got into the boat. But Uŋktomi said, "Brother, yonder are some nice ones, get them also." The young man replied, "No, we have now a great plenty." But Uŋktomi was persistent, so the young man went and got the eggs. In the meantime Uŋktomi had turned the head of the canoe outward and was starting home. "Halloo, Uŋktomi, bring the canoe here," he said. But Uŋktomi answered back, "What are you killing yourself about?" "Halloo, bring it here," he repeated, but he would not. Then he said, "Uŋktomi, bring the canoe here; when we reach home you shall have my sister for your wife." He replied, "That is what I am doing this for." The young man continued to plead. Uŋktomi bade him eat his own dung, which he would willingly do if the canoe would come for him. Uŋktomi laughed at him. Then the young man said, "You mean, bad fellow, you have deceived me," and so he reviled him. Uŋktomi answered, "Go away, you will see the Great Mosquito." Again he reviled him. "Go," said Uŋktomi, "you will see the Gray Bear." He repeated it, and Uŋktomi said, "Go away, you will see the Arm-awls." Again he cursed him, and the answer was, "Go, you will see His-many-dogs." Then for the last time he reviled Uŋktomi, who said, "Go, you will see the Two Women," and then he came home.

Then the young man also departed, and when he heard something above come whizzing along, the Great Mosquito fell into the water, and he threw himself under it. But, lo! something like a brown crane came and stood and said, "That thing that was moving about here as I was coming has gone somewhere. Indeed, if it were here I would do so to it," and he struck the mosquito with his bill. But as the bill stuck in, he (that is, the young man) in turn killed the crane, cut his bill off, and carried it along. Again the young man heard something, and the Gray Bear came crying out against him. But the young man changed himself into a dead fish and lay on the water. Then said the Gray Bear, "What was here moving about when I was coming has gone." The Gray Bear came, and saying, "I will eat whatever is yonder," he took the fish in his mouth. But, as it was flat, he turned it from one side of his jaws to the other, and finally swallowed it whole.

But in the belly of the bear the young man resumed his shape, took his knife, and cut the bear's heart to pieces, and so killed him. Then he cut a hole in the side and came out, and having cut off the two fore paws he took them along.

As he went along in the path there stood a bark lodge, from which smoke issued. He immediately thought, "These are what he called the Arm-awls," and so he wrapped his blanket up into a bundle, and placing it under his arm he went into the lodge and sat down in the back part, saying, "Lo! my grandmother, I would come into the house." Now, there were two old women sitting, one on either side, and making a disturbance about something at the door. Then, rising to his feet, he said, "Grandmother, I have come into the house, but you are not pleased; I will go out again." And as he said this he made pretense of going out, but threw his bundle at the door. And they with their elbows both pierced it, but, as it was only a blanket, they thrust through further than they had intended and stabbed each other. "My cousin, you have killed me," they both said. But he said, "Did such as you think you would kill me?" and at once he killed them both and went on.

Then he heard some one ahead saying aloud as he came, "Come, come, my dogs." And while he came on calling his dogs, the young man made his nose bleed and besmeared all his arrows with blood and spread them out in the path and lay down on his back. Then there came a lion and a great lynx and licked them. But the owner of the beasts said, "Let him alone, and go along, this is a poor child." So they passed on. Then the man came and said this: "Ah! my grandchild, you are the one that they say was left on the unvisited island. Go on, there are two of my dogs coming behind, those you may kill and eat." This was the one called His-many-dogs, because they say he has all things that move upon the earth for his dogs.

Then the young man rose and went on. And two raccoons came along, talking to each other. He killed them and carried them with him. Then he came to a bark-lodge which was standing in the path, and, laying down both the raccoons outside, he went in. There were two old women, one on either side of the house, and he sat down in the back part of the tent. Then they said: "Grandchild, are you the one who was cast away on the unvisited island?" These were good old women. Then one said: "Even if one is almost dead he eats; cook something for him." Then they boiled for him and gave him food and said: "Grandchild, you have come through many difficulties, but the hardest is yet to come." And he said, "Grandmother, I brought two raccoons and laid them outside, take them." So they took them and boiled them. Then one said to the other, "Give some counsel to my grandchild." Whereupon she said: "Grandchild, you will go to the house of The Two Women. They will treat you well, but at night they will seek to kill you. But we shall be there with you." Saying this, she pulled out a tooth and gave to him. And they say the other one gave him a bundle. The one who pulled the tooth and gave him was the Gopher; and the other who gave him the bundle was the Badger; he tied up his ear and gave him. Then one of the old women told him what to do. "When you lie with one of the Two Women and she covers you with a blanket so that you can not breathe, pierce a hole in the blanket with this tooth, and you shall breathe freely; then untie the bundle. When they give you food, you will look to the earth and say: 'Grandmother, whither have you gone, and at once we will be there with you.'"

Then he traveled till he reached a very large tent. And outside of it there was a bark lodge. He entered into the tent and sat down in the back part. But no one was there. But when the evening was coming on he heard young women laughing loudly. In the bark lodge he had seen an old woman, who now said; "Come quietly, you big-eyed courtezans." So when one of them would have entered she saw him there, and saying, "My house smells of something," she turned back. Again the other came and said the same thing and went again. But now, when both had come home, one of them went to cooking for him. And she gave him the half of a man cut up. This she put in a dish and placed before him. He bowed his head and looking to the earth said: "Grandmother, where have you gone?" Lo! from the earth there came a white mouth pushing up and sat down. So he emptied it all in and handed the dish back. And the young woman said, "My younger sister, now we two have mysterious man food." Then the other young woman also gave him her man-flesh, which he took, saying, "Grandmother, whither hast thou gone?" And from within the earth a white mouth came and sat down. So again he poured all the food in the mouth and handed the dish back. And the young woman said, "My older sister, now we two have mysterious man-food."

When it was now dark one of the young women lay down with him, and covered him with a blanket; but it was very heavy, so that he could not breathe. Then he pierced a hole through it with the gopher's tooth and with his nose through it he lay breathing. The woman thought something was wrong and touched him. But just then he untied the bundle, and the woman threw off the blanket and started off exclaiming, "A man has made a hole in my side." That blanket was the clear sky blanket.

Then the other young woman in turn lay down with him, and put over him a covering that was so very heavy that he could not breathe. Again he punched a hole in it with the gopher's tooth, and lay breathing. Again there was the touch. She thought he was dead. But he untied the bundle; when she suddenly exclaimed: "A man has made a hole in my side," and threw off the blanket. This was the black cloud blanket. In this way, as the story is told, he made them both good and married them both.

Then he said to them, "You must change your food." But, "What shall we eat?" they said. To which he replied; "No one should eat men; it is bad food; there are plenty of other things good to eat." And they believed him, and so left off eating men.

Now, in process of time they each had children, and both were boys. Then suddenly the husband thought of his old home and was sad and silent. The wives said to him, "Why are you silent?" He said, "Because I am sad." "It is not far away, we will go home with you," they said; and then they said to their mother, "Mother, burn soft stones. He is sad and we will take him home." So the old woman burned soft stone. Then the wives said, "Call father." So the mother-in-law stood by the side of the water and said; "Old man, come, my daughters will go to the main land." Then immediately something floated up from the water and came to the shore. The wives put their husband in a bag. What appeared was the husband of the old woman, and the young women were his children. They say it was Uŋktelii. So when the Uŋktelii had come to the shore, they filled both his eyes with the burnt stones, and on his many horns they piled the baggage, and their husband they placed among the baggage. He said, "My daughter, I smell some live thing." But they said, "Bad old man, what is there to be smelled?" To which he replied "Oh." Thus they set off. Moreover he said, "Let my grandchildren take little sticks and when I move slowly let them drum on my horns." He also said, "My daughters, keep a sharp lookout." This he said lest the Thunder should come. For the Thunder and the Uŋktelii are enemies.

Now, as they went over the water towards the mainland, he said, "My daughters, something overshadows me." He said this because it had clouded up and he knew it. But they said, "What is there to shade you; it is all clear sky." In saying this they deceived him, for already the clouds had come over. And now when they approached the shore the Thunder came nearer. But when they came to land they put ashore their husband first and then took off all the baggage; and then they said, "Go away, father; the Thunder is near." "Alas! my daughters, I thought so," he said, and started home. But just then the Thunder shot him, and the water all over turned to blood. The young man said, "Alas! my poor father-in-law!" But they said, "He will not die of that. Although that is done, he never dies."

They had now returned to the place whence he went out, but where the people had gone was not manifest. So he said, "Put up the tent here, while I go over yonder." He went towards the spring of water, when lo! he saw a woman with a head so large coming. "That is my sister," he said. She was coming—her head was the proper size, but her face was all broken out in sores. "Yes, that was my sister," he said; and as she said, "My brother that was," he embraced her, and said, "My sister, how is it?" "My brother," she said, "Uŋktomi has destroyed all our people. Me alone he has saved, but has treated me very badly. When I come thus for water and go back, he says, 'Now somebody has been courting you,' and he sprinkles hot ashes on my face, and so my face is all over sores." Then he said to her, "Go, take home water, and if he says that again, say to him, 'You have destroyed all the people; who is there alive to say anything to me?' Then throw the water on him, and come hither; I have pitched my tent here."

So she took the water home and went in; wherefore again Uŋktomi's face was flushed, and he said, "Now some one has been courting you indeed." But she replied,

"See, you have destroyed all the people; who is there alive to say anything to me?" And she dashed the water on him. He only laughed and said, "Woman, has my brother-in-law come home?" She replied, "If you had been left on the unvisited island would you ever have returned?" Then she left him and came to the tent of her brother, who commanded his wives to hasten with the preparations for his sister. So they heated water, washed her, combed her hair, put beautiful clothes on her, and placed her in the back part of the tent. Then the man said to his two boys, "Go, call Uŋktomi." They went and said, "Uŋktomi, we call you." He said, "Oh, how beautiful my nephews are," and followed them to the tent of his wife's brother. He was going in to see her who had been his wife, now dressed so beautifully and seated in the back part of the tent; but the young man said, "Sit there in the door." To which Uŋktomi made answer, "Yes, my brother-in-law, I will do what you say." When he was seated, the young man said, "Uŋktomi, eat your own dung." And they say he did so. This was done to be avenged, because Uŋktomi had once told him to do the same. Then the young man said, "Weave tamarack roots; weave the basket just your own size and make it come close around your neck." And Uŋktomi did so. "Sit down in it." And Uŋktomi sat down in it. So the young man pressed Uŋktomi in and hung it over the fire. Uŋktomi squirmed, but the young man said, "Pile on wood." So he killed Uŋktomi with the smoke, took out his heart and dried it, pounded it up fine and made medicine of it. Then he gave it to his two boys, and said, "Go, scatter it on the ruins of the village." And they did so.

When the next morning came, he said to them, "Go see the medicine you scattered." They returned and said, "Father, all over there are things like worms crawling." The next morning he sent them again. They returned and said, "Father, the things are now very large." On the third morning he sent them again. They brought back word, "Father, they are little men. 'Stand up! You are crooked,' they said to each other; and so they stumbled along," they said. On the fourth day the people were perfected, and at daybreak, with drum-beating, yelling, making proclamations, and great noise, they came and pitched their tents around the tent of the young man, whom they made their chief. Thus they say that by means of Uŋktomi's heart the people were brought to life again. That is all.

WAMNUḦA-ITAĠOŚA.

BEAD·SPITTER.

WRITTEN IN DAKOTA BY M. RENVILLE.

Hokśinćaŋtkiyapi waŋ hee tohan taġośa eća wamnuḣa oćaźe kiŋ owasiŋ
Boy-beloved   one   that is   when   he spits   then   beads   kinds   the   all

itaġośa eće; hećen taoyate kiŋ hena wokoyake yapi eće. Heoŋ oyate
he spits out always *or* so-that his-people the those clothes made-them always. Therefore people
regularly

ihdukśaŋ taŋhan wikośka owasiŋ hihnaye au eće. Uŋkaŋ wikośka waŋ
round about from young-women all to-marry they were always And young-woman one
him coming in *or* regu-
large num- larly.
bers.

iś hihnaye ya, uŋkaŋ iŋyuŋ hekta tuwe iḣa niyaŋpi. Hećen inaźiŋ;
she marry-him went, and behold behind who laughed they aloud. So-that she stopped;

uŋkaŋ wikośka nom en upi ḳa heyapi; Inama! Ćaŋktewiŋ den naźiŋ će,
and maidens two thither they and this-say; Wonderful! Heart-killer female here stands ,
were
coming.

eyapi: ḳa, Iho ye, Ćaŋktewiŋ, Wamnuḣa-itaġośa hihnaye uŋyaŋpi će,
they said: and, Come on, Heart-killer female, Beads-who-spits-out to-marry we are going ,

uŋyaŋpi kte, eyapi. Hećen om iyaye. Wikośka kiŋ denaoza Wiŋyaŋ-
we-go will, they said. So with them she went. Maiden the those-two Women

Noŋpapika ewićakiyapi. Oyate en ićaġapi śni, ituya ićaġapi; hena taku
Two they were called. People among they grew not, wildly they grew; these something

wakaŋ hećapi, hećen ćaźepi.
mysterious such they hence their name.
were,

Hećen hena om ya, ḳa om iwaŋka, waŋna ḣtayetu heoŋ. Hećen
So those with she went, and with she lay-down, now evening therefore. Thus
them

waŋna iśtiŋmapi kta, uŋkaŋ Wiŋyaŋ Noŋpapika kiŋ heyapi: Ihoŋye,
now they-sleep would, and Women-Two the this said: Come-on,

Ćaŋktewiŋ, haŋḣaŋna uŋkiktapi kiŋhaŋ taŋpa wakśića waŋ ohomni pahiŋ
Heart-killer female, morning we awake if birch-bark dish one around quills

oŋ akisoŋpi e psiŋ tona e pa kiŋ haŋ aŋpa kiŋhaŋ he Wamnuḣa-itaġośa
with braided that rice which that head the stands daylight if that Bead-spits-out
(?) ever (?)

hihnaye kta, eyapi. Tuka haŋḣaŋna uŋkaŋ Ćaŋktewiŋ e pa kiŋ en
husband have shall, they said. But morning then Heart-killer female that head the in

ećen haŋ, keyapi. Hećen yapi, ḳa mde waŋ yapi en taŋka, huta taŋiŋ
so stood, they say. So they-went, and lake one they went in large, shore appear

śni e en ipi. Ćaŋnaŋ wata waŋ taŋka yaŋka, hen Wamnuḣa-itaġośa
not that in they Out-on boat one large was (sitting), there Beads-spits-out
arrived.

144

toŋweye ćiŋ hetu; hećeŋ paŋpi, ka, Wamnuha-itaǵośa hihnaye uŋhipi ye,
dwells   the there: so   they called, and,   Beads-spits-out   to-marry   we have come,

eyapi. Hećen watopa waŋ u. Hi uŋkaŋ heyapi: Wamnuha-itaǵośa
they said.   Then   rower   one   was Arrived   and   this they say: Beads-spits-out
coming.

hihnaye uŋhipi će, eyapi. Uŋkaŋ, Iha, tuwe hećiyapi śta sdoŋwaye śni,
to-marry   we have come ,   they said.   Then,   No,   who   thus called although   I know him   not,

eye ća ioźuna wamnuha iyohnake ća tagośa iyeya: Uŋkaŋ wamnuha keya
he said, and mouth full   beads   he-placed   and   spit them out: Then   beads   abundantly
in his mouth

kada iyeya: Uŋkaŋ ihaha pahipi; ka hećeŋ Wiŋyaŋ Noŋpapi kiŋ napin
scattered were: And   laughing they picked and   so   Woman-Two   the   both
them up:

wata kiŋ opapi, ka waŋźi kiŋ kiśićapi, Ćaŋktewiŋ; Ako iyaya, eyapi, ka
boat   the   went-in, and   one   the   they sent her Heart-killer female: Away   go,   they said, and
away.

kići kihdapi. Tuka he Wamnuha-itaǵośa ee śni. Hećen uŋma koŋ ećeŋ
with they went home.   But   this   Beads-spits-out   that not.   So   other   the   thus
him   [aforesaid]

ćeya yaŋka. Uŋkaŋ, iŋyuŋ, wata waŋ hinaŋpa, uŋkaŋ nina wiyatpa, maza
crying was (sitting).   And,   lo,   boat   one   came-in-sight,   and   very   brilliant,   metal

wata nakaeś. Hećen u ka en hi: eke Wamnuha-itaǵośa hee; iye kiŋ
boat   indeed.   Thus   it was and there arrived: this   Beads-spits-out   that was;   he   the
coming

taku wiyatpa eće koyake nakaeś nina okitaŋiŋ. Hećen, Taku oŋ, wikośka,
some-   bright   alone   wears   indeed,   very   appears.   Then,   What for,   maiden,
thing

den yaćeya he, eya. Uŋkaŋ iś, Wamnuha-itaǵośa hihnaye hi keya; ka
here   you cry   ?   he said.   And   she,   Beads-spits-out   to-marry   came, she said: and

en Wiŋyaŋ Noŋpa token ećakićoŋpi he okiyake. Uŋkaŋ, Ho wo, uŋhde
these   Woman   Two   how   they did to her   that   she told him.   Then,   Come on,   we-two-
go-home

kta će eye ća kići ki.
will   , he said, and with he arrived
her   at his
home.

Ito uŋmapi kiŋ he omdake kta. Hećen Wiŋyaŋ Noŋpapi kiŋ wićaśta
Now   others   the that   I tell   will.   Thus   Women   Two   the   man

koŋ kići kipi. Uŋkaŋ kuŋkiśitku ti en ipi. Uŋkaŋ iŋyuŋ tuwe heya;
the   with they reached   Then   grandmother-his house in   they   And   lo   some one this said;
[aforesaid]   home.   came.

Siyaka, Wamnuha-itaǵośa nićo će, eya. Uŋkaŋ, Ho, token takeye se,
Teal,   Bead Spitter   you-calls ,   he-said.   Then,   Soho!   somehow what-he-   it
says   seems,

eya: Hećen upi śni po, he taku wakaŋyaŋ ećoŋpi eće e tuwena wiŋyaŋ
he said.   Hence   come ye not,   this something mysteriously   they-do always that   no-one   woman

waŋyake śni ećee će, eya ća iyaya. Tuka wiŋyaŋ koŋ heyapi: Taku
sees   not always ,   he said, and   went.   But   women   the   this said: What
[aforesaid]

wakaŋ keś waŋyag uŋyakoŋ ećee, ekta uŋye kte, eyapi, ka en yapi.
mysterious even   seeing   we-two-are   always,   to it   we-two-go will.   they said;   and there   went.

Uŋkaŋ nina oko e hećen wakeya ohdoka waŋ ohna etoŋwaŋpi, uŋkaŋ
Then   much   noise that   so   tent   hole   one   in   they looked,   and

hihnakupi koŋ hee nite kiŋ he awaćipi: uŋkaŋ tawićn kiŋ eyokasiŋpi e
husband-theirs   the   that-is back   the   that they danced on: and   wives-his   the   looking in   that
[aforesaid]

waŋwićayake; uŋkaŋ naźiŋ hiyaye ća, Miś siyaka nite awaćipi owapa, eye
them-he-saw;   and   he rose to his feet   and, ,   I   teal's   back   dancing on   I follow he said,

ća psipsića, keyapi. He magaksića waŋ siyaka eyapi ećee, hee keyapi.
and   jumped often,   they say.   This   duck   one   teal   called   always, that-is-it they say.

Heoŋ dehaŋyaŋ maǵaksića kiŋ he nite kiŋ ćepe śni: uŋkaŋ he oyate awaćipi
Therefore to-this-time   duck   the this back the   fat not: and   this people they danced
on him

ka hećeća, eyapi eće.
and so-it-is, they say regularly.

Hehan wiŋyaŋ koŋ hdićupi, ka śina nom, uŋma tuḣmaǵa mahen
Then   women   the they-started and blanket two, the one   bees'   within
[aforesaid] home,

ehnakapi, ka uŋma tažuśka mahen ehnakapi, ka iyayapi; ka uŋma wiŋyaŋ,
they-placed, and the other ants   within they-placed, and went on: and the other woman,

Ćaŋktewiŋ ećiyapi koŋ he hokśinćaŋtkiyapi kiŋ kići waŋkan yaŋka; tuka
Heart-killer she was the that   boy-beloved   the with above was [sitting]; but
female called [aforesaid]

yus taŋkan hiyuyapi, ka iye itaŋ-anog iyotaŋkapi.   Uŋkaŋ Śiyaka hde ća
taking outside they thrust her, and they on-each-side they sat down.   Then   Teal went- and
home

ki ka śina uŋmaŋ yuǵaŋ, tuka tuḣmaǵa koŋ yažipe.   Ake uŋma yuǵaŋ,
he and blanket the one opened, but   bees   the they-stung- Again the other opened,
reached   [aforesaid] him.
home

tuka tažuśka kiŋ yažipe.   Uŋkaŋ, Ećiŋ taku wakaŋ ota će, eye ća śina
but ants the they bit Then, Indeed what mysterious many , he said, and blank-
[aforesaid] him.   ets

yazamni, tuka tažuśka tuḣmaǵa ko ti ožuna; hećen owasiŋ wićakaḣapapi.
opened out, but ants bees also house full; so that all they were driven out.

Hećen ye ća Wamnuḣa-itaǵóśa Śiyaka tawićiu kiŋ napin om yaŋka en i;
So he- and Bead Spitter   Teal wives-his the both with [sitting] arrived;
went   was there he

ka, Ćiŋye, hakakta kiŋ he mićiu ye, eya.   Tuka ećaća tak eye śni.   Ake
and, Older brother, last the that return her to me, said. But no-way something said not. Again

eya keś ećaća tak eye śni.   Uŋkaŋ hećen Śiyaka kiŋ hde ća dowaŋ niyaŋ
he although not- some- said not. And so Teal the went- and he sang aloud
said   at-all thing

keyapi: Wamnuḣa-itaǵośa, wi hakakta mićiu wo; mde akasaŋpa keś ćaŋśuśka
they-say: Bead Spitter,   woman-last return her to me; lake across   even box-elder

ko okataŋtaŋ ihewaya će, eya dowaŋ niyaŋ.   Heon dehan woyazaŋ waŋ
also pounding-in-often I drive , he said he sang aloud. Therefore now sickness one

tukten toŋwićaye ća nina wićayazaŋ eće kiŋ he Śiyaka wićao, eyapi kiŋ
when pus-forms and very they sick always the that Teal then-shoots they-say the

hetaŋhaŋ he ićupi.
hence this they-take.

Hehan haŋyetu kehaŋ Igaŋgaŋheća isaŋ waŋ ićiu ka en ya: uŋkaŋ
Then   night when Sharp-grass knife one took and there went: And

Hokśinćantkiyapi kiŋ wiŋyaŋ kiŋ napin om iśtiŋma waŋka: tuka pa kiŋ
Boy-beloved   the women the both with sleeping he lay: but head the

tahu kiŋ en baksa iyeye ća hehan ti mahen wakeya kiŋ mahen yuha inažiŋ.
neck the in he-cut-off and there house-in tent the within having he stood
there.

Hehan oyate kiŋ sdoŋyapi. Hokśinćaŋtkiyapi koŋ pa ćona waŋka e hećen
Then   people the knew-it.   Boy-beloved   the head without lay that so
[aforesaid]

owodutatoŋ. Hećen Śiyaka ti kiŋ ekta yapi; uŋkaŋ koŋkiśitku koŋ
tumult-was   Thus Teal house the to they went; and grandmother-his the
[aforesaid]

owaŋćaya toki ye ća ti akan ekihde ka en yapi. Tuka hok'a ǵina waŋ
all-over some- she and house upon placed, and there they went. But heron brown one
where went

kiŋyaŋ iyaye, hećen waḣupakoza waŋ hok'aǵićana ećiyapi koŋ he śiyaka
flying went, so that   fowl one little brown heron is called the that teal
(snipe)   [aforesaid]

kuŋkiśitku ee. Hećen ćedi kahmiŋ waŋ en iyahe. Hećen oyate kiŋ en
grandmother his is.   Then reed corner one in she alighted. So people the thus
aye ća ćedi wita kiŋ ećelna inapaŋpi ka inakukapi. Hećen ćedi hute kiŋ
went and reed island the entirely tramped down and stamped out.   Hence reed roots the
owasiŋ śaśa eća kiŋ hena Śiyaka kuŋkiśitku we kiŋ hena ee, keyapi.
all red here when the those Teal grandmother-his blood the those are, they say.
and there

Hehan Śiyaka iś Hokśinćaŋtkiyapi pa kiŋ yuha wićaśtayatapi kiŋ
Then Teal he Boy-beloved head the having chief the
timahen wokeya kiŋ mahen yuha inaźiŋ. Uŋkaŋ Hokśinćaŋtkiyapi hoŋku
house-in tent the within having he stood there. And Boy-beloved mother
ćeye ća, Wahte śni, śića, mićinća kiŋ wowihahaye ća nite awaći wićakiye
his cried and. Worthless, bad, my-child the debauched and back on-dance them-he-made
ćikoŋ wahpanimaye, eya ćeya ća, Toki he miye nakaeś hećamoŋ, eya ećee.
that-one poor-me-made, said crying when, Well, I indeed that-I did, he-said always.
Uŋkaŋ Uŋktomi kićopi, ka hoŋku kiŋ heya ćeya ća; Toki iś heya niyaŋ
Then Uŋktomi they called, and mother-his the this-said crying when; Well, he this said aloud
eće, he miye naeś hećamoŋ, eya ećee; Eća iyukćaŋ wo, eyapi. Uŋkaŋ,
always, that I verily this I did, he said always; Indeed consider thou, they said. And
Uŋktomi witkotkoka ehapi će, tokeća idukćaŋpi śni he. De wakeya kiŋ
Uŋktomi a fool you say , why you consider not ? This tent the
mahen naźiŋ, heya. Uŋkaŋ wakeya kiŋ yuźuźupi, uŋkaŋ Śiyaka Hokśin-
within standing, he said. Then tent the they tore down, and Teal Boy-
ćaŋtkiyapi pa yuhe, ća uŋma iś isaŋ koŋ yuhe ća waŋkan inaźiŋ. Uŋkaŋ,
beloved head he-had. and other he knife the had and above he-stood there. Then,
[aforesaid]
Kun ku wo, yani kta će eyapi. Tuka waŋkan iyaye, ća haŋyetu wi kiŋ
Down come thou, you live shall , they said. But upward he-went, and night sun the
ćokaya inaźiŋ. Hećen tohan haŋyetu wi mima ća taku waŋ taŋiŋ kiŋ he
in-the-middle he-stood there. Thus when night sun round and something one appears the that
Śiyaka ee, nape saŋni Wamnuha-itagośa pa kiŋ yuhe ća uŋma iś Igaŋgaŋheća
Teal is, hand one Bead-Spitter head the holds, and other it Sharp-grass
isaŋ koŋ yuhe ća naźiŋ, keyapi.
knife the holds and he stands, they say.
[aforesaid]

NOTES.

1. The form, *Boy-beloved*, is said to be used only of the first-born or eldest son of a chief, and so would stand for Prince. It is 'hokśidaŋ,' *boy*, and 'ćantekiyá,' *to love.* This is put in the plural and passive form, and so means *Beloved-Son.*

2. This myth shows that plurality of wives is a custom of ancient date among the Dakota, and that the taking of sisters was a common form of it. Further, the myth shows a very low state of social morality. To the question, what laws or immemorial usages among the Dakota, restrain them in their matrimonial alliances, M. Renville answers, "There are no laws—that is, laws with penalties—to prevent a man from taking his sister to wife, or even his mother, but we simply say such a man is like a dog—he is a dog." That they often have largely transgressed the line of prescribed consanguinity, in taking wives, is evidenced by the name *Kiyuksa* being worn by a number of the sub-gentes in the Dakota nation. This *dividing* or *breaking* of custom is uniformly referred to their matrimonial alliances.

3. It is interesting to note in these myths the origin, or at least the explanation, of certain singular forms of speech in the language, which it is impossible to account for otherwise. For example, in this myth, we have 'Śiyaka-o,' *Teal-shot,*

which means *a boil*, the core of which is the mythical arrow of box-elder which the Teal drives in, even from beyond the lake.

4. Rather a beautiful mythical idea is that the roots of the tall reeds are made red by the blood of the snipe, which is the grandmother of the teal. Another, which is quite as good as our "man in the moon," is the translation of the Teal, with the gory head of Boy-beloved, together with Sharp-grass and his executioner's knife, to the broad land of the Night Sun.

TRANSLATION.

There was a Boy-beloved whose spittle was all kinds of beautiful beads. So abundant were they that his people arrayed themselves therewith. As the fame of this spread abroad, the young women of surrounding tribes were all anxious to have him for a husband. And as a certain maiden was going to make him her husband, if possible, she heard behind her some one laughing. She stopped, when lo! two women came up and said, "Why, here stands Heart-Killer." And they added, "Come along, Heart-Killer, we are going to make the Bead-Spitter our husband; let us go together." So she went with them.

These two young women were called—"The Two-Women." They did not grow from the people, but grew wildly and were supernatural beings, hence their name, "The Two-Women."

So Heart-Killer went with them and lay down with them, as it was now night. But before they went to sleep the two women said, "Look here, Heart-Killer, when the morning comes, at whosesoever head stands the birch-bark dish with quill work around it and filled with rice, she is the one who shall have Bead-Spitter for a husband." So when the morning came it was standing at the head of Heart-Killer, they say.

Then they went on and came to a large lake, whose farther shores could not be seen. Out on the water was a large canoe. And as this was where Bead-Spitter's village was they called and said, "We have come to get Bead-Spitter for our husband." Some one came rowing. When he arrived, they said, "We have come to make Bead-Spitter our husband." To which he replied, "I do not know any one by that name;" but at the same time he filled his mouth with beads, and then spat them out. The beads were scattered all around, and, laughing, they gathered them up. Then the two women went into the canoe, but the other they drove back, and said, "Go away, Heart-Killer." So they went home with the man, but he was not Bead-Spitter. Heart-Killer stood there crying, when, lo! another canoe came in sight. It was a very bright and beautiful one, for it was all metal. It came on and arrived. This was the Bead-Spitter, and, as he wore very bright clothing, the appearance was very splendid.

"Young woman, what are you crying for here?" he said. So she told him she had come to get Bead-Spitter for a husband and what the two women had done to her. Then he said, "Come on, we two will go home." So she went home with him. Let us return to the others.

The two women went home with the man whom they had met. His name was Teal-Duck, and he lived with his grandmother. By and by some one said, "Teal-Duck, Bead-Spitter calls you to a feast." The Teal said, "Indeed, somebody has said something;" and then to the women he said, "Do not come; they are making mystery; no woman looks at it." So he went. But the women said, "We, too, are accustomed to see the supernatural; we will go," and so they went. When they reached the place there was much noise, and they came and looked in by a hole of the tent, and lo! the inmates were dancing on the back of Teal-Duck. He saw his wives peeping in, and jumping up, said, "I, also, will join the dance on the Teal's back," and so he jumped about. They say this was the duck that is called the "Teal," and hence, to this day, that duck has no fat on its back, because the people danced on it, they say.

Then the two women started back, and, taking two blankets, they put bees in the one and ants in the other and went on. The other woman, who was called Heart-Killer, was with the Boy-Beloved. Her they took and thrust out, and then placed themselves on either side of him.

Then Teal-Duck came home, and when he had lifted one blanket the bees came out and stung him; when he lifted the other the ants came out and bit him. Then he said, "Indeed, here is much that is strange," and so he opened out the blankets and the ants and bees swarmed out and drove everybody from the house. So he went and found the two wives of Teal-Duck with Bead-Spitter, to whom he said, "My elder brother, give me back the younger one." There was no reply. Again he made the demand, but no answer came. And so Teal-Duck went home singing this song, they say:

> "You Spitter of-Pearls, give me back my younger wife;
> For over the lake I always drive box-elder pegs."

And from this has come down to us this form of speech, viz: When sores come out on people and pus is formed, they say, "Teal-Duck has shot them."

Now, when night came on, Sharp-Grass took his knife, and finding the Boy-Beloved sleeping with the two women, he cut off his head, and, holding it in his hand, took his station inside of the tent. When the people knew that the Boy-Beloved lay headless there was a great tumult. So they went to the house of the Teal, but his grandmother had placed him on the top of his tent. They went in, but only a little brown heron came flying out. Hence the fowl that is called Little-Brown-Heron (snipe) is the grandmother of the Teal-Duck. It flew away and alighted in the corner of a reed marsh. Then the people went and trod down and trampled up thoroughly the reed island. Hence, when all the roots of the reeds are red, they say this is the blood of the Teal's grandmother.

Then Teal-Duck, having the head of the Boy-Beloved, went and stood within the tent of the chief. And the mother of Boy-Beloved cried, and said, "You bad, worthless fellow who debauched my child and had people dance upon your own back, you have impoverished me." While she cried, some one said, "Indeed, and was it I who did this thing?" Then they called Uŋktomi, and when his mother said, crying, "Who is it who says this aloud, 'Indeed, and was it I who did it?'" Then Uŋktomi said, "Now, consider this: You say Uŋktomi is a fool; why, don't you understand this? It is he who stands within the tent who says this."

Then they tore down the tent and beheld Teal-Duck holding the head of Boy-Beloved and the other having the knife, and they stood up high. "Come down," they said, "you shall live;" but up they went and stood in the moon. And so now, when the moon is full, what appears in it is Teal-Duck holding the head of One-who-spits-out-pearls, and the other is Sharp-Grass holding the knife in his hands.

This is the Myth.

PARABLE OF THE PRODIGAL SON—Luke XV, 11–32.[1]

Wićaśta waŋ ćiŋhiŋtku noŋpa: uŋkaŋ hakakata kiŋ he atkuku kiŋ
Man   a   son-his   two: and   youngest   the   that father-his   the

hećiya: Ate, woyuha mitawa kte ćiŋ he mićumwo, eya. Uŋkaŋ woyuha
said-to-him: Father,   goods   mine   will-be the   that me-mine-give,   he-said.   And   goods

kiŋ yuakipam wićaku. Uŋkaŋ iyohakam aŋpetu tonana, ćiŋhiŋtku hakakta
the   dividing   them-he gave.   And   after   day   few,   son-his   youngest

koŋ he owasiŋ witaya tpahi, ka itehaŋyaŋ makoće waŋ ekta ićimani ya;
that- that   all   together gathered and   a-far-off   country   a   to   traveling   went;
was   his-own,

ka hen śihaŋ ohaŋyaŋpi kiŋ oŋ, taku yuhe ćiŋ owasiŋ hdutakuniśni. Uŋkaŋ
and there   bad   doings   the   by,   what   he-had the   all   he-destroyed-his-own.   And

owasiŋ waŋna hdusote ćehaŋ, makoće kiŋ he en wićaakihaŋ hiŋća; uŋkaŋ
all   now   he-had-spent when,   country   the   that in   famine   very;   and
his own

hiŋnakaha wićakiźa. Uŋkaŋ makoće kiŋ hen uŋpi kiŋ waŋźi ti kiŋ ekta
consequently he-was-in want.   And   country   the   there   dwelt   the   one house the   to

i, ka kići yaŋka; uŋkaŋ he maǧa kiŋ ekta kukuśe wo wićaku kte yeśi.
went, and   with   was;   and   that-one field   the   to   swine   food them-give should   sent.

Uŋkaŋ kukuśe taku yutapi kiŋ heeś oŋ wipiićiye waćiŋ; tuka tuwedaŋ
And   swine   what   eat   the   even-that with   fill-himself   desired;   but   some-one

dot oku śni. Uŋkaŋ waŋna ićiksuye ćehaŋ heya: Ate wićaśta opewićatoŋ
food gave- not.   And   now   remembered- when   this-said: My-   man   them-bought
him   himself   father

kiŋ heća tona wićayuha, ka hena aǧuyapi iyakićuya yuhapi, tuka miye ke
the   such how-many them-has,   and   those   bread   more-than-enough they have,   but   I   myself

wotektehdapi kiŋ oŋ atakuniśni amayaŋ će. Ito nawaźiŋ, ka ate ekta
hunger   .   the   by-   I am becoming feeble.   Lo!   I stand   and   my-   to
               means-of   (-arise),   father

wahde ća, hewakiye kta; Ate, mahpiya kiŋ ekta ka niye nakuŋ nitokam
I-go-home and,   to-him-I-say-this will: Father,   heaven   the   against and   thee   also   thee-before

wawahtani; ka detaŋhaŋ ćinćamayaye kta iyemaćeće śni; wićaśta
I-have-sinned;   and   from-this time,   child-me-thou-have shouldst   I am worthy   not;   man

opewićayatoŋ kiŋ heeś waŋźi iyećeća makaǧa wo, epe kta će, eya. Uŋkaŋ
hem-thou hast-bought the   even   one   like   me-make,   I-say will   ,   he-said.   And

naźiŋ hiyaye, ća atkuku ekta ki. Tuka nahahiŋ itehaŋ ku, atkuku
he rose to his feet,   and   father-his   to   went-home.   But   while-still   far-off   coming- father-his
                                                    home,

waŋhdake ća, oŋśikida ka, iŋyaŋg ye ća, poskin hduze ća, iikputaka. Uŋkaŋ
saw-him   and   had-compas-   and   running went, and by-the-neck clasped   and   kissed-him   And
his own   sion on his own,   his own,

ćiŋhiŋtku kiŋ hećiya: Ate, mahpiya kiŋ ekta ka niye nitokam wawahtani,
son-his   the   this-said-   Father,   heaven   the   to   and   thee   thee-before   I-have-sinned,

ka detaŋhaŋ ćinćamayaye kte ćiŋ he iyemaćeće śni, eya.
and from-this-time   child-me-thou-have shouldst the   that   I am worthy   not,   he-said.

---

[1] The accompanying interlinear translations from the Bible appeared in the edition of 1852, just after the Grammar.

Tuka atkuku kiŋ taokiye kiŋ hewićakiya: Śina iyotaŋ waśte kiŋ he
But   father-his the   his-servant the   this-to-them-said: Blanket most   good   the that

au-po, ḳa iŋkiya-po; ḳa mazanapćupe waŋ nape kiŋ en iyekiya-po; ḳa
bring ye, and put-on-him-ye; and finger-ring   a   hand the on   put-ye;   and

siha haŋpa ohekiya-po; ḳa pteźićadaŋ ćemyapi kiŋ he den au-po, ḳa kte-po;
feet moccasins put-on-him ye; and   cow-calf   fatted   the that here bring-ye, and kill-ye;

wauŋtapi ḳa uŋkiyuśkiŋpi kta će.   Mićiŋkśi kiŋ de ṭa, uŋkaŋ kini; taŋiŋśni
we-eat   and   we-rejoice   will .   My-son the this dead, and lives-again;   lost

ḳa iyeyapi, eya.   Uŋkaŋ hiŋnakaha wiyuśkiŋpi.
and is-found, he-said.   And   immediately   they-rejoiced.

Uŋkaŋ ćiŋhiŋtku tokapa ḳoŋ, he maġata uŋ : uŋkaŋ tikiyadaŋ ku ća
And   son-his   eldest that-was, that field-at was :   and   house-near-to was when
coming
home

dowaŋpi ḳa waćipi nahoŋ.   Uŋkaŋ ookiye waŋźi kipaŋ, ḳa hena token
singing   and dancing he-heard.   And   servant   one he-called-to, and these-things how

kapi hećiŋhaŋ, he iwaŋġa.   Uŋkaŋ hećiya : Nisuŋka hdi ; uŋkaŋ ni uŋ ḳa
meant   if,   that he-inquired.   And he-said-this- Thy-younger- has-   and alive is and
to-him: brother come-home;

zaniyaŋ hdi kiŋ ; heoŋ-etaŋhaŋ niyate pteźićadaŋ ćemyapi ḳoŋ he kikte će,
well   has- the;   therefore thy-father cow-calf   fatted that-was that killed ,
come-home   for him

eya.   Uŋkaŋ hećen śihda, ḳa tin kihde waćiŋ śni ; hehan atkuku kiŋ
he-said.   And   so he-was-angry, and into-the- he-go- desired not;   then father-his the
house   home

taŋkan hiyu ḳa ćekiya.   Uŋkaŋ hehan wayupte ća atkuku kiŋ hećiya :
out   came and besought-him.   And   then he-answered and father-his the this-said-to ;

Iho, waniyetu ota waŋna waoćićiye, ća iyae ćiŋ tohiŋni kawape śni ; hećeća
Lo! winter   many now I-have-helped-thee, and thy-word the   ever I-passed- not;   thus
bevond

eśta, kodawićawaye ćiŋ om wimduśkiŋ kta e tohiŋni taćiŋćadaŋ waŋźi
although, friend-them-I-have   the with I-rejoice might that at-any-time deer-child   one

mayaḳu śni će : Tuka nićiŋkśi witkowiŋpi kiŋ om woyuha nitawa kiŋ
me-thou-   not :   But thy-son   harlots   the with   property thy   the
gavest

temnićiye ćiŋ de hdi ća, waŋćake pteźićadaŋ ćemyapi kiŋ he yećićaṭa će,
eaten-up-for-thee the this come- when, at-once cow-calf   fatted   the that thou-for-him- ,
home   hast-killed

eya.   ·Uŋkaŋ hećiya ; Ćiŋś, ohiŋniyaŋ mići yauŋ ; ḳa taku mduhe ćiŋ he
he-said.   And this-he-said- Son, always me-with thou-art; and what I-have the that
to-him:

iyuhpa nitawa.   Nisuŋka kiŋ de ṭa uŋkaŋ kini ; taŋiŋśni, uŋkaŋ iyeyapi
all   thine.   Thy-younger- the this was- and has-come- was-lost, and   is-found
brother   dead   to-life;

kiŋ heoŋ etaŋhaŋ ito, ćaŋte uŋwaśtepi ḳa uŋkiyuśkiŋpi kte ćiŋ he hećetu
the   therefore lo! heart we-good   and   we-rejoice   should the that is-right

će, eya će.
, he-said .

THE LORD'S PRAYER.

Itaŋćaŋ tawoćekiye kin.
Lord   his-prayer   the.

Ateuŋyaŋpi mahpiya ekta naŋke ćiŋ ; Nićaźe ᴋiŋ wakaŋdapi kte;
Father-we-have   heaven   in thou-art the;   Thy-name the holy-regarded shall;

Nitokićoŋze kiŋ u kte.   Mahpiya ekta token nitawaćiŋ ećoŋpi kiŋ, maka akan
Thy-kingdom the come shall.   Heaven in how   thy-will   is-done the, earth upon

hećen ećoŋpi nuŋwe.   Aŋpetu kiŋ de taku-yutapi uŋḳu-po:[1] ḳa wauŋḣtanipi
so   done   may-it-be.   Day   the   this   food   us-give: and   our-trespasses

kiŋ uŋkićićaźuźu-po, uŋkiś iyećen toma ećiŋśniyaŋ uŋkokićihaŋyaŋpi hena
the   erase-for-us,   we   like-as as-may-as wrongly   have-done-to-us   those

iyećen wićuŋkićićaźuźupi kiŋ.   Wowawiyutaŋye kiŋ he en iyaye uŋyaŋpi
even-as   them-we-forgive   the,   Temptation   the   that into to-go us-cause

śni-po, ḳa taku śića etaŋhaŋ euŋhdaku-po.   Wokićoŋze kiŋ, wowaś'ake kiŋ,
not,   and what bad   from   us-deliver.   Kingdom   the,   strength   the,

wowitaŋ kiŋ, henakiya owihaŋke wanin ŋitawa nuŋwe.   Amen.
glory   the,   all-these   end   none   thine   may-be.   Amen.

THE FOURTH COMMANDMENT.

Woahope itopa.
Commandment   fourth.

Aŋpetu-okihpapi kiŋ he kiksuye ća wakaŋ da-wo.   Aŋpetu śakpe
Day-of-rest   the   that remember ' and holy regard thou.   Day   six

ḣtayani ḳa nitoḣtani kiŋ owasiŋ ećanoŋ kta.   Tuka aŋpetu iśakowiŋ kiŋ he
thou-labor and thy-work   the   all   thou-do shalt.   But   day   seventh   the that

aŋpetu-okihpapi, Yehowa Taku-Wakaŋ nitawa kiŋ he tawa, he en wićoḣtani
day-of-rest,   Jehovah   God   thy   the that his,   that in   work

takudaŋ ećanoŋ kte śni, niye ḳa nićiŋkśi, nićuŋkśi, wićaśta nitaokiye, wiŋyaŋ
some-little   thou-do shalt not, thou and thy-son,   thy-daughter,   man   thy-servant,   woman

nitaokiye, nitawoteća, ḳa tuwe tokeća nitatiyopa kiŋ en uŋ kiŋ henakiya.
thy-servant,   thy-cattle,   and whoever else   thy-door   the   in is the 'so-many.

Aŋpetu śakpe en Yehowa mahpiya, maka, miniwaŋća ḳa taku ohnaka
Day   six   in   Jehovah   heaven,   earth.   water-all   and what   is-in

ko owasiŋ kaǵa; uŋkaŋ aŋpetu iśakowiŋ kiŋ he en okihpa, hećen Yehowa
also   all   made;   and   day   seventh   the   that in   rested,   so   Jehovah

aŋpetu-okihpapi kiŋ he hdawaśte ḳa hduwakaŋ.
day-of-rest   the   that blessed   and hallowed
                               his own   his own.

---

[1] Some of the Dakota object to the use of the imperative in wo and po, in addressing God, pre-
ferring the ending ye, please.—J. O. D.

DAKOTA GRAMMAR, TEXTS, AND ETHNOGRAPHY.

PART THIRD.

ETHNOGRAPHY.

ETHNOGRAPHY.

CHAPTER I.

THE DAKOTA.

The introduction to the Dakota Grammar and Dictionary, published by the Smithsonian Institution in 1852, commences with this paragraph:

The nation of Sioux Indians, or Dakotas, as they call themselves, is supposed to number about 25,000. They are scattered over an immense territory, extending from the Mississippi River on the east to the Black Hills on the west, and from the mouth of the Big Sioux River on the south to Devils Lake on the north.. Early in the winter of 1837 they ceded to the United States all their land lying on the eastern side of the Mississippi; and this tract at present forms the settled portion of Minnesota. During the summer of 1851 the Commissioner of Indian Affairs, with Governor Ramsey, of Minnesota, negotiated with the Dakotas of the Mississippi and Minnesota, or St. Peters Valley, for all their land lying east of a line running from Otter-Tail Lake through Lake Traverse (Lac Travers) to the junction of the Big Sioux River with the Missouri; the Indians retaining for their own settlements a reservation on the upper Minnesota 20 miles wide and about 140 long. This purchase includes all the wooded lands belonging to the Dakotas, and extends, especially on the south side of the Minnesota River, some distance into the almost boundless prairie of the West. Beyond this, the Indians follow the buffaloes, which, although evidently diminishing in numbers, still range in vast herds over the prairies. This animal furnishes the Indian with food and clothing, and a house, and, during the summer, with the " bois de vache" for fuel. In the winter these sons of the prairie are obliged to pitch their tents at or in the little clusters of wood, which here and there skirt the margins of the streams and lakes.

The interval of thirty years has made such changes in this people as to require an almost entirely new statement. First, as regards numbers: The above statement was made mainly by estimation, and not on actual count. Only a small portion of the Dakota were at that time receiving annuities. In this case the estimate was largely under the truth. Since that time, when the western Dakota were at war with our Government, they were variously estimated as numbering from 40,000 upward. But as they are now gathered at the various agencies, viz, Cheyenne River, Crow Creek, Devils Lake, Lower Brule, Pine Ridge, Rosebud, Sisseton, Standing Rock, and Yankton, in Dakota Territory, with Poplar River in Montana, and Santee in Nebraska, they are reported at a little less than 30,000. This does not include the more than 100 families of homesteaders at Flandreau and Brown Earth. Nor does it include Sitting Bull's party, the greater part of which has recently returned to the United States. In addition to these, are, Dakota-speaking people beyond the line, the Stoneys, and Assiniboin, besides at least 1,000 of the refugees from our war of 1862, who have become permanent residents in the Queen's dominions. We now conclude that 40,000 will be a low estimate of those who speak the Dakota language.

Secondly, as regards habitat: This will be made plain by a brief statement of the migrations and history of the different tribes which constitute the Dakota nation.

TRIBES.

Their name, the Dakota say, means *leagued* or *allied;* and they sometimes speak of themselves as the "Oćeti śakowiŋ," *Seven council fires.* These are the seven principal bands which compose the tribe or nation, viz:

1. The Mdewakaŋtoŋwaŋ, *Village of the Spirit Lake.* Their name is derived from a former residence at Mdewakaŋ (*Spirit* or *Sacred Lake*), Mille Lacs, which are in Minnesota, at the head of Rum River. This was the old home of the nation, when Hennepin and Du Luth visited them two hundred years ago. As these so-called Spirit Lake villagers occupied the gateway of the nation, they were for a long time better known than the other portions of the tribe, and came to regard themselves as living in the center of the world. Thirty years ago this record was made of them:

They are divided into seven principal villages, three of which are still on the western bank of the Mississippi, and the others on or near the Minnesota, within 25 or 30 miles of Fort Snelling. This portion of the Dakota people have received annuities since the year 1838, and their number, as now enrolled, is about 2,000. They plant corn and other vegetables, and some of them have made a little progress in civilization.

In that same year of 1851 they sold their land to the Government and were removed to a reservation on the upper Minnesota, and were the principal actors in the *emeute* of 1862, which resulted in their capture and dispersion. Those who fled to the Dominion of Canada with Little Crow have, for the most part, remained there, while those who lived through the ordeal of captivity are now a civilized people at the Santee Agency, in Nebraska, and at the Flandreau Homestead Settlement on the Big Sioux.

The origin of the name Mdewakaŋtoŋwaŋ is accounted for by Mr. M. Renville as follows: In the east country there was a large lake, and in the lake there was a Taku-Wakaŋ, which was feared. But there they made their village. And when the planting time came this local god always made his appearance. But this gens dreamed of it and worshiped it, and no more feared it. Hence they got the name of "Sacred-Lake Villagers." This was an original gens of the Dakota people, which was afterwards divided into seven gentes, viz: (1) Ki-yu-ksa, *Breakers of custom* or *law*, said to refer to marrying into their own gens. (2) He-mni-ćaŋ (Hay-minnee-chan), *Hill-water-wood*, the name of Barn Bluff at Red Wing. (3) Ka-po-źa (Kaposia), *Light ones*, those who traveled unincumbered with baggage. (4) Ma-ġa-yu-te śni, *They who do not eat geese.* (5) He-ya-ta-toŋ-we, *The Back Villagers.* This was the Lake Calhoun band. (6) Oyate-śića, *Bad people.* (7) Tiŋ-ta-toŋ-we, *Prairie Villagers.*[1]

2. The Waȟpekute, *Leaf-shooters.* It is not now known from what circumstances the Waȟpekute received their name. Thirty years ago they were a roving band of about 500 or 600, who laid claim to the country of Cannon River, the head waters of the Blue Earth, and westward. They were guilty of the massacre of Spirit Lake, in Iowa, in 1857, and were so demoralized thereby that they became rovers, and have lost their place in the Dakota family. After the sale of their land, in 1851, they became connected with the Spirit-Lake band, and, disregarding their gentes, some of them are now at Santee Agency and some at Sisseton Agency, but the greater part have fled to the Missouri River and to Canada.

3. The Waȟpetoŋwaŋ, *Village in the Leaves*, probably obtained their name from the fact that formerly they lived only in the woods. The old home of this band was about the Little Rapids, which is some 45 miles by water from the mouth of the Minnesota River. Thirty years ago it was written:

About 300 still reside there, but the larger part of the band have removed to Lac-qui-parle and Big Stone Lake. In all they number about 1,000 or 1,200 souls. They all plant corn, more or less, and at Lac-qui-parle, one of the mission stations occupied by the American Board of Commissioners for Foreign Missions, they have made some progress in learning to read and write their own language, and have substituted, to some extent, the use of the plow for the hoe.

[1] Hake-waśte, a chief of the Mdewakaŋtoŋwaŋ, who was in Washington, D. C., in 1880, gave the fifth and seventh gentes as "Heyata otoŋwe" and "Tiŋta otoŋwe;" but since then Rev. A. L. Riggs has given the forms "Heyatatoŋwaŋ" and "Tiŋtatoŋwaŋ."—J. O. D.

These *Dwellers in the Leaves* were more or less mixed up in the outbreak of 1862. Some of them fled to Manitoba, where they now have a native church near Fort Ellin. Some of them were of the captivity, and carried letters and religion into the prison, while some were prominent in bringing about a counter revolution and in delivering the white captives. They are now mixed with Sisseton on the Sisseton and Devil's Lake Reservations and in the Brown Earth Homestead Settlement.

Mr. M. Renville accounts for the origin of the name *Leaf Villagers* in this wise: "First, tradition says the clan were in the habit of making booths with tree branches with the leaves attached. Secondly, when camping in a country of prairie and woods they were in the habit of making their camp in the wood. Hence their name. They were divided into three subgentes, viz: 1. Waḣpa-toŋ-waŋ.[1] 2. Ta-ka-psiŋ-tona. 3. Oteliatoŋna. They lived originally at Knife Lake, where there was a beautiful prairie. A part of the clan became famous ball players, and hence the name of Takapsintona. Another part were afraid of enemies, and so, when on journeys, they sought a *thicket* in which to make their camp. Hence they were called Otelii-atoŋwe, *Dwellers in Thickets*."

4. The Si-si-toŋ-waŋ. Formerly we were told that si-siŋ meant *swampy land;* and so we translated the name *Swamp Villagers*. But the evidence is in favor of another meaning and origin. M. Renville gives the following: At Traverse des Sioux, at the Blue Earth, and on the Big Cottonwood, they made their villages. They took many fish from the river and lakes. These they cut up and dried, throwing the scales and entrails in heaps, which appeared partly white and shining, and partly black and dirty. This appearance they called siŋ-siŋ. And hence when the young men of other villages would go to see them they said, Let us go to the Sisiatoŋwaŋ—those who live on the siŋsiŋ. Hence the people were called Sisseton.

They were divided thus into subgentes: The white people brought whiskey. The Sissetons got drunk and killed each other. By this means they were scattered. Some went up to Lake Traverse, and some went to the Two Woods west of Lac-qui-parle.

These last were called (1) Ti-zaptaŋna, *Five Lodges*. These were Thunder Face's people. Some were called (2) Okopeya. These were his brother's followers. A part of the gens remained at Traverse des Sioux

---

[1] The following is a full list of the gentes of the Waḣpetoŋwaŋ, as obtained from their missionary, Rev. Edward Ashley, in 1884: (1) Iŋyaŋ ćeyaka atoŋwaŋ, *Village at the Rapids;* (2) Takapsin toŋwaŋna, *Those who Dwell at the Shinny-ground;* (3) Wiyaka otina, *Dwellers on the Sand;* (4) Oteḣi atoŋwaŋ, *Village On-the-Thicket* (sic); (5) Wita otina, *Dwellers In-the-Island;* (6) Wakpa atoŋwaŋ, *Village On-the-River;* (7) Ćaŋ-kaġa otina, *Dwellers In-Log* (huts?). When they camped with the Sisitoŋwaŋ, a different order of these gentes was observed, as will be explained hereafter.—J. O. D.

and at Little Rock. These were called (3) Ćan-śda-ći-ḳa-na, *Little place bare of wood*.[1] These were Sleepy Eyes' and Red Iron's people. Another portion was called (4) Amdo-wa-pus-kiya. They lived at Lake Traverse and were great buffalo hunters. They often moved camp when their meat was not dried, and so spread it out on the horses' backs and on the thills, and hence were called *Dryers on the Shoulder*. These were Standing Buffalo's people. (5) Basdeće śni. (6) Kapoźa. (7) Ohdihe.

Previous to 1862 they numbered about 3,000. But, being involved in the uprising of that year, they fled to the Missouri River and to Canada. Some have returned, and are at the Sisseton and Devil's Lake agencies.[2]

These Mississippi and Minnesota Dakotas are called, by those on the Missouri, Isaŋties or Santies, from 'isaŋati' or 'isaŋyati;' which name seems to have been given them from the fact that they once lived at Isaŋtamde, *Knife Lake*, one of those included under the denomination of Mille Lacs.[3]

---

[1] Mr. Ashley says that these were Sleepy Eyes' division of the Kaḥmi atoŋwaŋ.—J. O. D.

[2] The following are the gentes and subgentes of the Sisitoŋwaŋ, as given by their missionary, Rev. Edw. Ashley, in 1884. Beginning at the north and to the right of the opening of the tribal circle the tents were pitched in the following order: 1. (*a*) Wita waziyata otina, *Dwellers at the Northern Island*. (*b*) Ohdihe. 2. (*a*) Basdeće śni, *Those who do not split* (the backbone of the buffalo). (*b*) Itokaḥ-tina, *Dwellers at the South*. 3. (*a*) Kaḥmi atoŋwaŋ, *Village at the Bend*. Part of these were called Ćaŋśda oiḳana. (*b*) Mani-ti, *Those who pitched their tents away from the main camp*. (*c*) Keze, *Barbed*, as a fishhook; a name of ridicule. The Keze tents were on the right of the south end of the tribal circle. On the left of them came: 4. Ćaŋkute, *Shooters at trees*, another name given in derision. 5. (*a*) Ti-zaptaŋ, *Five Lodges*. (*b*) Okopeya, *In danger*. 6. Kapoźa, *Those who travel with light burdens*. 7. Amdowapuskiyapi, *Those who place the meat on their shoulders in order to dry it*. These were divided into three subgentes, Maka ideya, Waŋmdiupi duta, and Waŋmdi nahotoŋ. When only a part of the tribe was together the following camping order was observed: The Wita waziyata otina pitched their tents from the right side of the opening at the north and as far as the east; next, the Itokaḥ-tina extended from the east to the south; the Kapoźa occupied the area from the south to the west, and the Amdo-wapus-kiyapi filled the space between them and the Wita waziyata otina.

When the Sisitoŋwaŋ and Waḥpetoŋwaŋ camped together it was in the following order, beginning at the right side of the opening at the north: 1. Wita waziyata otina (including Ohdihe). 2. Basdeće śni (including Itokaḥ tina). 3. Iŋyaŋ ćeyaka atoŋwaŋ. 4. Takapsin toŋwaŋna. 5. Wiyaka otina. 6. Oteḥi atoŋwaŋ. 7. Wita otina. 8. Wakpa atoŋwaŋ. 9. Ćaŋkaǵa otina (on the right of the south part of the circle). 10. Keze (on the left of the south part of the circle). 11. Kaḥmi atoŋwaŋ. 12. Ćaŋkute. 13. Okopeya. 14. Tizaptaŋ. 15. Kapoźa. 16. Amdo wapuskiyapi (on the left side of the opening at the north).—J. O. D.

[3] According to the context, we are led to make this last sentence of the author refer to four divisions of the Dakota: Mdewakaŋtoŋwaŋ, Waḥpekute, Waḥpetoŋwaŋ, and Sisitoŋwaŋ. But this is commented on in "The Word Carrier" for January, 1888, in a criticism of Kirk's Illustrated History of Minnesota:

"One such" error "we find on page 33, where the Mdewakantonwans are said to be one of the four bands of the Santees. Instead of this, the Mdewakantonwans are the Santees. It is true that white men on the Missouri River and westward, with utter disregard of the facts, call all the Minnesota Sioux 'Santees'; but a Minnesota writer should keep to the truth, if he knows it."

This led the undersigned to ask the editor of "The Word Carrier," Rev. A. L. Riggs, the following questions (in April, 1888): (1) Why do you say that the Mdewakaŋtoŋwaŋ are the (only) Santees? (2) How do you interpret the statement made in the first edition of 'The Dakota Language,' p. viii ('These

5. The Ihaŋktoŋwaŋ[1] or Yankton, *Village at the End*, were counted, thirty years ago, at about 240 lodges, or 2,400 persons. They are now reported at nearly that number by actual count. The outbreak did not disturb them and they continue to occupy their old home at the present Yankton Agency on the Missouri River, where they are making progress in civilization. This is the headquarters of Rev. J. P. Williamson's Presbyterian mission, and also of Bishop Hare's mission of the Episcopal Church.

6. The Ihaŋktoŋwaŋna, one of the *End Village* bands, were estimated at 400 lodges, or 4,000 souls. The Dakota tents on the Minnesota do not average more than about 6 inmates; but on the prairie, where, though the material for the manufacture of tents is abundant, tent-poles are scarce, they make their dwellings larger, and average, it is thought, about 10 persons to a lodge. The Ihaŋktoŋwaŋna are divided into the Huŋkpatina;[2] the Pabakse, *Cut Heads;* the Wazikute or Ćaŋona, *Pine Shooters;*[3] and the Kiyuksa, *Dividers* or *Breakers of Law.* Formerly they were the owners of

---

Mississippi and Minnesota Dakotas are called by those on the Missouri, Isanties,' to which your father added in 1882, 'or Santees')? Who were these Mississippi and Minnesota Dakotas at the date mentioned (1852) if not the Mdewakaŋtoŋwaŋ, Waḣpekute, Waḣpetoŋwaŋ, and Sisitoŋwaŋ? (3) Has there not been a change in the use of 'Santee' since 1852? (4) Are not all the Dakotas on the Santee reservation known as Santees, or were they not thus known from the time of their settlement on that reservation till they became citizens of the United States?"

To this Mr. Riggs replied as follows:

"The point I made with Prof. Kirk was this: That while there is a use of the name Santee in the Missouri River country to signify the Dakota Indians of the Minnesota and Mississippi, and those removed from there, yet the original meaning was more specific and limited. And that it was inexcusable in a Minnesota historian to have ignored the original and local signification of the term. This did not conflict in the least with the statement made by my father in the Dakota Dictionary * * * The Mdewakan and Isantamde are one and the same, *i. e.*, one of the Mille Lacs, from whence, as you know, came the names Mdewakantonwan and Isanyati. These Mdewakantonwan are the Santees of Santee Agency, Nebraska, who were removed from Minnesota."

Such testimony ought to be decisive; yet we find the father making the following statement (in 1882) in his "Argument of Migrations (derived) from Names" which will be found in the present volume: "Santee. For a century or more past there have been included in this name the Leaf Shooters (Waḣpekute) and also the Leaf Village (Waḣpetoŋwaŋ)."—J. O. D.

[1] The following names of the Yankton gentes were furnished by Heḣaka mani, a Yankton, in 1878: 1. Ćaŋ-kute, *Shooters at Trees.* 2. Ćaǧu, *Lights,* or, *Lungs.* 3. Wakmuha oiŋ, *Pumpkin-rind Earring.* 4. Iha isdaye, *Mouth Greasers.* 5. Waćeuŋpa, *Roasters.* 6. Ikmuŋ, *Wild Cat* (people). 7. Oyate śića, *Bad Nation.* 8. Waśićuŋ ćiŋća, *White Men's Sons,* or, *Half-Breeds* (a modern addition). In August, 1891, Rev. Joseph W. Cook, a missionary to the Yankton, obtained from several men the following order of their gentes in the camping circle:—On the right: 1. Iha isdaye. 2. Wakmuha oiŋ. 3. Ikmuŋ. On the left: 4. Waćeuŋpa. 5. Ćaŋ kute. 6. Oyate śića. 7. Ćaǧu. The first and seventh gentes always camped in the van.—J. O. D.

[2] See note under the next division—Huŋkpapa.

[3] It is said that the young men of a clan were poor shooters, and were led to practice by shooting at a mark, and that was a pine tree. Hence both these names—Ćaŋ-ona, *Hitting the Wood,* and Wazi-kute, *Shooting the Pine.* From this clan of *Pine Shooters* the *Assiniboin,* or "Hohe" of the Dakota, are said to have sprung.

the James River country. Now they are distributed in the villages along the Missouri, principally at Standing Rock.[1]

7. The Titoŋwaŋ. In its present form this might mean *House-dwellers*. But it is understood to be a contracted form of Tiŋta-toŋwaŋ, meaning *Dwellers on the Prairie*, or *prairie villages*. They constitute one-half or more of the whole Dakota nation. For many years they have followed the buffalo west of the Missouri River, and now they are mainly confined to the great Sioux Reserve in southwestern Dakota. Not a dozen years have passed since they began to take steps towards education and civilization. Hitherto the Episcopalians have done the most missionary work among them. Within two years past they have taken some interest in sending their children to Hampton and Carlisle to be educated. With the Shaiena Shahiyela, or Cheyennes, they have maintained friendly relations and intermarried. They are divided into seven principal tribes, viz: The Sićaŋgu, or Brules, *Burnt Thighs;* the Itazipćo, or Sans Arcs, *No Bows*, or *Without Bows*, as the word is understood to be contracted from Itazipa ćodaŋ; the Sihasapa, *Black-feet;* the Minikaŋye woźupi, or Minnekonjoos, *Who Plant by the Water;* the Oohenoŋpa, *Two Boilings* or *Two Kettles;* the Oglala, or Ogalala, and the Huŋkpapa. Each of these names has doubtless a history, which will be herewith given as far as we are able to trace it. Let us begin with the last:

Huŋkpapa: For a good many years we have been anxiously seeking to find out the meaning and origin of "Huŋkpapa," and its near neighbor "Huŋkpatina"—they both being names of large families or clans among the Titoŋwaŋ. But our investigations have hitherto been unsatisfactory. Sometimes it has seemed to us that they must be formed from "Huŋka," which is an honorable name for the older male relatives, and for ancestors generally: as in "Huŋkake" *ancestors*, and "Huŋkawaŋźi" *brothers*, and "Huŋkayapi" *elders*. The analysis would be reduced to its limit in "Huŋ" *mother*. "Huŋkpa" would be Huŋka-pa meaning Family-Head; and Huŋkpapa would be a reduplication, while Huŋkpatina would mean *Dwellers of Family Head.*

<hr/>

[1] In 1880, Nasuna taŋka, *Big Head*, and Mato noŋpa, *Two Grizzly Bears*, said that their people were divided into two parts, each having seven gentes. (I) Upper Ihaŋktoŋwaŋna includes the following: 1. Ćaŋ-ona, *Those who Hit the Tree*, or, Wazi-kute, *Shooters at the Pine*. 2. Takini. 3. Śikśićena, *Small bad ones of different kinds*. 4. Bakihoŋ, *Those who Gashed-Themselves*. 5. Kiyuksa, *Breakers of the Law* or *Custom*. 6. Pa-baksa, *Cut Heads* (divided into sub-gentes). 7. Name not remembered. (II) Huŋkpatina, or Lower Ihaŋktoŋwaŋna, includes the following: 1. Pute temini (*sic*), *Sweating Upper-Lips*. 2. Śuŋ ikćeka, *Common Dogs* (?). 3. Tahuha yuta, *Eaters of the Scrapings of Skins*. 4. Saŋona, *Those Who Hit Something White* or *Gray* (*in the distance*). These are called the Saŋonee (*One Siders?*) by the author. 5. Iha śa, *Red Lips*. 6. Ite gu, *Burnt Faces*. 7. Pte yute śni, *Eat no Buffalo*. The Ihaŋktoŋwaŋna are generally called Yanktonai.—J. O. D.

Then again we have endeavored to derive the words in question, from He-iŋkpa or He-oiŋkpa, which would give two meanings, *Horn-end* or *That-end*. In this case we have supposed the names might have originated from their dwelling on the upper or smaller part of the Missouri River. But as I said, neither of these have been quite satisfactory. Some other attempted explanations by Indians have been still less so.

But the other day, Paul Mazakutemani, who is largely acquainted with the habits and customs of the prairie Indians as well as the more eastern bands, gave what seems to be a very natural account of the origin of both the words. From time immemorial it has been the custom of the prairie Dakota to travel under strict camp regulations. The tribes of the children of Israel in the wilderness did not set forward with more formality, and camp with more precision. The "Tiyotipi" or Soldier's Lodge took the place of the Ark of the covenent. Under this leadership each band and each family took its appointed place in the encampment. In two lines they followed the lead of young men on horseback until the circle was completed. At the farther end of the circle a space was left in which was pitched the Tiyotipi. More commonly on the prairie this soldiers' tent was in the center of the area. The ends of this gateway, which would be well represented by the horns of a buffalo cow turning inwards, were called "Huŋkpa," evidently from *He-oiŋkpa*. The families camping on either side of this gateway were called *Huŋkpa-tina:* whence the name came to be attached to a clan of the Ihaŋktoŋwaŋna. The added "pa" in Huŋkpapa is probably only a reduplication.[1] This is decidedly the best and most satisfactory explanation of this difficult question in philology, that has come to my knowledge.

Oglala finds its corresponding term in Santee, in Ohdada, which means *to scatter one's own in;* and is understood to have originated in boys throwing sand in each others' eyes.

The following important information is furnished by Rev. J. Owen Dorsey:

In 1879 I received a letter from the Rev. John Robinson, missionary to the Oglala at Red Cloud Agency, giving the origin of the names Huŋkpapa, Oglala, etc., as told him by the Indians at that place:

" Huŋkpapa, those who camp at the head end of the (Dakota) circle; Huŋkpati, those who camp at the tail end of that circle. This latter probably includes both

---

[1] If there were a reduplication in this word, would not the form be "Huŋ-kpa-kpa," instead of Huŋ-kpa-pa? The final "pa" may be compared with the adverbial ending "wapa" in akowapa, etc., the locative ending "ta," and with the Biloxi endings "wa" and "wayaⁿ," denoting *direction.*—J. O. D.

Ihaŋktoŋwaŋ (Yankton), or ' End Village People,' and Ihaŋktoŋwaŋna (Yanktonnais), or ' People of the Smaller End Village.'

"Oglala originated in a quarrel between two women. One threw some flour (?) in the face of the other, thus giving rise to the name, which means ' She scattered her own.' The adherents of the injured woman separated from the rest, and since then their people have been called the Oglala."

The Oglala are called ' U-bȼa'-ȼa ' by the Ponka and Omaha tribes.

DIVISIONS OF THE TITOŊWAŊ.

A. Siȼaŋgu—*Burnt Thighs*, or *Brules*: List of Tataŋka wakaŋ (1880): (1) Iyaḳoza, Lump or Wart on a horse's leg; (2) Ćoka towela, Blue spot in the middle; (3) Śiyo taŋka, *Large Grouse;* (4) Homna, *Smelling of Fish;* (5) Śiyo subula, *Small (?) Grouse;* (6) Kaŋgi yuha, *Keeps the Raven;* (7) Pispiza wiȼaśa, *Prairie Dog People (?);* (8) Waleġa uŋ wohaŋ, *Boils with the Paunch Skin;* (9) Waȼeuŋpa, *Roasters;* (10) Sawala, *Shawnees* (descended from former Shawnee captives); (11) Ihaŋktoŋwaŋ, *Yanktons* (descended from Yanktons—refugees?); (12) Naḣpaḣpa, *Take down leggings* (after returning from war); (13) Apewaŋ taŋka, *Large Mane.*

List of Rev. W. J. Cleveland (1884): (1) Siȼaŋgu, *Burnt Thighs proper;* (2) Kaḳeġa, *Making a grating noise;* (3 a) Hiŋhaŋ śuŋwapa, *Towards the Owl Feather;* (b) Śuŋkaha napiŋ, *Wears dog-skin around the neck;* (4) Hihakaŋhaŋhaŋ wiŋ, *Woman the skir. of whose teeth dangles;* (5) Huŋku waniȼa, *Motherless;* (6) Miniskuya kiȼuŋ, *Wears Salt;* (7 a) Kiyuksa, *Breakers of the Law or Custom ("Breaks or Cuts in two his own");* (b) Tiglabu, *Drums-on-His-own Lodge;* (8) Waȼeoŋpa, *Roasters;* (9) Wagluhe, *Inbreeders;* (10) Isaŋyati, *Santees* (descended from the Mdewakaŋtoŋwaŋ?); (11) Wagmeza yuha, *Has Corn;* (12 a) Waleġa oŋ wohaŋ, *Boils with the Paunch Skin;* (b) Waḣna, *Snorters;* (13) Oglala iȼiȼaġa, *Makes himself an Oglala;* (14) Tiyoȼesli, *Dungs in the Lodge;* (15) Wazáza, *meaning not given (Osage?* or *Wash?);* (15) Ieska ȼiŋȼa, *Interpreters' Sons, Half-breeds;* (17) Ohe noŋpa, *Two Boilings,* or, *Two Kettles* (descended from the Oohe noŋpa?); (18) Okaġa wiȼaśa, *Southern People.*

B. Itazipȼo—*Sans Arcs*, or, *Without Bows:* (1) Mini śala, *Red Water;* or, Itazipȼo-ḣȼa, *Real Itazipȼo;* (2) Śina luta oiŋ, *Red cloth ear-pendant;* (3) Woluta yuta, *Eat dried venison or buffalo meat from the hind quarter;* (4) Maz pegnaka, *Piece of metal in the hair;* (5) Tataŋka ȼesli, *Buffalo Dung;* (6) Śikśiȼela, *Bad ones of different sorts;* (7) Tiyopa oȼaŋnuŋpa, *Smokes at the Door* (Rev. H. Swift, *fide* Waanataŋ, or, Charger).

C. Siha-sapa—*Black Feet:* (1) Ti-zaptaŋ, *Fire Lodges;* (2) Siha sapa ḣȼa, *Real Black Feet;* (3) Hohe, *Assiniboin,* or, *Rebels;* (4) Kaŋgi śuŋ pegnaka, *Raven Feather In-the-hair;* (5) Wazáze, "*Wash*," or, *Osage (?);* (6) Wamnuga oiŋ, *Shell ear-pendant* (of the shape of a conch, but very small); (7) Unknown or extinct (Rev. H. Swift, *fide* Charger, who denied that the last gens was called Glagla heȼa).

D. Minikoozu (Minneconjou)—*Those who Plant by the Water:* (1) Uŋkȼe yuta, *Dung Eaters;* (2) Glagla heȼa, *Untidy, Slovenly, Shiftless;* (3) Śuŋka yute śni, *Eat no Dog;* (4) Niġe taŋka, *Big Belly (fide* Charger); (5) Wakpokiŋyaŋ, *Flies along the creek;* (6) Iŋyaŋ-ha oiŋ, *Shell ear-ring, i. e.,* the muscle-shell one; (7) Śikśiȼela, *Bad ones of different sorts;* (8) Wagleźa oiŋ, *Water-snake ear-ring;* (9) Waŋ naweġa, *i. e.,* waŋhiŋkpe naweġa *Broken Arrows* (about extinct, *fide* Charger). All but Nos. 4 and 9 were obtained in 1880. All nine were given in 1884 by Rev. H. Swift.

E. Oohe noŋpa, *Two Kettles,* or, *Two Boilings:* (1) Oohe noŋpa; (2) Mawaḣota, *Skin smeared with whitish earth.* (Rev. H. Swift, *fide* Charger.)

F. Oglala: List of 1879–80: (1) Payabya (see 2 of next list); (2) Tapiśleca, *Spleen;* (3) Kiyuksa, *Breakers of the Law,* or, *Custom;* (4) Wazáza, see third list; (5) Ite śiȼa, *Bad Faces,* or, Oglala ḣȼa, *Real Oglala;* (6) Oiyuḣpe, see next list; (7) Wagluhe, *In-breeders* (commonly called *Loafers*). List of Rev. W. J. Cleveland (1884): (1) Ite śiȼa, *Bad Faces;* (2) Payabyeya, *Pushed aside;* (3) Oyuḣpe, *Thrown down,* or, *Unloaded;* (4) Tapiśleȼa, *Spleen;* (5) Peśla, *Bald-headed;* (6) Ćeḣ huha toŋ, *Pot with legs;* (7) Wableniȼa, *Orphans* (Rev. Mr. Swift makes this a society or order, not a gens); (8) Peśla pteȼela, *Short Bald-head;* (9) Taśnaheȼa, *Gophers;* (10) Iwayusota, *Used up by begging for,* or, *Used up with the mouth;* (11) Wakaŋ, *Mysterious;* (12 a) Iglaka teḣila, *Refused to remove the camp;* (b) Ite śiȼa, *Bad Faces;* (13) Ite śiȼa etaŋhaŋ, *Part of the Bad Faces;* (14) Zuzeȼa kiyaksa, *Bites the Snake in two;* (15) Waȼeoŋpa, *Roasters;* (16) Waȼape, *Stabbers;* (17) Tiyoȼesli, *Dungs in the lodge;* (18) Wagluhe, *In-breeders* (Cleveland renders, "Followers," or, "Loafers"); (19) Wagluhe; (20) Oglala; (21) Ieska śiŋȼa, *Interpreters' Sons,* or, *Half-breeds.*

Mr. Cleveland also gives as names for all the Oglala, Oiyuḣpe and Kiyaksa.

G. Huŋkpapa—List of 1880: (1) Ćaŋka oḣaŋ, *Broken backs* (?); (2) Će oḣba, *Sleepy membrum virile;* (3) Tinazipe śića, *Bad Bows;* (4) Talo napiŋ, *Fresh meat necklaces;* (5) Kiglaśka; (6) Ćeknake okisela, *Half a breechcloth;* (7) Śikśićela, *Bad ones of different sorts;* (8) Wakaŋ, *Mysterious;* (9) Huŋska ćaŋtoźuha, *"Tobacco-pouch leggins,"* probably so called from using leggins as tobacco pouches.

J. O. D.

(8) The Assiniboin: The majority of this tribe live north of the forty-ninth parallel, but some of them are mixed in with the Dakota proper at Poplar River and elsewhere. That they branched off from the Yanktonai some two centuries ago, is one of the traditions of the Dakota. They speak the language as purely as other portions of the parent stock. The name Assiniboin is said to be a combination of French and Ojibwa. The name given to the Dakota by their former enemies is "Bwaŋ." Hence the Assiniboin are *Stone Dakota.* The Dakota name for them is "Hohe," the origin and meaning of which we have hitherto failed to find out.[1]

PRIORITY.

Questions of priority and precedence among these bands are sometimes discussed. The Mdewakaŋtoŋwaŋ think that the mouth of the Minnesota River is precisely over the center of the earth, and that they occupy the gate that opens into the western world. These considerations serve to give them importance in their own estimation. On the other hand, the Sisitoŋwaŋ and Ihaŋktoŋwaŋ allege, that as they live on the great water-shed of this part of the continent, from which the streams run northward and eastward and southward and westward, *they* must be about the center of the earth; and they urge this fact as entitling them to the precedence. It is singular that the Titoŋwaŋ, who are much the largest band of the Dakota, do not appear to claim the chief place for themselves, but yield to the pretensions of the Ihaŋktoŋwaŋ, whom they call by the name of Wićiyela, which, in its meaning, may be regarded as about equivalent to *"they are the people."*

METHOD OF COUNTING.

Counting is usually done by means of their fingers. If you ask some Dakota how many there are of anything, instead of directing their answer to your organs of hearing, they present it to your sight, by holding up so many fingers. When they have gone over the fingers and thumbs of both hands, one is temporarily turned down for *one ten.* *Eleven* is *ten more one,* or more commonly *again one; twelve* is *again two,* and so on; *nineteen* is *the*

---

[1] According to Dr. J. Trumbull, the name Assiniboin is derived from two Ojibwa words, "asiŋni," *stone,* and "bwaŋ," *enemy.* Some of the Sihasapa Dakota are called Hohe.—J. O. D.

other nine. At the end of the next ten another finger is turned down, and so on. *Twenty* is *two tens, thirty* is *three tens*, etc., as will be seen by referring to the section on Numeral Adjectives in the Grammar. Opawiŋġe, *one hundred*, is probably derived from pawiŋġa, *to go round in circles* or *to make gyrations*, as the fingers have been all gone over again for their respective tens. The Dakota word for a *thousand*, kektopawiŋġe, may be formed of 'ake' and 'opawiŋġe,' *hundreds again*, having now completed the circle of their fingers in hundreds, and being about to commence again. They have no separate word to denote any higher number than a thousand. There is a word to designate *one-half* of anything, but none to denote any smaller aliquot part.

METHOD OF RECKONING TIME.

The Dakota have names for the natural divisions of time. Their years they ordinarily count by *winters*. A man is so many winters old, or so many winters have passed since such an event. When one is going on a journey, he does not usually say that he will be back in so many *days*, as we do, but in so many *nights* or *sleeps*. In the same way they compute distance by the number of nights passed in making the journey. They have no division of time into *weeks*. Their *months* are literally *moons*. The popular belief is that when the moon is full, a great number of very small mice commence nibbling on one side of it, which they continue to do until they have eaten it all up. Soon after this another moon begins to grow, which goes on increasing until it has reached its full size only to share the fate of its predecessor; so that with them the new moon is *really new*, and not the old one reappearing. To the moons they have given names, which refer to some prominent physical fact that occurs about that time in the year. For the names of the moons most commonly used by the Dakotas living in the Valley of the Minnesota, with their significations and the months to which they most nearly correspond, the reader is referred to the word "wi," Part I of the Dictionary.

Five moons are usually counted to the winter, and five to the summer, leaving only one each to the spring and autumn; but this distinction is not closely adhered to. The Dakotas often have very warm debates, especially towards the close of the winter, about what moon it is. The raccoons do not always make their appearance at the same time every winter; and the causes which produce sore eyes are not developed precisely at the same time in each successive spring. All these variations make room for strong arguments in a Dakota tent for or against Wićata-wi or Iśtawićayazaŋ-wi. But the main reason for their frequent difference of opinion in regard to this matter, viz., that twelve lunations do not bring them to the point from which they commenced counting, never appears to have suggested itself. In order to make their moons correspond with the seasons, they are obliged to pass over one every few years.

SACRED LANGUAGE.

The Dakota conjurer, the war prophet, and the dreamer, experience the same need that is felt by more elaborate performers among other nations of a language which is unintelligible to the common people, for the purpose of impressing upon them the idea of their superiority. Their dreams, according to their own account, are revelations made from the spirit-world, and their prophetic visions are what they saw and knew in a former state of existence. It is, then, only natural that their dreams and visions should be clothed in words, many of which the multitude do not understand. This sacred language is not very extensive, since the use of a few unintelligible words suffices to make a whole speech incomprehensible. It may be said to consist, first, in employing words as the names of thing which seem to have been introduced from other Indian languages; as, nide, *water;* paza, *wood,* etc. In the second place, it consists in employing descriptive expressions, instead of the ordinary names of things; as in calling a man *a biped,* and the wolf *a quadruped.* And thirdly, words which are common in the language are used far out of their ordinary signification; as, hepaŋ, *the second child, if a boy,* is used to designate *the otter.* When the Dakota braves ask a white man for an ox or cow, they generally call it *a dog;* and when a sachem begs a horse from a white chief, he does it under the designation of *moccasins.* This is the source of many of the figures of speech in Indian oratory; but they are sometimes too obscure to be beautiful.

ARE THE INDIANS DIMINISHING?

One view of the question, and that hitherto the most common one, considers that North America had a dense population before the coming of the white race, and that since the Indians have been brought in contact with the advance guard of civilization they have been diminishing, many tribes having disappeared. But another view is gaining ground among students of the Indian. It is now maintained that, in spite of wars, diseases, exposures, and migrations, there are nearly as many Indians to-day in the United States as there were in the same territory in 1520, when the Spaniards met the Indians of Florida.

While it must be conceded, as a matter of history, that some tribes and bands which once inhabited the country occupied by the people of these United States have greatly diminished, and a few have disappeared altogether, other tribes have been on the increase. War and "spirit water," and the diseases introduced among them by the white people, have wrought out their legitimate effects. A different course of treatment would undoubtedly have greatly modified or entirely changed the character of these results.

But there is one way in which a diminution of some tribes is taking place, viz, by ceasing to be Indians and becoming members of civilized society. In Minnesota all persons of mixed blood, *i. e.*, of white and Indian descent, are recognized as citizens. The same is true in other States; and the privilege is extended to those who are not mixed bloods. Also, under present homestead laws, Indians are becoming citizens by going off their reserves. Let a well-arranged severalty bill be enacted into a law, and Indians be guaranteed civil rights as other men, and they will soon cease to be Indians.

The Indian tribes of our continent may become extinct as such; but if this extinction is brought about by introducing them to civilization and christianity and merging them into our own great nation, which is receiving accretions from all others, who will deplore the result? Rather let us labor for it, realizing that if by our efforts they cease to be Indians and become fellow-citizens it will be our glory and joy.

CHAPTER II.

MIGRATIONS OF THE DAKOTA.

Of the aboriginal tribes inhabiting this country, George Bancroft, in his History of the United States, has assigned the first place, in point of numbers, to the Algonquin family, and the second place to the Dakota.

Those who have made a study of the ethnology and the languages of the races have almost uniformly come to the conclusion that the Indians of this continent are connected with the Mongolian races of Asia. The line across from Asia to America by Bering Straits is regarded as perfectly practicable for canoes. And in 10 degrees farther south, by the Aleutian Islands, the distances are not so great but that small boats might easily pass from one to the other, and so safely reach the mainland.

Lewis H. Morgan, of the State of New York, who has given much time and study to solving the question, "Whence came the Indians?" has adopted this theory, and makes them gather on the Columbia River, from whence they have crossed the Rocky Mountains and spread over these eastern lands. But it can be safely affirmed that, up to this time, ethnology and the comparative study of languages have not quite satisfactorily settled the question of their origin.

In discussing the question of the migrations of the Dakota or Sioux, there are two lines open to us, each entirely independent, and yet both telling the same story: First, the history, as written in books; second, the history, as found in names.

ARGUMENT FROM HISTORY.

The book history runs back nearly two and a half centuries. The first knowledge of the Dakota nation obtained by the civilized world came through the French traders and missionaries, and was carried along the line of the Great Lakes through New France.

Early in the seventeenth century, a young man of more than ordinary ability, by name Jean Nicolet, came from France to Canada. He had great aptness in acquiring Indian languages, and soon became Algonquin and

Huron interpreter for the colony of New France. In the year 1639 he visited the lake of the Winnebagos, or Green Bay, in the present state of Wisconsin, and concluded a friendly alliance with the Indians on Fox River. In the next year, Paul le Jeune, writing of the tribes who dwelt on Lake Michigan, says, "Still farther on dwell the Ouinipegon, who are very numerous." And, "In the neighborhood of this nation are the Naduessi and the Assiniponais." This appears to be the first mention made by voyagers of the Dakota and Assiniboin. Le Jeune's information was obtained from Nicolet, who claimed to have visited them in their own countries.

In 1641, at the Sault Ste. Marie, Jogues and Raymbault, of the "Society of Jesus," met Pottowattomies flying from the Dakota, and were told that the latter lived "about eighteen days' journey to the westward, nine across the lake, and nine up a river which leads inland."

Two adventurous Frenchmen, in 1654, went to seek their fortunes in the region west of Lake Michigan, and returning to Quebec two years afterwards, related their adventures among "the numerous villages of the Sioux." And in 1659, it is related that the two traders, as they traveled six days journey southwest from La Pointe in Lake Superior, came upon a Huron village on the shores of the Mississippi. These Hurons had fled from a fierce onslaught of the Iroquois, and for the time had taken refuge among the Dakota. In the vicinity of the Huron they saw the Dakota villages, "in five of which were counted all of 5,000 men."

From the beginning of the intercourse of white men with Indians on this continent the fur trade has been the chief stimulus to adventure and the great means by which the location and condition of the aboriginal populations were made known to the civilized world. Two other subsidiary motives operated to bring white men into connection with the great Dakota nation, viz, the desire to discover the great river on which they were said to dwell, and the zeal of the church of Rome to convert the savages.

In the summer of 1660 René Menard, the aged, burning with an apostolic desire to make converts from among the pagans, bore the standard of the cross to the shores of Lake Superior. At La Pointe, which was already a trading port, he wintered. But in the following spring he started on foot with a guide to visit "four populous nations" to the westward. By some means he became separated from his guide while passing through the marshes of northwestern Wisconsin and was lost. Many years afterwards a report was current in Canada that "his robe and prayer-book were found in a Dakota lodge," and were regarded as "wakan" or sacred.

The successor of Menard in the toils of missionary life was Father Claude Allouëz. He established the mission of the Holy Spirit at La Pointe and the Apostles' Islands in the year 1665, and four years later he commenced a mission among the Winnebago and others on Green Bay.

On reaching La Pointe, Allouëz found the Huron and Ojibwa villages in a state of great excitement. The Huron, who had fled to the Dakota of the Mississippi for protection from the tomahawk of the Iroquois some years before, had behaved ungraciously toward their protectors by taunting them with having no guns; whereupon the Dakota rose against them, massacred many of them in a swamp, and drove them all back to the shores of Lake Superior. The Ojibwa had formerly lived to the east of Lake Michigan, but had been driven westward by the victorious Iroquois. Now the Dakota, the Iroquois of the West, as they have been called, had shut them up to the lake shore. The young men were burning to be avenged on the Dakota. Here was gathered a grand council of the neighboring nations—the Huron, the Ojibwa, the Pottowattomi, the Sac and Fox, the Menomoni, and the Illinois. Allouëz commanded peace, in the name of the King of the French, and offered them commerce and alliance against the Five Nations.

In 1667 Father Allouëz met a delegation of Dakota and Assiniboin at the western end of Lake Superior, near where is now the town of Duluth. They had come, they said, from the end of the earth. He calls them "the wild and impassioned Sioux." "Above all others," he says, "they are savage and warlike; and they speak a language entirely unknown to us, and the savages about here do not understand them."

But Allouëz resolved to abandon his work at La Pointe, "weary of their obstinate unbelief," and was succeeded by the renowned Jacques Marquette. This enterprising and estimable man entered at once upon the work of perpetuating peace among the various tribes, and, in the autumn of 1669, sent presents and a message to the Dakota, that he wished them to keep a way open for him to the Great River and to the Assiniboin beyond. But not from the mission of the Holy Spirit was he to take his journey to the "Father of Waters." In the following winter it became apparent that the Huron were not safe on the southern shores of Lake Superior, and accordingly they abandoned their village, and at the same time Marquette retired to the Sault Ste. Marie, from which point, in the spring of 1672, he proceeded, with Louis Joliet, to find the Great River, the "Messipi."[1] They

---

[1] Probably in the language of the Illinois Indians, "messi," *great*, and "sepi," *river*.

proceeded by way of Green Bay. They entered the mouth of Fox River, followed up its windings, and were guided by Indians across to the head of the Wisconsin, which they descended to the mouth, and down the great river to the mouth of the Arkansas. They had wintered at Green Bay, and so it was the 17th of June, 1673, when their canoe first rode on the waters of the Mississippi. On their return they ascended the Illinois River, stopped to recruit at the famous Illinois village, and, crossing over to Lake Michigan, reached Green Bay in the latter end of September.[1]

The Jesuit relations of this period have much to say about the habits of the Dakota; that about 60 leagues from the upper end of Lake Superior, toward sunset, "there are a certain people, called Nadouessi, dreaded by their neighbors." They only use the bow and arrow, but use them with great skill and dexterity, filling the air in a moment. "They turn their heads in flight and discharge their arrows so rapidly that they are no less to be feared in their retreat than in their attack. They dwell around the great river *Messipi*. Their cabins are not covered with bark, but with skins, well dried, and stitched together so well that the cold does not enter. They know not how to cultivate the earth by seeding it, contenting themselves with a species of marsh rye (wild rice), which we call wild oats."

We now come to more definite information in regard to country occupied by the Dakota two hundred years ago. Du Luth and Hennepin approached the Dakota by different routes, and finally met each other at the great villages on Mille Lacs and Knife Lake, at the head of Run River.

Daniel Greysolon Du Luth, who built the first trading port on Lake Superior, "on the first of September, 1678, left Quebec" to explore the country of the Dakota and the Assiniboin. On July 2, 1679, he caused the King's arms to be planted "in the great village of the Nadouessioux, called Kathio, where no Frenchman had ever been, and also at Songaskicons and Houetbetons, 120 leagues from the former."[2]

In September of that year Du Luth held a council with Assiniboin and other nations, who came to the head of Lake Superior. And in the summer of 1680 he made another trip down to the Mississippi, where he met with Hennepin.

---

[1] Green Bay was called the Bay of the Puants, or Winnebago. In this neighborhood there were, at that time, the Winnebago, the Pottowattomi, the Menomoni, the Sac and Fox, the Miami, the Mascontin, the Kickapoo, and others. The Miami and Mascontin lived together and had their village on the Neenah or Fox River. The Miami afterwards removed to the St. Joseph River, near Lake Michigan. The Mascontin, or "Fire Nation," is now extinct.

[2] It is stated, on what appears to be good authority, that Du Luth this summer visited Mille Lac, which he called Lake Buade.

When Du Luth was fitting out his expedition by Lake Superior to the Dakota Nation and others, Robert La Salle was preparing to go to the great river of the West by the south end of Lake Michigan.[1] Louis Hennepin, a Franciscan priest of the Recollect order, accompanied him.

La Salle stopped to build a ship on Lake Erie, which he called the *Griffin*. This so detained his expedition that it was late in the fall of 1679 when they reached Green Bay. There the *Griffin* was left for the winter, and La Salle and Hennepin, with others, proceeded in canoes to the south end of the lake (Michigan), and thence by portage into the Illinois River. In the beginning of the year 1680, La Salle, after enduring incredible hardships, built a fort a little below where is now the town of Peoria, which he called "Créve Coeur," thus making his heart troubles historical.

In the month of February, La Salle selected Hennepin and two voyageurs named Michol Accau and the Picard du Gay, whose real name was Antoine Auguel, to undertake the discovery of the Upper Mississippi. On the last day of the month they embarked in a canoe laden with merchandise, and the venerable Ribourde took leave of Hennepin with the charge, "Viriliter age et confortetur cor tuum." On March 12 Hennepin and his companions turned their canoe up the stream of the Great River, and on April 11 they met a war party of 120 Dakota in thirty-three bark canoes. This meeting took place near the mouth of the Wisconsin, where Marquette had first seen the Mississippi, nearly seven years before. The Frenchmen had found wild turkeys abundant on their voyage, and were at this moment on the shore cooking their dinner. The Dakota approached with hostile demonstrations, and some of the old warriors repeated the name "Miamiha," giving the white men to understand that they were on the warpath against the Miami and Illinois. But Hennepin explained to them, by signs and marks on the sand, that these Indians were now across the Mississippi, beyond their reach.

The white men were the prisoners of the war party. What should be done with them? Not without much debate, did they decide to abandon the warpath and return home. Then, by signs, they gave the white men to understand that it was determined to kill them. This was the policy and the counsel of the old war chief, "Again-fills-the-pipe" by name, (Akepaǵidaŋ), because he was mourning the loss of a son killed by the Miami. Hennepin and his companions endeavored to obtain the mercy of their captors by giving them a large amount of presents. They spent an anxious night. But the next morning, better counsels prevailed, and a

---

[1] The great village which he calls "Kathio" must have been in that region.

younger chief, whose name was "Four Souls" (Naġi-topa), filled his pipe with willow bark and smoked with them. And then made them understand that, as the war against the Miami was abandoned, and they would now go back to their villages, the white men should accompany them.

This voyage up the Mississippi was not without continued apprehension of danger to the Frenchmen. When Hennepin opened his breviary in the morning, and began to mutter his prayers, his savage captors gathered about him in superstitious terror, and gave him to understand that his book was a "bad spirit" (Wakaŋ śiċa), and that he must not converse with it.

His comrades besought him to dispense with his devotions, or at least to pray apart, as they were all in danger of being tomahawked. He tried to say his prayers in the woods, but the Indians followed him everywhere, and said "Wakaŋ ċi," Is it not mysterious? He could not dispense with saying his office. But finally he chanted the Litany of the Virgin in their hearing, which charmed the evil spirit from them.

But the old chief, Again-fills-the-pipe, was still apparently bent on killing a white man to revenge the blood of his son. Every day or two he broke forth in a fresh fit of crying, which was accompanied with hostile demonstrations towards the captives. This was met by additional presents and the interceding of their first friend, Four Souls, in their behalf. It looks very much like a species of blackmailing—a device practiced by them—by which the goods of the white men should come into their possession without stealing. They were also required to bring goods to cover some bones, which old Akepaġidaŋ had with him, and over which they cried and smoked frequently. At Lake Pepin they cried all night, and from that circumstance, Hennepin called it the "Lake of Tears."

Thus they made their way up the Father of Waters where no white man had ever traveled before. Nineteen days after their capture they landed a short distance below where the city of St. Paul stands. Then the savages hid their own canoes in the bushes and broke the Frenchmen's canoe into pieces. From this point they had a land travel of five days, of suffering and starvation to the white men, when they reached the Dakota villages at Mille Lacs, which was then the home of the Mdewakantons. Hennepin estimated the distance they traveled by land at sixty leagues. But it was probably not over one hundred miles. They passed through the marshes at the head of Rum River, and were then taken by canoes "a short league" to an island in the lake, where were the lodges.

This lake the Dakota called "Mdewakaŋ," *mysterious lake*, from which came the name of this branch of the Dakota family, Mde-wakaŋ-toŋwaŋ. They also called it "Isaŋ-ta-mde," *Knife Lake*, because there they found their stone knives and arrowheads. From this came the name "Santee," which covers a much larger part of the tribe. (See footnote [3], pp. 159, 160.)

Thus, in Pere Louis Hennepin's narrative, we have the first exact locality of the eastern bands of the Dakota people, two hundred years ago. The principal chief, at that time, of this part of the tribe, is called by Hennepin "Washechoonde." If he is correct, their name for *Frenchmen* was in use, among the Dakota, before they had intercourse with them, and was probably a name learned from some Indians farther east.

The three white men, with their effects, were divided up among the various villages. And, strange to say, Hennepin was taken home by the old savage who had so much wished to kill him on the journey. He had now become his friend, even his father; his five wives became Hennepin's mothers. They treated him kindly—covered him with a robe made of dressed beaver skins, ornamented with porcupine quills, rubbed him down after his journey, and set before him a bark dish full of fish. As the Franciscan fell sick, his savage father made a sweating-cabin for him, and after the process of sweating naked by means of heated stones, he was rubbed down by four Indians. Thus he was reinvigorated.

As no mention is made by either Hennepin or the historian of Du Luth of any planting at these villages, we may be quite sure that they did not plant, but lived by hunting and fishing mainly, which was supplemented by gathering roots and berries and wild rice.

During the stay of the white men there came four Indians from the far west—Hennepin says, "500 leagues"—who reported the Assiniboin villages as only six or seven days' journey to the northwest. This would place this branch of the Dakota people, at that time, within the present limits of Minnesota, somewhere east of the Red River.

In the month of July the whole encampment of Dakota, numbering 250 men, with women and children, started on a buffalo hunt. The Frenchmen were to go with them. But Hennepin, anxious to make his escape, represented that a party of traders, "spirits" or "wakan men," were to be sent by La Salle to the mouth of the Wisconsin, and he wished to meet them there. The Indians gave them leave to go, but Accau, who disliked Hennepin, preferred to stay among the savages.

They all camped together on the banks of the Mississippi, at the mouth of Rum River, from which point Hennepin and Du Gay descended the great river in a small birch-bark canoe. At the falls, which Hennepin named St. Anthony, for his patron saint, they made a portage and saw half a dozen Dakotas, who had preceded them, offering buffalo-robes in sacrifice to Uŋktehi, the great water god.

As they paddled leisurely down the stream by the beautiful bluffs in this month of July, now and then shooting a wild turkey or a deer, they were suddenly overtaken by Hennepin's Dakota father, the old savage Akepagidaŋ, with 10 warriors in a canoe. The white men were somewhat alarmed, for he told them he was going down to the mouth of the Wisconsin to meet the traders, who were to be there according to the words of the Franciscan. They passed on rapidly, found no one at the place named, and, in a few days, they met them on their return, when the savage father only gave his son Hennepin a good scolding for lying.

They were then near the mouth of the Chippewa River, a short distance up which a large party of those with whom they had started were chasing buffalo. This information was given to the white men by the Indians as they passed up. Hennepin and Du Gay had but little ammunition, and for this reason they determined to turn aside and join the buffalo hunt. In this party they found their former comrade. A grand hunt was made along the borders of the Mississippi. The Dakota hunters chased the buffalo on foot and killed them with their flint-headed arrows. At this time they had neither guns nor horses. When they first saw the white men shoot and kill with a gun they called it "maza-wakaŋ," mysterious iron. And, in after years, when the horse came to their knowledge they called it "shuŋka wakaŋ," mysterious dog.

While they were thus killing the buffalo and drying the meat in the sun there came two Dakota women into camp with the news that a Dakota war party, on its way to Lake Superior, had met five "spirits"—washechooŋ.[1] These proved to be Daniel Greysolon Du Luth with four well-armed Frenchmen. In June they had started from Lake Superior, had probably ascended the Burnt Wood River, and from that made a portage to the St. Croix, where they met this war party and learned that three white men were on the Mississippi. As this was Du Luth's preempted trading country, he was anxious to know who the interlopers were, and at once started for the hunting camp. We can imagine this to have been a joyful meeting of Frenchmen.

The hunt was now over. The Indians, laden with dried meat and accompanied by the eight white men, returned to their resting place at Knife

---

[1] Wasicuŋ.

Lake. And when the autumn came the white men were permitted to leave, with the promise that in the following year they would return with goods to trade for the abundant peltries. They descended the Mississippi in bark canoes. At the Falls of St. Anthony two of the men took each a buffalo-robe that had been sacrificed to the god of the waters. Du Luth greatly disapproved of the act as both impolitic and wrong, but Hennepin justified it, saying they were offerings to a false god. As the white men were about to start up the Wisconsin River they were overtaken by a party of Dakota, again on the war-path against the Illinois. The white men, remembering the stolen robes, were alarmed, but the Dakota passed on and did them no harm.[1]

These Nadouessioux, or Sioux, of the east of the Mississippi, whose acquaintance we have now formed somewhat, appear at this time to have been divided into Matanton, Watpaaton, and Chankasketon. These are band names. But the headquarters of all was the Mde-wakaŋ or Isaŋ-ta-mde. From this point they issued forth on their hunting expeditions and their war parties. The latter penetrated into Iowa and central Illinois to Lake Superior and Lake Michigan. Sometimes we find them at peace with the Ojibwa and at war with the Fox. Then, again, we find the Fox and Ioway joining the Dakota war parties against the Ojibwa. The war which separated the Assiniboin from the Dakota had not ceased at this period, and the impression is that the separation had taken place not many years before they became known to history.

Nicholas Perrot was sent by the governor of Canada, in 1683, to take charge of the trading interests among the Ioway and Dakota. And in 1689 the first recorded public document was signed in which the land of the Dakota was claimed for the French king. In this document Father Marest, of the Society of Jesus, is spoken of as missionary among the Nadouessioux, and Mons. Le Sueur, to whom we are indebted for the next ten years of history, was present.

Le Sueur was first sent to La Pointe to maintain peace between the Ojibwa and Dakota. And in the year 1695 he erected a trading post on an island of the Mississippi, above Lake Pepin and below the mouth of St. Croix. In the summer of the same year he took to Montreal delegations from several western tribes, including one Dakota, "Tecoskatay"[2] by name. This man died in Montreal, and one hundred and fifty years afterward the

---

[1] Le Clercq, the historian of the Sieur Du Luth, corroborates the story of Hennepin in regard to their meeting at Knife Lake.

[2] Tioškate.

writer of this sketch heard him spoken of by those who claimed to be his descendants, then on the Minnesota River.

Becoming impressed with the idea that there were valuable mines in the land of the Dakota, Le Sueur obtained a royal license to work them. He was hindered in various ways, and not until the summer of 1700 do we find him ascending the Mississippi. On the 30th of July he met a war party of Dakota in seven canoes, who were on the warpath against the Illinois. Le Sueur bought them off with presents and turned them back home. Advancing up as far as the Galena River he called it the River Mino. On the 19th of September he entered the mouth of the Minnesota, or as he probably named it then, and long afterwards it continued to be called, the "St. Pierre." And by the 1st of October he had reached the Blue Earth River, where he built a trading post and expected to make his fortune out of the *blue earth* of its shores.

While Le Sueur was building his stockade on the Blue Earth he was visited by Dakota from the east of the Mississippi, who desired him to locate at the mouth of the St. Peter or Minnesota, since the country of the Blue Earth, they said, belonged to the western Dakota and to the Iowa and Oto. However, a short time after this Le Sueur was informed that the Iowa and Oto had gone over to the Missouri River to join the Omaha. At this time it is recorded that the Iowa and Oto planted corn, but the Dakota did not. Le Sueur offered to furnish corn to the latter for planting.

At the beginning of the eighteenth century we have the Dakota nation, so far as known, described by bands. Some of the names it is now impossible to read with certainty. Some have disappeared or given place to others, while some of them are old landmarks by which we can read the history of their migrations. Living at that time to the east of the Mississippi, whose headquarters were about Knife Lake, were the Spirit Lake Village (Mdewakaŋtoŋwaŋ), Great Lake Village (Matanton—perhaps originally Mdetaŋk-toŋwaŋ), Wild Rice Gatherers (Psiŋ-omani-toŋwaŋ), River Village (Watpatoŋwaŋ), Boat Village (Watomanitoŋwaŋ), Fortified Village (Caŋkaśkatoŋwaŋ). The Western Dakota are thus given, viz: Pole Village (Caŋhuasinton?), Red Wild Rice Village (Psiŋćatoŋwan), Small Band Village (Wagalespeton?), Great Wild Rice Village (Psiŋhutaŋkiŋ-toŋwaŋ), Grand Lodge Village (Titaŋka-kaġa-toŋ?), Leaf Village (Waħpetoŋwaŋ), Dung Village (Uŋkćekce-ota-toŋwaŋ), Teton Leaf Village (Waħpeton-Teton), and Red Stone Quarry Village (Hinhaneton). This last must be the Red Pipe Stone, and the Dakota who guarded it were doubtless the

Yankton.[1]   It is possible that the "Red Stone" may have signified the Des Moines River, which was so called.

These bands were all at that time within the present State of Minnesota, and mainly having their homes north of the forty-fifth parallel, except the last, who are said to have been living at the Red Stone Quarry.   This can be no other than the Red Pipe Stone in the neighborhood of the Big Sioux.   Le Sueur says the Assiniboin lived on the head waters of the Mississippi.

For the next fifty years the Dakota appear to have kept within their old limits, sometimes at war with the Ojibwa, and then again in league with them against the Fox and Sauk.   Already the quarrel between the English colonies and the French had commenced.   The Fox took the side of the English, but were defeated at the port of Detroit and elsewhere, and obliged to flee for protection to their enemies, the Dakota.   For a while it appears that the Fox hunted north of the Minnesota River.

The maps made in France about 1750 locate the Dakota, as we have already seen, partly on the east and partly on the west side of the Mississippi.   They occupied Leech Lake, Sandy Lake, and probably Red Lake at that time and for some years afterwards.   At the source of the Minnesota River there is put down a large lake called "Lake of the Teetons." Whether this was intended for Big Stone Lake, or for what we now call Devil's Lake, in Dakota, may admit of a doubt.   Besides this, these maps locate a portion of the Teton[2] (Titoŋwaŋ) and the Yankton (Ihaŋktoŋwaŋ) on the east side of the Missouri, down in Iowa, whence came the names of the streams, Big and Little Sioux.

In the "French and Indian war," the Dakota nation took no part.[3]   But very soon after the English came into possession of Canada and the French ports in the northwest, a company of Dakota braves visited Green Bay to solicit the trade of the Englishmen.   They told the officer in charge that if the Ojibwa or other Indians attempted to shut up the way to them (the Dakota), to send them word, and they would come and cut them off, "as all Indians were their dogs."

Previous to this time, the "Sioux of the East" had given the number

---

[1] Hiŋhaŋetoŋwaŋ approximates Ihaŋktóŋwaŋ.   Nasalizing the "n's" will make this change.— J. O. D.

[2] Perhaps the present Ihaŋktoŋwaŋ gens of the Siċaŋġu (Titoŋwaŋ)—see list of Taṭaŋka-wakaŋ—includes those whose ancestors intermarried with the Yankton proper, when part of the Titoŋwaŋ were neighbors of the Yankton.—J. O. D.

[3] The only thing I find which looks like participation at all, is a record of arrivals at Montreal in 1746, July 31.   "Four Sioux came to ask for a commandant."

of the "Sioux of the West" as "more than a thousand tepees." It is added, "They do not use canoes, nor cultivate the earth, nor gather wild rice. They remain generally in the prairies, which are between the Upper Mississippi and the Missouri Rivers, and live entirely by the chase."

Jonathan Carver, a native of New England, was the first English traveler who visited the country of the Dakota and added to our knowledge of their history. He left Boston in June of 1766, and by the way of Green Bay and the Wisconsin River he reached the Mississippi at the town whose name he writes "La Prairie les Chiens," consisting, as he says, of fifty houses This was then, and for many years after, the great fur mart of the Upper Mississippi. The villages of the Sauk and Fox he passed on the Wisconsin River. The Dakota he first met near the mouth of the St. Croix. For years past they had been breaking away from their old home on Knife Lake and making their villages along down the river. Hence the name of "River Bands," a term that then comprised the "Spirit Lake," the "Leaf Villagers," and the "Sisseton." The Nadouessies of the plains, he says, were divided into eight bands, not including the Assiniboin.

Carver ascended the St. Pierre River for some distance and wintered with a camp of Indians. In the spring he descended, with several hundred Dakota, to the mouth of the river. When they came to deposit their dead, in what seems to have been a general place of interment, in the cave, since called "Carver's Cave," Jonathan claims to have obtained from them a deed of the land. This purchase, however, has never been acknowledged by the Sioux.

Carver found, in 1766, the Dakota at war with the Ojibwa, and was told that they had been fighting forty years. Before the year 1800 the Ojibwa had driven the Dakota from what hold they had on the Sandy Lake and Leech Lake country. As the Indian goods commenced to come to them *up* the Mississippi, they were naturally drawn *down* to make more permanent villages on its banks. Then two forces united diverted the Dakota migration to the south and the west.

The Government of the United States, in the year 1805, sent into the Dakota and Ojibwa countries Lieut. Zebulon M. Pike, for the purposes of regulating the trade and making alliances with the Indians. He met the Dakota first at Red Wing, a short distance above Lake Pepin, and then at Kaposia, a short distance below where is now St. Paul. The respective chiefs were Red Wing and Little Crow. He also visited a Dakota village a short distance up the Minnesota River, and held a grand council with the Dakota assembled on the point where Fort Snelling was afterwards built.

On his downward trip in the following spring, he met Wabashaw's band, the Kiyuksa, below Lake Pepin. As he ascended the Mississippi as far as Leech Lake, and found the country above the Falls of St. Anthony, in the main, occupied by Ojibwa, the inference is that the Dakota had, in the previous years, been driven by their enemies from that part of the country. One reason for this was, that the Ojibwa were furnished with firearms before the Dakota A second reason was found in the drawing of the fur trade. And a third was the gradual disappearance of the buffalo in the wooded country of the Mississippi. At this date the Sisseton and Yankton were on the head waters of the Minnesota. Delegations of these bands met Lieut. Pike in the spring, and proceeded to a grand council at Prairie du Chien.

Old men still living relate how the Wahpeton, or Leaf Village, when they retired from the bullets of the Ojibwa on the east of the Mississippi, pitched their tents towards the northwest corner of what is now the State of Iowa, and when they returned they established their planting village at what has been called Little Rapids, on the lower part of the Minnesota River. In about 1810, a portion of them removed up to an island in Big Stone Lake, and afterwards a larger part settled at Lac qui Parle.

Until after the middle of this century, the habitats of the Dakota were, for the Mday-wakan-ton (Mde-wakaŋ toŋwaŋ), the Mississippi River from Winona to the Falls of St. Anthony, and up the Minnesota as far as Shakopee. The Leaf Shooters (Wahpekute) were on the Cannon River, where Faribault now is; and the Wahpeton (Leaf Village) were, as stated, at the Little Rapids, and Lac qui Parle and the lower end of Big Stone Lake. The Sisseton occupied the Blue Earth country and the southern bend of the Minnesota, while the great body of them were at the villages on Lake Traverse. The Yankton, Yanktonai, Cut-heads, and Titoŋwaŋ were on the great prairies to the westward.

When Lieut. Pike made his tour up the Mississippi, in the years 1805 and 1806, he found much of the trade, in the Dakota and Ojibwa countries, in the hands of men who were in sympathy with Great Britain. The traders, many of them, were Englishmen, and the goods were British goods. It is not strange then that, in the war of 1812, the Dakota, together with other Indians of the Northwest, were enlisted in the war against the United States. This was brought about mainly by Robert Dickson, a Scotchman, who was at this time at the head of the fur trade in this part of the country. Under his leadership the Dakota, the Ojibwa, the Winnebago, the Menomonie, the Sauk and Fox, and others, were brought into action, against the soldiers of the States, at Mackinaw, at Rock Island, and at Prairie du Chien. Of the Dakota villages, Little Crow and Wabashaw are especially mentioned. Joseph Renville, afterwards of Lac qui Parle, and other traders, were the lieutenants of Col. Dickson. History tells us of but two Dakota men who kept themselves squarely on the American side during the war. One of these was the special friend (Koda) of Lieut. Pike, his name being Ta-ma-he, meaning the pike fish. Probably he took that name as the friend of Pike. He went to St. Louis at the commencement of the war, and was taken into the employ of Gen. Clarke. He lived until after the middle of this century, always wore a stovepipe hat, had but one eye, and claimed to be the only "American" of his tribe.

It does not appear that the war of 1812 changed the location of Dakota. They still occupied the Mississippi above the parallel of $43\frac{1}{2}°$, and the Minnesota, and westward. In 1837–'38, the "Lower Sioux," as they were called, ceded to the Government their title to the land east of the great river. In 1851, all the Mississippi and Minnesota Dakota sold to the Government all their claim to the country as far west as Lake Traverse, except a reservation on the Upper Minnesota. A year or two afterwards they removed to this reservation, and were there until the outbreak of August, 1862, which resulted in the eastern Dakota, or those coming under the general name of Santees, being all removed outside of the lines of Minnesota. A part of those Indians fled to Manitoba, and a part across the Missouri, supposed to be now with (Tataŋka Iyotaŋke) Sitting Bull—a part were transported to Crow Creek on the Missouri, who afterwards were permitted to remove into the northeast angle of Nebraska. This is now the Santee Agency, from whence a colony of sixty families of homesteaders have settled on the Big Sioux. Still another portion were retained by the military as scouts, which have been the nuclei of the settlements on the Sisseton and Fort Totten reservations.

About what time the Dakota in their migrations westward crossed over the Missouri River, to remain and hunt on the western side, is a question not easily settled. There are various traditions of other neighbor tribes, which indicate pretty certainly that the Sioux were not there much over one hundred years ago.

Dr. Washington Matthews, of the U. S. Army, relates that the Berthold[1] Indians say, "Long ago the Sioux were all to the east, and none to the West and South, as they now are." In those times the western plains must have been very sparsely peopled with hostile tribes in comparison

---

[1] These may be the Hidatsa, Mandan, and Arikara tribes.—J. O. D.

with the present, for the old men now living, and children of men of the past generation, say that they traveled to the southwest, in search of scalps, to a country where the prairie ceased, and were gone from their village twenty-one moons.   Others went to the north to a country where the summer was but three moons long.

The French maps of this western country, made about one hundred and twenty-five years ago, are, in many things, very inaccurate, but may be received as indicating the general locality of Indians at that time.   In one of the maps the Ponka, Pawnee, and some of the Oto, together with the Panimaha,[1] are placed on the Platte and its branches.   Other villages of the Maha (Omaha) are placed, apparently, above the mouth of the James or Dakota River, on the eastern side of the Missouri.   The Iowa, the Oto, and the Yankton and Teton Dakota are placed down in what is now the State of Iowa.

When Lewis and Clarke ascended the Missouri, in the autumn of 1803, they met the Yankton Dakota about the mouth of the James or Dakota River, where Yankton now stands.   Their village was some distance above, perhaps about the site of Bon Homme.   They met the Teton Dakota at the mouth of the Teton or Little Missouri (Wakpa śića), where old Fort Pierre stood.   These were of the Oglala band.   Tradition says that the Oglala were the first to cross the Missouri, and that this was the place of crossing. At first they went over to hunt.   The buffalo were found to be more abundant.   They returned again.   But after several times going and returning they remained, and others followed.   At the commencement of this century some Teton were still on the east side of the river, but their home seems to have been then, as now, on the west side.

As this is the only notice of their meeting Teton on their ascent, we infer that the main body of them were not on the Missouri, but far in the interior.[2]

ARGUMENT FROM NAMES OF NATIONS, TRIBES, ETC.

In all primitive states of society the most reliable history of individuals and nations is found written in names.   Sometimes the removals of a people can be traced through the ages by the names of rivers or places

---

[1] Skidi or Pawnee Loup.

[2] In the winter count of American Horse (4th An. Rep. Bur. Eth., p. 130), Standing-Bull, a Dakota, discovered the Black Hills in the winter of 1775–'76.   The Dakota have of late years claimed the Black Hills, probably by right of discovery in 1775–'76; but the Crow were the former possessors, and were found in that region by the Ponka before the time of Marquette (i. e., prior to the date of his autograph map, 1673).—J. O. D.

which they have left behind them. The Dakota people, on the other hand, carry with them, to some extent, the history of their removals in the names of the several bands.

The Sioux people call themselves Dakota.[1] They say "Dakota" means "league" or "alliance"—they being *allied* bands. And this meaning is confirmed by other uses of the word in the language. The name Sioux, on the other hand, was given to them by their enemies. In the preceding account the word "Nadouessi," or "Nadouessioux," is of frequent occurrence. The Huron, and perhaps other western Indians, called the Iroquois Nadowe or Nottaway, which is said to mean enemy. Because they were ever on the war-path, as were the Six Nations, the Dakota were styled the Iroquois of the West, and, for distinction's sake, were called Nadouessioux, enemies. The last part of the word stuck, and has become a part of their history. The Ojibwa, it appears, called the Dakota by the name of Bwaŋ, which comes out in the name Assiniboin, Stone Dakota; and a small band, or family, of the Assiniboin are called Stoneys, living in the Dominion of Canada.

Spirit Lake Villages.—We have seen that Du Luth and Hennepin first visited the villages of the Dakota on the islands and shores of Mille Lacs, which was their Mde-wakaŋ, and hence the name Mde-wakaŋ-toŋwaŋ. This name has come down through more than two centuries, and still attaches to a portion of the people, and is abiding evidence of their having lived on the head of Rum River.

Not long after their first discovery by white men, if not at the time, a portion of this same band of Dakota were called Matanton, which name appears to be a contraction of Mde-taŋka-toŋwaŋ, meaning Village of the Great Lake. This was only a designation given to a portion of Mille Lacs.

Before the end of that century these people began to make their villages along down Rum River, and perhaps also on the Mississippi, and so obtained the name of Wakpa-atoŋwaŋ, Village on the River. But, after one hundred and fifty years, this, with the name preceding, passed out of use.

As previous to this time the Ojibwa had contented themselves with the shores of Lake Superior, but were now getting an advantage over the Dakota in the first possession of firearms, we find the Dakota, who pitched their tents westward and northward, toward Leech Lake and Sandy Lake, earning the name of "Choŋkasketons" (Ćaŋkaśke-toŋwaŋ), *Fortified Vil-*

In the Teton dialect this is Lakota.

lages.[1] From the name we read that they were in a wooded country and made wooden protections from the assaults of their enemies.

Some of the families appear to have made the gathering of the wild rice in the lakes a specialty, and so for a century or more we find them known as the Villages of Wild Rice Gatherers.

When the Frenchmen, in 1680, joined the buffalo hunt of the Dakota, they remarked that they killed them with stone-headed arrows and cut up the meat with stone knives. The sharp flint stone used for this purpose they found on the banks of the Thousand Lakes, and hence the name of "wakaŋ," or mysterious. And from this fact also they called the lake, or a part of it, by the name of " Isaŋ-ta-mde," Lake of Knives, or Knife Lake. From living there the whole of those eastern Sioux were called "Isaŋ-ya-ti"— Knife Dwellers—which has been modified to

SANTEE.

For a century or more past there has been included in this name The Leaf-shooters (Waḣpekute), and also Leaf Village (Waḣpetoŋwaŋ).[2] Both these last-named bands continued to dwell, for the most part, in the wooded country, as their names indicate. In the list of Dakota bands furnished by Le Sueur, about the beginning of the eighteenth century, the Waḣpatons, or Leaf Villages, are classed with what was then called " The Sioux of the West." And a somewhat singular combination occurs in the name "Wahpeton-Teton," indicating that some of the Leaf Village band had become " Dwellers on the Prairie."

Other names of divisions at that period, such as "Great Wild Rice Village," "Grand Lodge Village," "Dung Village," etc., have gone into disuse. Nor is it possible, at this time, to discover to what families they belonged.

Two hundred years ago, the Dakota nation was said to consist of seven Council Fires. Of these we have already spoken of three, viz: Spirit Lake (Mdewakaŋtoŋwaŋ), Leaf Shooters (Waḣpekute), and Leaf Village (Waḣpetoŋwaŋ).

SISSETON.

Coming next to these is the Sisseton band. The meaning of the name is not quite clear; but Mr. Joseph Renville, of Lac-qui-parle, in his day regarded as the best authority in Dakota, understood it to mean "Swamp

---

[1] Another version of this name is " Brave-hearts," as if from Ćaŋte, *heart*, and kaśka, *to bind.*
[2] See testimony of Rev. A. L. Riggs in foot-note [2] on pp. 159, 160.

Village."[1] This well accords with the early history, which places them in the marshy parts of the country. From the head waters of the Mississippi they journeyed southward to the country of Swan Lake and the Blue Earth, and above, on the Minnesota River. Here they were found early in the eighteenth century, and here a portion of them still remained until after 1850. But the great body of them had removed up to the Lake Traverse region before the war of 1812. The great Sisseton chief of those times was Red Thunder (Wakiŋyaŋ duta), still spoken of by his descendants. Since 1862 the Sisseton live on the Sisseton and Wahpeton Reservation, and at Devil's Lake, both of which are in Dakota.

YANKTON.

The Ihaŋktoŋwaŋ, now shortened to Yankton, were the "Villages of the Border." The "End," or "Border," appears to have been that of the wooded country. Connected with them, and to be treated in the same category, are the

YANKTONAI.

They were both Borderers. The name of the latter (Ihaŋktoŋwaŋna) is, in the Dakota, simply a diminutive of the former; but for more than a century—possibly more than two centuries—the distinction has been recognized. The Assiniboin branched off from the Yanktonai. Other divisions of them, reaching down to the present time, are the Sanonee[2] (or One Siders?), the Cut Heads (Pabakse); Kiyuksa or Dividers; Breakers of the law; the Pine Shooters (Waźikute), and the Huŋkpa-tina, or Hoonkpatee. This last name is explained in other parts of this volume. The same word is found in the name of one of the Teton divisions, now become somewhat notorious as the robber band of "Sitting Bull," viz: The Huŋkpapa, or, as it is incorrectly written, Unkpapa. Both of these bands have for many years roamed over the Upper Missouri country—one on the east and the other on the west side. The name of "Pine Shooters," by which one division of the Yanktonai is still called, they brought from the pine country of Minnesota,[3] and must have retained through at least two centuries.

As the Yankton, who now live on the Missouri River, at the Yankton Agency, claim to have been placed by the Taku Wakaŋ as guardians of

---

[1] For another explanation of this term, see "Sisitoŋwaŋ" in the preceding chapter, p. 158.

[2] The Saŋona. See p. 161, footnote.—J. O. D.

[3] The Omaha say that when their ancestors found the Great Pipe Stone Quarry, the Yankton dwelt east of them in the forest region of Minnesota, so they called them Jaⁿaȼa nikaciⁿga, or People of the forest. See 3d Rep. Bur. Eth., p. 212.—J. O. D.

the great Red Pipe Stone Quarry, there is scarcely a doubt but that they were the "Village of the Red Stone Quarry" mentioned in Le Sueur's enumeration. Fifty years after that, we find them placed on the French maps about the mouth of the Little Sioux River. In those times they hunted buffalo in the northwestern part of Iowa and down the Missouri to its mouth and up to their present location or above, and eastward over the James River and the Big Sioux to the Red Pipe Stone, where was the gathering of the nations.[1]

TETON.

These have been known for two hundred years—and how much longer we know not—as "Dwellers on the Prairie." The full name was *Tiŋtatoŋwaŋ*, Prairie dwelling, contracted now into Titoŋwaŋ, and commonly written Teton.

As we have already seen, the French, in their maps, made a great lake at the head of the Minnesota River, which they called "Lake of the Tetons." The name gives us nothing more than Inhabitants of the Prairie. There is abundant evidence that, as far back as our knowledge of the Dakota Nation extends, the Teton have formed more than half the tribe, and causes have been in operation which have increased their number, while in some cases the more eastern bands have been diminished. The buffalo hunt has always tended to increase the Teton somewhat by immigration; and by furnishing a supply of wild meat their children have grown up, while many of those who came to use flour and pork have died off. The late wars of the Minnesota Dakota with the whites have operated in the same way.

As the result of the massacre of Spirit Lake, on the border of Iowa, in the spring of 1857, a large portion of the small band of Leaf Shooters, under the leadership of Iŋkpaduta's family, have disappeared from the east of the Missouri and become absorbed by the Teton. The same thing is true of hundreds of those engaged in the massacre of 1862. While a large number fled north into the Dominion of Canada, others, in 1863, crossed

---

[1] Near the mouth of the Missouri, where in one of its bends it approaches the Mississippi, is a place called *Portage des Sioux*. Here, evidently, the Dakota, a century ago, carried their canoes across from one river to the other, when on their hunting and war expeditions. This fact quite agrees with what we are told of their war parties descending the Mississippi two centuries ago, to attack the Illinois and Miamis.

The Yanktonai passed over to the Upper Minnesota, and from thence, and from the Red River of the North, they have journeyed westward to the Missouri, led on by the buffalo, from which they have obtained their living for more than a century and a half. Thus they have occupied the country as it was vacated by the more numerous of the "Seven Council Fires."

the Missouri and joined the various northern divisions of the "Dwellers on the Prairie."

It is curious to find the number *seven* occurring so frequently in their tribal and family divisions.[1] Of the whole tribe there were seven bands or "council fires;" of the Spirit Lake band there were seven villages, and of this great body of the Dakota Nation there are still seven divisions or subgentes.

First.—The Brules: This is the French translation of Sićaŋgu—"Burnt Thighs." They occupy, at present, the mouth of Makaizite River[2] and up to Fort Thompson. The origin of this name is uncertain. They are divided into Uplanders and Lowlanders.

Second.—The Two Kettles, or Oohe noŋpa, literally, " Two Boilings :" One story is, that the name originated in a time of great scarcity of provisions, when the whole band had only enough of meat to put in two kettles. The present headquarters of this band, as well as of the two that follow, is at the Cheyenne Agency and at Standing Rock, on the Missouri.

Third.—The Minnekanjoo: The full name is Mini-kaŋye-woźupi (Water-near to-plant), " Planters by the Water." We ask, "What water?" They do not remember. It looks very much as though the name had a history—possibly in Minnesota—more than a century ago.

Fourth —The Sans Arcs: This is the French translation of their own name, Itazipćo; which written in full is, Itazipa-ćodaŋ, "Bows without" or "No Bows." It is easy to imagine a few families of Dakota appearing, at some time of need, without that necessary implement of the chase and war, and so, having fastened upon them a name, which they would not have chosen for themselves.

Fifth.—The Oglala, or Ogalala, meaning Scatterers: This name embodies the peculiar characteristics of the Teton dialect of the language, viz: The frequent use of the hard "g" and the "l."

Sixth.—The Black Feet, or Siha sapa: This band of the Western Dakota must not be confounded with the Black Feet[3] of the mountains, which are connected with the Piegans and Bloods. The Oglala and Black Feet Dakota mainly constitute the camps of Spotted Tail and Red Cloud. But the bands are all a good deal mixed up by marriage and otherwise.

Seventh.—The Huŋkpapa: This band has for many years roamed over

[1] I have found many examples of the use of mystic numbers among cognate tribes, *e. g.*, *seven* (4+3), *four*, *ten* (7+3), *twelve* (4×3), and, in Oregon, *five.* I hope to publish an article on this subject. See "A Study of Siouan Cults," in 11th An. Rep. of the Director, Bur. Ethn.—J. O. D.

[2] From maka, *earth*, and izita, *to smoke, i. e.*, the White Earth River of South Dakota.—J. O. D.

[3] Sĭk'-sĭk-a.

the country of the Upper Missouri.   The war of 1876 made it somewhat notorious under its war chief "Sitting Bull," or "Sitting Buffalo," as Tataŋka iyotaŋke ought to be translated.

This article, on the Migrations of the Dakota, will not be complete, without a brief notice of the affiliated tribes.   The Dakota family, as shown by similarity of language, is quite extensive.

ASSINIBOIN.

I. Evidently the first to claim our attention, outside of the Dakota themselves, is the Assiniboin tribe.   Indeed they are a part of the great Dakota Nation.   Their language differs less from the Dakota in general, than the dialects of the Dakota do from each other.   In our historical narrative of the Dakota, we found the knowledge of the Assiniboin coming to white people at the same time, and along with that of the Dakota proper. More than two centuries ago Assiniboin and Dakota met the French traders at the head of Lake Superior.   The Assiniboin are said to have broken off from the Pine Shooters (Wazikute), a branch of the Ihaŋktoŋwaŋna.

At that time the split, by which they ranged themselves as a separate people, appears to have been a recent thing.   The name "Bwaŋ," applied by the Ojibwa to the whole Dakota people, fastened itself on that branch. They are Stone Dakota.   And at the present time, we have information of a small family of the Assiniboin people living on the Saskatchewan, which goes by the name of Stonies.   The name given to the Assiniboin by the Dakota is Hohe,[1] the origin and meaning of which are in the darkness.

At the time we first learn anything of the Assiniboin, they appear to have been occupying the country of the Red River of the North, probably both on the eastern and western side.   Their migrations have been northward and westward.   About the middle of the seventeenth century a French pilot, by name Grosellier, roamed into the country of the Assiniboin, near Lake Winnipeg, and was taken by them to Hudson Bay.   In 1803 Lewis and Clarke met Assiniboin at their winter camp near where Fort Stevenson now is.   But their movement westward seems to have been mainly farther north up the Assiniboin and Saskatchewan rivers.   At present they are found in the neighborhood of Fort Peck, on the Upper Missouri, but the most of them are within the Dominion of Canada.

---

[1] Pronounced ho'-hay.   There is also a Hohe gens among the Sihasapa Titoŋwaŋ.   Hohe is said to mean "Rebels."—J. O. D.

WINNEBAGO.

Two centuries and a third ago the French traders and missionaries from Montreal and Quebec came in contact with the Puants, living on the "Bay of the Puants," now Green Bay, in Wisconsin. These Indians were called Winnepekoak, or "People of the fetid water," by their Algonkian neighbors; but their name for themselves is Hotcañgara, "People of the Original Speech," modified to Hotaŋke by the Dakota, and Huɹañga by the Omaha and Ponka, though these modified names signify "Big Voices" in their respective languages.

The Winnebago language is closely allied to the Dakota.[1] One can not but think that less than a thousand years ago they were a part of the same people.

They may have separated at an early period from these cognate tribes, and even reached "salt water," whence their Algonkian name. Examples of such separation are found in the Biloxi of Mississippi and the Yesa[n] or Tutelo, formerly of Virginia and North Carolina, now in Canada.

But, confining ourselves to history, two centuries ago the Winnebago were on Lake Michigan. During the eighteenth century they had drifted slowly across the State of Wisconsin. In 1806 Lieut. Pike met the Puants[2] with the Fox at Prairie du Chien. In the war of 1812 the Winnebago, with the tribes of the Northwest generally, ranged themselves on the side of the British. While a small portion of the tribe remained in the interior of Wisconsin, the majority were removed across the Mississippi into Iowa and located on Turkey River about the year 1840. Thence they were taken up to Long Prairie, in Minnesota. Not being at all satisfied with that country, they were again removed to what was to be a home in Blue Earth County, back of Mankato. They were supposed to have had some sympathy with the Dakota in their outbreak of 1862, and accordingly they were removed with the captured Dakota, in the spring following, to the Missouri River. Their location at Crow Creek was highly distasteful to them, and, accordingly, they made canoes and floated themselves down to the Omaha Reservation, in Nebraska, on a portion of which the Government arranged to have them remain.

It should be mentioned that the Winnebago were largely engaged in the French and Indian War. Forty-eight were present in 1757 at the

---

[1] See "Comparative Phonology of Four Siouan Languages," in Smithson. Rept., 1883.—J. O. D.

[2] The name Puants means Stinkers. There is no doubt but that the French traders at first understood the name Winnebago to mean stinking water. But it is believed they were in error, and that its proper meaning is salt water.

battle of Ticonderoga, together with large numbers of the Ojibwa and other Western bands.

OMAHA AND PONKA.

These tribes have a common dialect and are closely related to the Osage, Kansa, and Kwapa. The first are the Maha of the old French maps. The five tribes form the Çegiha (or Dhegiha) group of the Siouan family. According to their traditions, their ancestors dwelt east of the Mississippi River, on the Ohio and Wabash. When they reached the mouth of the Ohio, part went down the Mississippi, becoming the Kwapa (Uχaqpa, Ugaqpa), or " Down-stream People," who afterwards met De Soto. The others ascended the Mississippi; hence the name " Up-stream People," or U-maⁿ-haⁿ (Umaŋhaŋ), now Omaha, applied at first to those who subsequently became four tribes (Omaha, Ponka, Osage, and Kansa). Another separation occured near the mouth of the Osage River, where the Omaha and Ponka crossed the Missouri, and went north, being joined on the way by a kindred tribe, the Iowa. These three wandered through Iowa and Minnesota till they found the Great Pipestone Quarry, where they made a settlement. At that time the Yankton (perhaps including the Yanktonnai) dwelt in a wooded region near the source of the Mississippi, being called " People of the Forest" by the Omaha and Ponka.[1]

The three tribes were finally driven off by the Dakota, wandering westward and southwestward till they reached the Missouri River, which they followed as far as the mouth of White Earth River. There the Ponka left their allies, ascending the White Earth River till they drew near the Black Hills, which they found in the possession of the Crows. Retracing their course, they joined the Iowa and Omaha, and all three went down along the southwest side of the Missouri River till the Niobrara was reached. There was made the final separation. The Ponka remained at the mouth of the Niobrara; the Omaha settled on Bow Creek, Nebraska; the Iowa went beyond them till they reached Ionia Creek (probably *Iowa* Creek at first), where they made a village on the east bank of the stream, not far from the site of the present town of Ponka. The subsequent migrations of these tribes have been given in the paper mentioned in the preceding footnote ([1]), as well as in the Third Annual Report of the Bureau of Ethnology (p. 213). The three tribes occupied different habitats as far back as Marquette's time, and they are thus located in his autograph map of 1673.

---

[1] The migrations of the Kansa, Kwapa, Osage, etc., have been treated by the editor in a recent paper, "Migrations of Siouan Tribes," which appeared in the American Naturalist for March, 1886 (Vol. 22, pp. 211–222). See " Omaha Sociology," in the Third Ann. Rept. of the Director Bur. Eth., pp. 211–213.—J. O. D.

When, in 1803, Lewis and Clarke made their voyage up the Missouri and across the Rocky Mountains, they found the Ponka (Poncara) near their present location. They say, "The Maha (Omaha) were associated with them for mutual protection." But the Omaha were there only on a visit. It is quite certain that they had not lived together for many years previous to this. The Omaha were in northeastern Nebraska, south of Sioux City, Iowa.

IOWA AND OTO.

The two tribes Iowa and Oto are associated here because they are mentioned together by Le Sueur, in 1700, as having, previous to that time, had the occupancy and the hunters' right to the country of the Blue Earth and of southern Minnesota.[1] They appear to have retired before the aggressive Sioux down the Des Moines into central Iowa, the Oto going on to the Missouri and down into Kansas. While in possession of the country of the Blue Earth, we have notices of their having hunted on the St. Croix, in northern Wisconsin. It is also stated, which appears to be a matter of tradition only, that at a much later date, not far from the commencement of the present century, the Iowa, in war, cut off entirely a small tribe, which dwelt south of the St. Croix, called the Unktoka, which means, Our Enemies.

Ten Iowa warriors were present at the battle of Ticonderoga.

There are, near the Minnesota River, old fortifications, or earthworks, which were probably made by these tribes to protect themselves against the incursions of the more powerful Dakota. One such is found a few miles above the mouth of the Yellow Medicine River. But possibly this was an old Cheyenne fortification, which would seem to be the reading of Dakota tradition.

MANDAN AND HIDATSA.

These two small tribes live together at Fort Berthold in connection with the Ree. They are both small tribes. The Mandan at present number less than 400. Years ago they numbered many more, but wars and smallpox have almost annihilated them. From rather a remarkable fact, that many of this people have sandy hair, it has been affirmed that they are of Welsh origin—supposed to be a lost Welsh colony. George Catlin,

---

[1] This must have been long before 1673, the date of Marquette's autograph map. The Oto did not accompany the Iowa, Ponka, and Omaha. They were first met by the Omaha and Ponka, according to Joseph La Flèche, on the Platte River in comparatively recent times. —J. O. D.

the celebrated Indian portrait painter, takes this view of their parentage, and affirms that their language bears more than a likeness to the Welsh.[1]

The Mandan tradition of their origin is, that ages ago they lived underground by a great lake. The root of a grapevine pushed itself down through the crust of the earth. One by one they took hold of it and climbed up by its help, coming out into the light of day. By and by a very fat woman took hold of it and the vine broke, leaving the remainder of the Mandans by the lake underground. Could this legend have any connection with a passage over the ocean?

Ever since they have been known to the whites they have lived on the Upper Missouri. In the winter of 1803–'04, Lewis and Clarke wintered near their villages, only a short distance below where they now are.

The Hidatsa are better known by the names Minnetaree and Gros Ventres.[2] There is no apparent reason why the latter name should have been given them by the French. Minnetaree means "over the water," and was given to them when they crossed the Missouri, coming as they did from the northeast and crossing to the southwest. They number about 500. These Hidatsa have often been confounded with the "Minnetaree of the Plains," or "Gros Ventres," who belong to another linguistic family.

Both the Hidatsa and Mandan belong to the Siouan or Dakotan family. Whether it is from the common likeness to the tongue of their enemies, or for some other reason, it is a remarkable fact that many persons of each tribe can speak Dakota.

ABSAROKA OR CROW.

This tribe and the Hidatsa speak dialects of the same language. It is said that the Amahami, now extinct, were a branch of the Absaroka.

When the Ponka reached the Black Hills country, several hundred years ago, they found it in the possession of the Absaroka, whose habitat included the region now known as the western part of Dakota (south of the Missouri River) and the eastern part of Montana.

---

[1] I have made a careful examination of the Mandan vocabularies of Kipp, Hayden, Wied, and others. The following conclusions have been reached: (1) The Mandan is closely related to the Winnebago, Iowa, Oto, and Missouri dialects. (2) The fancied resemblance to the Latin, based on what was thought to be "sub" in three compound nouns, has no foundation. Suk, suke, kshuk, or kshuke means *small*.—J. O. D.

[2] *Big Paunch* (Gros Ventre) must have referred to a buffalo paunch over which a quarrel arose resulting in the separation of the Hidatsa and Crow. See Kihatsa in Matthews's Ethnog. and Philol. of the Hidatsa Indians.—J. O. D.

OSAGE, KANSA, KWAPA, AND, MISSOURI.

All these tribes belong to the Siouan stock. The Missouri, who call themselves Nyu-t'a-tci, speak a dialect allied to those of the Iowa and Oto, while the dialects of the others are related to that of the Omaha and Ponka.

The Osage connect themselves by tradition with the *beavers*. The first father of the Osage was hunting on the prairie all alone. He came to a beaver dam, where he saw the chief of all the beavers, who gave him one of his daughters to wife. From this alliance sprang the Osage.[1]

ARIKARA OR RICKAREE.

This tribe, commonly called Ree and sometimes Pawnee, has been heretofore counted as belonging to the Dakota family. But the Ree language, as spoken at Berthold, appears to have no resemblance to the Dakota, and indeed to be radically different in its construction. So that, without doubt we must deny them a place in the Dakota linguistic family. But the Ree, the northern branch of the tribe now at Fort Berthold, numbering more than 1,000 souls, have been for many years intermingling with the Dakota, and probably separated from their southern kindred, the Pawnee proper, on account of an intrusion of the Dakota.[2] In 1803 Lewis and Clarke found the Ree on the Missouri River, near the mouth of Grand River.

SHAYENNE OR CHEYENNEE.

This name is variously written. The tribe comes into the same category as the last named—Ree and Pawnee. We can not admit them into the Dakota linguistic family. The name they bear is of Dakota origin, by whom they are called "Sha-e-a-na."[3] Sha-e-a,[4] in Dakota, means "to talk red," that is, unintelligibly, as " Ska-e-a"[5] means "to talk white"—intelligibly—that is, to interpret. The Shayenne language then, we understand, is not like the Dakota. But, though sometimes enemies of the Dakota, they have more generally been confederates. Two hundred years

---

[1] This is probably the tradition of part of the Osage, the Beaver people, not that of the whole tribe. See "Osage Traditions" in the Sixth Ann. Rept. of the Director Bur. Eth., pp, 373–397.—J. O. D.

[2] According to Omaha tradition, the Ree and Skidi (or Pawnee Loups) were allies of the Winnebago and the ancestors of the Omaha, Ponka, Osage, Kansa, Kwapa, Iowa, etc., when all these people dwelt east of the Mississippi. It is doubtful whether the Ree were ever neighbors of the Grand, Republican, and Tappage Pawnee, since the latter have been west of the Missouri. The latter conquered the Skidi, with whom they do not intermarry, according to Joseph I a Flèche, formerly a head chief of the Omaha. The Skidi met the three southern Pawnee divisions at a comparatively late date, according to Pawnee tradition. If all five were ever together, it must have been at an early period, and probably east of the Mississippi River.—J. O. D.

[3] Śa-i-ye-na.   [4] Śa-ia.   [5] Ska-ia.

ago, or thereabouts, the Shayenne village was near the Yellow Medicine River in Minnesota, where are yet visible old earthworks.   From thence, according to Dakota tradition, they retired before the advancing Dakota, and made their village between Big Stone Lake and Lake Traverse.   Their next remove appears to have been to the south bend of the Cheyenne, a branch of the Red River of the North.   The fortification there is still very plain.   While there they seem to have had both the Ojibwa and Dakota for their enemies.   Bloody battles were fought and finally the Shayenne retired to the Missouri.   This is supposed to have been about one hundred years ago or more.   After that time the Dakota became friendly to them. The Shayenne stopped on the east side of the Missouri and left their name to the Little Cheyenne.   Soon after they crossed over and took possession of the country of the Big Cheyenne.   There they were, hunting out to the Black Hills, in 1803, when Lewis and Clarke ascended the Missouri.

CHAPTER III.

GENS AND PHRATRY OF THE DAKOTA.

THE GENS.

In the Dakota Nation the man is the head of the family; the woman was not considered worthy of honor. No Dakota woman ever aspired to be a chief. The chieftainship descended from the father to his sons, the eldest son taking the precedence. But in the making up of the *gens* the woman was an equal factor with the man. Thus a child counts his father's brothers all fathers, and his father's sisters all aunts; while his mother's sisters are all mothers, and his mother's brothers are only uncles. Hence, a man's brother's children are counted as his own children, and his sister's children are nephews and nieces. On the other hand, a woman's sister's children are counted by her as children, while her brother's children are nephews and nieces.[1] These same distinctions are carried down through the generations. In this circle intermarriages are not allowed by Dakota custom. This is the gens, but there is lacking the totem to bind them together. The real foundation for the totemic system exists among the Dakota as well as the Iroquois, in the names of men often being taken from mythical animals, but the system was never carried to perfection. Sometimes indeed a village was called through generations after the chief of the clan, as Black Dog's, Little Crow's, etc.

THE PHRATRY.

Among the eastern Dakota the Phratry was never a permanent organization, but resorted to on special occasions and for various purposes, such as war or buffalo hunting.

THE TIYOTIPI.

The exponent of the Phratry was the "Tiyotipi" or Soldiers' Lodge. Its meaning is the "Lodge of Lodges." There were placed the bundles of black and red sticks of the soldiers. There the soldiers gathered to talk and smoke and feast. There the laws of the encampment were enacted,

---

[1] See Kinship System of the Omaha in 3d Ann. Rept. of the Director, Bur. Eth., pp. 252–258.—J. o .D.

and from thence they were published by the camp crier. It is said that in the camps of the Prairie Dakota, the real buffalo hunters, the Soldiers' Lodge was pitched in the center of the circular encampment. This area was called ho-ćo-ka; and the gateway of the camp, which was always left at the front end, was called ho-a-na-pa. The encampment was then in the form of a horseshoe, or, more properly, in the form of the horns of a buffalo cow, which turn inward toward each other. The ends of the horns were called "Huŋ-kpa," from "he," *a horn*, and "iŋkpa," *small end*. Hence those camping at these ends of the horns would be called "Huŋkpa-tina." And hence the name of two of the gentes, which have developed into larger clans of the Dakota Nation, viz., the Huŋkpatina and the Huŋkpapa.

While, within the historical period, no political organization has been known to exist over the whole Dakota Nation, the traditional alliance of the "Seven Council Fires" is perpetuated in the common name Dakota.

FELLOWHOOD.

One of the customs of the olden time, which was potent both for good and for evil, and which is going into desuetude, was that of fellowhood. Scarcely a Dakota young man could be found who had not some special friend or Koda. This was an arrangement of giving themselves to each other, of the David and Jonathan kind. They exchanged bows, or guns, or blankets—sometimes the entire equipment. In rare cases they exchanged wives. What one asked of the other he gave him; nothing could be denied. This arrangement was often a real affection, sometimes fading out as the years pass by, but often lasting to old age.

In order to exhibit properly and as fully as may be Dakota national and individual life, I will here introduce a pen picture of a very prominent man of the last generation.

STANDING BUFFALO.

In connection with Standing Buffalo, the last great chieftain of the Sisseton Dakota, will be found a description of the "Tiyotipi," already referred to.

Ta-taŋ-ka-na-źiŋ, or Standing Buffalo, was the son of The Orphan, and hereditary chief of quite a large clan of Sisseton Dakota. Their planting place, before the outbreak in 1862, was in that rich and beautiful valley which lies between the head of Lake Traverse, whose waters communicate with the Red River of the North and Big Stone Lake, through which the

Minnesota River runs to the Mississippi. Through this isthmus, between the two lakes, now known as Brown's Valley, the Minnesota, as it comes down in small streams out of the Coteau, winds its way.

As soon as Standing Buffalo had come to man's estate, or when he was probably about twenty-five years old, the father abdicated his chieftainship in favor of his son. Henceforth he wore his father's medals, carried his father's papers, and was the recognized chief of his father's people. As already stated, the Dakota custom is that the rank and title of chief descend from father to son unless some other near relative is ambitious and influential enough to obtain the place. The same is claimed also in regard to the rank of soldier or brave, but this position is more dependent on personal bravery.

At the time of the outbreak Standing Buffalo was a man in middle life. He was tall and well-featured—rather a splendid looking Dakota. Previous to 1852 he and his people received no annuities, but raised a good deal of corn. Still they depended chiefly, both for food and clothing, on the buffalo, and much of the year they spent in the chase.

Although congregating in vast herds on the great prairies and moving in certain directions with a great deal of apparent force, the buffalo are nevertheless easily driven away. And hence the Indians find it necessary to protect the hunt by regulations which must be enforced. In this necessity probably originated the Ti-yo-ti-pi, or so-called Soldiers' Lodge, which is both the hall of legislation and the great feasting place.

Some patriotic woman vacates her good skin tent and goes into a poorer one that she may furnish the braves with a fitting place for their assemblies. This tipi is then pitched in some central place, or in the gateway of the circle, and the women take delight in furnishing it with wood and water and the best of the meat that is brought into camp, for every good deed done for this Soldiers' Lodge is proclaimed abroad by the crier or eyaŋpaha.

A good fire is blazing inside and we may just lift up the skin door and crawl in. Towards the rear of the tent, but near enough the fire for convenient use, is a large pipe placed by the symbols of power. There are two bundles of shaved sticks about 6 inches long. The sticks in one bundle are painted black and in the other red. The black bundle represents the real men of the camp—those who have made their mark on the warpath. The red bundle represents the boys and such men as wear no eagle feathers. Around this fire they gather together to smoke. Here they discuss all questions pertaining to the buffalo hunt and the removal of camp;

in short, all public interests. From these headquarters they send out from time to time runners, who bring back information of the whereabouts of the bison herds. From this lodge goes out the camp crier, who makes proclamation of the time and place of the buffalo surround. And from this same central place of power go forth the young men who are commissioned to cut up the tent and the blankets, or break the gun and kill the horse of one who has transgressed the laws of the Ti-yo-ti-pi. And when the hunt of the day is past, and the buffalo meat brought in, the breast or some nice piece is roasted or boiled here, and the young men gather to eat and smoke and sing and tell over the exploits of the day. It will not then surprise any one to know that this Soldiers' Lodge became the central force in the outbreak of 1862.

In the summer before the outbreak took place, there was quite a trouble at the Yellow Medicine. The payment was promised to these annuity Indians when the strawberries were ripe, that is the last of June or the first of July of each year. This season the Sisseton came down earlier perhaps than usual, and the annuity money and goods were delayed much beyond time. About 4,000 Indians were gathered at the Yellow Medicine, where they waited about six weeks. The small amount of provisions on hand Agent Galbraith wished to keep until the time of making the payment. The corn and potatoes planted by Indians living in the neighborhood had not yet matured. Consequently this multitude of men, women, and children were for more than a month on the borders of starvation. Some flour was obtained from traders, and the agent gave them small quantities; they gathered some berries in the woods and occasionally obtained a few ducks. But by all these means they scarcely kept starvation off. They said the children cried for something to eat.

Standing Buffalo was the principal chief of these northern Indians. They were encamped in a large circle on the prairie immediately west of the agency. It was now along in the first days of August. Hunger pressed upon them. They knew there was flour in the warehouse which had been purchased for them. It would not be wrong for them to take it in their present necessitous circumstances. Thus they reasoned; and although a detachment of soldiers from Fort Ridgeley had their camp near the warehouse, the Indians planned to break in and help themselves.

So it was, on a certain day, the men came down to the agency five or six hundred strong and surrounded the soldiers' camp. The white people thought they had come to dance; but while they stood around in great numbers, a selected few broke in the door of the warehouse with axes and carried out a large quantity of flour and pork. To this the attention of Agent Galbraith was immediately called, who made an ineffectual effort to have it carried back. The howitzer was turned towards the Indians and there was a prospect of a collision, but the numbers were so disproportionate that it was judged best to avoid it. Scarcely had they reached their own camp when those four hundred tents were struck, and all removed off to a distance of 2 or 3 miles. That was supposed to mean war.

The next morning the writer visited the agency, having heard something of the trouble. When I met the agent he said, "Mr. Riggs, if there is anything between the lids of the Bible that will help us out of this difficulty, I wish you would use it." I said I would try, and immediately drove up to Standing Buffalo's camp. I represented to him the necessity of having this difficulty settled. However perfect they might regard their right to the provisions they had taken, the Government would not be willing to treat them kindly until the affair was arranged. The breaking in of the warehouse was regarded as a great offense.

He promised to gather the chief men immediately and talk the thing over and come down to the agency as soon as possible.

It was afternoon when about fifty of the principal men gathered on the agent's porch. They said they were sorry the thing had taken place, but they could not restrain the young men, so great was the pressure of hunger in the camp. They wished, moreover, the agent to repair the broken door at their expense. Some of the young men who broke it down were present, but they did not want to have them punished. It was rather a lame justification, but Agent Galbraith considered it best to accept of it and to give them some more provisions, on condition that they would return immediately to their planting places at Big Stone Lake and Lake Traverse. This he desired them to do because the time when the payment could be made was unknown to him and their own corn patches would soon need watching. Standing Buffalo and his brother chiefs accepted the conditions, and in a couple of days the northern camp had disappeared.

Four or five weeks after this, these warriors came down again to the Yellow Medicine and the Red Wood; but it was not to meet the agent or any white people, but to see Little Crow and the hostile Indians and ascertain whereunto the rebellion would grow. It is reported that, on this occasion, Standing Buffalo told Little Crow that, having commenced hostilities with the whites, he must fight it out without help from him; and that, failing to make himself master of the situation, he should not flee through the country of the Sisseton.

But although as a whole these northern Dakota refused to go into the rebellion with the Santee, it is very certain that quite a number of their young men joined in the raids made upon the white settlements; and moreover, the attack upon Fort Abercrombie, at which several hundred Dakota warriors were said to have been present, must have been made almost entirely by these same Sisseton.

In the autumn which followed they all fled to the Upper Missouri country or into the Queen's dominions. It was reported soon after that Standing Buffalo had gone on the warpath and was killed.

THE TIYOTIPI.

[Translated from M. Renville's Dakota version.]

When Indians would hunt the buffalo, they do it in this way: Whenever they hear that there are buffalo, they look out a young man and ask him for his tent. If he consents, then no woman or child is allowed in the tent; men alone go into it. And so the man whose the tent is is called Tiyoti, and is the master in it.

Then also they do in this way: They shave out small round sticks all of the same length, and paint them red, and they are given out to the men. These are to constitute the Tiyotipi. This done, they choose four men whom they make the chiefs, who make all the arrangements. Also one who is called Eyaŋpaha (crier), who makes proclamation of everything that is determined on. In addition to these, they select two young men who are called Touchers. These attend to all the provisions that are brought to the Tiyotipi.

Then, of all the painted sticks that were given around, not one is brought in empty. When one is to be brought to the Tiyotipi, food is brought with it. And when these are all brought in, they are tied in a bundle. In the back part of the tent, by the fire, the ground is carefully cleaned off, and a pipe and a pipe rammer and incense leaves are all brought and placed together.

These are all completed in this way and then about two young men are selected, and the pipe is filled and passed to them, which is done by the Eyaŋpaha. When this ceremony is finished they are sent out into that part of the country in which they heard the buffalo were. Hence they are called Wakĉaŋya and also Wayeya, that is One-who-finds-out, and also One Sent.

Whither they were sent they go, and when they know the buffalo are there, they return to camp. When they come near they run, and by this it is known that they are bringing tidings. Thus they come directly to the Tiyotipi, which is already filled with those who want to hear. Then in the back part of the tent, which has been made sacred, where the pipe and the tobacco are, there the Eyaŋpaha fills the pipe and puts it to their mouths. Then privately they tell the news to the Eyaŋpaha, who says, "Hayen, hayen," and spreads his hands out to the earth. All in the tent do the same, and then the news is told openly. The Eyaŋpaha then goes out and makes proclamation to the whole camp. But this he does in a somewhat different style: "When a boy comes home to me from another place, and brings me word of so many large pieces of buffalo meat, let every ghost in all your families hear it; so far on the other side the earth is not visible, they say." While he cries this through the camp, all who are able whistle, which they do for joy.

When the Eyaŋpaha has returned to the Tiyotipi, then the four masters of the assembly consider and determine when they will go on the hunt. This being determined, the Eyaŋpaha again makes proclamation to all the people. This is what he says: "Bind on your saddle, for a piece of a day I will kill valuable children." Then all get themselves ready and they start out together.

Only the four chief men give the commands. When they come near to the buffalo, the party is divided and the approach is made from both sides. This is done whether there be one herd or two. They go on both sides. It is determined to conduct the chase in a proper manner. But if in doing this one side gets in a hurry and drives off the game, then their blankets and even their tents are cut to pieces. This they call "soldier killing."

When they come home from the buffalo chase, all who can bring fresh meat to the Tiyotipi. Then the Touchers cook it. When it is cooked they cut off some pieces and put in the mouths of the four chief men, and then they all eat as they please. In the meantime the Eyaŋpaha stands outside and praises those who brought the meat.

The summing up of the whole is this: The back part of the Tiyotipi, near the fire, is cleared off carefully; and there are placed two grass fenders, about a foot long each, on which the pipe is laid. The pipe is never laid back after the common custom.   Also they shave a round stick, sharpening one end and cutting the other off square.   This is driven in the ground, and on it, when the pipe is smoked out, they knock out the ashes.   They always do this.   Then of all the round-shaved sticks, some of which were painted black and some painted red, four are especially marked. They are the four chiefs of the Tiyotipi that were made.   And these men are not selected at random for this place; but men who have killed many enemies and are the most able, are chosen.   The things desired are, that the chase may be conducted in the best way, that the people may have a plenty of food, and that everything may be done properly—so they determined, and so they do.   The ashes of the pipe are not emptied out carelessly, so that when they command each other, and give each other the pipe, it may be done only in truth.   That is the reason for doing it.

Also in the deer hunt they have a Tiyotipi, but in that they do not send out persons to reconnoiter.   Nevertheless, in that also, if anyone goes to hunt on his own motion, they "soldier kill" him, that is, cut up his blanket and coat.

These are the customs of the Otiyoti.

Thus far the translation—to which may be added some words of explanation.

1. The special making of the sticks is done on the line of personal history.   Whatever is indicated by the kind of eagle feathers a man is entitled to wear in his head, and by the notches in them, this is all hiero-glyphed on his stick in the Tiyotipi.   Then these bundles of sticks are used for gambling.   The question is, "Odd or even?"   The forfeits are paid in meat for the Tiyotipi.

2. The announcements of the crier show the rhythmical character of the language.   This especially appears in the order for the hunt:

Akiŋ iyakaśka:
Śićeća teḣike,
Aŋpetu haŋkeya,
Ećawaliaŋ kta će.

The saddle bind:
Children dear,
For half a day,
I will kill.

CHAPTER IV.

UNWRITTEN DAKOTA LAWS.

THE FAMILY.

In the commencement and growth of the Dakota people and language we may properly assume that the words "a-te," *father*, and "i-na" and "huŋ," *mother* ("nihuŋ," *thy mother*, "huŋku," *his mother*), were among the very first. They are short, and not capable of further analysis. "Wića," *male*, and "wiŋ" or "wiŋna" and "wiŋyaŋ," *female*, would be the first words to designate the *man* and *woman*. From these would grow naturally the present names, wi-ća-śta,[1] or the Yankton and Teton form, "wi-ća-śa" (male-red), *man*, and winohiŋća[2] (female-very), *woman*. There would be *father-in-law* before *grandfather*; and hence we find the former designated by "tuŋ-kaŋ,"[3] the shorter one, and the latter by "tuŋ-kaŋ-śi-na." "Tuŋ-kaŋ" is also the name of the *stone god*, which may indicate some kind of worship of ancestors. The shortest word also is found in *mother-in-law*, "kuŋ" ("nikuŋ," *thy mother-in-law*, "kuŋku," *his mother-in-law*). A woman speaking of or to her mother-in-law and grandmother calls them both "uŋći," making the latter sometimes diminutive "uŋćina."

Some words for *child* should be at least as old, if not older than, father and mother. Accordingly we find the monosyllables "ćiŋś," *son*, and "ćuŋś," *daughter*, used by the parents when speaking to the children, while "ćiŋća" is the common form.

In the line of "wiŋ" being the oldest form word for *woman*, we have the Dakota man calling his wife "mitawiŋ," *my woman*. The word as wife is not used without the affixed and suffixed pronominal particles (mi-ta-wiŋ, nitawiŋ, tawiću), which would indicate property in the woman. On the

---

[1] While wića śa may mean " male red," how shall we render wića śta? Wića = nika (Ȼegiha), *c male of the human species;* and wića śa or wića śta = nikaciⁿga (Ȼegiha), *a person; an Indian.*—J. O D.

[2] Shortened to winohća.

[3] Tuŋkaŋśidaŋ, in Santee; tuŋkaŋśina, in Yankton; tuŋkaŋśila, in Teton.

other hand, the woman calls her husband "mihihna," *my husband.* The
latter part of the word we can not analyze satisfactorily.[1]

Thus we come into the family as constituted, the man calling his
woman "mi-tá-wiŋ," and she calling her man "mi-hihna," and each calling
the child "ćiŋś" or "ćuŋś," as the case may be. The taking of each
other makes each related to the family of the other. But somehow shame
has come into the tipi, and the man is not allowed to address or to look
towards his wife's mother, especially, and the woman is shut off from
familiar intercourse with her husband's father and others, and etiquette pro-
hibits them from speaking the names of their relatives by marriage. This
custom is called "wiśteŋ kiyapi," from "iśteća," *to be ashamed.* How it
grew is not apparent. But none of their customs is more tenacious of life
than this. And no family law is more binding.

THE HOUSEHOLD.

The "tipi" is the *house* or *living place.* There is no word for *home*
nearer than this. The Dakota woman owns the "tipi;" she dresses the
skins of which the "wakeya" or *shelter* is made; she pitches and takes down
the tipi, and carries it on her back oftentimes in the march. It should
belong to her. But when it is pitched and the ground covered with dry
grass, her man takes the place of honor, which is the back part opposite the
door. The wife's place is on the left side as one enters, the right side as
one sits in the back part. The children come in between the mother and
father. The place of the grandmother or mother-in-law or aunt is the
corner by the door opposite the woman of the house. If a man has more
wives than one, they have separate tipis or arrange to occupy the
different sides of one. When a daughter marries, if she remains in her
mother's tipi, the place for herself and husband is on the side opposite
the mother, and back near the "ćatku," the place of honor. The same
place is allotted to her in her husband's mother's tent. The back part of
the tent, the most honorable place, and the one usually occupied by the
father, is given to a stranger visitor.

---

[1] Mr. Dorsey is right, undoubtedly, in regarding "hna" as the root, or at least one root, of
"mi-hi-hná, *my husband,* "hi-hna-ku," *her husband.* And the meaning of it is rather that of *placing*
than of *deceiving,* relating it to "ohnaka" *to place in,* as if in the woman's family, rather than with
"hnayaŋ," *to deceive.* But what account shall we make of the "hi," or "hiŋ," as many Dakotas per-
sist in writing it? Does that mean *hair,* and so send the word back to an indelicate origin? Quite
likely.—S. R. R.

Compare the Dakota tawiŋtoŋ, tawiŋya, and tawitoŋ, "to have as his wife," used only of
coition. See footnote ([1]), p. 207.—J. O. D.

The young man who goes to live with his wife's relatives is called " wićawoha," which literally means *man-cached*, as if the man, by so doing, *buried himself.* Mothers, who have daughters to be married, are often desirous of having the sons-in-law come and live, for a while at least, with them, since, if the young man is a good hunter, this arrangement secures to them plenty of game. But on the other hand, the young man's parents are quite as likely to require his services and that of his wife in addition. So that, in this regard, there is no prevailing law. As soon as the young couple are able to procure a tent, and if the man is a good hunter and buffalo are plenty, that may be very soon, they set up for themselves. This usually takes place soon after their first child is born, if not before.

COURTSHIP AND MARRIAGE.

Before proceeding farther with the laws of the family, it is proper to describe how it becomes a family. Girls are sometimes taken very young, before they are of marriageable age, which generally happens with a man who has a wife already. The marriageable age is from fourteen years old and upward. The intercourse of young men with maidens is not always open and honorable, but the public sentiment of a Dakota community, while it does not prevent much that is illicit, makes it more or less dishonable, especially for the girl. A boy begins to feel the drawing of the other sex and, like the ancient Roman boys, he exercises his ingenuity in making a "ćotaŋke," or rude pipe, from the bone of a swan's wing, or from some species of wood, and with that he begins to call to his lady love, on the night air. Having gained her attention by his flute, he may sing this:

> Stealthily, secretly, see me,
> Stealthily, secretly, see me,
> Stealthily, secretly, see me;
> Lo! thee I tenderly regard;
> Stealthily, secretly, see me.

Or he may commend his good qualities as a hunter by singing this song:

> Cling fast to me, and you 'll ever have plenty;
> Cling fast to me, and you 'll ever have plenty;
> Cling fast to me.

When the family are abed and asleep, he often visits her in her mother's tent, or he finds her out in the grove in the daytime gathering fuel. She has the load of sticks made up, and when she kneels down to take it on her back possibly he takes her hand and helps her up, and then walks home by her side. Such was the custom in the olden time. Thus a mutual understanding is reached. He wants her and she wants him. He has seen her ability to supply the tipi with fuel as well as do other necessary things, and she has often seen him bringing to his mother's tent a back load of ducks, or, it may be, venison Capt. R. H. Pratt, of Carlisle school, tells a capital story of a Kiowa young man who, under a variety of circumstances, never "cared for girl." "But when Laura say she love me, then I begin to care for girl."

The young man then informs his father and mother, and they approving, together with other family friends, make up the *bundle-of-purchase.* It may be a horse. If so, it is led by one of his friends and tied by the tent of the girl's parents. Or guns and blankets are contributed, which are carried by an aunt or other female relative, and the load is laid down at the tent door. It is "wo-ḣpa-pi," *laying down,* and the young man thus *lays down* or *tenders* his offer for the girl. If this is not satisfactory, either from the small amount or the character of the young man, the offerings are carried back, and the young folks have a chance to elope, unless they are restrained by higher considerations.

Sometimes it happens that a young man wants a girl, and her friends are also quite willing, while she alone is unwilling. The purchase bundle is desired by her friends, and hence compulsion is resorted to. The girl yields and goes to be his slave, or she holds out stoutly, sometimes taking her own life as the alternative. Several cases of this kind have come to the personal knowledge of the writer. The legends of Winona and Black Day Woman are standing testimonies. The comely dark-eyed Winona wanted to wed the successful hunter, but the brilliant warrior was forced upon her, and therefore she leaped from the crag on Lake Pepin, which immortalizes her name. For a like reason, Black-Day Woman pushed her canoe out into the current, above the Falls of Saint Anthony, and sang her death song as it passed over. These are doubtless historical events, except that the years are not known.

When the offer is accepted the girl is taken by some relative to the tent of the buyer. In the olden time it is said the custom was that she rode on the back of some female friend. Thus they become man and wife, with the idea of property strongly impressed upon the mind of the man. He has purchased her, as he would do a horse, and has he not a right to command her, and even to beat her? The customs of his people allow it.

If she pleases him not, he may *throw her away* (eḣpeya), for is she not his property? Nevertheless this was the honorable way for a girl to be taken. On many accounts it was better than to be stolen or taken unlawfully. And this custom of wife-purchase maintains its hold upon the Dakota people until they have made much progress in civilization.

The difference in the pronouns used in *my wife* and *my husband* seems to mark the difference of the property idea. Two kinds of possession are indicated by the affixed possessive pronouns, one easily alienated, as in "mita-śuŋke," *my horse;* and the other not transferable, as in "mi-nape," *my hand.* The man uses the first form, where possession sits lightly, as "mitawiŋ;" while the woman uses the other, "mihihna."[1] But it must not be inferred from this that a Dakota woman does not often run away from her husband. In that case, unless he endeavors to win her back, the laws of his nation allow him to cut off her nose, or otherwise mutilate her for infidelity.

THE BABY.

The young father is away on purpose. He has gone to his own father's people, or perhaps on a hunt with his comrades. The mother is left with the older women, her own mother and other female relatives. Many of the middle-aged women become skillful mid-wives; and the Dakota women, who are healthy, have less labor at such times than women in more civilized communities. The baby is born, and, like the infant Saviour of the world, is wrapped in swaddling bands. "Hokśi" appears to be the root form of "ho-kśi-na," *boy,*[2] and hence to the "hokśi" is added "iyoḳopa," *the board to which the child is bound,* and we have the long descriptive name for "*baby*," "hokśiyoḳopa," and sometimes "hokśiyopa" and "hokśićopa." This board is shaved out nicely, and often ornamented in various ways, with beads and quills, having a stay board around the

---

[1] This is another instance of the necessity of observing great caution in the analysis of Indian words. Mitawiŋ hardly falls in the category to which mitaśuŋke belongs. It is better, for several reasons, not to lay too much stress upon the derivation of mitawiŋ from mita, *my*, and wiŋ, *woman*. (1) We should consider all the persons of each kinship term in any one language. (2) We should compare the Dakota terms with the corresponding ones in cognate languages. (3) We do not find any kinship terms which make their possessives in initial ta, but in final ku, ću, or tku (see what the author himself shows in § 69, b, p. 44). In Dakota we find, tahaŋ, *a* (not his) brother-in-law; tahaŋku, *his* ditto; tahaŋśi, *a* man's male cousin (or, *my* ditto); tahaŋśi-tku, *his* male cousin; tawi-ću, *his* wife; tawiŋ, *a* wife. Tawiŋ answers to the ˌɔiwere stem tami, in i-tami, *his wife*, where i- is the possessive fragment pronoun, *his* or *her*. Other ˌɔiwere kinship terms in which ta- occurs are as follows: i-takwa, his or her grandson; i-takwa-mi, his or her granddaughter; i-tahaⁿ, his brother-in-law, in all of which i-, not ta-, is the sign of the possessive.—J. O. D.

[2] Hokśidaŋ in Santee; hokśina in Yankton; hokśila in Teton. The initial 'ho' answers to 'to,' etc., of the cognate languages.—J. O. D.

foot, and a strap board or handle standing out over the head of the child, which serves both for protection and to tie the mother's strap to. In this nicely arranged cradle, which is often hung up in the daytime, the baby has his home for the most part, being taken out at night, and at other times when needing care. So it grows, crying sometimes as other babies do, but needing and receiving much less care than a civilized child. In the meantime the mother has, perhaps on the first day, or if not on that day very soon after, gone to the stream or lake and washed away her uncleanness. If it is winter she cuts a hole in the ice to do it. When they begin to take on civilized habits, the Dakota women find they can not continue to follow the customs of their grandmothers.

What will they call the baby? If it be a little girl, and is the first born, then it inherits the beautiful name of Winona. When the second child comes, if that is a girl, it is called "Ha′-paŋ;" the third, "Ha′-pistiŋna;" the fourth, "Waŋske;" and the fifth, "Wi-hake." Some of these names are said not to be used by the Sioux on the Missouri. On the other hand, if the first born is a boy, his inherited name is "Ćaske," and the second child, if a boy, will be called "He-paŋ;" and the third, "He-pi;" and the fourth, Ća-taŋ;" and the fifth, "Ha-ke." Some children have no other names given them, and wear these alone when they are grown up. But if all families were content with this limited circle, much confusion would exist, especially as they have no family name. Hence the necessity of giving other names. This is done often by the father, and sometimes by some relative of consideration. Frequently a feast is made by the father to mark the occasion, and the child's ears are bored that it may wear ornaments.

Girls' names generally terminate in "wiŋ" or "wiŋna," but not always. I recall a family of girls who were named "Aŋpao," *Morning*, "Ahiyaŋke-wiŋ," *Woman Come-to-stay*, "Maȟpi-wiŋna," *Cloud Woman*, "Haŋyetu-ku-wiŋ," *Coming Night Woman, etc.* But the boys, either in their childhood or when they are grown, receive the imposing and honorable names of ancestors, as, Gray Bear, Standing Buffalo, Standing Soldier, The Orphan, Burning Earth, etc. Oftentimes new names are given when young men signalize themselves in war or otherwise. Then there is feasting, music, and dancing.

CHILD LIFE.

The children have now come into the family. How will they grow up? What shall they be taught? Who shall be their teachers? What the father and mother do they will do. What the father and mother know they will know. What the father and mother are they will be. One can hardly say there is much government in a Dakota family. Children are scolded often, they are pushed, or shoved, or shaken sometimes, and they are whipped rarely. They are petted and indulged a good deal, but not more than children in civilized lands. But somehow or other, with exceptions, they manage to grow up affectionate and kind, the pride of father and mother. The love of the parents has wrought this. Not unfrequently the grandfather and grandmother are the principal teachers.

TRAINING OF THE BOY.

The old man sits in the tipi and shaves out a bow and arrow for the little boy. In the mean time he tells him stories of history and war. The boy's father, it may be, has been killed by the enemy. The grandfather tells the story over and over again. It burns itself into the boy's heart. It becomes the animus of his life. He shoots his first bird and brings it into the tent. He is praised for that. "When you become a man you must kill an enemy," the old man says. "Yes; I will kill an enemy," is the boy's reply. He dreams over it. He witnesses the "Scalp Dance" and the "No Flight Dance" in his village. His heart is growing strong. When he is fifteen or sixteen he joins the first war party and comes back with an eagle feather in his head, if so be he is not killed and scalped by the enemy. All this is education. Then there are foot racings, and horse racings, and ball playing, and duck hunting, and deer hunting, or it may be the whole village goes on a buffalo chase.

These are the schools in which the Dakota boy is educated. In the long winter evenings, while the fire burns brightly in the center of the lodge and the men are gathered in to smoke, he hears the folk lore and legends of his people from the lips of the older men. He learns to sing the love songs and the war songs of the generations gone by. There is no new path for him to tread, but he follows in the old ways. He becomes a Dakota of the Dakota. His armor is consecrated by sacrifices and offerings and vows. He sacrifices and prays to the stone god, and learns to hold up the pipe to the so-called Great Spirit. He is killed and made alive again, and thus is initiated into the mysteries and promises of the Mystery Dance. He becomes a successful hunter and warrior, and what he does not know is not worth knowing for a Dakota. His education is finished. If he has not already done it, he can now demand the hand of one of the beautiful maidens of the village.

TRAINING OF THE GIRL.

Under the special care and tuition of the mother and grandmother and other female relatives the little girl grows up into the performance of the duties of tent life. She plays with her "made child," or doll, just as children in other lands do. Very soon she learns to take care of the baby; to watch over it in the lodge, or carry it on her back, while the mother is away for wood or dressing buffalo robes. Little girl as she is, she is sent to the brook or lake for water. She has her little workbag with awl and sinew, and learns to make small moccasins as her mother makes large ones. Sometimes she goes with her mother to the wood and brings home her little bundle of sticks. When the camp moves she has her small pack as her mother carries the larger one, and this pack is sure to grow larger as her years increase. When the corn is planting, the little girl has her part to perform. If she can not use the hoe yet, she can at least gather off the old cornstalks. Then the garden is to be watched while the god-given maize is growing. And when the harvesting comes, the little girl is glad for the corn roasting. So she grows. She learns to work with beads and porcupine quills and to embroider with ribbons. She becomes skilled in the use of vermilion and other paints. A stripe of red adorns her hair and red and yellow spots are over her eyebrows and on her cheeks. Her instincts teach her the arts of personal adornment. She puts cheap rings on her fingers and tin dangles in her ears and strands of beads around her neck. Quite likely a young man comes around and adds to her charms as he sings:

> Wear this, I say;
> Wear this, I say;
> Wear this, I say;
> This little finger ring,
> Wear this, I say.

Thus our Dakota girl becomes skilled in the art of attracting the young men, while she is ambitious in the line of carrying bundles as well as in cooking venison. In all these ways she is educated to be a woman among Dakota women. It is a hard lot and a hard life, but she knows no other.

WHEN DEATH COMES.

In the wild life of the Dakota the birth rate exceeded the death rate. So that, without doubt, notwithstanding famines sometimes and pestilences and wars, the Dakota nation has increased for the last two hundred years. This has been proved true within the last few decades at villages where actual count has been made. But in their entering upon the habits and environments of civilization, it is usually found that a wave of death goes over the people. They do not know how to live in the changed conditions, and the death rate is fearfully increased. "We die, we all die, we are consumed with dying," is the sad refrain of many a Dakota family.

Living much in the outdoors and within airy tipis, and subsisting on wild meats and such roots and fruits as they could gather, the children usually lived. But, nevertheless, even then death came. The baby in the mother's arms or strapped to her back sickened; or the little boy or girl occasionally succumbed under the hardships and privations; or the mother was taken with insidious consumption. The young father, it may be, ran too long and hard after that deer; he never ran again, but sickened and died. Then the old and the blind and the lame passed away, because they had reached the limits of life. So death comes to Indian tipis as to white men's hovels and palaces. But it is no more welcome in the one case than in the other. The Dakota mother loves her infant as well as the white woman her baby. When the spirit takes its flight a wild howl goes up from the tent. The baby form is then wrapped in the best buffalo calf-skin or the nicest red blanket and laid away on a scaffold or on the branch of some tree. Thither the mother goes with disheveled hair and the oldest clothes of sorrow—for she has given away the better ones—and wails out her anguish, in the twilight, often abiding out far into the cold night. The nice kettle of hominy is prepared and carried to the place where the spirit is supposed to hover still. When it has remained sufficiently long for the wanagi to inhale the ambrosia, the little children of the village are invited to eat up the remainder.

But let us take another case. A young man is lying sick in yonder tent. He has been the best hunter in the village. Many a time he has come in carrying one, two, or more deer on his back, and has been met and relieved of his burden by his wife or mother. The old men have praised him as swifter than the antelope, while they have feasted on his venison. But now some spirit of wolf or bear has come into him and caused this sickness. The doctors of the village or conjurers are tried, one after another. The blankets, the gun, and the horse have all been given to secure the best skill; but it is all in vain; the hunter dies. The last act of the conjurer is to sing a song to conduct the spirit over the wanagi taćaŋku, *the spirit's road*, as the milky way is called. The friends are inconsolable. They give away their good clothes, and go into mourning with ragged clothes and bare feet, and ashes on their heads. Both within the lodge and without there is a great wailing. Mićiŋkśi, mićiŋkśi, *my son, my son*, is the lamentation in Dakota land, as it was in the land of Israel.

The departed is wrapped in the most beautifully painted buffalo robe or the newest red or blue blanket. Dakota custom does not keep the dead long in the tipi. Young men are called and feasted, whose duty it is to carry it away and place it on a scaffold, or, as in more recent times, to bury it. The custom of burial, however, soon after death was not the Dakota custom. It would interfere with their idea that the spirit had not yet bidden a final farewell to the body. Therefore the laying up on a scaffold which was erected on some mound, where it would have a good view of the surrounding country. After a while the bones could be gathered up and buried in the mound and an additional quantity of earth carried up to cover it. This is partly the explanation of burial mounds made since the period of the mound-builders.

Thus the lodge is made desolate. It must be taken down and pitched in a new place. The young wife cries and cuts her flesh. The mother and other female relatives wail out their heart sadness on the night air. The father, the old man, leans more heavily on his staff as he goes on to the time of his departure. The brothers or cousins are seen wending their way, in the afternoon, to the place of the dead, to lay down a brace of ducks and to offer a prayer. A near relative makes up a war party. The feathers and other ornament, together with the clothing of the young man, are taken by this company on the warpath and divided among themselves in the country of their enemies. This is honoring the dead. If they succeed in bringing home scalps their sorrow is turned into joy. For will not this make glad the spirit of the departed? So, then, this will be gladness to the dead and glory to the living. The young men and maidens dance around the war trophies until the leaves come out in the spring or until they fall off in the autumn.[1]

THE SPIRIT-WORLD.

If sorrow brings mankind into a common kinship, a white man may understand something of an Indian's feelings as he stands by the side of his

---

[1] For Teton burial customs, etc., see "Teton Folk-lore," translated by the editor and published in the Amer. Anthropologist for April, 1889, pp. 144–148.—J. O. D.

dead and looks over into the land of spirits. What has gone? And whither has it gone? The belief of the Dakotas in the *existence* of spirit is deeply inwrought into their language. The "naġi," or *shadow*, in the concrete form, meaning primarily the *shade* or *shadow* made by any material thing in the sunlight, is used to indicate the human soul or spirit, as well as the spirit of all living beings. It is, moreover, put into the abstract form as "wanaġi," and also into the human absolute, "wiċa-naġi," *human spirit.* They speak also of the "wanaġi tipi," *house of spirits,* and say of one who has died, "wanaġiyata iyaya," *gone to the spirit land.* And the road over which it passes is called "wanaġi taċaŋku," *spirit's path.* The war prophet also, in his incantations, sings:

> I have cast in here a soul;
> I have cast in here a soul;
> I have cast in here a buffalo soul;
> I have cast in here a soul.

In the sacred language of conjuring man is designated by the "mythic buffalo."

Thus we have abundant evidence, in the language and customs of the people, of the common belief of the nation in the existence of spirits. But having said that, there is little more that can be said. The vista is dark. No light shines upon the path. But looking out into this dark avenue, the sad heart of the Dakota sings a song for the dead. Take this mourning song of Black-Boy for his grandson as a specimen. The object appears to be that of introducing the freed spirit of the child to his comrades in the world of spirits.

"The unearthliness of the scene," says Mr. Pond, "can not be described, as, in the twilight of the morning, while the mother of the deceased boy, whose name was Makadutawiŋ, *Red-Earth-Woman,* was wailing in a manner which would excite the sympathies of the hardest heart, Hoksidaŋ-sapa, *Black-boy,* standing on the brow of a hill, addressed himself to the ghostly inhabitants of the spirit-world, in ghostly notes, as follows:

> "Friend, pause and look this way;
> Friend, pause and look this way;
> Friend, pause and look this way;
> Say ye,
> A grandson of Black-boy is coming."

CHAPTER V.

THE SUPERHUMAN.

The existence of spirits and the necessity for the superhuman are facts fully recognized by the Dakotas. The unknown and unknowable form a broad belt in which humbuggery can be practiced by the Dakotas as well as other nations. The powers are evil. The lightning strikes suddenly and kills. The thunder god is angry and merciless. The north god sweeps down upon them with terrible snow storms, and buries their encampments, killing their ponies, and making buffalo hunting impossible. Or in the spring floods, the Uŋktehi, or god of the waters, is malignant and kills now and then a man or a child. And all through the year the demon spirits of the wolf and the bear and the lynx and the owl and the snake are doing their mischievous work, scattering disease and death everywhere. Who shall cope with these evil-minded powers? How shall deliverance come to the people? Will not fasting and praying and self-inflicted suffering bring the needed power? To the Dakota thought this is surely among the possibilities. Hence, naturally, grows up the *wakaŋ* man, or the so-called "medicine man." His applied power and skill are denominated *renewing* or *fixing over*—"wapiyapi;" and the man is called a *renewer*. He works rather by magic than by medicine. His singing, and rattling the gourd shell, and sucking the place where the pain is, are all for the purpose of driving out the evil spirits. It is a battle of spirits. The greater a man's spirit power is the more successful he is as a doctor. And the secret of spirit power is the alliance with other spirits. Hence the efficacy of fasting and praying. Praying is "crying to." Hence also the augmented power obtained in the Sun Dance. The singing, the back cuttings, the thongs, the buffalo head, the dancing unto entire exhaustion, all these bring one into the realm of the spirits. Also the experiences in passing through the death and the resurrection of the Mystery Dance must bring added super-human power. Still more, the vision seeking, the fasting, the prayer to the night winds, the standing on a mound where men have been buried, or getting down into a hole nearer the bones, this will surely bring communications from the spirit world. Thus, armed by all these experiences and aids, the man becomes a wićaśta wakaŋ indeed, a man of mystery, a healer of diseases, a war-prophet and a leader on the war-path.

The conjuring, the powwowing, that is, the magic of the healing art, may always have called to its aid, in some small degree, a knowledge and use of barks and roots and herbs. But as the magic declined the use of roots and medicines increased, so that the doctor comes to be designated Peźihuta wićaśta, *the Grass Root Man*. As the knowledge of letters and Christianity have come in, their faith in vision seeking and necromancy has been undermined and the power, they say, has departed.

The Dakota beliefs in regard to diseases, and the common way of treating them, as well as the progress of thought, and change of practice, consequent upon the introduction of Christianity, will be well illustrated in the following sketch of a full blood Dakota man, who was a member of the Presbyterian General Assembly of 1880, and who before that body made a speech on Indian rights in the capitol of Wisconsin.

EHNA-MANI.

The "One who walks through," as his name means, is now a man of fifty winters or more and the pastor of the Pilgrim Church at the Santee Agency, in Knox County, Nebraska. He was born at Red Wing on on the Mississippi, which place the Dakotas called He-mini-ćaŋ—*hill-water-wood*—thus finely describing the hill, standing so close to the water, with its river side covered with trees.

At his baptism Ehna-mani was called *Artemas*. Tall and athletic, energetic and swift of foot, as a young man, he appears to have made his mark on the war path, in the deer hunt, on the ball ground, and in the dancing circles. Even now he can sing more Dakota songs of love, war songs, and songs of the sacred mysteries, than any other man I have seen. During last summer I journeyed with Artemas and others, on horseback, many hundred miles up the Missouri River, and across to Fort Wadsworth and Minnesota, and often beguiled the tedious prairie rides with listening to these songs, hearing his explanation of the enigmatical words, and then stopping my pony to note them down.

Because of the light that came through the increasing intercourse of the Dakotas with white people, the father of Artemas was afraid he might be induced to forsake the religion of his ancestors, and so made him promise that, while he had his children educated in the civilization and

Christianity brought to them by the missionaries, he himself would be true to his ancestral faith.   Under all ordinary providences, Artemas thinks he should have so lived and died.

But when the trouble came in 1862, he found himself at the ferry, without gun or war-club, when Captain Marsh's men were fired upon and nearly half of them killed, and because he too was wounded there, he was imprisoned. This change of circumstances produced a change of life. With the younger men he learned to read and write, became a Christian, and was elected elder or leader of the Red Wing class, while in prison at Davenport, Iowa. This place he filled with great credit to himself and profit to others.

It was during the last winter of their imprisonment that the question of conjuring came before them in its moral and religious aspects.   Will Christianity grapple successfully with the customs of the fathers?   Will it modify or abolish this system of Dakota conjuring?

Among all the nations of men disease and death are common.   Heathens die as fast as Christians, perhaps faster.   And when sickness comes into a family it would be inhuman not to make some efforts to alleviate and cure. This feeling belongs to our humanity.   It is greatly influenced and shaped, but not created, by the Christian religion.

Among the Dakotas, and probably all Indian tribes, the method of treating the sick is that known to us as powwowing or conjuring.   Disease, they say, comes from the spirit world.   The gods are offended by acts of omission or commission, and the result is that some spirit of animal, bird, or reptile is sent, by way of punishment, and the man is taken sick.   The process of recovering must accord with the theory of disease.   It will not be met by roots and herbs, but by incantations.   Hence the Indian doctor must be a wakaŋ man; that is, he must be inhabited by spiritual power which will enable him to deliver others from the power of spirits.   The process includes chants and prayers and the rattling of the sacred gourd shell.

From the commencement of the Dakota mission we had never taken any fancy to powwowing.   It seemed to us that such terrible screeching, groaning, singing, rattling, and sucking would make a well man sick rather than a sick man well.   This was education.   An Indian did not think so. But, soberly, we thought it was not a civilized and Christian way of approaching a sick person.

We had also an opinion about it as wrong and wicked thus to come in contact with the evil spirits over the suffering body of one sick. Hence Dr. Williamson always refused to practice medicine in a case where the conjurer was also employed. And it had been generally understood that we regarded the Dakota method of treating the sick as inconsistent with a profession of Christianity. Still the question could not be considered as settled.

In October of 1865 it came up for discussion and settlement in the prison on this wise: During the previous summer, when no missionary was with them, a number of men had yielded to various temptations. Some had drunk beer, and perhaps something stronger, to an extent that they could hardly be sober. Some had been persuaded and hired by white men to dance an Indian dance, and others had either powwowed or been the subjects of the powwow.

In the adjustment of these cases, one man admitted that he had practiced as a Dakota conjurer, and claimed that it was right. His fathers practiced in this way, and were often successful in healing the sick. He grew up in this system of doctoring, and had also practiced it with success. He was not skilled in any other mode of treating disease. The white people had their medicine men. No one was willing to see a friend die without making some efforts to prolong his life. It was merciful, it was right. Jesus Christ when on earth healed the sick and cast out devils.

Besides, they—the prisoners—were in peculiar circumstances. More than one hundred had died since their first imprisonment. And the white doctor, who was appointed to treat their sick, cared not whether they died or lived. Indeed, they thought he would rather have them die. When a good many of them were sick and dying with smallpox, he had been heard to say that his Dakota patients were doing very well! Thus they were under the necessity of endeavoring to heal their own sick, by the only method in which they were skillful. This was the argument.

The missionary would not decide the case, but referred it to the elders—Ehnamani and his brethren. After two weeks they signified that they were prepared to give their decision. When they were come together for this purpose, they were told that the Gospel of Christ molded the customs and habits of every people by whom it was received. There might be some wrong things in a national custom which could be eliminated, and the custom substantially retained. Or the custom might be so radically absurd and wrong, that it could not be redeemed. In that case, Christian-

ity required its abandonment.   It was for them, with their knowledge of
the teachings of the Bible, and the requirements of Christ's religion, to
decide on the character of this custom of their fathers.

There were twelve elders.   Very deliberately each one arose and stated
his opinion.   Two thought the circumstances were such that they could
not altogether give up this, their ancestral method of curing disease.   They
were shut up to it.   But Artemas and nine others agreed in saying that
the practice of conjuring was wrong, and inconsistent with a profession of
the Christian religion.   They said the notion entertained by the Dakotas,
that disease was caused by spirits, they believed to be erroneous; that
sickness and death, they now understand, come not out of the ground, but
by the appointment of the Great Spirit; and that the system of conjuring
brings men into contact with the evil spirits and tends to lead them away
from Christ.

This decision was regarded as a finality in the prison on that point,
and is accepted throughout the mission churches.

When the prisoners were released, Artemas met his wife and family
with great gladness of heart; and as soon thereafter as possible he was
married according to the Christian form.   For he said that, when a heathen
he thought she was his wife, but the Bible had taught him that he had not
truly taken her.

A few months after this he was licensed to preach the gospel, and in
the next year was ordained as one of the pastors of the Pilgrim church.
In the autumn of 1868, he attended a large gathering of ministers at Minneapolis, and was cordially received by all classes of Christians.   The
Congregational and Methodist Sunday Schools were entertained with the
story of his turning from the warpath to the "strait and narrow way;" and
from seeking after a chaplet of eagle's feathers as the reward of prowess
on the battlefield, to his reaching forth for the prize of the high calling in
Christ—even the crown of Life.

CHAPTER VI.

ARMOR AND EAGLE'S FEATHERS.

For more than two hundred years we know that the Dakota have been noted as the most warlike nation of the northwest. Hennep'n and his comrades were captured by a flotilla of canoes coming down to make war on the Illini and Miami of Illinois. And the reputation of good fighters has come down to recent times, as we know from the Custer massacre. The making and keeping them a nation of warriors has, in my judgment, been accomplished mainly by three customs, viz: The scalp dance, the wearing of eagle's feathers, and consecrated armor. In their natural order the last comes first.

In the ancient times the exhortation to a young man was, "Guard well your sacred armor;" and that consisted of the spear, an arrow, and a bundle of paint, with some swan's down painted red, to which were sometimes added some roots for the healing of wounds. These were wrapped together in strips of red or blue cloth, and could be seen in pleasant days carefully set up outside of the lodge. These were given by an older man, who was believed to have power over spirits, and who had, in the act of consecration, made to inhere in them the spirit of some animal or bird, as the wolf, the beaver, the loon, or the eagle. Henceforth these, or rather the one which became each one's tutelar divinity and his armor god, were sacred and not to be killed or eaten until certain conditions were fulfilled. Certain customs of this kind are finely illustrated in the following personal narrative of

SIMON ANAWANG-MANI.

Simon was all that a Dakota brave could be. In his early years he must have been daring even to recklessness. There was in him a strong will, which sometimes showed itself in the form of stubbornness. His eye, even in a later day, showed that there had been evil, hatred, and maliciousness there   He was a thorough Indian, and for the first dozen years of his manhood, or from his eighteenth to his thirtieth year, no one of his comrades had followed the warpath more, or reaped more glory on it, than he had. None had a right to wear so many eagle's feathers; no other one was so much honored.

Dakota war-honors are distributed in this manner: A party of young men have gone on the warpath against the Ojibwa. They find a man and kill him. Five braves may share this honor and be entitled therefor to wear each a feather of the royal eagle. The one who shoots the enemy is one of the five, but is not the chief. He who runs up and first plunges his battle-ax or scalping knife into the foe is counted the first. Then others may come up and strike him and be partakers of the glory. Each wears for that act an eagle's feather. If it is only a woman that is killed and scalped, the mark of honor is only a common eagle's feather.

There is another distinction worth noting. The only real punishment existing among the Dakota, having the sanction of law or immemorial usage comes under the name of "soldier-killing." This is carrying out the decrees of the braves or warriors. The shape it takes is the destruction of property, cutting up blankets or tents, breaking guns, or killing horses. But the same immemorial custom places an estoppage on this power. A man who has killed more enemies than anyone else in the camp can not be "soldier-killed" by anyone else. Or if he has killed an enemy in more difficult circumstances than the others, as, for instance, if he has climbed a tree to kill one, and no other man has performed a like feat, no one has a right to execute on him any decree of the "Soldiers' lodge." In this way he is placed above the execution of law.

To this eminence Simon had risen. By the customs of the nation no one in that part of the country had a right to publicly cut up his blanket or tent, or break his gun, or kill his horse. This was surely an honorable distinction

Another custom prevails among the Dakota which may be mentioned in connection with Simon. The reception of the wo-ta-we, or armor, by the young man places him under certain pledges which he must, if possible, redeem in after life. It taboos or consecrates certain parts of an animal, as the heart, the liver, the breast, the wing, etc. Whatever part or parts are tabooed to him he may not eat until by killing an enemy he has removed the taboo. Simon had removed all taboos, and in this respect was a free man. His armor was purified and made sacred by the blood of his enemies. His manhood was established beyond all dispute. All things were lawful for him.

This Dakota name, Anawaŋg-mani, means "One who walks[1] gallop-ing upon." It may have had its significance. It may have been given after his war exploits, and had reference to the fury with which he rushed upon the foe. This is a common thing. Young men distinguish themselves on the warpath, and come home with the scalps of their enemies. Their boy-names are thrown away and new names given to them. And so the giving and receiving of a new name was not among them a new or strange thing. It was a mark of distinction. Hence the desire that all had, when making a profession of the Christian religion, to have new names—Christian names—given them. They were to be new people. There was a fitness in it, for Christ had said, "I will write upon him my new name."

At his baptism the "One who walks galloping upon" was called Simon, and by that name he is extensively known among white people and Indians. He learned to read and write in the first years of the mission at Lac-qui-parle, though he never became as good a scholar as many others, and he became a convert to Christianity about the beginning of the year 1840. The energy and independence which had characterized him on the hunt and the warpath he carried with him into his new relations. By dressing like a white man and going to work, he showed his faith by his works. This was all contrary to the customs of his people, and very soon brought on him a storm of opposition. He built for himself a cabin, and fenced a field and planted it. For this his wife's friends opposed and persecuted him.

It is true, as already stated, no man in the village had more Dakota honors than he had. No one had taken more Ojibwa scalps, and no one could cover his head with so many eagle feathers; and hence no one could "soldier-kill" him. But now he had cut off his hair and abjured his Dakota honors, and no one was found so poor as to do him reverence. As he passed through the village, going to his work, he was laughed at, and the children often said, "There goes the man who has made himself a woman." The men who before had honored him as a Dakota brave now avoided him and called him no more to their feasts. But those forms of opposition he met bravely and was made stronger thereby.

It happened that, about the beginning of the year 1844, Simon went down with his family to the then new mission station at Traverse des Sioux. While there he cut rails for the mission and taught as an assistant in the Dakota school. The Dakota men at this place, although even more openly opposed to the new religion than were those at Lac-qui-parle, never-

[1] That is, continues.—J. O. D.

theless pursued a very different course with Simon. They honored him and invited him to their dog feasts. They praised him; told him he was a good fellow; that he had taken many Ojibwa scalps, and so they wanted him to drink spirit water with them. How much Simon resisted the importunities is not known. He fell. He was ashamed. He put off his white man's clothes and for some time was an Indian again.

For several years his history in regard to fire water was one of sinning and repenting. Again and again he was drawn away. His appetite for spirit water would return, and the desire to obtain horses by trading in it led him farther astray So we mourned sadly over his fall. He repented and promised reformation only to fall again; and each time he appeared to go down deeper than before. For years he seemed to work iniquity with greediness. Yet during all this time we had hope in his case. We often urged him to come back to the path of life; and something seemed to say, "Simon will yet return." Sometimes we obtained from him a promise, and sometimes he came to church, but was so much ashamed that he could not be persuaded to enter, but would sit down on the doorstep.

Thus he came up gradually, getting more and more strength and courage. And so in 1854 he returned to the dress and customs of the white men and to his profession of love to Jesus Christ. Since that time he has witnessed a good confession before many witnesses as a ruling elder and class leader, and recently as a licensed local preacher.

When the outbreak of 1862 occurred Simon and his family were living in a brick house near the Hazelwood mission station. Subsequently Little Crow and the whole camp of hostile Indians removed up to that part of the country, and they forced the Christian Indians to leave their houses, which were all afterwards burned. While the hostile and loyal parties were camped there near together on Rush Brook, Mrs. Newman, one of the captives, and her three children, came to seek food and protection in Simon's tipi. She had been badly treated by her captors, and now cast off to go whither she could. She afterwards told me that she felt safe when she found herself and children in a family where they prayed and sang praise to the Great Spirit.

Little Crow ordered the camp to be removed from the vicinity of Hazelwood up to the mouth of the Chippewa. At this time, when all had started, Simon fell behind, and leaving his own family to take care of themselves, he and one of his sons placed Mrs. Newman and her children in a little wagon and brought them safely down to Gen. Sibley's camp at Fort Ridgley.

The bringing in of these and some others not only caused great gladness in our camp, but gave us hope that God would enable us to rescue the remaining captives. Indeed, this was to us the first certain knowledge of that counter revolution, which was brought about by the daring and energy of the Christian Indians. It was the lifting up of the dark cloud of almost despair that had for weeks been setting down upon us.

CHAPTER VII.

DAKOTA DANCES.

The function of the dance among the Dakota may be stated as four-fold: First, amusement; secondly, gain; thirdly, superhuman help; and, fourthly, worship. Two or more of these objects may be combined in one dance, but usually one idea is predominant. In a purely heathen Dakota camp there is always a great deal of drumming, some by day and more by night. This is a kind of practice and preparation for more important occasions as well as a nightly amusement for the young men. All dances have musical accompaniments.

SINGING TO.

There is one especially, which is called "Ádowaŋ" and "Wádowaŋ," that is, Singing to or over. This is a begging dance. Sometimes it is called "Zitkadaŋ pa adowaŋ," Singing over the heads of birds. A man gathers some beautiful woodpeckers' heads and sings over them to another person. They are a gift to that person, and, of course, the honorable deeds of that person are mentioned and his praises sung. In return a horse or something quite valuable is expected. It has been related to me that articles of clothing or other skins or curiously wrought pipes were, in years gone by, taken by the Dakota of Minnesota to the Missouri, and this ceremony of singing over was practiced upon the heads of a man's children, who, in return for the honor, gave several horses.

BEGGING DANCE.

But the common begging dance, which was often seen among the eastern Dakota forty years ago, included a variety of fashionable dances, all of which were made for the purpose of begging. Sometimes it was called the buffalo dance, when the dancers made themselves look hideous by wearing the horns and long hair of that animal. Doubtless women alone could dance a begging dance, but all that I ever saw were of men alone. Dressed in their best clothes and painted in the most approved styles, with all their eagle's feathers properly arranged in their heads, the

224

men collect and dance in a ring. Their bodies lean forward, and their knees are bent accordingly, and thus with a motion up and down, keeping time to the drum and the deer-hoof rattle, they dance and sing their almost monotonous song, concluding with a shout and the clapping of the mouth with the hand. Then some warrior steps out into the middle, and, with abundance of gesture, recites some war exploit. This is received with a shout, and the dance begins again. Presently, at one of these intervals, an old man, sitting outside, makes a speech in praise of the man or the people who are expected to make the presents. If the dance is made to a trader, he loses no time in sending out tobacco, or powder and lead, or provisions, or, it may be, all together. If one Indian village is dancing to another village, the women hasten to bring their presents of food and clothing from the different lodges. Another dance of thanks is made, the presents are distributed, and the party breaks up or goes elsewhere. Considering that begging dances must be very demoralizing, white men have often been greatly to blame for encouraging them.

NO-FLIGHT DANCE.

In the organization of an army and its preparation for effective service a large amount of drill[1] is found necessary. Something very like this, in its objects, is resorted to by the Dakota war captain in preparing the young men and boys for the warpath. It is called the "No flight dance."[1] This gathers in the young men who have not yet made their mark on the battle field, and drills them by the concerted motions of the dance, while, by the recital of brave deeds, their hearts are fired and made firm for the day of battle. The instructions given are lessons in Indian warfare.

All this is preparatory to the war prophet's organizing a party for the warpath. But before starting he must propitiate the spirits of evil and obtain the help of the gods. This was sought for in a variety of ways, one of which was by the "Yumni Waćipi," or Circle dance.

CIRCLE DANCE.

A preparation for this, and for god-seeking in general, was through the purification of the vapor bath or initipi. This finished, the wakaŋ man had a tent set for him, joined to which a circle was made of about forty feet in diameter, by setting sticks in the ground and wreathing them with willows. Four gateways were left. In the center stood a pole twenty

---

[1] Nape śni kaġapi, literally, They pretend not to flee.

feet high, with bark images suspended at the top.   Near the foot of this
the ground was scooped out and a small willow booth made over it.   At
the entrance to this was a fire of coals, a stone painted red, and a pipe.
When everything was thus prepared, and the night previous had been spent
in drumming and fasting and praying, the old man came out of the tent,
naked except a wisp of grass around his loins.   He carried his drum and
rattles.   Before the painted stone he stood and trembling prayed, "Grandfather have mercy on me!"   This done, he entered the little booth and
commenced to sing and drum.   The dancers then entered the circle and
danced around, a dozen or more at once, and all fixed up in paint and
feathers.   Three or four women followed.   The men sang and the women
answered in a kind of chorus.   This continued for ten minutes perhaps,
and they retired for a rest.   The dance was resumed again and again, each
time with an increased frenzy.   When the last act was finished several men
who had guns shot the wolf image at the top of the pole, when the old
man gave forth his oracle, and the dance was done.

SCALP DANCE.

When the spirits had been propitiated and the vision had appeared,
the leader made up his party and started for the country of the enemy.
We will suppose they have been successful, and have obtained one or more
scalps.   They come home in triumph.   This is wakte-hdipi, *having killed,*
they come home.   But having killed enemies, they paint themselves black
and let their hair hang down.   Before reaching their village they sit down
on some knoll and sing a war dirge to the souls they have disembodied,
when they are met by some of their own people and stripped of their
clothes, which is called wayuzapi or taking-all.   And their blankets may
be taken from them on each occasion of painting the scalps red, which
ceremony is commonly performed four times.

Then the scalp dance commences.   It is a dance of self-glorification,
as its name, "Iwakićipi," seems to mean.   A hoop 2 feet in diameter, more
or less, with a handle several feet long, is prepared, on which the scalp is
stretched.   The young men gather together and arrange themselves in a
semicircle; those who participated in taking the scalp are painted black,
and the others are daubed with red or yellow paint, according to their
fancy; and all dance to the beat of the drum.   On the other side of the
circle stand the women, arranged in line, one of whom carries the scalp of
the enemy.   The men sing their war chants and praise the bravery and

success of those who have returned from the warpath, and the women, at intervals, sing an answering chorus. As with other nations a new song is often made for the occasion; but the old ones are not forgotten. This may serve as a sample:

> Something I've killed, and I lift up my voice;
> Something I've killed, and I lift up my voice;
> The northern buffalo I've killed, and I lift up my voice;
> Something I've killed, and I lift up my voice.

The "northern buffalo" means a black bear; and the "black bear" means a man. The "lifting up the voice" is in mourning for the slain enemy. Night after night is the dance kept up by the young men and women, until the leaves fall, if commenced in the summer; or, if the scalp was brought home in the winter, until the leaves grow again. On each occasion of painting the scalp a whole day is spent dancing around it. And these days are high days—days of making gifts, feasting, and general rejoicing.

The influence of the scalp dance on the morality of the people is quite apparent. In so loose a state of society as that of the Dakotas, such frequent and long-continued night meetings tend greatly to licentiousness. But the great wrong o᷉ the scalp dance consists in its being a crime against our common humanity. "If thine enemy hunger feed him, and if he thirst give him drink." What a contrast is the spirit of those divine words with the spirit of the "Iwakićipi." The eagle's feather and the scalp dance tended greatly to keep up the intertribal wars among the Indians.

Since the "circle dance" and the "scalp dance" have become things of the past among our partly civilized Dakotas, what is called the "grass dance" has been revived. It is said to have derived its name from the custom, in ancient times, of dancing naked, or with only a wisp of grass about the loins. Only the men appeared in this nude state. It is a night dance, and regarded as extremely licentious, although now they are represented as dancing in their Indian dress or even clothed as white men.

MYSTERY DANCE.[1]

This is a secret organization, which is entered through mysterious death and mysterious resurrection. As it appears to have been confined mainly to the eastern portion of the Dakota Nation, it is supposed to have been derived from some other Indians at no very remote date. The

---

[1] Wakaŋ waćipi. [See Mandan feast, p. 273, and Wacicka dance, pp. 342–6, 3d. Ann. Rept. of the Director Bur. Eth—J. O. D.]

Dakota themselves, however, claim that it was communicated to them by the great Uŋktehi or god of the waters. It is a form of religion which has doubtless largely supplanted older forms of worship. The badge of the order is the "wakaŋ" sack, or sack of mystery. The great water god ordained that this should be the skin of the otter, raccoon, weasel, squirrel, loon, or a species of fish and of snakes. It should contain four kinds of medicine and represent fowls, quadrupeds, herbs, and trees. Thus grass roots, the bark of tree roots, swan's down, and buffalo hair are the symbols which are carefully preserved in the medicine sack. This combination is supposed to produce

> A charm of powerful trouble,
> Like a hellbroth, boil and bubble.

Certain good rules, in the main, are laid down, which must govern the conduct of members of this organization: They must revere the "wakaŋ" sack; they must honor all who belong to the dance; they must make many "sacred feasts;" they must not steal nor listen to slander, and the women must not have more than one husband. The rewards promised to those who faithfully performed the duties were honor from their fellow members, frequent invitations to feasts, abundance of fowl and venison, with supernatural aid to consume it, long life here with a crown of silver hair, and a dish and spoon in the future life.

After the proper instruction in the mysteries, the neophyte practiced watchings and fastings and was purified for four successive days by the vapor bath. Then came the great day of initiation. The ceremonies were public. A great deal of cooked provisions was prepared. At the sacred dance which I witnessed four decades ago, there were a half dozen large kettles of meat. The arrangements for the dance consisted of a large tent at one end, whose open front was extended by other tents stretched along the sides, making an oblong with the outer end open. Along the sides of this inclosure sat the members, perhaps a hundred in number, each one having his or her "sack of mystery." At a given signal from the officiating old men, all arose and danced inward until they became a solid mass, when the process was reversed and all returned to their seats. Near the close of the performance those who were to be initiated were shot by the "sacks of mystery," and falling down they were covered with blankets. Then the mysterious bean or shell which they claimed had produced death was extracted by the same mysterious power of the sack of mystery, and the persons were restored to a new life. But this new life came only after the throes and the bitterness of death. Then he has a "sack" given him, and is thenceforth a member of the order of the sacred mysteries.

A necessary adjunct of the Wakaŋ-waćipi is the "Wakaŋ-wohaŋpi," or Sacred Feast. This is made very frequently when there is a plenty of food in the village. Of course, as a general thing, only those are invited who belong to the order. Forty years ago I was honored with an invitation to one of their feasts, in a wild Teton village at Fort Pierre on the Missouri. It is in part a worship. The pipe is lighted and held up to the gods with a prayer for mercy. Then they smoke around, after which the food is dished out. The guests bring their own wooden bowl and horn spoon. Each one must eat up all that is given him or pay a forfeit. This is a blanket or gun or such article as the person can give. I have known a community, in time of plenty, run wild over the idea of stuffing each other and getting all the forfeits possible. Their god is their belly.

Quite likely there are other forms of the dance in other parts of the Dakota country, or dances which have other names than those spoken of here; but these are sufficient. There remains, however, to be mentioned the greatest exemplification of self-sacrifice and worship in the sun-dance.

SUN-DANCE.

The following graphic account of the sun-dance held in June, 1880, by the Teton under Red Cloud, is an abstract of what was published in the Daily Journal of Sioux City, Iowa. It is a very trustworthy and more than usually vivid description of a ceremony which is becoming rarer under the influence of Christianity.

This sun-dance began at 5 a. m., June 24, 1880. The lodges, 700 in number, were arranged in a circle of about six miles in circumference on a level plain near White Clay Creek, Nebraska. The dance began with a grand charge within the circle. It is estimated that about 4,000 men and women took part in the charge. Nearly all were on horseback, and they charged back and forth over the ground, yelling for an hour, for the alleged purpose of frightening away the ghosts and bad spirits from the grounds. A hard rain set in at 6 o'clock, and nothing more was done until 1 o'clock, when the sky cleared and the people went up on a branch of White Clay Creek to cut the sacred pole. Around the tree to be felled a ring was formed, and no living object was allowed to enter therein except the persons who took part in felling the tree. The master of ceremonies was a colored man, captured when a child, and at the time of this dance attached to the band of Little Wound. It was his duty to keep intruders out of the circle. After much ceremony, dancing, and giving away of horses, six men walked slowly up to the tree and each gave it a hack, after which it was felled by the wife of Spider. When it went down a charge was made on it, and the tree, branches and all, was taken up and carried by men and women to the sun-dance grounds, a distance of two miles. On reaching the grounds, they made another charge to drive away any ghosts that might be lingering there. Then Taśuŋke kokipapi,[1] the younger (commonly called Young-Man-Afraid-of-his-Horses), announced that there was nothing more to be seen till 10 o'clock on the following day, Friday, June 25.

The evening of the 24th and the forenoon of the 25th were spent in raising the pole and erecting a tabernacle. The latter was formed in a circle of about 500 yards in circumference, 12 feet high, and was constructed by putting posts in the ground and covering them with green boughs. The pole was placed in the center and decorated with red, white, and blue flags, said to be gifts to the Great Spirit. There were within the inclosure about 1,000 men sitting around, and 300 dancers, besides 25 men riding their horses around the ring. The 300 dancers marched around the pole, dancing, singing, and shooting up at the pole. Each man had from one to three belts of cartridges strung around his body. He had little clothing besides his breechcloth, and his bare body and limbs were painted in various colors. This performance lasted for two hours, then all firing ceased, and twenty children entered the ring to have their ears pierced. The parents of each child gave away two horses to the poor. When a horse was turned loose, the first man who caught hold of it owned it. Persons competing for the horses were placed outside the gate of the inclosure in two parallel rows 30 feet apart, one row on each side of the road. When a horse was turned out there was a scramble to see who could reach it first.

The child to be honored was laid by its mother on a pile of new calico. Then six old men sprinkled water on its head, repeating the following words: "O Wakaŋtaŋka, hear me! this man has been a good and brave man, and the mother is a good woman. For their sake let this child live long, have good luck and many children." Then, with a long, slender, sharp-pointed knife, two holes were made through each ear, wherein were

---

[1] Literally, They (the foe) fear even his horse.—J. O. D.

placed rings of German silver. When all the children had had their ears pierced, ten men placed by the pole the skull of some large animal, crying over it and making sundry passes. Then all the young unmarried maidens who had obeyed their parents and had been chaste during the year went up and touched the tree, raised their right hands to the sun, bowed to the skull, and then retired from the inclosure. The young women had been told that if any of them had been unchaste the touching of the tree would insure fatal consequences to them, as the large animal represented by the skull would carry them off to the spirit land.

At 8 o'clock the sun-dancers proper, seventeen in number, entered the ring. These men had been fasting, no food or water having been given them for three days and nights previous to their entering the inclosure. Men who take part in this dance say what they are going to do before they are placed on record—*i. e.*, they intend going one, two, or more days without food and water, and whether they intend being cut and tied up to the pole. After making such a declaration they lose all control of their own wills. They are obliged to fast, and are placed on buffalo robes in a sweat-house until they become as gaunt as grayhounds. In this condition were the seventeen brought into the ring by guards, and each one had a whistle placed in his mouth and a banner with a long staff placed in his hand. Then ten large bass drums, beaten by sixty men, struck up a hideous noise, the seventeen men danced, whistled, gazed steadily at the sun, and kept time with the drums. This scene was kept up with little or no change until the morning of the third day.

The white visitors reached the grounds at 10 a. m. Saturday, the 26th. The same noise was there, and the seventeen were still dancing and whistling. The clubs used as drumsticks had horses' tails fastened to them instead of the scalps which would have been used in earlier days. At 11 a. m. seven of the seventeen were laid down on blankets, and after much ceremony and giving away of horses and calico, each man was cut and tied up to the pole. This operation was performed by raising the skin of the right breast and then that of the left, cutting a hole about an inch long through the skin at each place. A round wooden skewer was inserted through each hole, fastened by sinews, the sinews tied to a rope, and the rope to the pole. One fellow had pins inserted in each arm, tied with sinews, and fastened to a horse which was standing beside him. The first and second dancers seemed to be veterans, as they went forward to the pole, made a short prayer, and then ran backward, breaking loose and falling flat on their backs. The third man, seeing the others break loose, took courage, braced up, and made a desperate struggle. He succeeded not only in breaking from the pole, but also from the horse. This feat pleased the Indians, who shouted lustily. Little Big Man, who was mounted, was so delighted that he shot an arrow straight up into the air, whooping with all his might. The arrow came down on the back of a large fat woman, who was standing outside the inclosure. The old woman jumped up and ran howling across the prairie. An Indian on the outside happened to be on horseback, so he ran up to her and held her while the others extracted the arrow. Little Big Man was obliged to part with three horses to satisfy the woman.

The four remaining dancers were young and inexperienced, so they could not break their bonds. Consequently they gave away three horses each and were cut loose. One of them fainted, and on being resuscitated he became unruly, making a break from the ring, tumbling over several women, and when finally seized he was standing among several infants that had been stowed away under blankers in the corner of the lodge. He was brought back, a whistle made of an eagle's feather was put into his mouth, and he was set to dancing. Then an old man with a looking-glass in his hand and a buffalo skull on his head performed mystery rites over him, to drive out the evil spirit which they thought had entered into the young man. Meantime two breathless infants were taken out into the air and resuscitated. Another old man said that he was ready to give to any worthy woman the mysterious anointing. A large number went up and received this ancient rite. This was administered by cutting a hole in the right arm and introducing medicine under the skin. Women entitled to this privilege were those who had at any period of their lives held a horse or borne arms in battle. At 6 P. M. the sun disappeared under the clouds, and the old man with the buffalo skull on his head uttered a few words and dismissed the audience. Then the dance ended, and an hour later the lodges were taken down and most of the Indians started homeward.

INDEX.

233

○